SOURCES FOR FRAMEWORKS OF WORLD HISTORY

SOURCES FOR FRAMEWORKS OF WORLD HISTORY

VOLUME ONE: TO 1550

Lynne Miles-Morillo
WABASH COLLEGE

Stephen Morillo
WABASH COLLEGE

NEW YORK OXFORD
OXFORD UNIVERSITY PRESS

Oxford University Press is a department of the University of Oxford.
It furthers the University's objective of excellence in research,
scholarship, and education by publishing worldwide.

Oxford New York
Auckland Cape Town Dar es Salaam Hong Kong Karachi
Kuala Lumpur Madrid Melbourne Mexico City Nairobi
New Delhi Shanghai Taipei Toronto

With offices in
Argentina Austria Brazil Chile Czech Republic France Greece
Guatemala Hungary Italy Japan Poland Portugal Singapore
South Korea Switzerland Thailand Turkey Ukraine Vietnam

For titles covered by Section 112 of the US Higher Education
Opportunity Act, please visit www.oup.com/us/he for the latest
information about pricing and alternate formats.

Published by Oxford University Press
198 Madison Avenue, New York, New York 10016
http://www.oup.com

Library of Congress Cataloging-in-Publication Data
Sources for Frameworks of world history : networks, hierarchies,
culture / edited by Stephen Morillo, Lynne Miles-Morillo.
pages cm
Includes bibliographical references and index.
ISBN 978-0-19-933227-4
1. World history—Sources. I. Morillo, Stephen, editor of compilation.
II. Miles-Morillo, Lynne, editor of compilation. III. Morillo, Stephen.
Frameworks of world history.
D21.M85 2013 Suppl.
909—dc23

2013046091

To students everywhere who are *doing* history.
(And a debt of gratitude to our patient progeny, who lived
with this project for many moons indeed.)

CONTENTS

INTRODUCTION

This is a book of primary sources designed to accompany *Frameworks of World History.* Primary sources are the basic working material for working historians, including student historians. Historical sources are pieces of the past that have come down to us today and that allow us to reconstruct, at least partially, a model of the time and place of their origin. They are the evidence that historians use to construct hypotheses of the past. But sources do not really speak for themselves: historians must interpret them, and historical interpretation involves many possible steps. Two sources can corroborate each other, if they agree, assuming that they are truly independent sources (i.e., that one is not a copy of the other or that both are copies of a lost original). Interpreting any source requires an explanatory model of the world to guide that interpretation. The *Frameworks* model of networks, hierarchies, and cultural frames and screens is one such model, and the text makes the model explicit so that you can examine it, determine whether you agree with it, and use it to interpret the evidence in this book. You can also invert the use of the evidence and the model by using the evidence to test and refine the *Frameworks* model. That's how science works—including historical interpretation.

Let's help you get into this process by exploring two questions. First, what is a *primary* source? Second, how do you go about interpreting a primary source?

WHAT IS A PRIMARY SOURCE?

Historians generally talk about two kinds of sources, *primary* sources and *secondary* sources. "Primary" and "secondary" do ***not*** refer to the importance of a given source, either in general or for the purposes of a particular historical investigation. **In the most basic terms, *primary sources* are sources *from the time, place, and people under investigation.*** Thus, Abbot Guibert of Nogent's autobiography, which he wrote himself during his life in the early 1100s (to be utterly clear to the point of silliness), is a fine primary source for Guibert's life and even for the events he reports on and the people he tells us about. We can even consider him a primary source for aspects of the First Crusade, even though he did not witness it personally, because the information he gives us come from the time of the First Crusade. When his reports are secondhand, however, we must be skeptical of the reliability of his information more than we are of his personal narrative, and other sources, ideally eyewitnesses, should corroborate any such information in his story. (We are skeptical of the reliability of his personal narrative as well, but one person's own biases about his or her own life are easier to assess than the biases of any secondhand information.)

This definition of a *primary source* is idealized, of course. Things are not always simple or straightforward. Sometimes we accept certain accounts as primary sources because they are as close to the time period as we can get. Our sources for the life of Alexander the Great include only a handful of truly primary sources: a brief inscription that mentions him in passing, a handful of coins he issued, and the archaeological remains of his activities, including cities and, in one spectacular case, a coastline that he altered. (He built a causeway out into the Mediterranean during his siege of the island city of Tyre in 332 BCE. It remained after the siege, silted up, and the island is now a peninsula.) But the major narratives we have of his life and campaigns are Roman, they date from several hundred years after Alexander's time, and they do not show a particularly good understanding of his time. They refer to and sometimes even incorporate bits and summaries of narratives written during Alexander's time. We still accept these Roman sources as "primary sources" for Alexander's life because they are the closest we can get.

What we've just said about sources for Alexander also demonstrates that primary sources need not be written sources. *Anything* from the time and place we are studying can be a primary source: works of art, archaeological finds, scientific data about the natural world (the natural world being, after all, an aspect of a time and place), and so forth. Even written evidence comes in many forms beyond self-conscious narratives. Government documents, fictional writing, daily newspapers, and mundane bits of writing such as grocery lists or restaurant menus—all of these can be primary sources.

Primary can of course still have its ordinary, non-history–specific meaning of "chief" or "main": "The primary source for my paper on Abraham Lincoln is the movie *Abraham Lincoln: Vampire Hunter.*" *Primary* here indicates that the film was the main source of information you consulted. However, this would not a *primary* source in terms of types of historical sources (nor would using primarily that source be a very good idea).

What then is a *secondary source,* if so many things can count as primary sources? *Secondary sources* are sources that discuss the topic, the time, place, and people under study, but on the basis of primary sources or of other second-hand accounts. Thus, if you were writing a paper about Alexander the Great, any biography of him written by a current day historian (indeed, any biography written after the Roman accounts that we characterized above as "just about almost primary") would be a secondary source, no matter how useful, informative, or well-written a secondary source. And of course, like primary sources, not all secondary sources are created equal. A scholarly biography of Alexander might be a *good* secondary source; a medieval epic poem about Alexander consisting mostly of legends or a movie such as Oliver Stone's 2004 *Alexander?* Not so much. To introduce a further complication, however: what if your research topic were on "the historical reception of Alexander the Great from medieval times to the present", in which you examine what people at different times and places thought of Alexander, whether what they thought were true or not? In that case, both that legend-encrusted medieval epic and today's Hollywood dreck would be excellent primary sources. And what if your research topic is something going on today (or close enough to be called "contemporary history"—topics involving people who are still alive)? In that case you gain the possibility of oral interviews, news footage, and so forth, as primary sources. But another historian's synthesis of such information, even though it is from the time of the topic, has already become a secondary source. Journalism, sometimes called "the first draft of history," lies in an interesting gray zone here.

Confused? Let's sum up. *Primary sources* are sources whose information about a topic comes, as closely as possible, from the time, place, and participants in the topic. For most purposes, that will work for you. But this definition says nothing about the *quality* of the information a source offers. To evaluate that, we need to say a few things about how to read and evaluate a primary source.

HOW TO READ A PRIMARY SOURCE

There are, as we have noted, many different kinds of primary sources. The interpretation of some primary sources, such as the archaeological remnants of buildings and, even more, ancient bones and other natural substances, requires at least some specialized knowledge. We will focus here on the most common kinds of sources selected for inclusion in this book, written documents. The principles for reading these works for many visual sources as well, especially ones such as paintings or drawings that tell a story.

Reading a source is like interrogating a witness in a trial. Reading a source productively—so that its story gets you closer to understanding "what happened"—requires answering two fundamental questions. First, how reliable is the source, that is, does its story give us a reasonably accurate representation of the reality it describes? Second, what information can we derive from the source? These questions of assessment and interpretation are tied together.

Assessing the reliability of a source that purports to tell a factual story involves answering the same questions you would ask of a living witness. Who is the witness? In other words, who wrote or compiled the source? Sometimes we can't answer this question precisely, as with a routine government document (author: nameless bureaucrat) or an oral epic poem (author: many people in a culture). But we can get a sense of what kind of person or persons created the source.

When and where did the author create the source? Were they close, temporally and chronologically, to the events the source describes? Generally, the closer the better.

Finally, what can we know about why the author wrote the document? What audience did the author intend to address and for what reason? How do these factors shape the story the author tells? What you are trying to figure out with such questions is what the author's *perspective* is and whether the author has a *bias*. As the "Issues in Doing World History" box in Chapter 27 of *Frameworks* says about historians, everyone has a *perspective* that comes from where that person exists in time, place, social position, and so forth. The world will look different to an elite male author than to even a privileged woman, to any peasant, to a slave, or to a member of an ethnic or religious minority. That an author has a perspective does not mean the source is unreliable. Perspective is inevitable: a historian has to account for what a source author's perspective allows him or her to see well, and what conversely that perspective might obscure. An author with a *bias,* on the other hand, is intentionally telling a distorted story, such as an author writing a very partisan account from within a heated political battle.

Once you have done a rough assessment of the reliability of the source, you can begin to extract information from your witness. (These two steps often occur at the same time, of course, because evidence from within the source can tell you about the source's reliability.) What can the source tell us?

One basic division among sources is between those that purport to tell a factual story and those that are overtly fictional. In some ways, fictional sources are easier to deal with (including sources that purport to tell a true story but obviously do not), because you can stop worrying about the "truth" of the story. Instead, if the story comes from the time and place you are studying and is reasonably representative of its time (and yes, that's another hard question), you can generally get two sorts of information fairly easily. First, what was "normal" at the time in terms of everyday life? This is the social history question. You see this by ignoring the main story and looking at the background details, the ones that are there because that's what the author assumed was normal about the world without thinking much about it. Suppose, for example, you read the following passage in a murder mystery.

Investigator: Where were you on Thursday evening last week between 7 and 10?

Suspect: I was home watching *The Simpsons* on TV.

What do we know? We know nothing about what the suspect might actually have been doing. Maybe he was at home, maybe he was out committing the heinous murder at the heart of the plot. He's an unreliable witness. But his very unreliability means that he will want his story about what he was doing to sound plausible. Thus, we know about the people in this society at this time that they had an easily observed system of timekeeping, that they had TVs, that watching TV was a normal activity, that *The Simpsons* was probably a well-known show, and that living in a private home was probably normal. So we know quite a bit.

The other thing we can learn from fictional sources is even more obvious. What did the society believe? This is the cultural history question. From our brief passage above we can infer something about beliefs regarding privacy, for example. But even more, if we step back and observe that the passage came from a best-selling mystery novel, we can infer that mysteries were a form of popular entertainment. You can then interpret the whole story for at least some of the beliefs, concerns, and outlooks of the culture from which the story came.

You can ask these same questions about nonfiction sources. But you can also ask further questions about the particular events the source narrates. What happened? Who wanted what to happen to whom? Why? When it comes to such factual questions, there are ways to assess how reliable this particular information is. The two main ways are to test the source against physical reality and against what other sources say. The physical reality test is especially good at evaluating the often unreliable numbers in older sources: Herodotus claims that the Persian king Xerxes marched a million men across a pontoon bridge on his way to invading Greece. Not possible. Testing against other sources can mean using not just individual sources, but what other similar sources say in general. This is what the *Frameworks* model is: a generalization based on many primary sources. So test a source against the model. Does what it describes fit the model? If so, that suggests a reliable source. If it doesn't, perhaps the source is unreliable, or perhaps the model needs some modification. Your call.

Let's finish this with a brief example of extracting information from a source. These are a well known pair of judgments from *The Code of Hammurabi:*

> 196. If a man put out the eye of another man, his eye shall be put out.
>
> 199. If he put out the eye of a man's slave, or break the bone of a man's slave, he shall pay one-half of its value.

This is the famous "eye for an eye" judgment and a less well-known but similar clause. What do they tell us? The easy answers are that the Babylonians dealt with crime by means of physical punishment, and that their society had slaves, and that the punishment for a crime varied with the status of the victim. In other words, this was a society with class divisions. Other pieces of the Code confirm and extend those conclusions, which fit the general patterns of early state-level complex societies.

What else can we learn? Well, we know that the "code" looks on close reading more like a set of judgments or precedents than a set of laws, so we can safely assume that the crimes mentioned not only happened, but probably happened frequently enough that is was worth the king's while to advertise the punishment. They were carved into a massive pillar set in the middle of Hammurabi's city. We can therefore infer that at least some people in the society could read. Those who couldn't, we can guess, might have been impressed by the size and complexity of the pillar. The Code therefore served to display royal power—again, a common theme for early states (and later ones, too).

There is even more to learn from these passages (see Chapter 3 of *Frameworks* for what this passage says about limiting vengeance, for example). The sources collected here, in other words, are rich in information about many of the people and places of the past. Dig in and enjoy doing history.

SOURCES FOR FRAMEWORKS OF WORLD HISTORY

CHAPTER 1

Early Humans and the Origins of Complex Systems: to 8000 BCE

INTRODUCTION

Written sources do not exist for the period covered by this chapter. In their place, we examine various kinds of visual evidence and one modern reconstruction of the lives of people living in the late Hunter-Gatherer Era. Interpreting visual evidence is not as different from interpreting written evidence as you might think, especially when you are viewing works of art that have authors, intended audiences, and points of view. But ancient archaeological artifacts, which are simply surviving physical evidence of the past, are more complicated. To be comprehensible, scientific study of the objects must be brought to bear. These sources illustrate both kinds of objects that survive and the kinds of conclusions different scientists can draw from them.

HOMININ RECONSTRUCTIONS

The remains of our predecessors in the primate-hominin-homo part of the evolutionary bush are usually presented as fragmentary skeletal remains: femurs (thighbones, which can give clues about whether the species in question walked upright, for example), teeth (the toughest and thus most common kind of remain, which can tell us about diet), and, most interestingly, skulls. But imagining the humanity, the sense of relatedness, of one of our predecessor species from a skull is difficult. Combining a number of strands of forensic paleoarchaeology and medical advances, a team at Yale created reconstructions of twenty two extinct species of "humans" from such skeletal remains. We present four here in chronological order.

1.1a: Australopithecus

East Africa, between 4 and 2 million years ago.

1.1b: Homo Erectus Georgicus

Caucasus, 1.8 million years ago; a subspecies of Homo erectus.

1.1c: Homo Floresiensis

Island of Flores (Indonesia), c. 100,000 to 12,000 years ago; probably a speciation from homo erectus by island dwarfism.

1.1d: Homo Neanderthalensis

Europe and Southweast Asia; c. 500,000 to 27,000 years ago.

a

b

c

d

From: Deak,Viktor, *The Last Human*, (Yale UP, 2007), pp. 75, 155, 181, 213.

QUESTIONS:

1. What physiological changes from Australopithecus to Neanderthals stand out most clearly in these reconstructions? How do these changes seem significant?
2. How "human" does each reconstruction seem? If modern humans are a "10" on the humanity scale, where does each of these rate? If forced into a yes/no answer, which ones would you give a "yes" to?

1.2: Movements of Early Human Language Groups

Two kinds of evidence converge to support the "out of Africa" hypothesis of the origins of the modern human species. The first is genetic: genetic diversity is far higher in Africa than anywhere else in the world, with the rest of the world therefore presumably descending from a subset of Africans who migrated. The second is linguistic, with the evidence of language diversity telling the same story that genetics does. One specific part of that evidence has to do with the number of distinct sounds, or phonemes, languages have. The languages with the most separate phonemes, as this map shows, are African. Those with the fewest are those farthest from their African origins. Linguists have found that new sounds are rarely added to languages, but that sounds are regularly lost. The implication is that language, and the entire Cognitive Linguistic Revolution, started in Africa.

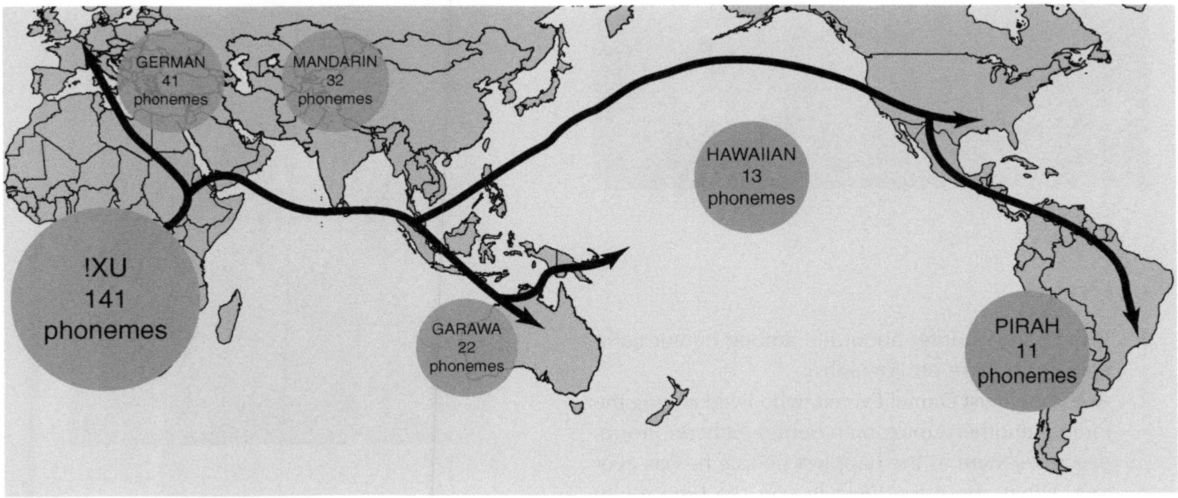

From: http://www.dailymail.co.uk/sciencetech/article-1377150/Every-language-evolved-single prehistoric-mother-tongue-spoken-Africa.html.

QUESTIONS:

1. What does the high density of separate phonemes in African languages suggest about early language and the communication systems that preceded it?
2. In later languages in perfectly complex cultures but with far fewer phonemes (such as Hawaiian), what mechanisms, linguistic or cultural, might enable a language/culture to make up for the paucity of phonemes in allowing people to express themselves as fully as anyone else?

1.3: Hunter-Gatherers

Studies of the few remaining hunter-gatherer peoples of today's world can provide some evidence of what life might have been like for our pre-agricultural ancestors, though interpreting that evidence is fraught with dangers. (In a nutshell, we cannot simply read today's hunter-gatherers back into the past because inevitably they have been affected by contact, however tenuous, with the industrial world, if only through anthropologists studying them!) But the evidence is not useless, and can help us ask better questions of the archaeological evidence we have. These pictures are of a Hadzabe hunter in Tanzania, in the East African Rift region where the modern human species may have first evolved, and a Huaorani Indian carrying hunted howler monkeys and coati in Yasuni National Park, Amazon rainforest, Ecuador.

1.3a: Bow Hunter

1.3b: Hunter

QUESTIONS:

1. What can you infer about life among hunter gatherers from these photographs?
2. Anthropologist Daniel Everett, who lived among the Pirahá, another Amazonian hunter-gatherer group, describes them as the happiest people he has ever met. What about the lifestyle you see here might contribute to high levels of personal satisfaction?

1.4: Cave Paintings

The Cognitive Linguistic Revolution made humans not only better hunters, as the Hadzabe and Huaorani demonstrate, but also gave us the capacity to make art, religion, and other forms of meaning (though not all people automatically invent all such forms: the Pirahá have no belief in the supernatural, it seems). Among the earliest and most impressive evidence for "modern" cognitive-linguistic capacities among early Homo sapiens populations are the cave paintings in parts of France and Spain. These paintings of a horse and a bull in Lascaux cave in France are excellent examples.

1.4a: Lascaux Bull

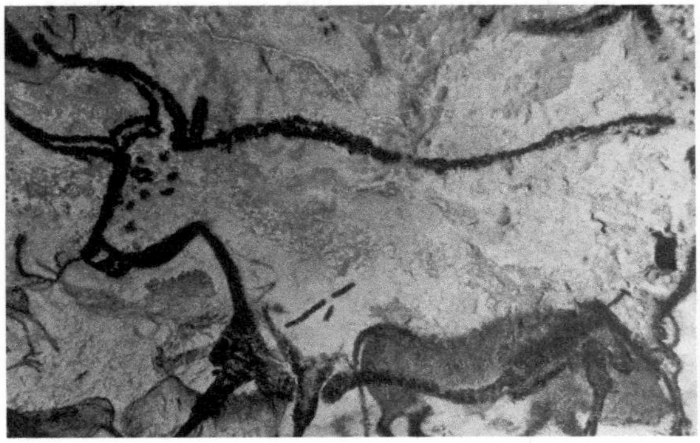

1.4b: Lascaux Horse

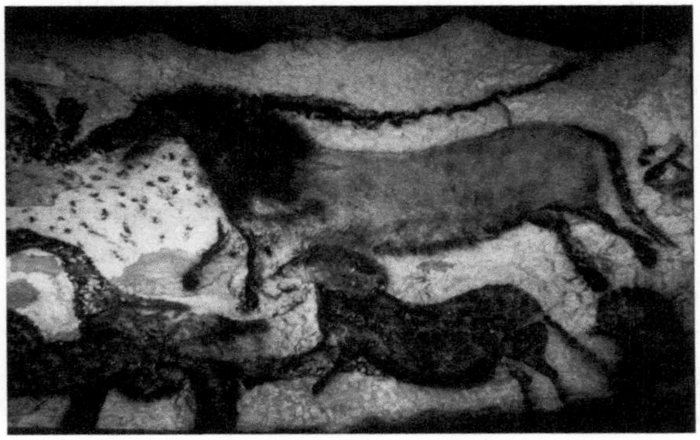

From: Art Resource, NY.

QUESTIONS:

1. Based on these two pictures, make a list of what you know about the people who made them.
2. What do you think of these paintings as art? What does your answer assume about what art is for?

1.5: Last of the Cave Painters

The question of what the cave paintings were for has generated debate among experts for decades. In this brief selection, anthropologist Steven Mithen offers his answer. It comes from his book *After the Ice,* which surveys the changes in habitation, lifestyle, technology, and culture among various human communities in the period from about 20,000 years ago, when the last Ice Age began to give way to global warming, to about 10,000 years ago on the eve of the Agricultural Revolution.

LAST OF THE CAVE PAINTERS

Economic, Social and Cultural Change in Southern Europe, 9600–8500 BC

The date is 9500 BC. Somewhere in southern Europe the last of the ice-age cave artists is at work. He or she is mixing pigments and painting upon a wall, perhaps a horse or a bison, perhaps a line of dots or merely touching up a painting made long ago. And that will be it: more than 20,000 years of cave painting—perhaps the greatest art tradition humankind has ever known—will have come to an end. . . .

The tradition of painting and carving animals, especially horse and bison, together with abstract signs and human figures, had lasted for more than 20,000 years. It had extended from the Urals to southern Spain, and produced masterpieces by the score: the painted bison of Altamira, the lions of Chauvet, the horses of Lascaux, the carved ibex from Mas d'Azil. For more than 800 generations, artists had inherited the same concerns and the same techniques. It was by far the longest-lived art tradition known to humankind, and yet it virtually disappeared overnight with global warming.

Had the closed woodlands also closed people's minds to artistic expression? Was the Mesolithic a time when ancient knowledge was forgotten—'the dark age' of the Stone Age? Well, no, not at all. The cave art tradition ended simply because there was no longer a need to make such art. The paintings and carvings had never been mere decoration; nor had they been the inevitable expression of an inherent human creative urge. They had been much more than this—a tool for survival, one as essential as tools of stone, clothes of fur, and the fires that crackled within the caves.

The ice age had been an information age—the carvings and paintings the equivalent of our CD-ROMs today. Ambush and bloody slaughter had been easy: as long as the right people were in the right place at the right time, ample supplies of food could be acquired. Rules were then required to ensure distribution without conflict. An abundance of food in one region had meant scarcity elsewhere—groups had to be willing to join together and then to split apart; to do so they needed to know which group was where, and to have friends and relations that could be relied upon in times of need. Because herds of animals are prone to unpredictable extinctions the hunters required alternative hunting plans, always ready to put into practice.

To solve such problems, information was crucial—knowledge about the location and movements of animals, about who was living and hunting where, about future plans, about what to do in times of crisis. The art, the mythology and the religious ritual served to maintain the constant acquisition and flow of information.

When groups joined together once or twice a year for ceremony, painting and ritual, such as at Pech Merle, Mas d'Azil and Altamira, they also exchanged vital information about animal movements. Such groups would have spent the previous year living apart, some in the uplands, some on the coastal plains; some had made long treks to visit distant relations, others had watched for the arrival of migratory birds. There was a lot to tell and even more to find out. The religious beliefs of the hunter-gatherers provided sets of rules for the sharing of food when necessary. Cave paintings had not only depicted the tracks of animals, but had shown them in the act of defecating, and with their antlers and fatty parts exaggerated. Such pictures were the stimulus for accounts of what had been seen, for teaching the children; they contained the signs that a hunter must look for when searching for prey and selecting a victim in the months to come. The mythological stories contained survival strategies for those inevitable but unpredictable years of hardship.

So, for as long as the annual ceremonies and rituals were performed, and people had opportunities to gossip, to swap ideas and observations, to recount tales of hunters' exploits, to reaffirm social bonds, to learn yet more about the animals around them, information flowed and society flourished—as far as it could under the constraints of an ice-age climate.

Life in thick woodland after 9600 BC did not exact the same demands. Animals were now largely hunted on a one-to-one basis; with no mass kills there were no surpluses to manage. Narrow valleys and river crossings no longer had the same significance; there was no longer a need to have people in precisely the right place at the right time. Neither was there the need to know what was happening many miles away, either in the natural or in the social world. Hunting could effectively take place anywhere, any time, by anyone. And if animals could not be found, there were plenty of plant foods to gather and limpets to collect. Just like the red deer, people began to live in smaller, more scattered groups, becoming increasingly self-sufficient.

Periodic gatherings still took place but these were to solve problems of maintaining social ties, to allow people to marry, to exchange raw materials and food, to learn and teach new techniques of basketry and weaving. There was no longer the need for these group activities to be conducted under the gaze of painted beasts.

The ending of the cave-art tradition should not be attributed to cultural disintegration, social collapse, or the arrival of a dark age when minds were closed to the arts. The cessation of cave painting is a remarkable testament to the ability of people to rewrite the rules of their society when the need arises. It is one that we must recall as global warming threatens our planet today.

From: Mithen, Steven, *After the Ice* (New York: Orian, 2003), Ch. 16, pp. 143–49.

QUESTIONS:

1. What does the wide range and persistence of the cave painting tradition tell you about cultural networks during Ice Age Europe?
2. Connect what Mithen says to the paintings in the previous source. Does what he says fit the paintings? Does it go beyond them?

CHAPTER 2

Patterns and Parameters: Development of the Agrarian World since 10,000 BCE

INTRODUCTION

This chapter presents two kinds of sources. First, there are visual sources related to the changing world brought about by the Agricultural Revolution, including human settlement patterns that in some places began to replace the nomadic life of hunter-gatherers. Second, we present a set of sources from a wide chronological range that illustrate one of the consequences of dense and permanent settlement: epidemic disease.

ÖTZI THE ICE MAN MUMMY

Ötzi, whose story is described in Chapter 2 of *Frameworks*, was discovered as a frozen mummy. These first two pictures ask you to think about the process by which that mummy revealed its secrets and became a modern educational display.

2.1a: A Scientist Working with the Actual Mummy of the Ice Man

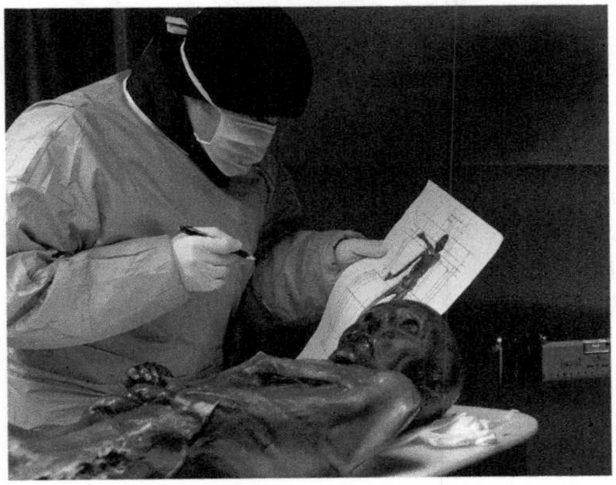

2.1b: Workers Putting the Reconstruction of the Ice Man on Display

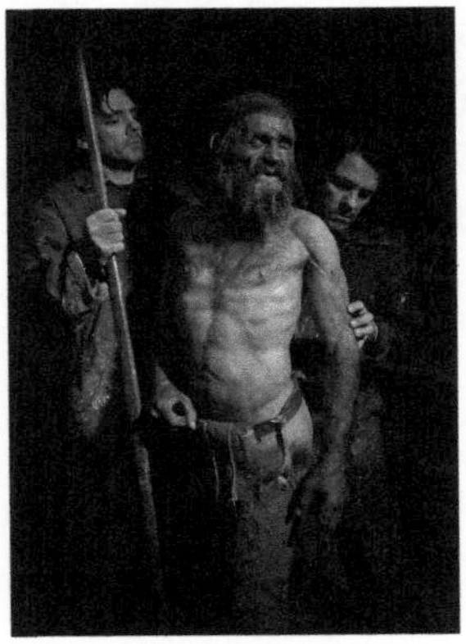

From: copyright is mentioned: © South Tyrol Museum of Archaeology.

QUESTIONS:

1. Faced with a mummy like this, what kinds of scientific specialists would you want to investigate it? How would you ensure that such scientific study had as little impact on the integrity and survival of the mummy as possible?
2. This picture shows people arranging of the Iceman reconstruction. Judging from the reconstruction, what choices—what authorial perspective on the evidence—did the people setting up the display make? Put another way, what do you think of the pose, the facial expression, and other details of the display not dictated by the evidence?

EARLY SETTLEMENTS

Agriculture was accompanied by the growth of permanent human settlements. The forms of those settlements offer evidence about the social organization, hierarchy, network connections, and culture of the people who lived in them. Here we present three such settlements.

2.2a: Çatal Höyük

Anatolia, c. 7500–5700 BCE

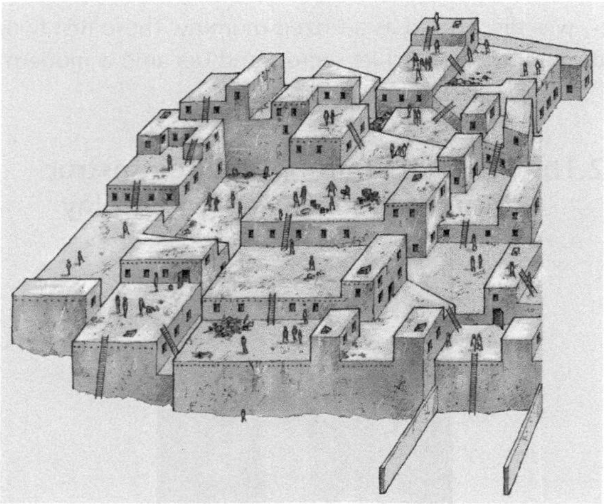

From: Library of Congress.

2.2b: Togolok 21

Margiana (Turkmenistan), c. 2300–1700 BCE

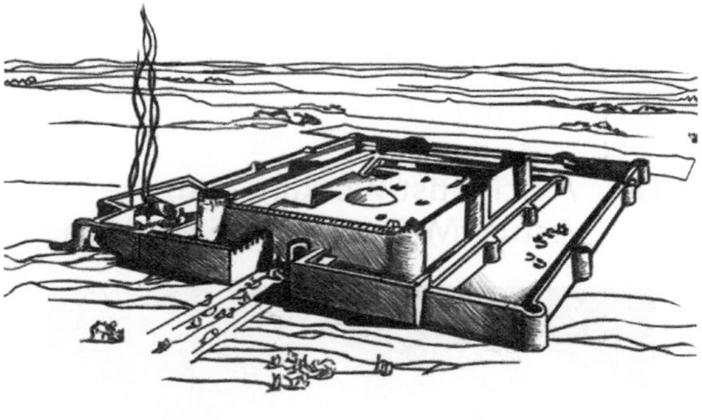

From: Anthony, David W. The horse, the wheel, and language: how bronze-age riders from the Eurasian steppes shaped the modern world, (Princeton, NJ: Princeton University Press, 2007), pp. 424 (Fig. 16.4).

2.2c: Mohenjo Daro

Indus valley, c. 2600–1900 BCE

From: National Museum of Pakistan, Karachi.

2.2d: A Temple Ziggurat

Agargouf, Iraq. Reconstruction.

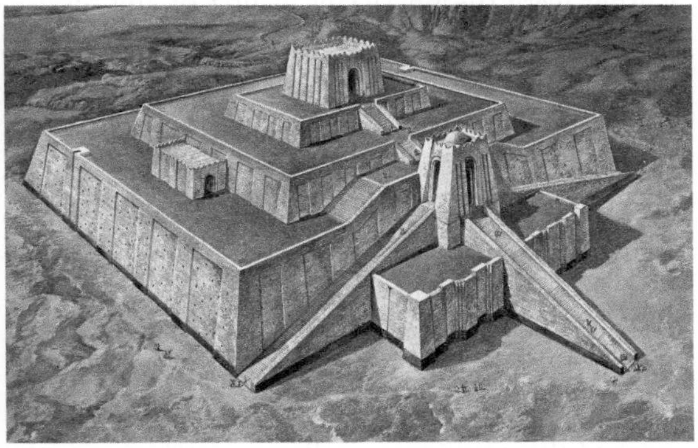

From: © DeA Picture Library / Art Resource, NY.

QUESTIONS:

1. Judging from these reconstructions and photos, what factors shaped the layout of early settlements? That is, what concerns did the builders of these settlements have? Did they change over time?
2. What information can these reconstructions and pictures not tell us? What would you like to know about these settlements that this kind of evidence cannot tell you?

EPIDEMIC DISEASE

2.3a: "The Plague in Athens" from *History of the Peloponnesian War* (Thucydides, 431 BCE)

Thucydides (c. 46–c. 395 BCE) was, along with Herodotus, one of the founders of the Greek tradition of history writing. His *History of the Peloponnesian War* recounts the great struggle between alliances of Greek city-states led by Athens and Sparta. The way he, along with Herodotus, approached the writing of history forms the foundation of the European historical tradition. He relied on eyewitness accounts (including his own) and other verifiable evidence, and he analyzed that evidence in terms of material cause and effect. These aspects of his approach are evident in the next source, in which he describes a plague that broke out in Athens during a Spartan siege of the city early in the war. His account makes clear the link between both network connections (note where the plague came from) and war in the spread of epidemic disease.

In the first days of summer the Lacedaemonians and their allies, with two-thirds of their forces as before, invaded Attica, under the command of Archidamus, son of Zeuxidamus, King of Lacedaemon, and sat down and laid waste the country. Not many days after their arrival in Attica the plague first began to show itself among the Athenians. It was said that it had broken out in many places previously in the neighborhood of Lemnos and elsewhere; but a pestilence of such extent and mortality was nowhere remembered. Neither were the physicians at first of any service, ignorant as they were of the proper way to treat it, but they died themselves the most thickly, as they visited the sick most often; nor did any human art succeed any better. Supplications in the temples, divinations, and so forth were found equally futile, till the overwhelming nature of the disaster at last put a stop to them altogether.

It first began, it is said, in the parts of Ethiopia above Egypt, and thence descended into Egypt and Libya. . . . Suddenly falling upon Athens, it first attacked the population in Piraeus—which was the occasion of their saying that the Peloponnesians had poisoned the reservoirs, there being as yet no wells there—and afterwards appeared in the upper city, when the deaths became much more frequent. All speculation as to its origin and its causes, if causes can be found adequate to produce so great a disturbance, I leave to other writers, whether lay or professional; for myself, I shall simply set down its nature, and explain the symptoms by which perhaps it may be recognized by the student, if it should ever break out again. This I can the better do, as I had the disease myself, and watched its operation in the case of others.

That year then is admitted to have been otherwise unprecedentedly free from sickness; and such few cases as occurred all determined in this. As a rule, however, there was no ostensible cause; but people in good health were all of a sudden attacked by violent heats in the head, and redness and inflammation in the eyes, the inward parts, such as the throat or tongue, becoming bloody and emitting an unnatural and fetid breath. These symptoms were followed by sneezing and hoarseness, after which the pain soon reached the chest, and produced a hard cough. When it fixed in the stomach, it upset it; and discharges of bile of every kind named by physicians ensued, accompanied by very great distress. In most cases also an ineffectual retching followed, producing violent spasms, which in some cases ceased soon after, in others much later. Externally the body was not very hot to the touch, nor pale in its appearance, but reddish, livid, and breaking out into small pustules and ulcers. But internally it burned so that the patient could not bear to have on him clothing or linen even of the very lightest description; or indeed to be otherwise than stark naked. What they would have liked best would have been to throw themselves into cold water; as indeed was done by some of the neglected sick, who plunged into the rain-tanks in their agonies of unquenchable thirst; though it made no difference whether they drank little or much. Besides this, the miserable feeling of not being able to rest or sleep never ceased to torment them. The body meanwhile did not waste away so long as the distemper was at its height, but held out to a marvel against its ravages; so that when they succumbed, as in most cases, on the seventh or eighth day to the internal inflammation, they had still some strength in them. But if they passed this stage, and the disease descended further into the bowels, inducing a violent ulceration there accompanied by severe diarrhea, this brought on a weakness which was generally fatal. For the disorder first settled in the head, ran its course from thence through the whole of the body, and, even where it did not prove mortal, it still left its mark on the extremities; for it settled in the privy parts, the fingers and the toes, and many escaped with the loss of these, some too with that of their eyes. Others again were seized with an entire loss of memory on their first recovery, and did not know either themselves or their friends.

But while the nature of the distemper was such as to baffle all description, and its attacks almost too grievous for human nature to endure, it was still in the following circumstance that its difference from all ordinary disorders was most clearly shown. All the birds and beasts that prey upon human bodies, either abstained from touching them (though there were many lying unburied), or died after tasting them. In proof of this, it was noticed that birds of this kind actually disappeared; they were not about the bodies, or indeed to be seen at all. But of course the effects which I have mentioned could best be studied in a domestic animal like the dog.

Such then, if we pass over the varieties of particular cases which were many and peculiar, were the general features of the distemper. Meanwhile the town enjoyed an immunity from all the ordinary disorders; or if any case occurred, it ended in this. Some died in neglect, others in the midst of every attention. No remedy was found that could be used as a specific; for what did good in one case, did harm in another. Strong and weak constitutions proved equally incapable of resistance, all alike being swept away, although dieted with the utmost precaution. By far the most terrible feature in the malady was the dejection which ensued when any one felt himself sickening, for the despair into which they instantly fell took away their power of resistance, and left them a much easier prey to the disorder; besides which, there was the awful spectacle of men dying like sheep, through having caught the infection in nursing each other. This caused the greatest mortality. On the one hand, if they were afraid to visit each other, they perished from neglect; indeed many houses were emptied of their inmates for want of a nurse: on the other, if they ventured to do so, death was the consequence. This was especially the case with such as made any pretensions to goodness: honour made them unsparing of themselves in their attendance in their friends' houses, where even the members of the family were at last worn out by the moans of the dying, and succumbed to the force of the disaster. Yet it was with those who had recovered from the disease that the sick and the dying found most compassion. These knew what it was from experience, and had now no fear for themselves; for the same man was never attacked twice—never at least fatally. And such persons not only received the congratulations of others, but themselves also, in the elation of the moment, half entertained the vain hope that they were for the future safe from any disease whatsoever.

An aggravation of the existing calamity was the influx from the country into the city, and this was especially felt by the new arrivals. As there were no houses to receive them, they had to be lodged at the hot season of the year in stifling cabins, where the mortality raged without restraint. The bodies of dying men lay one upon another, and half-dead creatures reeled about the streets and gathered round all the fountains in their longing for water. The sacred places also in which they had quartered themselves were full of corpses of persons that had died there, just as they were; for as the disaster passed all bounds, men, not knowing what was to become of them, became utterly careless of everything, whether sacred or profane. All the burial rites before in use were entirely upset, and they buried the bodies as best they could. Many from want of the proper appliances, through so many of their friends having died already, had recourse to the most shameless sepultures: sometimes getting the start of those who had raised a pile, they threw their own dead body upon the stranger's pyre and ignited it; sometimes they tossed the corpse which they were carrying on the top of another that was burning, and so went off.

Nor was this the only form of lawless extravagance which owed its origin to the plague. Men now coolly ventured on what they had formerly done in a corner, and not just as they pleased, seeing the rapid transitions produced by persons in prosperity suddenly dying and those who before had nothing succeeding to their property. So they resolved to spend quickly and enjoy themselves, regarding their lives and riches as alike things of a day. Perseverance in what men called honor was popular with none, it was so uncertain whether they would be spared to attain the object; but it was settled that present enjoyment, and all that contributed to it, was both honorable and useful. Fear of gods or law of man there was none to restrain them. As for the first, they judged it to be just the same whether they worshipped them or not, as they saw all alike perishing; and for the last, no one expected to live to be brought to trial for his offences, but each felt that a far severer sentence had been already passed upon them all and hung ever over their heads, and before this fell it was only reasonable to enjoy life a little.

. . .

During the whole time that the Peloponnesians were in Attica and the Athenians on the expedition in their ships, men kept dying of the plague both in the armament and in Athens. Indeed it was actually asserted that the departure of the Peloponnesians was hastened by fear of the disorder; as they heard from deserters that it was in the city, and also could see the burials going on. Yet in this invasion they remained longer than in any other, and ravaged the whole country, for they were about forty days in Attica.

. . .

From: Thucydides, and Richard Crawley, trans., *The history of the Peloponnesian war*. (London: Longmans, Green, and Co. 1876), Book II, Chapter VII, http://classics.mit.edu/Thucydides/pelopwar.2.second.html.

QUESTIONS:

1. Despite Thucydides' careful description of the symptoms of this disease, modern scientists have been unable to identify the disease. Why might this be?
2. The social effects of the plague are central to Thucydides' account. What were they? Do the behaviors he describes constitute "true" human nature, revealed when social convention breaks down, or is social convention more indicative of "true" human nature? Why (not)?

2.3b: "The Plague of Justinian" from *History of the Wars of Justinian* (Procopius, c. 552)

Procopius of Caesarea (c. 500–c. 565) was a Late Roman historian whose works are central to our understanding of the time of the Emperor Justinian (r. 527–565). As with Thucydides's writing, the focus of most of his work is on the wars and politics of his time, including a history of the building programs of Justinian, a fine demonstration of the importance of public works in Agrarian-Era exercise of power. But also like Thucydides, he witnessed a plague, which in this case is identifiable as bubonic plague, that struck Constantinople and much of the Eastern Mediterranean world in 542. Genetic studies suggest that China was the ultimate origin of the plague, which again demonstrates the impact of growing network connections on the spread of pathogens.

[542 A.D.] During these times there was a pestilence, by which the whole human race came near to being annihilated. Now in the case of all other scourges sent from Heaven some explanation of a cause might be given by daring men. . . . But for this calamity it is quite impossible either to express in words or to conceive in thought any explanation, except indeed to refer it to God. For it did not come in a part of the world nor upon certain men, nor did it confine itself to any season of the year, so that from such circumstances it might be possible to find subtle explanations of a cause, but it embraced the entire world, and blighted the lives of all men, though differing from one another in the most marked degree, respecting neither sex nor age. For much as men differ with regard to places in which they live, or in the law of their daily life, or in natural bent, or in active pursuits, or in whatever else man differs from man, in the case of this disease alone the difference availed naught. And it attacked some in the summer season, others in the winter, and still others at the other times of the year. Now let each one express his own judgment concerning the matter, both sophist and astrologer, but as for me, I shall proceed to tell where this disease originated and the manner in which it destroyed men.

It started from the Egyptians who dwell in Pelusium. Then it divided and moved in one direction towards Alexandria and the rest of Egypt, and in the other direction it came to Palestine on the borders of Egypt; and from there it spread over the whole world, always moving forward and travelling at times favorable to it . . . and if it had passed by any land, either not affecting the men there or touching them in indifferent fashion, still at a later time it came back; then those who dwelt round about this land, whom formerly it had afflicted most sorely, it did not touch at all. . . . And in the second year it reached Byzantium in the middle of spring, where it happened that I was staying at that time. And it came as follows.

Apparitions of supernatural beings in human guise of every description were seen by many persons, and those who encountered them thought that they were struck by the man they had met in this or that part of the body, as it happened, and immediately upon seeing this apparition they were seized also by the disease. . . . But in the case of some the pestilence did not come on in this way, but they saw a vision in a dream and seemed to suffer the very same thing at the hands of the creature who stood over them, or else to hear a voice foretelling to them that they were written down in the number of those who were to die. But with the majority it came about that they were seized by the disease without becoming aware of what was coming either through a waking vision or a dream. And they were taken in the following manner. They had a sudden fever, some when just roused from sleep, others while walking about, and others while otherwise engaged, without any regard to what they were doing. And the body showed no change from its previous color, nor was it hot as might be expected when attacked by a fever, nor indeed did any inflammation set in, but the fever was of such a languid sort from its commencement and up till evening that neither to the sick themselves nor to a physician who touched them would it afford any suspicion of danger. It was natural, therefore, that not one of those who had contracted the disease expected to die from it. But on the same day in some cases, in others on the following day, and in the rest not many days later, a bubonic swelling developed; and this took place not only in the particular part of the body which is called "bubon," that is, below the abdomen, but also inside the armpit, and in some cases also beside the ears, and at different points on the thighs.

Up to this point, then, everything went in about the same way with all who had taken the disease. But from then on very marked differences developed; and I am unable to say whether the cause of this diversity of symptoms was to be found in the difference in bodies, or in the fact that it followed the wish of Him who brought the disease into the world. For there ensued with some a deep coma, with others a violent delirium, and in either case they suffered the characteristic symptoms of the disease. . . . And those who were attending them were in a state of constant exhaustion and had a most difficult time of it throughout. For this reason everybody pitied them no less than the sufferers, not because they were threatened by the pestilence in going near it (for neither physicians nor other persons were found to contract this malady through contact with the sick or with the dead, for many who were constantly engaged either in burying or in attending those in no way connected with them held out in the performance of this service beyond all expectation, while with many others the disease came on without warning and they died straightway); but they pitied them because of the great hardships which they were undergoing. . . . And when water chanced to be near, they wished to fall into it, not so much because of a desire for drink (for the most of them rushed into the sea), but the cause was to be found chiefly in the diseased state of their minds. They had also great difficulty in the matter of eating, for they could not easily take food. And many perished through lack of any man to care for them, for they were either overcome by hunger, or threw themselves down from a height. And in those cases where neither coma nor delirium came on, the bubonic swelling became mortified and the sufferer, no longer able to endure the pain, died. . . . Now some of the physicians who were at a loss because the symptoms were not understood, supposing that the disease centered in the bubonic swellings, decided to investigate the bodies of the dead. And upon opening some of the swellings, they found a strange sort of carbuncle that had grown inside them.

Death came in some cases immediately, in others after many days; and with some the body broke out with black pustules about as large as a lentil and these did not survive even one day, but all succumbed immediately. With many also a vomiting of blood ensued without visible cause and straightway brought death. Moreover I am able to declare this, that the most illustrious physicians predicted that many would die, who unexpectedly escaped entirely from suffering shortly afterwards, and that they declared that many would be saved, who were destined to be carried off almost immediately. So it was that in this disease there was no cause which came within the province of human reasoning; for in all cases the issue tended to be something unaccountable. For example, while some were helped by bathing, others were harmed in no less degree. And of those who received no care many died, but others, contrary to reason, were saved. And again, methods of treatment showed different results with different patients. Indeed the whole matter may be stated thus, that no device was discovered by man to save himself, so that either by taking precautions he should not suffer, or that when the malady had assailed him he should get the better of it; but suffering came without warning and recovery was due to no external cause. And in the case of women who were pregnant death could be certainly foreseen if they were taken with the disease. For some died through miscarriage, but others perished immediately at the time of birth with the infants they bore. However, they say that three women in confinement survived though their children perished, and that one woman died at the very time of child-birth but that the child was born and survived.

Now in those cases where the swelling rose to an unusual size and a discharge of pus had set in, it came about that they escaped from the disease and survived, for clearly the acute condition of the carbuncle had found relief in this direction, and this proved to be in general an indication of returning health; but in cases where the swelling preserved its former appearance there ensued those troubles which I have just mentioned. And with some of them it came about that the thigh was withered, in which case, though the swelling was there, it did not develop the least suppuration. With others who survived the tongue did not remain unaffected, and they lived on either lisping or speaking incoherently and with difficulty.

XXIII Now the disease in Byzantium ran a course of four months, and its greatest virulence lasted about three. And at first the deaths were a little more than the normal, then the mortality rose still higher, and afterwards the tale of dead reached five thousand each day, and again it even came to ten thousand and still more than that. Now in the beginning each man attended to the burial of the dead of his own house, and these they threw even into the tombs of others, either escaping detection or using violence; but afterwards confusion and disorder everywhere became complete. For slaves remained destitute of masters, and men who in former times were very prosperous were deprived of the service of their domestics who were either sick or dead, and many houses became completely destitute of human inhabitants. For this reason it came about that some of the notable men of the city because of the universal destitution remained unburied for many days. And it fell to the lot of the emperor, as was natural, to make provision for the trouble. He therefore detailed soldiers from the palace and distributed money. . . . So those who had not as yet fallen into complete destitution in their domestic affairs attended individually to the burial of those connected with them. But Theodorus, by giving out the emperor's money and by making further expenditures from his own purse, kept burying the bodies which were not cared for. . . . At that time all the customary rites of burial were overlooked. For the dead were not carried out escorted by a procession in the customary manner, nor were the usual chants sung over them. . . . At that time, too, those of the population who had formerly been members of the factions laid aside their mutual enmity and in common they attended to the burial rites of the dead, and they carried with their own hands the bodies of those who were no connections of theirs and buried them. . . . [But] as soon as they were rid of the disease and were saved, and already supposed that they were in security, since the curse had moved on to other peoples, then they turned sharply about and reverted once more to their baseness of heart, and now, more than before, they make a display of the inconsistency of their conduct, altogether surpassing themselves in villainy and in lawlessness of every sort. . . . And work of every description ceased, and all the trades were abandoned by the artisans, and all other work as well, such as each had in hand. Indeed in a city which was simply abounding in all good things starvation almost absolute was running riot. . . .

From: Procopius, and H. B. Dewing, trans., *Procopius*, (London: W. Heinemann, 1914), pp. 451–73.

QUESTIONS:

1. What does Procopius's description of the plague tell us about social structures and class attitudes in the Late Roman Empire? What other cultural values can you identify that shape his description?
2. Compare Procopius's plague account with the account by Thucydides. How does each historian describe the social reactions to the plague? Procopius modeled his description on Thucydides's. Does that make it less valuable as a source? Why (not)?

2.3c: "*Rat Death*" (Shih Tai-nan, 1792)

Plagues have a long history in China, the bubonic plague in particular, with regular outbreaks recorded from as early as 125 during the Han Dynasty and lasting well into the twentieth century. In 1792, a major outbreak occurred in Yunnan. A local poet, Shih Tai-nan, wrote a description of the plague shortly before he himself succumbed to the disease. Although it is much briefer than the accounts by Thucydides and Procopius, it is just as evocative of the suffering and the social breakdown that accompanied major epidemics.

Dead rats on the east,
Dead rats on the west!
Dear rats are more fiercesome than tigers.
After several days
After the death of the rats—corpses litter
the steppe.
Countless dead by day!
In their fear people no longer notice the sun.
If three persons work together
Two of them fall dead
At a distance of ten paces.
Numberless dead by night:
No one dares to mourn the dead.
After a visit of the demon plague

Lamps suddenly flicker out,
Leaving the soul and body in darkness.
The crows croak endlessly,
Mournfully howl the dogs.
Man and spirit are one,
when the soul has left the body.
The earth is covered with human bones,
In the field are left ungathered harvests.
Even the landlords do not collect taxes.
I wish to leave on the red dragon,
In order to meet with the Gods in the heavens
And ask them to send a heavenly moisture
And again revive the dead.

From: "Rat Death" (Chinese, 1792) in http://www.dtic.mil/cgi-bin/GetTRDoc?AD=AD0648103, pp. 3–4.

QUESTIONS:

1. How does Shih Tai-nan's attitude towards the plague compare to the attitudes of Thucydides and Procopius? What does the poetic form convey differently from prose descriptions?
2. What social effects of the plague does Shih Tai-nan describe? How does this differ from the social effects Thucydides and Procopius describe?

CHAPTER 3

The World of Early Complex Societies: 4000 BCE to 600 BCE

INTRODUCTION

The invention of agriculture laid the foundations for the development of more complex societies. The sources in this chapter come from the earliest societies to reach state-level hierarchical structure. They give us examples of some of the political and social concerns of early states, and they also show us some of the cultural images of themselves these early state projected onto their cultural screens.

3.1: *The Punitive Expedition of Yin from Shu Jing* (The Classic of History, c. 600 BCE, purporting to be from 2159-2147 BCE)

The *Shu Jing,* known in English by several names including *The Classic of History,* is a compilation of documents purporting to be from the early dynastic history of China (traditionally beginning as early as 2900 BCE and historically from around 1700 BCE), but many of the documents are actually forgeries from the period 600–300 BCE. While they portray traditions from the earlier era, they also have an overlay of ideological concerns from the later period. The collection probably began to come together before 600; Confucius quoted versions of it in his *Analects,* and it achieved the status of one of the Confucian classics during the Former Han Dynasty (206 BCE–9 CE). In this selection, the king orders the marquis of Tin to punish the court astrologers Hsi and Ho, who have neglected their duties and failed to predict an autumnal eclipse of the sun.

1. When Kung Khang commenced his reign over all within the four seas, the marquis of Yin was commissioned to take charge of the (king's) six hosts. (At this time) the Hsi and Ho had neglected the duties of their office, and were abandoned to drink in their (private) cities; and the marquis of Yin received the king's charge to go and punish them.

2. He made an announcement to his hosts, saying, 'Ah! ye, all my men, there are the well-counselled instructions of the sage (founder of our dynasty), clearly verified in their power to give stability and security:—"The former kings were carefully attentive to the warnings of Heaven, and their ministers observed the regular laws (of their offices). All the officers

(moreover) watchfully did their duty to assist (the government), and their sovereign became entirely intelligent." Every year, in the first month of spring, the herald, with his wooden-tongued bell, goes along the road, (proclaiming). "Ye officers able to instruct, be prepared with your admonitions. Ye workmen engaged in mechanical affairs, remonstrate on the subjects of your employments. If any of you do not attend with respect (to this requirement), the country has regular punishments for you."

'Now here are the Hsi and Ho. They have allowed their virtue to be subverted, and are besotted by drink. They have violated the duties of their office, and left their posts. They have been the first to let the regulating of the heavenly (bodies) get into disorder, putting far from them their proper business. On the first day of the last month of autumn, the sun and moon did not meet harmoniously in Fang. The blind musicians beat their drums; the inferior officers galloped, and the common people (employed about the public offices) ran about. The Hsi and the Ho, however, as if they were (mere) personators of the dead in their offices, heard nothing and knew nothing;—so stupidly went they astray (from their duties) in the matter of the heavenly appearances, and rendered themselves liable to the death appointed by the former kings. The statutes of government say, "When they anticipate the time, let them be put to death without mercy; when (their reckoning) is behind the time, let them be put to death without mercy."

'Now I, with you all, am entrusted with the execution of the punishment appointed by Heaven. Unite your strength, all of you warriors, for the royal House. Give me your help, I pray you, reverently to carry out the dread charge of the Son of Heaven.

'When the fire blazes over the ridge of Khwăn, gems and stones are burned together; but if a minister of Heaven exceed in doing his duty, the consequences will be fiercer than blazing fire. While I destroy, (therefore), the chief criminals, I will not punish those who have been forced to follow them; and those who have long been stained by their filthy manners will be allowed to renovate themselves.

'Oh! When sternness overcomes compassion, things are surely conducted to a successful issue. When compassion overcomes sternness, no merit can be achieved. All ye, my warriors, exert yourselves, and take warning, (and obey my orders)!'

From: James Legge, transl, *The Sacred Books of China: The Texts of Confucianism*, in F. Max Mueller, ed., *The Sacred Books of the East*, 50 vols., (Oxford: Clarendon, 1879–1910), Vol 5 (1899). pp. 81–83.

QUESTIONS:

1. Why would court astrologers have been so important to the court of a Chinese king?
2. What cultural values does the document promote? What should people believe in order to make a kingdom run smoothly?

3.2: *The Code of Hammurabi* (unknown author, 1792–1750 BCE)

The "Code of Hammurabi" is a set of 282 laws (or, more accurately, a group of judgment records set out as precedents) with a prologue and an epilogue dating to the reign of the Babylonian king Hammurabi (r. c. 1792–50 BCE). The Code was inscribed on a stone stele meant for public display, and fragments on various clay tablets have survived as well. Its provisions cover crimes and punishments, family law (including inheritance and property disputes), and commerce and contracts. The provisions about commerce and contracts are especially numerous: network activity was a central concern in the world's earliest cities.

PROLOGUE

When Anu the Sublime, King of the Anunaki, and Bel, the lord of Heaven and earth, who decreed the fate of the land, assigned to Marduk, the over-ruling son of Ea, God of righteousness, dominion over earthly man, and made him great among the Igigi, they called Babylon by his illustrious name, made it great on earth, and founded an everlasting kingdom in it, whose foundations are laid so solidly as those of heaven and earth; then Anu and Bel called by name me, Hammurabi, the exalted prince, who feared God, to bring about the rule of righteousness in the land, to destroy the wicked and the evil-doers; so that the strong should not harm the weak; so that I should rule over the black-headed people like Shamash, and enlighten the land, to further the well-being of mankind.

. . .

CODE OF LAWS

1. If any one ensnare another, putting a ban upon him, but he can not prove it, then he that ensnared him shall be put to death.
2. If any one bring an accusation against a man, and the accused go to the river and leap into the river, if he sink in the river his accuser shall take possession of his house. But if the river prove that the accused is not guilty, and he escape unhurt, then he who had brought the accusation shall be put to death, while he who leaped into the river shall take possession of the house that had belonged to his accuser.
3. If any one bring an accusation of any crime before the elders, and does not prove what he has charged, he shall, if it be a capital offense charged, be put to death.
4. If he satisfy the elders to impose a fine of grain or money, he shall receive the fine that the action produces.
5. If a judge try a case, reach a decision, and present his judgment in writing; if later error shall appear in his decision, and it be through his own fault, then he shall pay twelve times the fine set by him in the case, and he shall be publicly removed from the judge's bench, and never again shall he sit there to render judgement.
6. If any one steal the property of a temple or of the court, he shall be put to death, and also the one who receives the stolen thing from him shall be put to death.
7. If any one buy from the son or the slave of another man, without witnesses or a contract, silver or gold, a male or female slave, an ox or a sheep, an ass or anything, or if he take it in charge, he is considered a thief and shall be put to death.
8. If any one steal cattle or sheep, or an ass, or a pig or a goat, if it belong to a god or to the court, the thief shall pay thirtyfold therefor; if they belonged to a freed man of the king he shall pay tenfold; if the thief has nothing with which to pay he shall be put to death.
9. If any one lose an article, and find it in the possession of another: if the person in whose possession the thing is found say "A merchant sold it to me, I paid for it before witnesses," and if the owner of the thing say, "I will bring witnesses who know my property," then shall the purchaser bring the merchant who sold it to him, and the witnesses before whom he bought it, and the owner shall bring witnesses who can identify his property. The judge shall examine their testimony—both of the witnesses before whom

the price was paid, and of the witnesses who identify the lost article on oath. The merchant is then proved to be a thief and shall be put to death. The owner of the lost article receives his property, and he who bought it receives the money he paid from the estate of the merchant.

10. If the purchaser does not bring the merchant and the witnesses before whom he bought the article, but its owner bring witnesses who identify it, then the buyer is the thief and shall be put to death, and the owner receives the lost article.
11. If the owner do not bring witnesses to identify the lost article, he is an evil-doer, he has traduced, and shall be put to death.
12. If the witnesses be not at hand, then shall the judge set a limit, at the expiration of six months. If his witnesses have not appeared within the six months, he is an evil-doer, and shall bear the fine of the pending case.

. . .

14. If any one steal the minor son of another, he shall be put to death.
15. If any one take a male or female slave of the court, or a male or female slave of a freed man, outside the city gates, he shall be put to death.
16. If any one receive into his house a runaway male or female slave of the court, or of a freedman, and does not bring it out at the public proclamation of the major domus, the master of the house shall be put to death.
17. If any one find runaway male or female slaves in the open country and bring them to their masters, the master of the slaves shall pay him two shekels of silver.
18. If the slave will not give the name of the master, the finder shall bring him to the palace; a further investigation must follow, and the slave shall be returned to his master.
19. If he hold the slaves in his house, and they are caught there, he shall be put to death.
20. If the slave that he caught run away from him, then shall he swear to the owners of the slave, and he is free of all blame.

. . .

102. If a merchant entrust money to an agent (broker) for some investment, and the broker suffer a loss in the place to which he goes, he shall make good the capital to the merchant.
103. If, while on the journey, an enemy take away from him anything that he had, the broker shall swear by God and be free of obligation.
104. If a merchant give an agent corn, wool, oil, or any other goods to transport, the agent shall give a receipt for the amount, and compensate the merchant therefor. Then he shall obtain a receipt form the merchant for the money that he gives the merchant.
105. If the agent is careless, and does not take a receipt for the money which he gave the merchant, he can not consider the unreceipted money as his own.
106. If the agent accept money from the merchant, but have a quarrel with the merchant (denying the receipt), then shall the merchant swear before God and witnesses that he has given this money to the agent, and the agent shall pay him three times the sum.
107. If the merchant cheat the agent, in that as the latter has returned to him all that had been given him, but the merchant denies the receipt of what had been returned to him, then shall this agent convict the merchant before God and the judges, and if he still deny receiving what the agent had given him shall pay six times the sum to the agent.
108. If a tavern-keeper [female] does not accept corn according to gross weight in payment of drink, but takes money, and the price of the drink is less than that of the corn, she shall be convicted and thrown into the water.
109. If conspirators meet in the house of a tavern-keeper [female], and these conspirators are

not captured and delivered to the court, the tavern-keeper shall be put to death.

110. If a "sister of a god" open a tavern, or enter a tavern to drink, then shall this woman be burned to death.

111. If an inn-keeper furnish sixty ka of usakani-drink to . . . she shall receive fifty ka of corn at the harvest.

. . .

137. If a man wish to separate from a woman who has borne him children, or from his wife who has borne him children: then he shall give that wife her dowry, and a part of the usufruct of field, garden, and property, so that she can rear her children. When she has brought up her children, a portion of all that is given to the children, equal as that of one son, shall be given to her. She may then marry the man of her heart.

138. If a man wishes to separate from his wife who has borne him no children, he shall give her the amount of her purchase money and the dowry which she brought from her father's house, and let her go.

139. If there was no purchase price he shall give her one mina of gold as a gift of release.

140. If he be a freed man he shall give her one-third of a mina of gold.

141. If a man's wife, who lives in his house, wishes to leave it, plunges into debt, tries to ruin her house, neglects her husband, and is judicially convicted: if her husband offer her release, she may go on her way, and he gives her nothing as a gift of release. If her husband does not wish to release her, and if he take another wife, she shall remain as servant in her husband's house.

142. If a woman quarrel with her husband, and say: "You are not congenial to me," the reasons for her prejudice must be presented. If she is guiltless, and there is no fault on her part, but he leaves and neglects her, then no guilt attaches to this woman, she shall take her dowry and go back to her father's house.

143. If she is not innocent, but leaves her husband, and ruins her house, neglecting her husband, this woman shall be cast into the water.

144. If a man take a wife and this woman give her husband a maid-servant, and she bear him children, but this man wishes to take another wife, this shall not be permitted to him; he shall not take a second wife.

145. If a man take a wife, and she bear him no children, and he intend to take another wife: if he take this second wife, and bring her into the house, this second wife shall not be allowed equality with his wife.

146. If a man take a wife and she give this man a maid-servant as wife and she bear him children, and then this maid assume equality with the wife: because she has borne him children her master shall not sell her for money, but he may keep her as a slave, reckoning her among the maid-servants.

147. If she have not borne him children, then her mistress may sell her for money.

. . .

EPILOGUE

In future time, through all coming generations, let the king, who may be in the land, observe the words of righteousness which I have written on my monument; let him not alter the law of the land which I have given, the edicts which I have enacted; my monument let him not mar. If such a ruler have wisdom, and be able to keep his land in order, he shall observe the words which I have written in this inscription; the rule, statute, and law of the land which I have given; the decisions which I have made will this inscription show him; let him rule his subjects accordingly, speak justice to them, give right decisions, root out the miscreants and criminals from this land, and grant prosperity to his subjects.

From: The Code of Hammurabi, L. W. King, transl., with commentary from Charles F. Horne, PhD (1915), online at: http://avalon.law.yale.edu/ancient/hamframe.asp.

QUESTIONS:

1. What provisions of the Code reflect the hierarchical structure of Babylonian society? Can you map particular provisions onto the *Framework* pyramid diagram of state-level Agrarian societies?
2. What cultural values does the Code express? Is the Code idealized or realistic?

3.3: *A Peace Treaty between Ramses II and Hattusili III, the Egyptian Version* (1258 BCE)

The international politics of the great Bronze Age chariot kingdoms of Egypt, Hatti (the Hittite Empire), and Babylon produced the world's first known peace treaty. After a coup in Hatti, the ousted king fled to Egypt, precipitating a diplomatic crisis. The Egyptian pharaoh Ramses II (c. 1303–1213 BCE) ended the crisis by negotiating a peace treaty with Hattusili III (r. 1267–1237 BCE), king of Hatti. The agreement was recorded in both languages; the two versions are nearly identical except that each claims that the other party sued for peace. We present the Egyptian version here. The treaty seems to have worked: the frontier between the two kingdoms remained peaceful for the remainder of Ramses' long reign.

Year 21, first month of the second season, twenty-first day, under the majesty of the King of Upper and Lower Egypt: Usermare-Setepnere, Son of Re: Ramses-Meriamon, given life, forever and ever, beloved of Amon-Re-Harakhte, Ptah-South-of-His-Wall, lord of "Life-of-the-Two-Lands," Mut, mistress of Ishru, and Khonsu-Neferhotep; shining upon the Horus-throne of the living, like his father, Harakhte, forever and ever.

On this day, lo, his majesty was at the city (called): "House-of-Ramses-Meriamon," performing the pleasing ceremonies of his father, Amon-Re-Harakhte-Atum, lord of the Two Lands of Heliopolis; Amon of Ramses-Meriamon, Ptah of Ramses-Meriamon, "— great in strength, son of Mut," according as they gave to him eternity in jubilees, everlastingness in peaceful years, all lands, and all countries being prostrate beneath his sandals forever. There came the king's messenger, the deputy and butler —, together with the king's messenger — [bringing (?) to the king] Ramses II [the messenger (?)] of [Kheta, Ter] teseb and the [second messenger (?)] of Kheta [bearing (?) a silver tablet] which the great chief of the Kheta, Khetasar [caused] to be brought to Pharaoh, L. P. H., to crave peace [fro]m [the majesty] of the King of Upper and Lower Egypt, Ramses II, given life, forever and ever, like his father, Re, every day.

Copy of the silver tablet, which the great chief of Kheta, Khetasar caused to be brought to Pharaoh, L. P. H., by the hand of his messenger, Terteseb, and his messenger, Ramose, to crave peace from the majesty of Ramses II, the Bull of rulers, making his boundary as far as he desires in every land.

The treaty which the great chief of Kheta, Khetasar, the valiant, the son of Merasar, the great chief of Kheta, the valiant, the grandson, of Seplel, [the great chief of Kheta], the valiant, made, upon a silver tablet for Usermare-Setepnere (Ramses II), the great ruler of Egypt, the valiant, the son of Menmare (Seti II), the great ruler of Egypt, The valiant, the grandson of Menpehtire (Ramses I), the great ruler of Egypt, the valiant; the good treaty of peace and of brotherhood, setting peace [between them (?)], forever.

1. Now, at the beginning, since eternity, the relations of the great ruler of Egypt with the great chief of Kheta were (such) that the god prevented hostilities between them, by treaty. Whereas, in the time of Metella, the great chief of Kheta, my brother, he fought w[ith Ramses II], the great ruler of Egypt, yet afterward, beginning with this day, behold, Khetasar, the great chief of Kheta, is [in] a treaty- relation for establishing the relations which the Re made, and which Sutekh made, for the land of Egypt, with the land of Kheta, in order not to permit hostilities to arise between them, forever.
2. Behold then, Khetasar, the great chief of Kheta, is in treaty relation with Usermare-Setepnere (Ramses II), the great ruler of Egypt, beginning with this day, in order to bring about good peace and good brotherhood between us forever, while he is in brotherhood with me, he is in peace with me; and I am in brotherhood with him, and I am in peace with him, forever. Since Metella, the great chief of Kheta, my brother, succumbed to his fate, and Khetasar sat as great chief of Kheta upon the throne of his father, behold, I am together with Ramses-Meriamon, the great ruler of Egypt, and he is [with me in (?)] our peace and our brotherhood. It is better than the former peace and brotherhood which were in the land.

   Behold, I, even the great chief of Kheta, am with [Ramses II], the great ruler of Egypt, in good peace and in good brotherhood.

   The children of the children of the great chief of Kheta shall be in brotherhood and peace with the children of the children of Ramses-Meriamon, the great ruler of Egypt, being in our relations of brotherhood and our relations [of peace], that the [land of Egypt] may be with the land of Kheta in peace and brotherhood like ourselves, forever.
3. There shall be no hostilities between them, forever. The great chief of Kheta shall not pass over into the land of Egypt, forever, to take anything therefrom. Ramses-Meriamon, the great ruler of Egypt, shall not pass over into the land of Kheta, to take [anything] therefrom, forever.
4. As for the former treaty which was in the time of Seplel, the great chief of Kheta, likewise the former treaty which was in the time of Metella the great chief of Kheta, my father, I will hold to it. Behold, Ramses-Meriamon, the great ruler of Egypt, will hold [to it] with us [together (?)] beginning with this day. We will hold to it, and we will deal in this former manner.
5. If another enemy come against the lands of Usermare-Setepnere (Ramses II), the great ruler of Egypt, and he shall send to the great chief of Kheta, saying; "Come with me as reinforcement against him," the great chief of Kheta shall [come], and the great chief of Kheta shall slay his enemy. But if it be not the desire of the great chief of Kheta to come, he shall send his infantry and his chariotry, and shall slay his enemy.
6. Or if Ramses-Meriamon, [the great ruler of Egypt], be provoked against [delinquent (?)] subjects, when they have committed some other fault against him, and he come to slay them, then the great chief of Kheta shall act with the lord of Egypt [— —].
7. If another en[emy come] against the great chief of Kheta, [and he shall send] to the great chief (sic!) [of Egypt], Usermare-Setepnere [for reinforcements (?) then he] shall come to him as reinforcement, to slay his enemy. But if it be [not] the desire of Ramses-Meriamon, the great ruler of Egypt, to come, he shall [send] his infantry and his chariotry [and shall slay his enemy (?)]. [Or] —— — seeing them, besides returning answer to the land of Kheta.

8. Now if subjects of the great chief of Kheta transgress against him, and Ramses-Meriamon, the great ruler of Egypt, shall ——/ the land of Kheta and the land of Egypt ——/, that is to say; "I will come after [their punishment (?)] to Ramses-Meriamon, the great ruler of Egypt, living forever, — — — the land of Kheta." . . . . their appointing him for them, to be lord, to cause that Usermare-Setepnere, the great ruler of Egypt, shall be silent from his speech forever. If he — his — — the land of Kheta, and he shall turn back [again to (?)] the great chief of Kheta ——//.
9. [If any great man of the land of Egypt shall flee and shall come to] the great chief of Kheta, from either a town [or] — of the lands of Ramses-Meriamon, the great ruler of Egypt, and they shall come to the great chief of Kheta, then the great chief of Kheta shall not receive them, (but) the great chief of Kheta shall cause them to be brought to Usermare-Setepnere, the great ruler of Egypt, [their] lord therefor.
10. Or if there flee a man, or two men who are unknown—, and they shall come to the land of Kheta, to become foreign subjects, then they shall not be settled in the land of Kheta, but they shall be brought to Ramses-Meriamon, the great ruler of Egypt,
11. Or if any great man shall flee from the land of Kheta, [and he shall come to] Usermare-Setepnere, the great ruler of Egypt, (from) either a town or a district, or [any region of] those belonging to the land of Kheta, and they shall come to Ramses-Meriamon, the great ruler of Egypt, then Usermare-Setepnere, the great ruler of Egypt, shall not receive them, (but) Ramses-Meriamon, the great ruler of Egypt, shall cause them to be brought to the great chief of Kheta. They shall not be settled.
12. Likewise, if there flee a man, or two, or three, [who are not] known, and they shall come to the land of Egypt, to become foreign subjects, then Usermare-Setepnere, the great ruler of Egypt, shall not settle them, (but) he shall cause them to be brought to the great chief of Kheta.
13. As for the words of this [contract (?)] of the great chief of Kheta, with Ramses-Meriamon, the great ruler [of Egypt], written upon this silver tablet; as for these words, a thousand gods of the male gods and of the female gods, of those of the land of Kheta, together with a thousand gods, of the male gods and of the female gods of those of the land of Egypt, they are with me as witnesses [to (?)] these words: the Sun-god, lord of the heavens, the Sun-god, of the city of Ernen (ArnnA), Sutekh, the lord of the heavens, Sutekh of Kheta, Sutekh of the city of Ernen, Sutekh of the city Zepyerened, Sutekh of the city of Perek, Sutekh of the city of Khesesep, Sutekh of the city Seres, Sutekh of the city of Aleppo, Sutekh of the city of Rekhsen, Sutekh [of the city of—], ——, Sutekh of the city of Sekhpen, Antheret of the land of Kheta, the god of Zeyethekhrer, the god of Kerzet —, the god of Kherpenteres, the goddess of the city of Kerekhen — n —, the goddess of [Khewek], the goddess of Zen—, the god of Zen—wet, the god of Serep~ the god of Khenbet, the queen of the heavens, gods, lords of swearing, the goddess, the mistress of the soil, the mistress of swearing, Teskher, the mistress of the mountains, and the rivers of the land of Kheta, the gods of the land of Kezweden, Amon, the Sun-god, Sutekh, the male gods and the female gods of the mountains and the rivers of the land of Egypt, of the heavens, the soil, the great sea, the wind, and the storms.
14. Now, these words, which are upon this silver tablet, are for the land of Kheta and for the land of Egypt. As for him who shall not keep them, the thousand gods of the land of Kheta, and the thousand gods of the land of Egypt shall desolate his house, his land, and his subjects.

15. Now as for him who shall keep these words, which are upon this silver tablet, whether they be of Kheta, or whether they be people of Egypt, and they shall not devise (aught) against them; the thousand gods of the land of Kheta, together with the thousand gods of the land of Egypt, shall preserve his health, and his life, together with his issue, with his land, and his subjects.
16. If a man flee from the land of Egypt, or two or three, and come to the great chief of Kheta, the great chief of Kheta shall seize upon them, and shall cause them to be brought back to Usermare-Setepnere, the great ruler of Egypt. Now, as for the man who shall be brought (back) to Ramses-Meriamon, the great ruler of Egypt, let not his crime be set up against him; let not his house be injured, nor his wives, nor his children, [let] him [not be killed], and let no injury be done to his eyes, to his ears, to his mouth, nor to his feet. Let not any crime be set up against him.
17. Likewise if a man flee from the land of Kheta, be it one, be it two, (or) be it three, and they shall come to Usermare-Setepnere, the great ruler of Egypt, let Ramses-Meriamon, the great ruler of Egypt, seize [upon them, and let him cause] that they be brought to the great chief of Kheta; and the great chief of Kheta shall not set up their crime against them; let not his house be injured, nor his wives, nor his children, let him not be killed, and let no injury be done to his ears, to his eyes, to his mouth, nor to his feet. Let not any crime be set up against him.
18. That which is in the middle of this silver tablet: on its front side is a figure in the likeness of Sutekh embracing the likeness of the great chief of Kheta, surrounded by the following [words (?)]: "The seal of Sutekh, the ruler of the heavens; the seal of the treaty which Khetasar, the great chief of Kheta, the valiant, the son of Merasar the valiant, the great chief of Kheta, the valiant, made." That which is in the midst of the surrounding design is the seal [of Sutekh, the ruler of the heavens]. [That which is [in the middle on] its other side is a figure, in the likeness of [—] of Kheta, embracing the figure of the princess of Kheta, surrounded by the following words: "The seal of the Sun-god of the city of Ernen, the lord of the land; the seal of Petkhep, the princess of the land of Kheta, the daughter of the land of Kezweden, the — — — of Ernen, the mistress of the land, the votress of the goddess. That which is in the midst of the surrounding design is the seal of the Sun-god of Ernen, the lord of every land."

From: J. H. Breasted, *Ancient Records of Egypt*, vol. 3, 367–91, pp. 163–73.

QUESTIONS:

1. In what ways do the two sides in this treaty recognize and honor each other's cultural differences in order to make a lasting agreement?
2. How do the provisions of the treaty reflect the hierarchical structures of the two kingdoms?

3.4: The Hymn to Purusha from The Rig Veda

The Hymn to Purusha is one of the creation myth hymns contained in the Rig Veda, an ancient Indian sacred text that became one of the four sacred texts of Hinduism. Based on linguistic evidence, the Rig Veda was composed (or emerged from an oral tradition) as early as around 2500 BCE. It has since been passed down by methods of memorization that generated the world's first studies of linguistics. The first written versions of those memorized texts date to the Gupta period between 300 and 600 CE.

HYMN XC. Purusha.

1. A THOUSAND heads hath Purusha, a thousand eyes, a thousand feet.
   On every side pervading earth he fills a space ten fingers wide.
2. This Purusha is all that yet hath been and all that is to be;
   The Lord of Immortality which waxes greater still by food.
3. So mighty is his greatness; yea, greater than this is Purusha.
   All creatures are one-fourth of him, three-fourths eternal life in heaven.
4. With three-fourths Purusha went up: one-fourth of him again was here.
   Thence he strode out to every side over what cats not and what cats.
5. From him Virāj was born; again Purusha from Virāj was born.
   As soon as he was born he spread eastward and westward o'er the earth.
6. When Gods prepared the sacrifice with Purusha as their offering,
   Its oil was spring, the holy gift was autumn; summer was the wood.
7. They balmed as victim on the grass Purusha born in earliest time.
   With him the Deities and all Sādhyas and Ṛshis sacrificed.
8. From that great general sacrifice the dripping fat was gathered up.
   He formed the creatures of-the air, and animals both wild and tame.
9. From that great general sacrifice Ṛcas and Sāma-hymns were born:
   Therefrom were spells and charms produced; the Yajus had its birth from it.
10. From it were horses born, from it all cattle with two rows of teeth:
    From it were generated kine, from it the goats and sheep were born.
11. When they divided Purusha how many portions did they make?
    What do they call his mouth, his arms? What do they call his thighs and feet?
12. The Brahman was his mouth, of both his arms was the Rājanya made.
    His thighs became the Vaiśya, from his feet the Śūdra was produced.
13. The Moon was gendered from his mind, and from his eye the Sun had birth;
    Indra and Agni from his mouth were born, and Vāyu from his breath.
14. Forth from his navel came mid-air the sky was fashioned from his head
    Earth from his feet, and from his car the regions. Thus they formed the worlds.
15. Seven fencing-sticks had he, thrice seven layers of fuel were prepared,
    When the Gods, offering sacrifice, bound, as their victim, Purusha.
16. Gods, sacrificing, sacrificed the victim these were the earliest holy ordinances.
    The Mighty Ones attained the height of heaven, there where the Sādhyas, Gods of old, are dwelling

From: Purushasukta, *Hinduism: the Rig Veda,* Ralph T. H. Griffith, transl., 1896, pp. 602–3, from Bk X, Hymn XC.

QUESTIONS:

1. Purusha sacrifices himself to create the cosmos, meaning that god and creation are not separate. What are the implications of such a view?
2. Creation of the cosmos includes creation of hierarchical social order. How might making social order part of nature appeal to those lower in that order?

3.5: *Harappan Unicorn Seal* (c. 2300 BC)

A widespread complex of cities arose in the Indus Valley in the third millennium BCE, with the most famous sites being Harappa and Mohenjo Daro. Although extensive archaeological excavation has revealed vast ground plans and impressive structures (see Source 2c in Chapter 2), less is known about this early center of civilization than about others such as Mesopotamia, Egypt, and China because the Harappan script, of which we have only small fragments, has never been deciphered. What we have appears on seals such as this one. Such seals have been discovered throughout the Indus Valley and as far away as Mesopotamia, indicating perhaps that the seals played some role in trade.

From: http://www.harappa.com/indus2/145.html.

QUESTIONS:

1. What visual elements of the seal seem significant to you? What might they represent?
2. What can be inferred from this seal about Harappan society that is similar to other early state-level societies?

CHAPTER 4

The Axial Age: 600 BCE to 300 BCE

INTRODUCTION

The spread and development of state-level complex societies slowly created a more complex world, especially in the most populous core of Afro-Eurasia. This more complex world posed new challenges and inspired intellectual responses to questions about the meaning of the cosmos, social order, and individual ethics. The responses were sophisticated enough to form the foundations of cultural traditions still relevant today. This chapter presents examples of this intellectual activity.

MEDICINE

4.1a: *On the Sacred Disease* (Hippocrates, c. 400 BCE)

Hippocrates (c. 460–c. 377 BCE) is considered "the father of Western medicine" and the creator of the Hippocratic Oath. There is in a sense more screen image than reality to this reputation, because almost everything we know about him comes from the writings and practices of his followers. But if we assume that his followers in fact built on Hippocrates' own teachings, the screen image is at least reasonable. In the following selection, Hippocrates writes about epilepsy, which many Greeks at the time attributed to divine causes, calling it "The Sacred Disease". Hippocrates sets out to show that it was like any other disease.

It is thus with regard to the disease called Sacred: it appears to me to be nowise more divine nor more sacred than other diseases, but has a natural cause from the originates like other affections. Men regard its nature and cause as divine from ignorance and wonder, because it is not at all like to other diseases. And this notion of its divinity is kept up by their inability to comprehend it, and the simplicity of the mode by which it is cured, for men are freed from it by purifications and incantations. But if it is reckoned divine because it is wonderful, instead of one there are many diseases which would be sacred; for, as I will show, there are others no less wonderful and prodigious, which nobody imagines to be sacred. The quotidian, tertian, and quartan fevers, seem to me no less sacred and divine in their origin than this disease, although they are not reckoned so wonderful. And I see men become mad and demented from no manifest cause, and at the same time doing many things out of place; and I have known many persons in sleep groaning and crying out, some in a state of suffocation, some jumping up and fleeing out of doors, and deprived of their reason until they awaken, and afterward becoming well and rational as before, although they be pale and weak; and this will happen not once but frequently. And there are many and various things of the like kind, which it would be tedious to state particularly.

They who first referred this malady to the gods appear to me to have been just such persons as the conjurors, purificators, mountebanks, and charlatans now are, who give themselves out for being excessively religious, and as knowing more than other people. Such persons, then, using the divinity as a pretext and screen of their own inability to of their own inability to afford any assistance, have given out that the disease is sacred, adding suitable reasons for this opinion, they have instituted a mode of treatment which is safe for themselves, namely, by applying purifications and incantations, and enforcing abstinence from baths and many articles of food which are unwholesome to men in diseases. . . .

But this disease seems to me to be no more divine than others; but it has its nature such as other diseases have, and a cause whence it originates, and its nature and cause are divine only just as much as all others are, and it is curable no less than the others, unless when, the from of time, it is confirmed, and has became stronger than the remedies applied. Its origin is hereditary, like that of other diseases. For if a phlegmatic person be born of a phlegmatic, and a bilious of a bilious, and a phthisical of a phthisical, and one having spleen disease, of another having disease of the spleen, what is to hinder it from happening that where the father and mother were subject to this disease, certain of their offspring should be so affected also? . . .

In these ways I am of the opinion that the brain exercises the greatest power in the man. This is the interpreter to us of those things which emanate from the air, when it (*the brain*) happens to be in a sound state. But the air supplies sense to it. And the eyes, the ears, the tongue and the feet, administer such things as the brain cogitates. For in as much as it is supplied with air, does it impart sense to the body. It is the brain which is the messenger to the understanding. For when the man draws the breath (*pneuma*) into himself, it passes first to the brain, and thus the air is distributed to the rest of the body, leaving in the brain its acme, and whatever has sense and understanding. For if it passed first to the body and last to the brain, then having left in the flesh and veins the judgment, when it reached the brain it would be hot, and not at all pure, but mixed with the humidity from flesh and blood, so as to be no longer pure. . . .

And the disease called the Sacred arises from causes as the others, namely, those things which enter and quit the body, such as cold, the sun, and the winds, which are ever changing and are never at rest. And these things are divine, so that there is no necessity for making a distinction, and holding this disease to be more divine than the others, but all are divine, and all human. And each has its own peculiar nature and power, and none is of an ambiguous nature, or irremediable. And the most of them are curable by the same means as those by which any other thing is food to one, and injurious to another. Thus, then, the physician should understand and distinguish the season of each, so that at one time he may attend to the nourishment and increase, and at another to abstraction and diminution. And in this disease as in all others, he must strive not to feed the disease, but endeavor to wear it out by administering whatever is most opposed to each disease, and not that which favors and is allied to it. For by that which is allied to it, it gains vigor and increase, but it wears out and disappears under the use of that which is opposed to it. But whoever is acquainted with such a change in men, and can render a man humid and dry, hot and cold by regimen, could also cure this disease, if he recognizes the proper season for administering his remedies, without minding purifications, spells, and all other illiberal practices of a like kind.

From: Hippocrates, *The Genuine Works of Hippocrates*, Charles Darwin Adams, transl. (Dover: New York, 1868), pp. 355–70.

QUESTIONS:

1. According to Hippocrates, what factors contribute to causing epilepsy? How does he relate those causes to treatments?
2. What method of inquiry lies behind Hippocrates' ideas about epilepsy? How does Hippocrates connect individual patients to the laws or patterns of nature? What does this imply about prevention and treatment?

4.1b: *The Great Treatise on the Harmony of the Atmosphere of the Four Seasons with the (Human) Spirit* from *The Yellow Emperor's Classic of Internal Medicine* (between 475 BCE and 220 CE)

The Yellow Emperor is pure screen image: he is one of the legendary founders of Chinese civilization, who according to tradition ruled from 2697–2597 BCE and invented the Chinese state along with many of the advanced arts, including medicine. His cult was particularly popular in Axial Age (Warring States) China, when his image provided the (apparently) traditional foundation for the codification of Chinese medical thought. This selection lays out general rules for maintaining health.

The three months of Spring are called the period of the beginning and development of life. The breaths of Heaven and Earth are prepared to give birth; thus everything is developing and flourishing.

After a night of sleep people should get up early in the morning; they should walk briskly around the yard; they should loosen their hair and slow down their movements; by these means they can fulfill their wish to live healthfully.

During this period one's body should be encourage to live and not be killed; one should give to it freely and not take away from it; one should reward it and not punish it.

All this is in harmony with the breath of Spring and all this is the method for the protection of one's life.

Those who disobey the laws of Spring will be punished with an injury of the liver. For them the following Summer will bring chills and bad changes; thus they will have little to support their development in Summer.

The three months of Summer are called the period of luxurious growth. The breaths of Heaven and Earth intermingle and are beneficial. Everything is in bloom and begins to bear fruit.

After a night of sleep people should get up early in the morning. They should not weary during daytime and they should not allow their minds to become angry. They should enable the best parts of their body and spirit to develop; and they should act as though they loved everything outside.

All this is in harmony with the atmosphere of Summer and all this is the method for the protection of one's development.

Those who disobey the laws of Summer will be punished with an injury of the heart. For the Fall will bring intermittent fevers; thus they will have little support them for harvest in Fall; and hence, at Winter solstice they will suffer from grave disease.

The three months of Fall are called the period of tranquility of one's conduct. The atmosphere of

Heaven is quick and the atmosphere of the Earth is clear.

People should retire early at night and rise early in the morning with the crowing of the rooster. They should have their minds at peace in order to lessen the punishment of Fall. Soul and spirit should be gathered together in order to make the breath of Fall tranquil; and to keep their lungs pure they should not give vent to their desires.

All this is in harmony with the atmosphere of Fall and all this is the method for the protection of one's harvest.

Those who disobey the laws of Fall will be punished with an injury of the lungs. For them Winter will bring indigestion and diarrhea; thus they will have little to support their storing of Winter.

The three months of Winter are called the period of closing and storing. Water freezes and the Earth cracks open. One should not disturb one's Yang. People should retire early at night and rise late in the morning and they should wait for the rising of the sun. They should suppress and conceal their wishes, as though they had not internal purpose, as though they had been fulfilled. People should try to escape the cold and they should seek warmth, they should not perspire upon the skin, they should let themselves be deprived of breath of the cold.

All this is in harmony with atmosphere of Winter and all this is the method for the protection one's storing.

Those who disobey (laws of Winter) will suffer an injury of the kidneys; for them Spring will bring impotence, and they will produce little.

The breath of Heaven is pure and light. Heaven always maintains its original virtue; thus it never comes to fall. If Heaven opened up completely then sun and moon would never be bright, evil would come during this period of emptiness, the atmosphere of Yang would close up and the Earth would lose its brightness, clouds and fog would be unable to undergo changes and as a consequence white dew would not fall, and the circulation of the natural elements would not communicate with the life of everything in creation. This situation would be called "not bestowing," and as a consequence of "not bestowing" all vegetation would perish. Furthermore, the noxious air would not disappear, wind and rain would not be harmonious, white dew would not fall, so that the vegetation would never again flourish There would always be violent winds and sudden squalls of rain, and Heaven and Earth and the four seasons would be unable to protect each other, they would lose Tao and would soon be destroyed.

The sages followed the laws of nature and therefore their bodies were free from strange diseases; they did not lose anything which they had received by nature and their spirit of life was never exhausted.

Those who do not conform with the breath of Spring will into bring to life the region of the lesser Yang. The atmosphere of their liver will change their constitution.

Those who do not conform with the atmosphere of Summer will not develop their greater Yang. The atmosphere of their heart will become empty.

Those who do not conform with the atmosphere of Fall will not harvest their greater Yin. The atmosphere of their lungs will be blocked from lower burning space.

Those who do not conform with the atmosphere of Winter will not store their lesser Yin. The atmosphere of their kidneys will be isolated and decreased.

Thus the interaction of the four seasons and the interaction of Yin and Yang [the two principles in nature] is the foundation of everything in creation. Hence the sages conceived and developed their Yang in Spring and Summer, and conceived and developed their Yin in Fall and Winter in order to follow the rule of rules; and thus the sages, together with everything in creation, maintained themselves at the gate of life and development.

Those who rebel against the basic rules of the universe sever their own roots and ruin their true selves. Yin and Yang, the two principles in nature, and the four seasons are the beginning and the end of everything and they are also the cause of life and death. Those who disobey the laws of the universe will give rise to calamities and visitations, which those who follow the laws of the universe remain free form dangerous illness, for they are the ones who have obtained Tao, the Right Way.

Tao was practiced by the sages and admired by the ignorant people. Obedience to the laws of Yin and Yang means life; disobedience means death. The obedient ones will rule while the rebels will be in disorder and confusion. Anything contrary to harmony with nature is disobedience and means rebellion to nature.

Hence the sages did not treat those who were already ill; they instructed those who were not yet ill. They did not want to rule those who were already rebellious; they guided those who were not yet rebellious. This is the meaning of the entire preceding discussion. To administer medicines to diseases which have already developed and to suppress revolts which have already developed is comparable to the behavior of those persons who begin to dig a well after they have become thirsty, and of those who begin to cast weapons after they have already engaged in battle. Would these actions not be too late?

From: Veith, Ilza, *Huang ti nei ching su wên = The Yellow Emperor's classic of internal medicine.* (Berkeley: University of California Press, 2002), pp. 102–5.

QUESTIONS:

1. Which do the rules in this source stress more, prevention or treatment? If you read this as a political treatise, what are the implications of this view of medicine?
2. What relationship of individual patients to the laws or patterns of nature does this treatise assume? How does this compare to Hippocrates?

4.2: *The Analects* (Confucius, written between 475 BCE and 220 CE)

The most influential of Chinese philosophers was Kung Fu Tzu (Master Kung Fu, 551–479 BCE), whose name was Latinized by the Jesuits in the seventeenth century to Confucius. Confucius traveled widely, looking for a ruler who would heed his advice on good rulership and restoring the harmony to Chinese civilization. His students collected and eventually wrote his teachings as *The Analects*. His prescriptions for reform advocate a return to the virtues of an earlier Golden Age, but his teachings stress the importance of education and the malleability of human nature. This offers openings for further interpretation of tradition and his own teachings. His teachings also give a coherent account of social relationships and individual responsibility within them, and they became central to the Chinese tradition.

BOOK 1

1.1. The Master said, To learn and at due times to repeat what one has learned, is that not after all a pleasure? That friends should come to one from afar, is this not after all delightful? To remain unsoured even though one's merits are unrecognized by others, is that not after all what is expected of a gentleman?

1.2. Master Yu [a disciple of Confucius] said, Those who in private life behave well towards their parents and elder brothers, in public life seldom show a disposition to resist the authority of their superiors. And as for such men starting a revolution, no instance of it has ever occurred. It is upon the root that a gentleman works. When that is firmly planted, the Way grows. And surely proper behavior towards parents and elder brothers is the root of humanity.

1.5. The Master said, A country of a thousand war-chariots cannot be administered unless the ruler attends strictly to business, punctually observes his promises, is economical in expenditure, shows affection towards his subjects in general, and uses the labor of the common people only at the proper times of year.

1.6. The Master said, A young man's duty is to behave well to his parents at home and to his elders abroad, to be cautious in giving promises and punctual in keeping them, to have kindly feelings towards everyone, but to associate with humane men. If, when all that is done, he has any energy to spare, then let him study the polite arts [*wen*].

BOOK 2

2.1. The Master said, He who rules by virtue [*te*] is like the pole-star, which remains in its place while all the lesser stars do homage to it.

2.2. The Master said, If out of the three hundred *Songs* I had to take one phrase to cover all my teaching, I would say 'Let there be no evil in your thoughts.'

2.3. The Master said, Govern the people by regulations, keep order among them by chastisements, and they will flee from you, and lose all self-respect. Govern them by virtue, keep order among them by ritual, and they will keep their self-respect and come to you of their own accord.

2.4. The Master said, At fifteen I set my heart upon learning. At thirty, I had taken my stance. At forty, I no longer suffered from perplexities. At fifty, I knew what were the biddings of Heaven [*t'ien-ming*]. At sixty, I heard them with docile ear. At seventy, I could follow the dictates of my own heart; for what I desired no longer overstepped the boundaries of righteousness.

2.5. Meng Yi Tzu [a disciple] asked about the treatment of parents. The Master said, Never disobey! When Fan Ch'ih [another disciple] was driving his carriage for him, the Master said, Meng asked me about the treatment of parents and I said, Never disobey! Fan Ch'ih said, In what sense did you mean it? The Master said, While they are alive, serve them according to ritual. When they die, bury them according to ritual, and sacrifice to them according to ritual.

2.13. Tzu-kung [a disciple] asked about the true gentleman. The Master said, He does not preach what he practices till he has practiced what he preaches.

2.14. The Master said, A gentleman can see a question from all sides without bias. The small man is biased and can see a question only from one side.

2.15. The Master said, He who learns but does not think, is lost. He who thinks but does not learn is in great danger.

BOOK 3

3.3. The Master said, A man who is not humane, what can he have to do with ritual [*li*]? A man who is not humane, what can he have to do with music?

3.7. The Master said, Gentlemen never compete. You will say that in archery they do so. But even then they bow and make way for one another when they are going up to the archery-ground, when they are coming down, and at the subsequent drinking-bout. Thus even when competing, they still remain gentlemen.

BOOK 6

6.16. The Master said, When inborn qualities prevail over culture, you get the boorishness of the rustic. When culture prevails over inborn qualities, you get the pedantry of the scribe. Only when culture and inborn qualities are duly blended do you get the true gentleman.

BOOK 8

8.2. The Master said, Courtesy not bounded by the prescriptions of ritual becomes tiresome. Caution not bounded by the prescriptions of ritual becomes timidity, daring becomes turbulence, inflexibility becomes harshness. The Master said, When gentlemen deal generously with their own kin, the common people are incited to humanity. When old dependents are not discarded, the common people will not be fickle.

8.9. The Master said, The common people can be made to follow it; they cannot be made to understand it.

BOOK 13

13.3. Tzu-lu said, If the prince of Wei were waiting for you to come and serve in his government, what would be your first measure? The Master said, It would certainly be the rectification of names. Tzu-lu said, Can I have heard you aright? Surely what you say has nothing to do with the matter. Why should names be rectified? The Master said, Tzu-lu! How boorish you are! With regard to things he does not understand, a gentleman should maintain an attitude of reserve. If names are not rectified, then what is said does not correspond to what is meant. If what is said does not correspond to what is meant, then what is to be done will not be accomplished. If what is to be done cannot be accomplished, then ritual and music will not flourish. If ritual and music do not flourish, then punishments will go astray. If punishments go astray, then the common people will not know where to put hand and foot. Thus the gentleman gives to things only those names which can be used in speech, and says only what can be carried out in practice. A gentleman, in what he says, leaves nothing to mere chance.

BOOK 15

15.14. The Master said, To demand much from oneself and little from others is the way for a ruler to banish discontent.

15.20. The Master said, The demands that a gentleman makes are upon himself. Those that a small man makes are upon others.

15.21. The Master said, A gentleman is proud, but not quarrelsome, allies himself with individuals, but not with parties.

15.23. Tzu-kung asked saying, Is there any single saying that one can act upon all day and every day? The Master said, Perhaps the saying about consideration: 'Never do to others what you would not like them to do to you.'

15.29. The Master said, To have faults and to be making no effort to amend them is to have faults indeed!

15.31. The Master said, A gentleman, in his plans, thinks of the Way. He does not think how he is going to make a living. Even farming sometimes entails times of shortage; and even learning may incidentally lead to high pay. But a gentleman's anxieties concern the progress of the Way. He has no anxiety concerning poverty.

15.35. The Master said, When it comes to being humane, one need not avoid competing with one's teacher.

BOOK 17

17.2. The Master said, By nature men are pretty much alike; it is learning and practice that set them apart.

From: The Analects of Confucius, Arthur Waley, transl. (Knopf Doubleday Publishing Group, 1989), pp. 83–84, 88, 90–91, 94–95, 119, 132, 134, 171–72, 196–200, 209.

QUESTIONS

1. What are the foundations of social order for Confucius? What models of authority and obedience does he cite?
2. What sort of social order would emerge if everyone strictly followed his advice? What is the relationship for Confucius between individual behavior and social order? Would Confucian government benefit the common people as he claims?

4.3: *The Bhagavad Gita*

The most famous and fundamental of all Hindu religious texts is the epic poem known as the *Bhagavad Gita*, which tells the story of Arjuna, a great warrior-king fighting in a civil war. The poem opens just as Arjuna is about to go into battle against his cousins and kinsmen from the opposing family line, which sets up the central moral problem of the story. Arjuna's *dharma*, or duty, as a warrior is to fight, but his dharma as a family member (and his emotions) tells him not to kill relatives. Faced with this dilemma, Arjuna freezes in indecision before the battle. Fortunately for Arjuna, he has a charioteer named Krishna who is in fact the god Vishnu in disguise. Time stops, in effect, and Krishna holds a dialog with Arjuna in which he explains why and how he must do his duty as a warrior. This involves his explaining first the fundamental nature of birth, death and rebirth and second the three yogas, or disciplines, by which one may attain the proper mental and emotional attitude towards one's dharma. The point of the poem is to show how to solve a conflict of dharmas, which has metaphorical application to any moral conflict of principles, not only Arjuna's particular dilemma. It is *the* Hindu text on individual ethical decision making and social order.

The Dilemma
Arjuna
I see omens of chaos,
Krishna; I see no good
In killing my kinsmen
in battle.
Evil will haunt us if we kill them,
Even though their bows are drawn to kill.

Honor forbids us to kill
Our cousins. . . .

When the family is ruined,
The timeless laws of family duty
Perish; and when duty is lost,
Chaos overwhelms the family.

In overwhelming chaos, Krishna,
Women of the family are corrupted;
And when women are corrupted,
Disorder is born in society.

The sins of men who violate
the family create disorder in society
That undermines the constant laws
Of caste and family duty.

Death and Rebirth
Lord Krishna
Why this cowardice
In time of crisis, Arjuna?
The cowardice is ignoble, shameful,
foreign to the ways of heaven.

You grieve for those beyond grief,
And you speak words of insight,
But learned men do not grieve
For the dead or the living.

Never have I not existed,
Nor you, nor these kings;
And never in the future
Shall we cease to exist.

Just as the embodied self
Enters childhood, youth, and old age,
So does it enter another body. . . .

Arjuna, when a man knows the self
To be indestructible, enduring, unborn,
Unchanging, how does he kill
Or cause anyone to kill?

Death is certain for anyone born,
And birth is certain for the dead;
Since the cycle is inevitable,
You have no cause to grieve!

Look to your own duty;
Do not tremble before it;
Nothing is better for a warrior
Than a battle of sacred duty.

The Yoga of Action
Lord Krishna
Understanding is defined in terms of
philosophy;
Now hear it in spiritual discipline.

Armed with this understanding, Arjuna,
You will escape the bondage of action.

Be intent on action,
Not on the fruits of action;
Avoid attraction to the fruits
and attachment to inaction!

Wise men disciplined by understanding
Relinquish the fruit born of action;
Freed from those bonds of rebirth,
They reach a place beyond decay.

A man cannot escape the force
Of action by abstaining from actions;
He does not attain success
just by renunciation.

No one exists for even an instant
without performing an action. . . .

Always perform with detachment
Any action you must do;
Performing action with detachment,
One achieves supreme good.

These worlds would collapse
If I did not perform action;
I would create disorder in society,
Living beings would be destroyed.

The Yoga of Knowledge

Lord Krishna

Without doubt, the mind
Is unsteady and hard to hold,
But practice and dispassion
Can restrain it, Arjuna.

The Yoga of Devotion

Lord Krishna

Without faith in sacred duty,
Men fail to reach me, Arjuna;
They return to the cycle
Of death and rebirth.

If he is devoted solely to me,
Even a violent criminal
Must be deemed a man of virtue,
For his resolve is right.

I am time grown old,
Creating world destruction,
Set in motion
To annihilate the worlds;

Even without you,
All these warriors
Arrayed in hostile ranks
Will cease to exist.

Therefore, arise
And win glory!
Conquer your foes
And fulfill your kingship!
They are already
Killed by me.
Be just my instrument,
The archer at my side!

Acting only for me, intent on me,
Free from attachment,
Hostile to no creature, Arjuna,
A man of devotion comes to me.

Action in sacrifice, charity,
And penance is to be performed,
Not relinquished—for wise men,
They are acts of sanctity.

But even these actions
should be done by relinquishing to me
Attachment and the fruit of action—
This is my decisive idea.

Conclusion

Lord Krishna

The actions of priests, warriors,
Commoners, and servants
Are apportioned by qualities
Born of their intrinsic being.

Tranquility, control, penance,
Purity, patience and honesty,
Knowledge, judgment, and piety
Are intrinsic to the action of a priest.

Heroism, fiery energy, resolve,
Skill, refusal to retreat in battle,

Charity, and majesty in conduct
Are intrinsic to the action of a warrior.

Farming, herding cattle, and commerce
Are intrinsic to the action of a commoner,
Action that is essentially service
Is intrinsic to the servant.

Each one achieves success
By focusing on his own action. . . .

Better to do one's own duty imperfectly
Than to do another man's well;
Doing action intrinsic to his being
A man avoids guilt.

Arjuna
Krishna, my delusion is destroyed,
And by your grace I have regained memory;
I stand here, my doubt dispelled,
Ready to act on your words.

Sanjaya
Where Krishna is lord of discipline
And Arjuna is the archer,
There do fortune, victory, abundance,
And morality exist, so I think.

From: The Bhagavad Gita, Barbara Stoller Miller, transl. (Bantam Books, Random House, 1986), pp. 25–26, 29, 31–36, 41, 43–44, 67, 83, 87, 103–4, 109, 143–44, 149, 153–54.

QUESTIONS:

1. What is it about the nature of death and rebirth makes it acceptable for Arjuna to kill his relatives? How do the three yogas explain how he is supposed to perform this action?
2. What is the relationship of individual ethical choice to social order presented in the *Gita?* Which side of the equation seems more important to you? What sort of society would result if everyone followed the advice of the *Gita*?

4.4: *The Teachings of the Buddha: The Four Noble Truths*

The Buddha was born Gautama Siddhartha, prince and heir to a small kingdom at the foot of the Himalayas in modern Nepal. But we know little else for certain about his life, for the sources all were written long after his death and reflect conflicting oral traditions. Though they agree that he lived to the age of 80, different traditions place his birth as early as 624 BCE or as late as 448 BCE. The sources agree on the outlines of his career: he had an early life of sheltered luxury, then he had a deeply disturbing encounter with the universal suffering which is caused by sickness, old age, and death, and after this he went on a quest to find the cause of (and to alleviate) this suffering. His answer to the problem of suffering is presented below, in a version of his first sermon, along with a lesson about what his teachings do not address, and why such things are unimportant. The key concept in Buddhism is variously translated as "desire," "craving," "thirst," or perhaps most appropriately, simply "attachment." For the Buddha, nonattachment was the key to understanding individual action and its relation to social order.

The world is full of suffering. Birth is suffering, old age is suffering, sickness and death are sufferings. To meet a man whom one hates is suffering. To be separated from a beloved one is suffering. To be vainly struggling to satisfy one's needs is suffering. In fact, life that is not free from desire and passion is always involved with distress. This is called the Truth of Suffering.

The cause of human suffering is undoubtedly found in the thirsts of the physical body and in the illusions of worldly passion. If these thirsts and illusions are traced to their source, they are found to be rooted in the intense desires of physical instincts. Thus, desire, having a strong will-to-live as its basis, seeks that which it feels desirable, even if it is sometimes death. This is called the Truth of the Cause of Suffering.

If desire, which lies at the root of all human passion, can be removed, then passion will die out and all human suffering will be ended. This is called the Truth of the Cessation of Suffering.

In order to enter into a state where there is no desire and no suffering, one must follow a certain Path. The stages of this Noble Eightfold Path are: Right Understanding, Right Purpose, Right Speech, Right Behavior, Right Livelihood, Right Effort, Right Mindfulness, and Right Concentration. This is called the Truth of the Noble Path to the Cessation of the Cause of Suffering.

People should keep these Truths clearly in mind, for the world is filled with suffering, and if anyone wishes to escape from suffering, he must sever the ties of worldly passion, which is the sole cause of suffering. The way of life which is free from all worldly passion and suffering can only be known through Enlightenment, and Enlightenment can only be attained through the discipline of the Noble Eightfold Path.

THE SEARCH FOR ENLIGHTENMENT

In the search for truth there are certain questions that are unimportant. Of what material is the universe constructed? Is the universe eternal? Are there limits or not to the universe? In what way is this human society put together? What is the ideal form of organization for human society? If a man were to postpone his searching and practicing for Enlightenment until such questions were solved, he would die before he found the path.

Suppose a man were pierced by a poisoned arrow, and his relatives and friends got together to call a surgeon to have the arrow pulled out and the wound treated.

If the wounded man objects, saying, "Wait a little. Before you pull it out, I want to know who shot this arrow. Was it a man or a woman? Was it someone of noble birth, or was it a peasant? What was the bow made of? Was it a big bow or a small bow that shot the arrow? Was it made of wood or bamboo? What was the bowstring made of? Was it made of fiber or of gut? Was the arrow made of rattan or of reed? What feathers were used? Before you extract the arrow, I want to know all about these things." Then what will happen?

Before all this information can be secured, no doubt the poison will have time to circulate all through the system and the man may die. The first duty is to remove the arrow, and its poison prevented from spreading.

When a fire of passion is endangering the world, the composition of the universe matters little. What is the ideal form for the human community is not so important to deal with.

The question of whether the universe has limits or is eternal can wait until some way is found to extinguish the fires of birth, old age, sickness, and death. In the presence of lamentation, sorrow, suffering, and pain, one should first search for a way to solve these problems and devote oneself to the practice of that way.

The Buddha's teaching teaches what is important to know and not what is unimportant. That is, it teaches people that they must learn what they should learn, remove what they should remove, train for what they should become enlightened about.

Therefore, people should first discern what is of the first importance, what problem should first be solved, what is the most pressing issue for them. To do all this, they must first undertake to train their minds; that is, they must first seek mind-control.

Those who seek the true path to Enlightenment must not expect an easy task or one made pleasant by offers of respect and honor and devotion. And further, they must not aim with a slight effort, at a trifling advance in calmness or knowledge or insight.

First of all, one should get clearly in mind the basic and essential nature of this world of life and death.

HUMAN LIFE

There is an allegory that depicts human life. Once there was a man rowing a boat down a river. Someone on the shore warned him, "Stop rowing so gaily down the swift current. There are rapids ahead and a dangerous whirlpool, and there are crocodiles and demons lying in wait in rocky caverns. You will perish if you continue."

In this allegory, "the swift current" is a life of lust. "Rowing gaily" is giving rein to one's passion. "Rapids ahead" means the ensuing suffering and pain. "Whirlpool" means pleasure. "Crocodiles and demons" refers to the decay and death that follow a life of lust and indulgence. "Someone on the shore" who calls out is Buddha.

Everything is changeable, everything appears and disappears. There is no blissful peace until one passes beyond the agony of life and death.

From: The Teachings of the Buddha (Tokyo: Buddhist Promoting Foundation, 1980).

QUESTIONS:

1. What is the cause of all suffering for Buddha? How is suffering then eliminated? Do you agree with Buddha's diagnosis? Do you agree with his prescription for dealing with the problem?
2. What things are unimportant to the Buddha? Why are they unimportant to him? What implications for the relationship of right individual conduct to social order are contained in these views?

4.5: *Zoroastrianism: Yasna 19*

The traditions of the religion that became known as Zoroastrianism (from Zoroaster, the Greek version of the name of the prophet Zarathustra who first preached its basic tenets) put the prophet's life in the half century just after 600 BCE, but the internal linguistic evidence of the earliest sayings of the prophet point to a much earlier date. Complicating the picture is the fact that most of the *Avesta,* the holy written text of Zoroastrianism, dates to after 224 CE. Thus, the true role of Zarathustra in the creation of this religion is largely unknowable. The religion's rise to prominence does fit squarely into the era of world history covered by this chapter, however, as it became the official religion of the Persian royalty under Darius the Great (r. 522–486 BCE). The following selections come from the Yasnas, or liturgical texts, of the *Avesta,* some of which contain some of the *Gathas,* or sayings of the Prophet.

15. The evil one at once arose (to oppose Him), but He (Ahura) repelled that wicked one with His interdict, and with this repelling renunciation: Neither our minds are in harmony, nor our precepts, nor our comprehensions, nor our beliefs, nor our words, nor our actions, nor our consciences, nor our souls!

16. And this saying, uttered by Mazda, has three stages, or measures, and belongs to four classes (of men as its supporters), and to five chiefs (in the political world, without whom its efficiency is marred), and it has a conclusion ending with a gift.

(Question.) How are its measures (constituted)?

(Answer.) The good thought, the good word, and the good deed.

17. *(Question.)* With what classes of men?

(Answer.) The priest, the charioteer (as the chief of warriors), the systematic tiller of the ground, and the artisan. These classes therefore accompany the religious man throughout his entire duty with the correct thought, the truthful word, and the righteous action. These are the classes and states in life which give attention to the rulers, and fulfill the (laws) of religion; (yea, they are the

guides and companions of that religious man) through whose actions the settlements are furthered in righteousness.

18. *(Question.)* How are the chiefs (constituted)?

(Answer.) They are the house-chief, the village-chief, and the tribe-chief, the chief of the province, and the Zarathushtra [Zoroastrian priests] as the fifth. That is, so far as those provinces are concerned which are different from, and outside of the Zarathushtrian regency, or domain. Ragha which has four chiefs (only) is the Zarathushtrian (district) [The Persian homeland, which had no provincial governor]

(Question.) How are the chiefs of this one constituted?

(Answer.) They (are) the house-chief, the village-chief, the tribe-chief, and the Zarathushtra as the fourth.

19. *(Question.)* What is the thought well thought?

(Answer.) (It is that which the holy man thinks), the one who holds the holy thought to be before all other things.

(Question.) What is the word well spoken?

(Answer.) It is the Mathra Spenta, the bounteous word of reason.

(Question.) What is the deed well done?

(Answer.) It is that done with praises, and by the creatures who regard Righteousness as before all other things.

20. *(Question.)* Mazda made a proclamation, whom did He announce?

(Answer.) Some one who was holy, and yet both heavenly and mundane.

(Question.) What was His character, He who made this sacred enunciation?

(Answer.) He who is the best (of all), the ruling one.

(Question.) Of what character (did He proclaim him the coming one)?

(Answer.) As holy and the best, a ruler who exercises no wanton or despotic power.

From: Sacred Books of the East, L. H. Mills, transl., American Edition, 1898.

QUESTIONS:

1. What sorts of beliefs and behaviors does Ahura Mazda demand of his followers? What are the consequences of obedience or disobedience to Mazda's wishes?
2. How do the injunctions about individual choice and behavior connect to social order? What is the role of Mazda's act of creation in structuring the cosmos and society?

4.6: *The Hebrews: Second Isaiah*

One of the peoples the Persians conquered were the Chaldeans, who in 586 BCE had themselves conquered the kingdom of Judah and its capital of Jerusalem. Judah was the remaining southern kingdom of the Hebrews, the larger kingdom of Israel to its north having fallen to the Assyrians a century and a half earlier. The Chaldeans destroyed Jerusalem and sent many of the Hebrew elites into exile in their capital at Babylon. But after Cyrus the Great, king of the Persians, destroyed the Chaldean Empire, he freed the Hebrews from what became known as the Babylonian Captivity in 538 BCE. An otherwise unknown prophet of the time named Isaiah took the lead in interpreting these events from the perspective of earlier Hebrew history and faith. His reinterpretation (and the impression the Babylonian Captivity made on the Hebrew elite) proved central to the transformation of early Hebrew religion into the faith now called Judaism. Isaiah's interpretation put morality, or "righteousness" at the center of his story's (and history's) meaning.

ISAIAH 44

24. Thus saith the LORD, thy redeemer, and he that formed thee from the womb, I am the LORD that maketh all things; that stretcheth forth the heavens alone; that spreadeth abroad the earth by myself;

25. That frustrateth the tokens of the liars, and maketh diviners mad; that turneth wise men backward, and maketh their knowledge foolish;

26. That confirmeth the word of his servant, and performeth the counsel of his messengers; that saith to Jerusalem, Thou shalt be inhabited; and to the cities of Judah, Ye shall be built, and I will raise up the decayed places thereof:

27. That saith to the deep, Be dry, and I will dry up thy rivers:

28. That saith of Cyrus [The Persian king who liberated the Hebrews from Babylon], He is my shepherd, and shall perform all my pleasure: even saying to Jerusalem, Thou shalt be built; and to the temple, Thy foundation shall be laid.

ISAIAH 45

1. Thus saith the LORD to his anointed, to Cyrus, whose right hand I have holden, to subdue nations before him; and I will loose the loins of kings, to open before him the two leaved gates; and the gates shall not be shut;

2. I will go before thee, and make the crooked places straight: I will break in pieces the gates of brass, and cut in sunder the bars of iron:

3. And I will give thee the treasures of darkness, and hidden riches of secret places, that thou mayest know that I, the LORD, which call thee by thy name, am the God of Israel.

4. For Jacob my servant's sake, and Israel mine elect, I have even called thee by thy name: I have surnamed thee, though thou hast not known me.

5. I am the LORD, and there is none else, there is no God beside me: I girded thee, though thou hast not known me:

6. That they may know from the rising of the sun, and from the west, that there is none beside me. I am the LORD, and there is none else.

7. I form the light, and create darkness: I make peace, and create evil: I the LORD do all these things.

8. Drop down, ye heavens, from above, and let the skies pour down righteousness: let the earth open, and let them bring forth salvation, and let righteousness spring up together; I the LORD have created it.

9. Woe unto him that striveth with his Maker! Let the potsherd strive with the potsherds of the earth. Shall the clay say to him that fashioneth it, What makest thou? or thy work, He hath no hands?

11. Thus saith the LORD, the Holy One of Israel, and his Maker, Ask me of things to come concerning my sons, and concerning the work of my hands command ye me.

12. I have made the earth, and created man upon it: I, even my hands, have stretched out the heavens, and all their host have I commanded.

13. I have raised him up in righteousness, and I will direct all his ways: he shall build my city [Jerusalem], and he shall let go my captives, not for price nor reward, saith the LORD of hosts.

15. Verily thou art a God that hidest thyself, O God of Israel, the Saviour.

16. They shall be ashamed, and also confounded, all of them: they shall go to confusion together that are makers of idols.

17. But Israel shall be saved in the LORD with an everlasting salvation: ye shall not be ashamed nor confounded world without end.

19. I have not spoken in secret, in a dark place of the earth: I said not unto the seed of Jacob, Seek ye me in vain: I the LORD speak righteousness, I declare things that are right.

20. Assemble yourselves and come; draw near together, ye that are escaped of the nations: they have no knowledge that set up the wood of their graven image, and pray unto a god that cannot save.

ISAIAH 56

1. Thus saith the LORD, Keep ye judgment, and do justice: for my salvation is near to come, and my righteousness to be revealed.

2. Blessed is the man that doeth this, and the son of man that layeth hold on it; that keepeth the sabbath from polluting it, and keepeth his hand from doing any evil.

ISAIAH 57

1. The righteous perisheth, and no man layeth it to heart: and merciful men are taken away, none considering that the righteous is taken away from the evil to come.

2. He shall enter into peace: they shall rest in their beds, each one walking in his uprightness.

15. For thus saith the high and lofty One that inhabiteth eternity, whose name is Holy; I dwell in the high and holy place, with him also that is of a contrite and humble spirit, to revive the spirit of the humble, and to revive the heart of the contrite ones.

16. For I will not contend for ever, neither will I be always wroth: for the spirit should fail before me, and the souls which I have made.

17. For the iniquity of his covetousness was I wroth, and smote him: I hid me, and was wroth, and he went on frowardly in the way of his heart.

18. I have seen his ways, and will heal him: I will lead him also, and restore comforts unto him and to his mourners.

19. I create the fruit of the lips; Peace, peace to him that is far off, and to him that is near, saith the LORD; and I will heal him.

20. But the wicked are like the troubled sea, when it cannot rest, whose waters cast up mire and dirt.

21. There is no peace, saith my God, to the wicked.

From: Holy Bible, RSE 1952, pp. 756–58, 769, 770–71.

QUESTIONS:

1. What is the relationship of individual righteousness to social order in Isaiah? How is this relationship complicated by the Jews' subject status in the Persian Empire? How does Isaiah explain the role of the Persians?
2. Like Ahura Mazda, Yahweh is presented here not as the particular god of the tribes of Hebrews, but as the universal and only god, creator of the universe. What is the role of the Hebrews in the history of Yahweh's universe?

4.7: Book 3, Chapter 3 from *The Nichomachean Ethics* (Aristotle, c. 340)

Aristotle (384–22 BCE) was the quintessential Axial Age thinker. He wrote on politics, art, biology, cosmology, metaphysics, and ethics, among other things. He invented formal logic in a form that remained basically unchallenged until advances in mathematical logic in the late nineteenth century. A student of Plato, he was tutor to Alexander the Great and remained the most influential thinker in the western European tradition until the Scientific Revolution of the seventeenth century. In this selection from his *Nichomachean Ethics,* he discusses philosophical method itself.

Do we deliberate about everything, and is everything a possible subject of deliberation, or is deliberation impossible about some things? We ought presumably to call not what a fool or a madman would deliberate about, but what a sensible man would deliberate about, a subject of deliberation.

Now about eternal things no one deliberates, e.g. about the material universe or the incommensurability of the diagonal and the side of a square. But no more do we deliberate about the things that involve movement but always happen in the same way, whether of necessity or by nature or from any other cause, e.g. the solstices and the risings of the stars; nor about things that happen now in one way, now in another, e.g. droughts and rains; nor about chance events, like the finding of treasure. But we do not deliberate even about all human affairs; for instance, no Spartan deliberates about the best constitution for the Scythians. For none of these things can be brought about by our own efforts.

We deliberate about things that are in our power and can be done; and these are in fact what is left. For nature, necessity, and chance are thought to be causes, and also reason and everything that depends on man. Now every class of men deliberates about the things that can be done by their own efforts. And in the case of exact and self-contained sciences there is no deliberation, e.g. about the letters of the alphabet (for we have no doubt how they should be written); but the things that are brought about by our own efforts, but not always in the same way, are the things about which we deliberate, e.g. questions of medical treatment or of money-making. And we do so more in the case of the art of navigation than in that of gymnastics, inasmuch as it has been less exactly worked out, and again about other things in the same ratio, and more also in the case of the arts than in that of the sciences; for we have more doubt about the former. Deliberation is concerned with things that happen in a certain way for the most part, but in which the event is obscure, and with things in which it is indeterminate. We call in others to aid us in deliberation on important questions, distrusting ourselves as not being equal to deciding.

We deliberate not about ends but about means. For a doctor does not deliberate whether he shall heal, nor an orator whether he shall persuade, nor a statesman whether he shall produce law and order, nor does any one else deliberate about his end. They assume the end and consider how and by what means it is to be attained; and if it seems to be produced by several means they consider by which it is most easily and best produced, while if it is achieved by one only they consider how it will be achieved by this and by what means this will be achieved, till they come to the first cause, which in the order of discovery is last. For the person who deliberates seems to investigate and analyse in the way described as though he were analysing a geometrical construction (not all investigation appears to be deliberation—for instance mathematical investigations—but all deliberation is investigation), and what is last in the order of analysis seems to be first in the order of becoming. And if we come on an impossibility, we give up the search, e.g. if we need money and this cannot be got; but if a thing appears possible we try to do it. By 'possible' things I mean things that might be brought about by our own efforts; and these in a sense include things that can be brought about by the efforts of our friends, since the moving principle is in ourselves. The subject of investigation is sometimes the instruments, sometimes the use of them; and similarly in the other cases—sometimes the means, sometimes the mode of using it or the means of bringing it about. It seems, then, as has been said, that man is a moving principle of actions; now deliberation is about the things to be done by the agent himself, and actions are for the sake of things other than themselves. For the end cannot be a subject of deliberation, but only the means; nor indeed can the particular facts be a subject of it, as whether this is bread or has been baked as it should; for these are matters of perception. If we are to be always deliberating, we shall have to go on to infinity.

The same thing is deliberated upon and is chosen, except that the object of choice is already determinate, since it is that which has been decided upon as a result of deliberation that is the object of choice. For every one ceases to inquire how he is to act when he has brought the moving principle back to himself and to the ruling part of himself; for this is what chooses. This is plain also from the ancient constitutions, which Homer represented; for the kings announced their choices to the people. The object of choice being one of the things in our own power which is desired after deliberation, choice will be deliberate desire of things in our own power; for when we have decided as a result of deliberation, we desire in accordance with our deliberation.

From: Aristotle, *Nicomachean Ethics*, W. D. Ross, transl. (Oxford: Clarendon Press, 1908).

QUESTIONS:

1. What are the implications of Aristotle's method of inquiry for "Truth"? In this sense, how does he compare to the other sources in this chapter?
2. What does Aristotle's method imply about politics and the relationship of individual ethics to social order?

CHAPTER 5

The Age of Empires: 500 BCE to 400 CE

INTRODUCTION

The philosophical advances of the Axial Age contributed to the emergence of large, influential hierarchies, hence the Age of Empires. The sources presented in this chapter show the application of the ideas of the Axial Age (as well as some principles of practical politics) to the problems of running such empires. In the Age of Empires, hierarchies employed ideology as a technology of social control and management.

5.1: *Correspondence with Trajan* (Pliny the Younger, c. 100 CE)

Pliny the Younger (c. 61–112 CE) was a lawyer, prolific writer, and magistrate of the Roman Empire under the emperor Trajan (r. 98–117). He served in Syria and Anatolia (Asia minor) and gained a reputation as an efficient, honest magistrate. Trajan, the thirteenth emperor of the Roman Empire, was from a nonelite Spanish family. He rose through the ranks of the army to become emperor. He not only expanded Rome to its greatest territorial extent, he gained a reputation as a generous and good ruler who was concerned with building public works and social welfare programs. The selections presented here from the correspondence between the emperor and his magistrate give us a window into the everyday administration of a great empire.

XLII — To THE EMPEROR TRAJAN

WHILE I was making a progress in a different part of the province, a most extensive fire broke out at Nicomedia, which not only consumed several private houses, but also two public buildings; the town-house and the temple of Isis, though they stood on contrary sides of the street. The occasion of its spreading thus far was partly owing to the violence of the wind, and partly to the indolence of the people, who, manifestly, stood idle and motionless spectators of this terrible calamity. The truth is the city was not furnished with either engines, buckets, or any single instrument suitable for extinguishing fires; which I have now however given directions to have prepared. You will consider, Sir, whether it may not be advisable to institute a company of fire-men, consisting only of one hundred and fifty members. I will take care none but those of that business shall be admitted into it, and that the privileges granted them shall not be applied to any other purpose. As this corporate body will be restricted to so small a number of members, it will be easy to keep them under proper regulation.

XLIII — TRAJAN TO PLINY

YOU are of opinion it would be proper to establish a company of firemen in Nicomedia, agreeably to what has been practiced in several other cities. But it is to be remembered that societies of this sort have greatly disturbed the peace of the province in general, and of those cities in particular. Whatever name we give them, and for whatever purposes they may be founded, they will not fail to form themselves into factious assemblies, however short their meetings may be. It will therefore be safer to provide such machines as are of service in extinguishing fires, enjoining the owners of houses to assist in preventing the mischief from spreading, and, if it should be necessary, to call in the aid of the populace.

XLIV — To THE EMPEROR TRAJAN

WE have acquitted, Sir, and renewed our annual vows for your prosperity, in which that of the empire is essentially involved, imploring the gods to grant us ever thus to pay and thus to repeat them.

XLV — TRAJAN TO PLINY

I RECEIVED the satisfaction, my dearest Secundus, of being informed by your letter that you, together with the people under your government, have both discharged and renewed your vows to the immortal gods for my health and happiness.

XLVI — To THE EMPEROR TRAJAN

THE citizens of Nicomedia, Sir, have expended three millions three hundred and twenty-nine sesterces in building an aqueduct; but, not being able to finish it, the works are entirely falling to ruin. They made a second attempt in another place, where they laid out two millions. But this likewise is discontinued; so that, after having been at an immense charge to no purpose, they must still be at a further expense, in order to be accommodated with water. I have examined a fine spring from whence the water may be conveyed over arches (as was attempted in their first design) in such a manner that the higher as well as level and low parts of the city may be supplied. There are still remaining a very few of the old arches; and the square stones, however, employed in the former building, may be used in turning the new arches. I am of opinion part should be raised with brick, as that will be the easier and cheaper material. But that this work may not meet with the same ill-success as the former, it will be necessary to send here an architect, or some one skilled in the construction of this kind of waterworks. And I will venture to say, from the beauty and usefulness of the design, it will be an erection well worthy the splendor of your times.

XLVII — TRAJAN TO PLINY

CARE must be taken to supply the city of Nicomedia with water; and that business, I am well persuaded, you will perform with all the diligence you ought. But really it is no less incumbent upon you to examine by whose misconduct it has happened that such large sums have been thrown away upon this, lest they apply the money to private purposes, and the aqueduct in question, like the preceding, should be begun, and afterwards left unfinished. You will let me know the result of your inquiry.

XLVIII — To THE EMPEROR TRAJAN

THE citizens of Nicea, Sir; are building a theatre, which, though it is not yet finished, has already exhausted, as I am informed (for I have not examined the account myself), above ten millions of sesterces; and, what is worse, I fear to no purpose. For either from the foundation being laid in soft, marshy ground, or that the stone itself is light and crumbling, the wails are sinking, and cracked from top to bottom. It deserves your consideration, therefore, whether it would be best to carry on this work, or entirely discontinue it, or rather, perhaps, whether it would not be most prudent absolutely to destroy it: for the buttresses and foundations by means of which it is from time to time kept up appear to me more expensive than solid. Several private persons have undertaken to build the compartment of this theatre at their own expense, some engaging to erect the portico, others the galleries over the pit: but this design cannot be executed, as the principal building which ought first to be completed is now at a stand. This city is also rebuilding, upon a far more enlarged plan, the gymnasium, which was burnt down before my arrival in the province. They have already been at some (and, I rather fear, a fruitless) expense. The structure is not only irregular and ill-proportioned, but the present architect (who, it must be owned, is a rival to the person who was first employed) asserts that the walls, although twenty-two feet in thickness, are not strong enough to support the superstructure, as the interstices are filled up with quarrystones, and the walls are not overlaid with brickwork. Also the inhabitants of Claudiopolis are sinking (I cannot call it erecting) a large public bath, upon a low spot of ground which lies at the foot of a mountain. The fund appropriated for the carrying on of this work arises from the money which those honorary members you were pleased to add to the senate paid (or, at least, are ready to pay whenever I call upon them) for their admission. As I am afraid, therefore, the public money in the city of Nicea, and (what is infinitely more valuable than any pecuniary consideration) your bounty in that of Nicopolis, should be ill applied, I must desire you to send hither an architect to inspect, not only the theatre, but the bath; in order to consider whether, after all the expense which has already been laid out, it will be better to finish them upon the present plan, or alter the one, and remove the other, in as far as may seem necessary: for otherwise we may perhaps throw away our future cost in endeavoring not to lose what we have already expended.

XLIX — TRAJAN TO PLINY

YOU, who are upon the spot, will best be able to consider and determine what is proper to be done concerning the theatre which the inhabitants of Nicea are building; as for myself, it will be sufficient if you let me know your determination. With respect to the particular parts of this theatre which are to be raised at a private charge, you will see those engagements fulfilled when the body of the building to which they are to be annexed shall be finished.—These paltry Greeks are, I know, immoderately fond of gymnastic diversions, and therefore, perhaps, the citizens of Nicea have planned a more magnificent building for this purpose than is necessary; however, they must be content with such as will be sufficient to answer the purpose for which it is intended. I leave it entirely to you to persuade the Claudiopolitani as you shall think proper with regard to their bath, which they have placed, it seems, in a very improper situation. As there is no province that is not furnished with men of skill and ingenuity, you cannot possibly want architects; unless you think it the shortest way to procure them from Rome, when it is generally from Greece that they come to us.

L — To THE EMPEROR TRAJAN

WHEN I reflect upon the splendor of your exalted station, and the magnanimity of your spirit, nothing, I am persuaded, can be more suitable to both than to point out to you such works as are worthy of your glorious and immortal name, as being no less useful than magnificent. Bordering upon the territories of the city of Nicomedia is a most extensive lake; over which marbles, fruits, woods, and all kinds of materials, the commodities of the country, are brought over in boats up to the high-road, at little trouble and expense, but from thence are conveyed in carriages to the sea-side, at a much greater charge and with great labor. To remedy this inconvenience, many hands will be in request; but upon such an occasion they cannot be wanting: for the country, and particularly the city, is exceedingly populous; and one may assuredly hope that every person will readily engage in a work which will be of universal benefit. It only remains then to send hither, if you shall think proper, a surveyor or an architect, in order to examine whether the lake lies above the level of the sea; the engineers of this province being of opinion that the former is higher by forty cubits, I find there is in the neighborhood of this place a large canal, which was cut by a king of this country; but as it is left unfinished, it is uncertain whether it was for the purpose of draining the adjacent fields, or making a communication between the lake and the river. It is equally doubtful too whether the death of the king, or the despair of being able to accomplish the design, prevented the completion of it. If this was the reason, I am so much the more eager and warmly desirous, for the sake of your illustrious character (and I hope you will pardon me the ambition), that you may have the glory of executing what kings could only attempt.

LI — TRAJAN TO PLINY

THERE is something in the scheme you propose of opening a communication between the lake and the sea, which may, perhaps, tempt me to consent. But you must first carefully examine the situation of this body of water, what quantity it contains, and from whence it is supplied; lest, by giving it an opening into the sea, it should be totally drained. You may apply to Calpurnius Macer for an engineer, and I will also send you from hence some one skilled in works of this nature.

From: Pliny the Younger, *Letters*, William Melmoth, transl.; rev. F. C. T. Bosanquet, vol. IX, part 4, The Harvard Classics (New York: P.F. Collier & Son, 1909–14). pp. 1033–44.

QUESTIONS:

1. What functions do public works and organizations play in the administration of the empire, according to these letters? What problems do Pliny and Trajan face in promoting public works?
2. How do the proposals and decisions visible in these letters reflect the *Frameworks* pyramid model of hierarchy? How do they reflect the fundamental constraints ("low and slow") on the Agrarian societies that the model portrays?

5.2: *Res Gestae Divi Augusti: The Achievements of the Divine Augustus* (Augustus Caesar, c. 13 CE)

Augustus Caesar (63 BCE–14 CE, reigned 27 BCE–14 CE) founded the empire that Trajan and Pliny administered a century later. Nephew of the dictator Julius Caesar, Augustus triumphed in the civil wars that followed his uncle's assassination. The political settlement which he arranged to end the wars was a political masterpiece: Augustus managed to establish the mechanisms and, perhaps more important, the prestige of one-man rule while projecting the image of being the savior of the anti-monarchical Roman Republic. The title he gave himself, *princeps* (First Citizen), reflected that successful balancing act. His *Res Gestae* was his autobiographical funerary inscription, designed to cement his reputation and stabilize the Empire after his succession. It is thus one of the great screen images in history.

1. At the age of nineteen on my own responsibility and at my own expense I raised an army, with which I successfully championed the liberty of the republic when it was oppressed by the tyranny of a faction. . . . In the same year, when both consuls had fallen in battle, the people appointed me consul and triumvir for the organization of the republic.

2. I drove into exile the murderers of my father, avenging their crime through tribunals established by law; and afterwards, when they made war on the republic, I twice defeated them in battle.
3. I undertook many civil and foreign wars by land and sea throughout the world, and as victor I spared the lives of all citizens who asked for mercy. When foreign peoples could safely be pardoned I preferred to preserve rather than to exterminate them. The Roman citizens who took the soldier's oath of obedience to me numbered about 500,000. I settled rather more than 300,000 of these in colonies or sent them back to their home towns after their period of service; to all these I assigned lands or gave money as rewards for their military service. . . .
4. I celebrated two ovations and three curule triumphs and I was twenty-one times saluted as imperator. The senate decreed still more triumphs to me, all of which I declined. . . .
5. The dictatorship was offered to me by both senate and people in my absence and when I was at Rome . . ., but I refused it. . . .
6. . . . [T]he senate and people of Rome agreed that I should be appointed supervisor of laws and morals without a colleague and with supreme power, but I would not accept any office inconsistent with the custom of our ancestors. . . .
8. . . . By new laws passed on my proposal I brought back into use many exemplary practices of our ancestors which were disappearing in our time, and in many ways I myself transmitted exemplary practices to posterity for their imitation.
9. The senate decreed that vows should be undertaken every fifth year by the consuls and priests for my health. . . .
13. It was the will of our ancestors that the gateway of Janus Quirinus should be shut when victories had secured peace by land and sea throughout the whole empire of the Roman people; from the foundation of the city down to my birth, tradition records that it was shut only twice, but while I was the leading citizen the senate resolved that it should be shut on three occasions.
15. To each member of the Roman plebs I paid under my father's will 300 sesterces, and in my own name I gave them 400 each from the booty of war in my fifth consulship, and once again in my tenth consulship I paid out 400 sesterces as a largesse to each man from my own patrimony, and in my eleventh consulship bought grain with my own money and distributed twelve rations apiece, and in the twelfth year of my tribunician power I gave every man 400 sesterces for the third time. These largesses of mine never reached fewer than 250,000 persons. . . .
16. I paid cash to the towns for the lands that I assigned to soldiers. . . . The sum amounted to about 600,000,000 sesterces paid for lands in Italy, and about 260,000,000 disbursed for provincial lands. . . . I paid monetary rewards to soldiers whom I settled in their home towns after completion of their service, and on this account I expended about 400,000,000 sesterces.
17. Four times I assisted the treasury with my own money, so that I transferred to the administrators of the treasury 150,000,000 sesterces. . . .
18. From the consulship of Gnaeus and Publius Lentulus onwards, whenever the taxes did not suffice, I made distributions of grain and money from my own granary and patrimony, sometimes to 100,000 persons, sometimes to many more.
20. I restored the Capitol and the theatre of Pompey, both works at great expense without inscribing my own name on either. I restored

the channels of the aqueducts, which in several places were falling into disrepair through age, and I brought water from a new spring into the aqueduct called Marcia, doubling the supply. . . . In my sixth consulship I restored eighty-two temples of the gods in the city on the authority of the senate, neglecting none that required restoration at that time. In my seventh consulship I restored the Via Flaminia from the city as far as Rimini, together with all bridges except the Mulvian and the Minucian.

21. I built the temple of Mars the Avenger and the Forum Augustum on private ground from the proceeds of booty. I built the theatre adjacent to the temple of Apollo on ground in large part bought from private owners. . . .

22. I gave three gladiatorial games in my own name and five in that of my sons or grandsons; at these games some 10,000 men took part in combat. Twice in my own name and a third time in that of my grandson I presented to the people displays by athletes summoned from all parts. I produced shows in my own name four times and in place of other magistrates twenty-three times. . . .

23. I produced a naval battle as a show for the people at the place across the Tiber now occupied by the grove of the Caesars, where a site 1,800 feet long and 1,200 broad was excavated. There thirty beaked triremes or biremes and still more smaller vessels were joined in battle. About 3,000 men, besides the rowers, fought in these fleets.

24. After my victory, I replaced in the temples of all the cities of the province of Asia the ornaments which my late adversary, after despoiling the temples, had taken into his private possession. Some eighty silver statues of me, on foot, on horse and in chariots) had been set up in Rome; I myself removed them, and with the money that they realized I set golden offerings in the temple of Apollo, in my own name and in the names of those who had honored me with the statues.

25. I made the sea peaceful and freed it of pirates. In that war I captured about 30,000 slaves who had escaped from their masters and taken up arms against the republic, and I handed them over to their masters for punishment. . . .

26. I extended the territory of all those provinces of the Roman people on whose borders lay peoples not subject to our government. I brought peace to the Gallic and Spanish provinces as well as to Germany, throughout the area bordering on the Ocean from Cadiz to the mouth of the Elbe. I secured the pacification of the Alps from the district nearest the Adriatic to the Tuscan sea, yet without waging an unjust war on any people. My fleet sailed through the ocean eastwards from the mouth of the Rhine to the territory of the Cimbri, a country which no Roman had visited before either by land or sea. . . . At my command and under my auspices two armies were led almost at the same time into Ethiopia and Arabia Felix; vast enemy forces of both peoples were cut down in battle and many towns captured. Ethiopia was penetrated as far as the town of Nabata, which adjoins Meroe; in Arabia the army advanced into the territory of the Sabaeans to the town of Mariba.

27. I added Egypt to the empire of the Roman people. . . . I recovered all the provinces beyond the Adriatic sea towards the east, together with Cyrene, the greater part of them being then occupied by kings. I had previously recovered Sicily and Sardinia which had been seized in the slave war.

28. I founded colonies of soldiers in Africa, Sicily, Macedonia, both Spanish provinces, Achaea, Asia, Syria, Gallia Narbonensis and Pisidia. Italy too has twenty-eight colonies founded by my authority, which were densely populated in my lifetime.

29. By victories over enemies I recovered in Spain and in Gaul, and from the Dalmatians several standards lost by other commanders. I compelled the Parthians to restore to me the spoils and standards of three Roman armies and to ask as suppliants for the friendship of the Roman people. Those standards I deposited in the innermost shrine of the temple of Mars the Avenger.
31. Embassies from kings in India were frequently sent to me; never before had they been seen with any Roman commander. . . .
32. While I was the leading citizen very many other peoples have experienced the good faith of the Roman people which had never previously exchanged embassies or had friendly relations with the Roman people.
34. In my sixth and seventh consulships, after I had extinguished civil wars, and at a time when with universal consent I was in complete control of affairs, I transferred the republic from my power to the dominion of the senate and people of Rome. For this service of mine I was named Augustus by decree of the senate, and the door-posts of my house were publicly wreathed with bay leaves and a civic crown was fixed over my door and a golden shield was set in the Curia Julia, which, as attested by the inscription thereon, was given me by the senate and people of Rome on account of my courage, clemency, justice and piety. After this time I excelled all in influence [auctoritas], although I possessed no more official power [potestas] than others who were my colleagues in the several magistracies.
35. In my thirteenth consulship the senate, the equestrian order and the whole people of Rome gave me the title of Father of my Country, and resolved that this should be inscribed in the porch of my house and in the Curia Julia and in the Forum Augustum below the chariot which had been set there in my honor by decree of the senate. At the time of writing I am in my seventy-sixth year.

From: Augustus, P. A. Brunt and J. M. Moore, *Res gestae divi Augusti: the achievements of the divine Augustus*, (London: Oxford University Press, 1967), pp. 19–37.

QUESTIONS:

1. What evidence does the *Res Gestae* provide about the practicalities of running a huge empire? Does it help explain why collective rule by the Roman Senate was no longer practical by the time of Augustus?
2. What are the key elements of Augustus' screen image of himself? What achievements does he stress most, and what values does he appeal to?

5.3: *Rock Edict XIII from the Rock and Pillar Edicts* (Ashoka, from between 269 BCE and 231 BCE)

Ashoka (304–232 BCE) was third king of the Mauryan dynasty. After taking the throne, he initially pursued the expansionist policies of his father Bindusara and his grandfather Chandragupta Maurya. With the conquest of the kingdom of Kalinga on India's southeastern coast, Ashoka brought almost the whole of the subcontinent under Mauryan rule. But the cost of that campaign in human lives and misery led Ashoka to a spiritual crisis and conversion to Buddhism. He foreswore offensive warfare (but did retain his large army and the will to use it defensively when necessary), and instead he committed himself and his government to spiritual conquest, the welfare of his subjects, and the promotion of dharma. As described in Chapter 4, dharma is usually translated as "sacred duty," but the term has a number of different meanings in Hindu and Buddhist traditions. Ashoka construed the term broadly and with toleration for religious variety. Adopting the reign name *Priyadarsi* ("One who looks after the welfare of others"), he had stone pillars erected throughout his realms inscribed with his precepts on dharma. This selection comes from those Rock and Pillar Edicts.

Beloved-of-the-Gods, King Priyadarsi, conquered the Kalingas eight years after his coronation. One hundred and fifty thousand were deported, one hundred thousand were killed and many more died (from other causes). After the Kalingas had been conquered, Beloved-of-the-Gods came to feel a strong inclination towards the Dharma, a love for the Dharma and for instruction in Dharma. Now Beloved-of-the-Gods feels deep remorse for having conquered the Kalingas.

Indeed, Beloved-of-the-Gods is deeply pained by the killing, dying and deportation that take place when an unconquered country is conquered. But Beloved-of-the-Gods is pained even more by this—that Brahmans, ascetics, and householders of different religions who live in those countries, and who are respectful to superiors, to mother and father, to elders, and who behave properly and have strong loyalty towards friends, acquaintances, companions, relatives, servants and employees—that they are injured, killed or separated from their loved ones. Even those who are not affected (by all this) suffer when they see friends, acquaintances, companions and relatives affected. These misfortunes befall all (as a result of war), and this pains Beloved-of-the-Gods.

There is no country, except among the Greeks, where these two groups, Brahmans and ascetics, are not found, and there is no country where people are not devoted to one or another religion. Therefore the killing, death or deportation of a hundredth, or even a thousandth part of those who died during the conquest of Kalinga now pains Beloved-of-the-Gods. Now Beloved-of-the-Gods thinks that even those who do wrong should be forgiven where forgiveness is possible.

Even the forest people, who live in Beloved-of-the-Gods' domain, are entreated and reasoned with to act properly. They are told that despite his remorse Beloved-of-the-Gods has the power to punish them if necessary, so that they should be ashamed of their wrong and not be killed. Truly, Beloved-of-the-Gods desires non-injury, restraint and impartiality to all beings, even where wrong has been done.

Now it is conquest by Dharma that Beloved-of-the-Gods considers to be the best conquest. And it (conquest by Dharma) has been won here, on the borders, even six hundred yojanas away, where the Greek king Antiochos rules, beyond there where the four kings named Ptolemy, Antigonos, Magas and Alexander rule, likewise in the south among the Cholas, the Pandyas, and as far as Tamraparni. Here in the king's domain among the Greeks, the Kambojas, the Nabhakas, the Nabhapamkits, the Bhojas, the Pitinikas, the Andhras and the Palidas, everywhere people are following Beloved-of-the-Gods' instructions in Dharma. Even where Beloved-of-the-Gods' envoys have not been, these people too, having heard of the practice of Dharma and the ordinances and instructions in Dharma given by Beloved-of-the-Gods, are following it and will continue to do so. This conquest has been won everywhere, and it gives great joy—the joy which only conquest by Dharma can give. But even this joy is of little consequence. Beloved-of-the-Gods considers the great fruit to be experienced in the next world to be more important.

I have had this Dharma edict written so that my sons and great-grandsons may not consider making new conquests, or that if military conquests are made, that they be done with forbearance and light punishment, or better still, that they consider making conquest by Dharma only, for that bears fruit in this world and the next. May all their intense devotion be given to this which has a result in this world and the next.

From: Edict XIII: *The Edicts of King Asoka*, Ven. S. Dhammika, transl. (Kandy, Sri Lanka: Buddhist Publication Society, 1993).

QUESTIONS:

1. What evidence does this Edict provide about the challenges of ruling a vast Agrarian empire? How is the erection of monumental edicts an active form of administration?
2. What screen image of himself do Ashoka's Edicts project? How does it differ, and how is it similar, to the images projected by Augustus and Trajan?

5.4: *"The First Emperor"* from *The Records of the Grand Historian* (Sima Qian, c. 105 BCE)

Sima Qian (c. 145 to after 91 BCE) is to Chinese history writing what Herodotus and Thucydides combined are to Western historical writing. A scholar and official under the Han, he began collecting historical records and sources early in his career. He was eventually appointed Grand Historian of the Han Court in 107 BCE, in which office he composed The Records of the Grand Historian. Based on extensive research in the Imperial Library and on the sources he collected, this monumental work traces Chinese history from the legendary Five Sage Emperors down to Sima Qian's own times. A central section of the work, from which this selection comes, deals with the rise and fall of the Qin Dynasty (221–206 BCE) and its founder, the fearsome First Emperor, Qin Shi Huangdi (256–210 BCE). Although the Han abolished many of the Qin's harshest measures, in many ways it retained the structure of government set in place by the Qin. But it cloaked the iron hand of the Chinese state in a Confucian velvet glove. (It also implemented, for a time, a rather Taoist—what we might call laissez faire—economic policy that worked for a time to promote prosperity.) It was this synthesis that would survive into subsequent dynasties, in part because of the view of history promoted by Sima Qian and his successors as official court historians.

. . . [W]hen the power of the Zhou dynasty waned, the Qin rose to prominence, building its capital in the western borderland. From the time of Duke Mu on, it gradually ate away at the domains of the other feudal rulers until the process was finally completed by the First Emperor. . . . In the case of Qin, however, while it was in a flourishing state, its manifold laws and stern punishments caused the empire to tremble. But when its power declined, then the people eyed it with hatred and the whole area within the seas rose up in revolt.

Duke Xiao of Qin, relying upon the strength of Mt. Yao and the Hangu Pass and basing himself in the area of Yongzhou, with his ministers held fast to his land and eyed the house of Zhou, for he cherished a desire to roll up the empire like a mat, to bind into one the whole world, to bag all the land within the four seas; he had it in his heart to swallow up everything in the eight directions. At this time he was aided by Lord Shang, who at home set up laws for him, encouraged agriculture and weaving, and built up the instruments of war, and abroad contracted military alliances and attacked the other feudal lords. Thus the men of Qin were able with ease to acquire territory east of the upper reaches of the Yellow River.

After the death of Duke Xiao, kings Huiwen and Wu carried on the undertakings of their predecessor and, following the plans he had laid, seized [a state] in the south and [states] in the west, and acquired rich land in the east and provinces of strategic value. The other feudal lords in alarm came together in council to devise some plan to weaken Qin, sparing nothing in gifts of precious objects and rich lands to induce men from all over the empire to come and join with them in a "vertical alliance", and pool their strength. . . . [The leading] four lords were all men of intelligence and loyalty, generous and kind to others, who honored worthy men and took good care of their followers. They rejected the Horizontal Alliance and instead formed the Vertical Alliance, which united all the forces of [nine] states. . . . With a force of 1,000,000 soldiers drawn from an area ten times that of Qin, they beat upon the Pass and pressed forward toward Qin. But the men of Qin opened the Pass to entice the enemy in, and the armies of the Nine States fled and did not dare advance. Qin, without expending a single arrow or losing a single arrowhead, threatened the feudal rulers of the entire empire.

With this the Vertical Alliance collapsed, its treaties came to naught, and the various states hastened to present Qin with parts of their territory as bribes for peace. With its superior strength Qin pressed the crumbling forces of its rivals, pursued those who had fled in defeat, and overwhelmed and slaughtered the army of 1,000,000 until their shields floated upon a river of blood. Following up the advantages of its victory, Qin gained mastery over the empire and divided up its mountains and rivers. The powerful states begged to submit to its sovereignty and the weaker ones paid homage at its court.

Then followed kings Xiaowen and Zhuangxiang, whose reigns were short and uneventful. After this came the First Emperor who, carrying on the glorious spirit of his six predecessors, cracked his long whip and drove the universe before him, swallowed up the eastern and western Zhou, and overthrew the feudal lords. He ascended the throne of honor and ruled the six directions, scourging the world with his lash, and his might shook the four seas. In the south he seized the land of the hundred tribes . . . and made of it [two] provinces, and the lords of the hundred [tribes] bowed their heads, hung halters from their necks, and pleaded for their lives with the lowest officials of Qin. Then he sent [a general] north to build the Great Wall and defend the borders, driving back the Xiongnu over 700 li, so that the barbarians no longer ventured to come south to pasture their horses and their men dared not take up their bows to vent their hatred.

Thereupon he discarded the ways of the former kings and burned the books of the hundred schools of philosophy in order to make the black-headed people ignorant. He destroyed the walls of the great cities, put to death the powerful leaders, and collected all the arms of the empire, which he had brought to his capital at Xianyang, where the spears and arrowheads were melted down and cast to make twelve human statues. All this he did in order to weaken the black-headed people. After this he ascended and fortified Mt. Hua, set up fords along the Yellow River, and strengthened the heights and precipices overlooking the fathomless valleys, in order to secure his position. He garrisoned the strategic points with skilled generals and strong crossbowmen and stationed trusted ministers and well-trained soldiers to guard the land with arms and question all who passed back and forth. When he had thus pacified the empire, the First Emperor believed in his heart that, with the strength of his capital within the passes and his walls of metal extending 1,000 miles, he had established a rule that would be enjoyed by his sons and grandsons for 10,000 generations.

For a while after the death of the First Emperor the memory of his might continued to awe the common people. Yet Chen She, born in a humble hut with tiny windows and a wattle door, a day laborer in the fields and a garrison conscript, whose abilities could not match even the average, who had neither the worth of Confucius . . . nor wealth . . ., stepped from the ranks of the common soldiers, rose up from the paths of the fields, and led a band of some hundred poor, weary soldiers in revolt against Qin. They cut down trees to make their weapons and raised their flags on garden poles, and the whole world gathered like a cloud, answered like an echo to a sound, brought them provisions, and followed after them as shadows follow a form. In the end the leaders east of the mountains rose up together and destroyed the house of Qin.

. . . Qin, beginning with an insignificant amount of territory, reached the power of a great kingdom and for 100 years made the ancient eight provinces pay homage at its court. Yet, after it had become master of the six directions and established its palaces within the passes, a single commoner opposed it and its seven ancestral temples toppled, its ruler died by the hands of men, and it became the laughing stock of the world. Why? Because it failed to rule with humanity and righteousness, and did not realize that the power to attack, and the power to retain what one has thereby won, are not the same.

. . . [T]he First Emperor was greedy and short-sighted, confident in his own wisdom, never trusting his meritorious officials, never getting to know his people. He cast aside the kingly Way and relied on private procedures, outlawing books and writings, making the laws and penalties much harsher, putting deceit and force foremost and humanity and righteousness last, leading the whole world in violence and cruelty. In annexing the lands of others, one may place priority on deceit and force, but insuring peace and stability in the lands one has annexed calls for a respect for authority. Hence I say that seizing, and guarding what you have seized, do not depend upon the same techniques.

. . . So it is said, a people who feel secure may be led into righteous ways, but a people who feel threatened easily turn to evil. . . .

From: Sima Qian, *Records of the Grand Historian*, Burton Watson, transl. (New York: Columbia University Press,1993), pp. 74–83.

QUESTIONS:

1. Sima Qian writes that "the power to attack, and the power to retain what one has thereby won, are not the same". What are the implications of such a view for the administration of a vast Agrarian empire? How does the role of the military in Chinese government compare to that in Rome under Augustus?
2. The First Emperor was a great conqueror and unifier. In other civilizations he might have been regarded as a martial hero. Why is he not seen this way in the Chinese tradition? What screen image of The First Emperor does Sima Qian project?

5.5: *Discourses on Salt and Iron* (Huan Kuan, c. 80 BCE)

The laissez faire economic policies of the early Han, noted in the introduction to the previous source, gave way under Emperor Han Wudi (r. 156–87 BCE) to a more interventionist economic policy. The state established monopolies on the sale of salt and iron as well as other key commodities and set up price stabilization schemes. After Wudi died, Huo Guang, the regent for Wudi's eight-year-old heir, called together scholars and officials to debate economic policy. Huan Kuan, one of the scholars, wrote a record of the debates. Two sides emerged. The Confucian scholars, called The Literati in the source, argued for a traditionalist position of abolishing the monopolies. The other side, represented in the source by The Lord Grand Secretary, argued for maintaining the newer policies. The source therefore gives us a fascinating glimpse at a philosophical policy debate.

THE BASIC ARGUMENT

a. It so happened that in the sixth year of the *shih-yüan* era an Imperial edict directed the Chancellor and the Imperial secretaries to confer with the recommended Worthies and Literati, and to enquire of them as to the rankling grievances among the people.

b. The Literati responded as follows: It is our humble opinion that the principle of ruling men lies in nipping in the bud wantonness and frivolity, in extending wide the elementals of virtue, in discouraging mercantile pursuits, and in displaying benevolence and righteousness. Let lucre never be paraded before the eyes of the people; only then will enlightenment flourish and folkways improve.

c. But now, with the system of the salt and iron monopolies, the liquor excise, and *equable marketing* established in the provinces and the demesnes, the Government has entered into financial competition with the people, dissipating primordial candor and simplicity and sanctioning propensities to selfishness and greed. As a result few among our people take up the fundamental pursuits of life, while many flock to the non-essential. Now sturdy natural qualities decay as artificiality thrives, and rural values decline when industrialism flourishes. When industrialism is cultivated, the people become frivolous; when the values of rural life are developed, the people are simple and unsophisticated. The people being unsophisticated, wealth will abound; when the people are extravagant, cold and hunger will follow. We pray that the salt, iron and liquor monopolies and the system of *equable marketing* be abolished so that the rural pursuits may be encouraged, people be deterred from entering the secondary occupations, and national agriculture be materially and financially benefited.

d. The Lord Grand Secretary said: When the Hsiung Nu rebelled against our authority and frequently raided and devastated the frontier settlements, to be constantly on the watch for them was a great strain upon the soldiery of the Middle Kingdom; but without measures of precaution being taken, these forays and depredations would never cease. The late Emperor, grieving at the long suffering of the denizens of the marches who live in fear of capture by the bar barians, caused consequently forts and seried signal stations to be built, where garrisons were held ready against the nomads. When the revenue for the defence of the frontier fell short, the salt and iron monopoly was established, the liquor excise and the system of *equable marketing* introduced; goods were multiplied and wealth increased so as to furnish the frontier expenses.

e. Now our critics here, who demand that these measures be abolished, at home would have the hoard of the treasury entirely depleted, and abroad would deprive the border of provision for its defence; they would expose our soldiers who defend the barriers and mount the walls to all the hunger and cold of the borderland. How else do they expect to provide for them? It is not expedient to abolish these measures!

f. The Literati: Confucius observed that *the ruler of a kingdom or the chief of a house is not concerned about his people being few, but about lack of equitable treatment; nor is he concerned about poverty, but over the presence of discontentment*. Thus the Son of Heaven should not speak about *much and little*, the feudal lords should not talk about *advantage and detriment*, ministers about *gain and loss*, but they should cultivate benevolence and righteousness, to set an example to the people, and extend wide their virtuous conduct to gain the people's confidence. Then will nearby folk lovingly flock to them and distant peoples joyfully submit to their authority. Therefore *the master conqueror does not fight; the expert warrior needs no soldiers; the truly great commander requires not to set his troops in battle array*. Cultivate virtue in the temple and the hall, then you need only to show a bold front to the enemy and your troops will return home in victory. The Prince who practices benevolent administration should be matchless in the world; for him, what use is expenditure?

g. The Lord Grand Secretary: The Hsiung Nu, savage and wily, boldly push through the barriers and harass the Middle Kingdom, massacring the provincial population and killing the keepers of the Northern Marches. They long deserve punishment for their unruliness and lawlessness. . . . I again assert that the proposal to do away with the salt and iron monopoly and *equable marketing* would grievously diminish our frontier supplies and impair our military plans. I can not consider favorably a proposal so heartlessly dismissing the frontier question.

h. The Literati: The ancients held in honor virtuous methods and discredited resort to arms. Thus Confucius said: *If remoter people are not submissive, all the influences of civil culture and virtue are to be cultivated to attract them to be so; and when they have been so attracted, they must be made contented and tranquil?* Now these virtuous principles are discarded and reliance put on military force; troops are raised to attack the enemy and garrisons are stationed to make ready for him. It is the long drawn-out service of our troops in the field and the ceaseless transportation for the needs of the commissariat that cause our soldiers on the marches to suffer from hunger and cold abroad, while the common people are burdened with labor at home. The establishment of the salt and iron monopoly and the institution of finance officials to supply the army needs were not permanent schemes; it is therefore desirable that they now be abolished.

i. The Lord Grand Secretary: The ancient founders of the Commonwealth made open the ways for both fundamental and branch industries and facilitated equitable distribution of goods. Markets and courts were provided to harmonize various demands; there people of all classes gathered together and all goods collected, so that farmer, merchant, and worker could each obtain what he desired; the exchange completed, everyone went back to his occupation. *Facilitate exchange so that the people will be unflagging in industry* says the Book of Changes. Thus without artisans, the farmers will be deprived of the use of implements: without merchants, all prized commodities will be cut off. The former would lead to stoppage of grain production, the latter to exhaustion of wealth. It is clear that the salt and iron monopoly and *equable marketing* are really intended for the circulation of amassed wealth and the regulation of the consumption according to the urgency of the need. It is inexpedient to abolish them.

j. The Literati: Lead the people with virtue and the people will return to honest simplicity; entice the people with gain, and they will become vicious. Vicious habits would lead them away from righteousness to follow after gain, with the result that people will swarm on the road and throng at the markets. *A poor country may appear plentiful, not because it possesses abundant wealth, but because wants multiply and people become reckless*, said Lao-tzŭ. Hence the true King promotes rural pursuits and discourages branch industries; he checks the people's desires through the principles of propriety and righteousness and provides a market for grain in exchange for other commodities, where there is no place for merchants to circulate useless goods, and for artisans to make useless implements. Thus merchants are for the purpose of draining stagnation and the artisans for providing tools; they should not become the principal concern of the government.

. . .

m. The Lord Grand Secretary: Formerly the Princes in the Provinces and the demesnes sent in their respective products as tribute. The transportion was vexacious and disorganized; the goods were usually of distressingly bad quality, often failing to replay their transport costs. Therefore Transportion Officers have been provided in every province to assist in the delivery and transportion and for the speeding of the tribute from distant parts. So the system came to be known as *equable marketing*. A Receiving Bureau has been established at the capital to monopolize all the commodities, buying when prices are low, and selling when prices are high, with the result that the Government suffers no loss and the merchants cannot speculate for profit. This is therefore known as the *balancing standard*. With the *balancing standard* people are safeguarded from unemployment; with the *equable marketing* people have evenly distributed labor. Both of these measures are intended to equilibrate all goods and convenience the people, and not to open the way to profit and provide a ladder to popular misdemeanor.

n. The Literati: The Ancients in levying upon and taxing the people would look for what the latter were skilled in, and not seek for those things in which they were not adept. Thus the farmers contributed the fruits of their labor, the weaving women, their products. Now the Government leaves alone what the people have and exacts what they have not, with the result that the people sell their products at a cheap price to satisfy demands from above. Recently in some of the provinces and demesnes they ordered the people to make woven goods. The officers then caused the producers various embarassments and bargained with them. What was collected by the officers was not only the silk from Ch'i and T'ao, or cloth from Shu and Han, but also other goods manufactured by the people which were mischievously sold at a standard price. Thus the farmers suffer twice over while the weaving women are doubly taxed. We have not yet seen that your marketing is "equable". As to the second measure under discussion, the government officers swarm out to close the door, gain control of the market and corner all commodities. With commodities cornered, prices soar: with prices rising, the merchants make private deals by way of speculation. Thus the officers are lenient to the cunning capitalists, and the merchants store up goods and accumulate commodities waiting for a time of need. Nimble traders and unscrupulous officials buy in cheap to get high returns. We have not yet seen that your standard is "balanced." For it seems that in ancient times *equable marketing* was to bring about equitable division of labor and facilitate transportation of tribute; it was surely not for profit or to make trade in commodities.

FRONTIERS, THE GREAT CONCERN

a. The Lord Grand Secretary: You say, oh Literati, that the Enlightened Ruler is concerned when the Empire is not at peace and the states are not at rest. To be sure, the Prince should consider the Empire as if it formed a single household. Even if one man find not his proper position in life, he cannot be happy. Consequently, he is not a Benevolent Prince who lets his people drown in distress without making an attempt to rescue them; and he is not a loyal minister who shows no concern for the misfortunes of his state. To hold fast to his charge in defeat, even unto death, is the duty of a minister; to clothe the cold and feed the hungry is the way of a kindly father.

b. At present as our sons and younger brothers, far from home, suffer privations on the borders, the Ruler of Men feels uneasy for them day and night; and all the ministers turn all their energies to the consideration of methods whereby the state revenue might be increased. Thus it came about that the Keeper of the Privy Treasury proposed to establish the liquor excise, in order to provide for the frontier, supply the needs of our fighting men, and bring succor to the people in distress. Out of sheer humanity, could we, their fathers and elder brothers, help but do it? But it has been found insufficient to have thus economized in the interior on prime necessities, in order to relieve the need abroad. If we follow your repeated suggestions to abolish these sources of revenue, and to decrease thereby the provisions for the frontier, we would certainly be acting contrary to the ways of kindly fathers or worthy elder brothers.

c. The Literati: In the period of Chou's decline, the Emperor's power grew weak and the feudal lords ruled by force. Consequently, princes sat uneasy on their thrones, and their counsellors rushed restlessly about. Why? Because, threatened by enemy countries on all sides, the Dynasty was in constant danger. At present, however, the Nine Provinces are enclosed within one boundary and the whole Empire is under one rule. Your Majesty can leisurely promenade through Your lofty halls, while the ministers advance their exhaustive proposals. In unison the hymns and chants sound within Your court, and the jingling bells of Your chariot resound merrily outside. Your pure virtue is as illuminating as that of Yao and Shun; Your illustrious deeds will flow down to posterity. How could the barbarian tribes of the Man or Mai, and their barren lands, be worth all this trouble and worry that brings us back to the uncertainty of the Warring States period. Should Your Majesty be unwilling to abandon them to their fate, You have but to manifest Your virtue towards them and extend Your favors to cover them, and the northern barbarians will undoubtedly come of their own accord to pay You tribute at the Wall. If held to be our "outside subjects", then the Hsiung Nu will never in all their lives lack the sustenance they need.

. . .

g. The Lord Grand Secretary: I have heard that a minister should execute his duties with all loyalty, and a son should assume his patrimony with due filial piety. When the ruler commits some error, the minister should cover it. When the father does some wrong, the son should aid and abet. Thus, when the ruler dies, the minister does not change his policy. When the father dies, the son does not alter his ways. The *Spring and Autumn* disapproved of the destruction of the Ch'üan Tower, because the work of the ancestors was destroyed; and this created the impression of a wrong act of old by rulers and fathers.

h. Now the salt and iron monopoly and the *equable marketing* are long standing. To abolish them, would that be possible without destroying the achievement of His late Majesty, and thus aspersing the virtue of the Enlightened Ruler! The officials, therefore, are *biased in favor of* the ways of loyalty and filial piety. This is how their ways "differ" from, and why they cannot "deliberate" with, the Literati.

i. The Literati: Enlightened persons adapt themselves to the times. The wise devise systems to conform with the needs of their contemporaries. Confucius said: *A linen cap is the prescribed form, but nowadays silk is worn. This saves expense and I follow the general usage.* Therefore the Sages and the Worthies without departing from antiquity, follow custom but without being partial to what is convenient. Duke Ting of Lu arranged his ancestors' tablets in the order of his remote progenitors and immediate ancestors. Duke Chao dismissed his ministers and officers to save expense. No one could call this a change in their ancestors' policies or in their father's ways. On the other hand, the Second Emperor wasted money in elaborating the O-pang Palace to promote the prestige of the House, and Chao Kao piled up the legislation of Ch'in to extend its awesomeness. No one could call them a loyal minister and a filial son.

From: Huan Kuan, *Discourses on Salt and Iron*, Esson M. Gale, transl. (Brill, 1931), pp. 1–11, 75–80.

QUESTIONS:

1. How do the two sides argue? What authorities or evidence do they appeal to in their arguments, and what screen image of the Chinese state and culture do they project?
2. What frame values shape this debate? What do the two sides in this debate implicitly agree on without even thinking about it?

CHAPTER 6

Societies and Peoples: Everyday Life in the Agrarian World

INTRODUCTION

This chapter presents sources about everyday life in the Agrarian Era, or at least some aspects of everyday life among some classes. The Great Cultural Divide in Agrarian Era hierarchies means that it is difficult for us to learn about the lives and perspectives of people in all social classes. There are plenty of sources that discuss the lives of elite men, who dominated the cultural screen of Agrarian societies. But most women and peasant men were illiterate and so left no writings about themselves, and elite men who did write paid little attention to women and peasants. Thus, the limited information we have comes from a few elite women who wrote about themselves, from some elite men who wrote prescriptions about how women should live, and from some state administrators who wrote about peasants as a class, mostly in order to ensure that they remained productive taxpayers. This chapter presents sources of these types.

6.1: *Lessons for Women* (Ban Zhao, c. 106)

Ban Zhao (45–c. 116 CE) is introduced at the beginning of Chapter 6 of *Frameworks*. Her father and brother were court historians to the Han dynasty, a role she assumed after their deaths. She could do so because her father had given her a classical Confucian education and her husband had died, freeing her of her duties to him. In addition to writing official histories, she wrote *Lessons for Women* for her daughters. The advice is deeply Confucian and gives a fine example of the expectations placed on elite women.

I, the unworthy writer, am unsophisticated, unenlightened, and by nature unintelligent, but I am fortunate both to have received not a little favor from my scholarly Father, and to have had a cultured mother and instructresses upon whom to rely for a literary education as well as for training in good manners. More than forty years have passed since at the age of fourteen I took up the dustpan and the broom in the Cao family [the family into which she married]. During this time with trembling heart I feared constantly that I might disgrace my parents, and that I might multiply difficulties for both the women and the men of my husband's family. Day and night I was distressed in heart, but

I labored without confessing weariness. Now and hereafter, however, I know how to escape from such fears.

Being careless, and by nature stupid, I taught and trained my children without system. Consequently I fear that my son Gu may bring disgrace upon the Imperial Dynasty by whose Holy Grace he has unprecedentedly received the extraordinary privilege of wearing the Gold and the Purple, a privilege for the attainment of which by my son, I a humble subject never even hoped. Nevertheless, now that he is a man and able to plan his own life, I need not again have concern for him. But I do grieve that you, my daughters, just now at the age for marriage, have not at this time had gradual training and advice; that you still have not learned the proper customs for married women. I fear that by failure in good manners in other families you will humiliate both your ancestors and your clan. I am now seriously ill, life is uncertain. As I have thought of you all in so untrained a state, I have been uneasy many a time for you. At hours of leisure I have composed . . . these instructions under the title, "Lessons for Women." In order that you may have something wherewith to benefit your persons, I wish every one of you, my daughters each to write out a copy for yourself.

From this time on every one of you strive to practice these lessons.

HUMILITY

On the third day after the birth of a girl the ancients observed three customs: first to place the baby below the bed; second to give her a potsherd [a piece of broken pottery] with which to play; and third to announce her birth to her ancestors by an offering. Now to lay the baby below the bed plainly indicated that she is lowly and weak, and should regard it as her primary duty to humble herself before others. To give her potsherds with which to play indubitably signified that she should practice labor and consider it her primary duty to be industrious. To announce her birth before her ancestors clearly meant that she ought to esteem as her primary duty the continuation of the observance of worship in the home.

These three ancient customs epitomize woman's ordinary way of life and the teachings of the traditional ceremonial rites and regulations. Let a woman modestly yield to others; let her respect others; let her put others first, herself last. Should she do something good, let her not mention it; should she do something bad let her not deny it. Let her bear disgrace; let her even endure when others speak or do evil to her. Always let her seem to tremble and to fear. When a woman follows such maxims as these then she may be said to humble herself before others.

Let a woman retire late to bed, but rise early to duties; let her nor dread tasks by day or by night. Let her not refuse to perform domestic duties whether easy or difficult. That which must be done, let her finish completely, tidily, and systematically, When a woman follows such rules as these, then she may be said to be industrious.

Let a woman be correct in manner and upright in character in order to serve her husband. Let her live in purity and quietness of spirit, and attend to her own affairs. Let her love not gossip and silly laughter. Let her cleanse and purify and arrange in order the wine and the food for the offerings to the ancestors. When a woman observes such principles as these, then she may be said to continue ancestral worship.

No woman who observes these three fundamentals of life has ever had a bad reputation or has fallen into disgrace. If a woman fail to observe them, how can her name be honored; how can she but bring disgrace upon herself?

HUSBAND AND WIFE

The Way of husband and wife is intimately connected with Yin and Yang [these are the two basis elements of the Universe: Yin, the soft yielding feminine element, and Yang the hard aggressive male element. Every substance contains both elements in varying proportions]. and relates the individual to gods and ancestors. Truly it is the great principle of Heaven and Earth, and the great basis of human relationships. Therefore the "Rites" [The Classic of Rites] honor union of man and woman; and in the "Book of Poetry" [The Classic of Odes] the "First Ode" manifests the principle of marriage. For these reasons the relationships cannot but be an important one.

If a husband be unworthy, then he possesses nothing by which to control his wife. If a wife be unworthy, then she possesses nothing with which to serve her husband. IF a husband does not control his wife, then the rules of conduct manifesting his authority are abandoned and broken. If a wife does not serve her husband, when the proper relationship between men and women and the natural order of things are neglected and destroyed. As a matter of fact the purpose of these two [the controlling of women by men, and the serving of men by women] is the same.

Now examine the gentlemen of the present age. They only know that wives must be controlled, and that the husband's rules of conduct manifesting his authority must be established. They therefore teach their boys to read books and study histories. But they do not in the least understand that husbands and masters must also be served, and that the proper relationship and the rites should be maintained. Yet only to teach men and not to teach women—is that not ignoring the essential relation between them? According to the "Rites," it is the rule to begin to teach children to read at the age of eight years, and by the age of fifteen years they ought then to be ready for cultural training. Only why should it not be that girls' education as well as boys' be according to this principle?

RESPECT AND CAUTION

As Yin and Yang are not of the same nature, so man and woman have different characteristics. The distinctive quality of the Yang is rigidity; the function of the Yin is yielding. Man is honored for strength; a woman is beautiful on account of her gentleness. Hence there arose the common saying: "A man though born like a wolf may, it is feared, become a weak monstrosity; a woman though born like a mouse may, it is feared, become a tiger."

Now For self-culture nothing equals respect for others. To counteract firmness nothing equals compliance. Consequently it can be said that the Way of respect and acquiescence is woman's most important principle of conduct. So respect may be defined as nothing other than holding on to that which is permanent; and acquiescence nothing other than being liberal and generous. Those who are steadfast in devotion know that they should stay in their proper places; those who are liberal and generous esteem others, and honor and serve chem.

If husband and wife have the habit of staying together, never leaving one another, and following each other around within the limited space of their own rooms, then they will lust after and take liberties with one another. From such action improper language will arise between the two. This kind of discussion may lead co licentiousness. But of licentiousness will be born a heart of disrespect to the husband. Such a result comes from not knowing that one should stay in one's proper place.

Furthermore, affairs may be either crooked or straight; words may be either right or wrong. Straightforwardness cannot but lead to quarreling; crookedness cannot but lead to accusation. If there are really accusations and quarrels, then undoubtedly there will be angry affairs. Such a result comes from not esteeming others, and not honoring and serving them.

If wives suppress not contempt for husbands, then it follows that such wives rebuke and scold their husbands. If husbands stop not short of anger, then they are certain to beat their wives. The correct relationship between husband and wife is based upon harmony and intimacy, and conjugal love is grounded in proper union. Should actual blows be dealt, how could matrimonial relationship be preserved? Should sharp words be spoken, how could conjugal love exist? If love and proper relationship both be destroyed, then husband and wife are divided.

WOMANLY QUALIFICATIONS

A woman ought to have four qualifications: (1) womanly virtue; (2) womanly words; (3) womanly bearing; and (4) womanly work. Now what is called womanly virtue need not be brilliant ability, exceptionally different from others. Womanly words need be neither clever in debate nor keen in conversation. Womanly appearance requires neither a pretty nor a perfect face and form. Womanly work need not be work done more skillfully than that of others.

To guard carefully her chastity; to control circumspectly her behavior; in every motion to exhibit modesty; and to model each act on the best usage, this is womanly virtue.

To choose her words with care; to avoid vulgar language; to speak at appropriate times; and nor to weary others with much conversation, may be called the characteristics of womanly words.

To wash and scrub filth away; to keep clothes and ornaments fresh and clean; to wash the head and bathe the body regularly, and to keep the person free from disgraceful filth, may be called the characteristics of womanly bearing.

With whole-hearted devotion to sew and to weave; to love not gossip and silly laughter; in cleanliness and order to prepare the wine and food for serving guests, may be called the characteristics of womanly work.

These four qualifications characterize the greatest virtue of a woman. No woman can afford to be without them. In fact they are very easy to possess if a woman only treasure them in her heart. The ancients had a saying: "Is love afar off? If I desire love, then love is at hand!" So can it be said of these qualifications.

IMPLICIT OBEDIENCE

Whenever the mother-in-law says, "Do not do that," and if what she says is right, unquestionably the daughter-in-law obeys. Whenever the mother-in-law says, "Do that," even if what she says is wrong, still the daughter-in-law submits unfailingly to the command. Let a woman not act contrary to the wishes and the opinions of parents-in-law about right and wrong; let her not dispute with them what is straight and what is crooked. Such docility may called obedience which sacrifices personal opinion. Therefore the ancient book, "A Pattern for Women," says: "If a daughter-in-law who follows the wishes of her parents-in-law is like and echo and shadow, how could she not be praised?"

From: Nancy Lee Swann, *Pan Chao: Foremost Woman Scholar of China* (New York: Century Company, 1932), pp. 111–14.

QUESTIONS:

1. According to Ban Zhao, what are the most important characteristics of proper womanly behavior and virtue? How do these virtues fit women into a larger social structure?
2. What screen image of herself does Ban Zhao project? What frame values inform that screen image?

6.2: *The Law of Manu* (c. second to third century CE)

The Law of Manu dates from the late second or early third century CE, just after a time of disorder in the Hindu societies of northern India. It represents an attempt to reimpose order in all spheres of life, and as for many Agrarian societies, establishing proper gender roles was an essential aspect of order. The Manu of the title is the legendary "first man" of Hindu culture (Manu and the English word man are related linguistically), who established human laws in accordance with both human traditions and divine sanctions. Thus, it bases traditional values on religious authority. If the *Bhagavad Gita* establishes the basic ethical framework for the Hindu notion of dharma, or duty, the Law of Manu, excerpted here, clarifies the dharma of proper womanhood.

Hear now the duties of women.

By a girl, by a young woman, or even by an aged one, nothing must be done independently, even in her own house.

In childhood a female must be subject to her father, in youth to her husband, when her lord is dead to her sons; a woman must never be independent.

She must not seek to separate herself from her father, husband, or sons; by leaving them she would make both (her own and her husband's) families contemptible.

She must always be cheerful, clever in (the management of her) household affairs, careful in cleaning her utensils, and economical in expenditure.

Him to whom her father may give her, or her brother with the father's permission, she shall obey as long as he lives, and when he is dead, she must not insult (his memory). . . .

[B]etrothal (by the father or guardian) is the cause of (the husband's) dominion (over his wife).

The husband who wedded her with sacred texts, always gives happiness to his wife, both in season and out of season, in this world and in the next.

Though destitute of virtue, or seeking pleasure (elsewhere), or devoid of good qualities, (yet) a husband must be constantly worshipped as a god by a faithful wife.

No sacrifice, no vow, no fast must be performed by women apart (from their husbands); if a wife obeys her husband, she will for that (reason alone) be exalted in heaven.

A faithful wife, who desires to dwell (after death) with her husband, must never do anything that might displease him who took her hand, whether he be alive or dead. . . .

[L]et her emaciate her body by (living on) pure flowers, roots, and fruit; but she must never even mention the name of another man after her husband has died.

Until death let her be patient (of hardships), self-controlled, and chaste, and strive (to fulfill) that most excellent duty which (is prescribed) for wives who have one husband only.

A virtuous wife who after the death of her husband constantly remains chaste, reaches heaven, though she have no son, just like those chaste men.

But a woman who from a desire to have offspring violates her duty towards her (deceased) husband, brings on herself disgrace in this world, and loses her place with her husband (in heaven). . . .

By violating her duty towards her husband, a wife is disgraced in this world, (after death) she enters the womb of a jackal, and is tormented by diseases (the punishment of) her sin. . . .

[A] female who controls her thoughts, speech, and actions, gains in this (life) highest renown, and in the next (world) a place near her husband.

Women must particularly be guarded against evil inclinations, however trifling (they may appear); for, if they are not guarded, they will bring sorrow on two families. . . .

No man can completely guard women by force; but they can be guarded by the . . . (following) expedients: Let the (husband) employ his (wife) in the collection and expenditure of his wealth, in keeping (everything) clean, in (the fulfilment of) religious duties, in the preparation of his food, and in looking after the household utensils.

Women, confined in the house under trustworthy and obedient servants, are not (well) guarded; but those who of their own accord keep guard over themselves, are well guarded. . . .

Through their passion for men, through their mutable temper, through their natural heartlessness, they become disloyal towards their husbands, however carefully they may be guarded in this (world).

(When creating them) Manu allotted to women (a love of their) bed, (of their) seat and (of) ornament, impure desires, wrath, dishonesty, malice, and bad conduct. . . .

The production of children, the nurture of those born, and the daily life of men, (of these matters) woman is visibly the cause.

Offspring, (the due performance on religious rites, faithful service, highest conjugal happiness and heavenly bliss for the ancestors and oneself, depend on one's wife alone.

He only is a perfect man who consists (of three persons united), his wife, himself, and his offspring; thus (says the Veda), and (learned) Brahmanas propound this (maxim) likewise, 'The husband is declared to be one with the wife.' . . .

The husband receives his wife from the gods, (he does not wed her) according to his own will; doing what is agreeable to the gods, he must always support her (while she is) faithful.

'Let mutual fidelity continue until death,' this may be considered as the summary of the highest law for husband and wife.

Let man and woman, united in marriage, constantly exert themselves, that (they may not be) disunited (and) may not violate their mutual fidelity.

From: The Law of Manu, in *The Sacred Books of the East,* vol. XXV, G. Bühler, transl. (Oxford, England: Clarendon Press, 1886): 194–97, 328–30, 332, 335, 344–45.

QUESTIONS:

1. What are the duties of a virtuous woman, according to the Law of Manu? Does caste or class matter? How do these duties compare to those of a Chinese woman in Ban Zhao's writing?
2. What does this source tell us about the relationship and interdependence of the front and back halves of the Agrarian pyramid? How are women recognized as necessary even as their place is strictly defined?

6.3: *The Life of St. Thomaïs of Lesbos* (Anonymous, mid-tenth century?)

Nothing is known of St. Thomaïs except from her two hagiographies (saints lives), the longer and more detailed of which is excerpted here. The *Life* seems to have been written about twelve years after her death, but it may have been revised in the following century. Its anonymous author was educated. Judging from the internal evidence from the *Life*, St. Thomaïs probably lived in the first half of the tenth century and spent most of her life in Constantinople, the capital of the Byzantine Empire. She achieved sainthood on the basis of her daily life, so the *Life* affords us a rare glimpse into the ordinary world of a merchant-class woman. She died when she was about thirty eight years old.

1. Since the Holy Scriptures say that the *memory of the righteous is praised,* should we not praise one who is an adornment to the female sex? I exclude from <this> discussion the Mother of God, She Who has been lifted above the cherubim, since She is beyond all created beings. As I said then, we should praise one who was more righteous than all the righteous women, the admirable Thomaıs. . . . By her family and life she was well known to all, she who was adorned by all forms of virtue and sparkled like a light. By her holy habits, modest character, still more modest lifestyle, as well as her asceticism,

Thomaıs adorned her family by her ways, rather than being one who was adorned by her family's glory, renown, and brilliance.

. . .

3. Her father, a man who lived in a way pleasing to God and maintained an angelic lifestyle, was named Michael. He was upright in character, holy in his way of life, firm of purpose, prematurely gray-haired, possessed of a perfect and advanced understanding because of his mature age. . . .

His wife and life companion was Kale, who was most beautiful in character, and more beautiful in soul. <She was> quite temperate, and, to speak truly, was of one mind with her husband. She <was> praiseworthy in conduct, intelligent in her mind, and good in her disposition. . . . They had enough wealth and money that they were neither enslaved by poverty, nor were they swollen by the weight of money, but they proceeded along in a middle path, which is a clear sign, I think, of their virtue.

4. The fetter of sterility strongly grieved this <couple>, as of old the shackle of childlessness had bound the forefathers of the Lord. It agitated them mightily, upset them deeply, and tore apart their soul. They constantly went to the holy churches, remaining all night singing hymns, indeed singing to the Lord both night and day. For they had not turned to marriage for the sake of bodily pleasure, quite the contrary, but out of desire for a good child; I speak of the wondrous Thomaıs, toward whom this account is hastening. . . .

This good <couple> suffered <then>, being troubled by their desire for a child, as had the ancestors of my Lord Christ. You surely know <who they are>; <my> account has alluded to some of them. They were afflicted with despondency and composed words of lamentation. They entreated God unceasingly. . .

Thus the Lord looked down from heaven and hearkened to the lamentation of this couple which was bound <in sterility>, and He loosed the fetters of childlessness. . .

5. . . . [O]ne night the all-immaculate and ever-virginal Virgin was seen in a dream by the wondrous woman Kale, truly good in character and manner, and said these very words: "Do not be of sad countenance about these things, O woman, and do not be upset on account of your childlessness. In a short while you shall bear a female child, who will chase as far as possible from you all despondency, O good woman." . . . The name "Thomaıs" <was given> to her, a child who was born in accord with a promise, who by nature was female, but by virtue and ascetic discipline much more male than men.

6. . . . As <Thomaıs> grew up, she continued to be strengthened in the virtues, devoted to the worship of God, and adorned by all forms of goodness. She disclosed her hidden beauty by its external manifestation and revealed the grace of her soul by her bodily features; <revealing her> invisible <virtues> by the visible, her internal <virtues> by her external <beauty>. One could see in her a perfect bodily harmony, which suggested the spiritual beauty <of her soul>. She was not raised in an ignoble manner by her parents, but with discipline, understanding, and frequent admonition.

After <Thomaıs> was thus reared and trained and reached the age of about twenty-four years, she was forced by her parents to take a husband even though she preferred to remain a virgin; she wished to remain ignorant of bodily pleasure and to trample on fleshly desires so as to present herself as a pure and undefiled temple to the pure God. But she had both to *guard her virginity* and to *respect marriage,* since these things are appreciated and revered by all.

<And so> she obeyed her parents. Agreeing to marriage, she bowed her head to the <marriage> crown and took a lawful husband. But he, who was Stephen by name, but not by <his> lifestyle, did not devote himself to her as companion but as an opponent, not as a helpmate but rather as an enemy. . . .

But what a noble mind she had, what a staunch spirit, what praiseworthy judgment again of her way of life! She did not cease to give thanks continually to God, to spend her free time in the divine churches, to take care of the poor, to pour out her wealth, and to give back her own <property> to God. . . . She put her whole hand to the spindle. She worked skillfully and artfully to weave on the loom fabrics of various colors. Her hands made cloth and the bellies of the poor ate to their content. Her hands labored for the sake of the poor and wove tunics for the naked. Her feet walked eagerly to the divine churches and kept vigil there all the night. . . .

7. . . . And one could see in this situation an unusual married couple; for the wife was manly and masculine in virtue, and strove to surpass her own nature [i.e., sex] by works of zeal <done> for virtue's sake. . . . <Thomaıs was> always stretching her hands up to heaven, kneeling, weeping, conversing with God, and kindling the divine love without interruption. And in doing the things pleasing to God—clothing the naked, raising up and encouraging those who had fallen—in this way she used every effort, she sought out every method, she devised every purpose through which she might bring to fruition the teachings of the Lord, even though she might be hindered by Stephen, to whom she was married, as our account has related above. For he opposed completely the wondrous intentions of Thomaıs, and while she was hastening to give away her wealth to the poor, he was opposing her like a Satan. . . .

<And> he [Stephen] used to strike the noble <Thomaıs> frequently, mocking greatly and sneering <at her>. . . .

8. . . . <Once>, as she was going to a holy church, she encountered a poor and naked man who was pierced with the greatest poverty. But look at what she did about it. She stripped off her own garments, and went naked for the sake of Christ; indeed, she suffered for the sake of Christ. And <as a result> she was beaten by Stephen so that she might obtain from Christ the lordly crown, <for> this <act of charity> was made known to her husband, and <consequently> the wondrous Thomaıs endured many blows. . . .

. . .

13. *Miracle 4.* . . . A woman who lived wantonly and licentiously in every way [as a prostitute] suffered from hemorrhaging for more than six years and was terribly afflicted by this sickness. But the holy woman, realizing that the woman's illness <came> from God, spoke to her as follows: "If you, woman, desire to be released from this illness which afflicts you, abandon all intercourse with men during the divine and great feasts, and <abandon also> the prohibited activities you habitually perform. Cast as far away as possible your wallowing in the mud of passions." When the woman then promised to abstain from these activities and rejected with loathing her filthy acts, the holy <Thomaıs> healed the woman, anointing her with the usual oil. So the words and counsel of the saint released the longsuffering woman from her serious affliction. And after having been sick for so many years, she was restored to health and promised to sin no longer. . . . For she realized that it was indecent to engage in sexual pleasure and intercourse.

. . .

15. But let our account pause a little and recount in detail her husband's treatment of her. Her husband used to lie in wait then, like a violent tyrant with beetled brows, grimly regarding the blessed <Thomaıs>, and with furrowed brows displaying a wild-looking glance and the coarse nature of his face. She suffered terrible beatings. . . . For her husband viewed her actions in a contrary fashion and reckoned them extravagant, and he condemned her for living in a prodigal fashion and criticized and scorned her for squandering their livelihood. But <her actions> were rather charity, carrying out mercy in accordance with the divine and holy scriptures. . . .

He considered such <charitable work> to be in vain. . . . For while her aforementioned husband lived in a rustic manner, earned their daily bread by going to sea, and enjoyed a modest standard of living, the following occurred: whenever he returned home, he made inquiry about the expenditure of his assets and, calculating on a daily basis, he reckoned up how much of their livelihood she was spending. And he constantly tried to prevent her from <carrying out> the <charitable> activity I have frequently described <above>. For one could see her each day abundantly supplying gifts to the poor: clothing the naked and giving those in rags splendid clothes; distributing food to orphans; and furnishing the necessities of life to the destitute. . . .

16. . . . Thus after the saint had endured her many afflictions for a considerable time (for she had already borne for thirteen years that violent abuse, painful wounds, <those> immoderate bruises <and> blows), she received her blessed end and was transported to the ageless life without end, having lived in all thirty-eight years of the present life, <it being> the first day of January, when she departed to the Lord.

. . .

25. *Miracle 14.* I should also mention the sufferings of her [Thomaıs'] husband, and not be silent about them nor pass over them, but should in the present account make plain and describe to the best of my ability the kind of compensation he had to pay for his most wicked and base life. For he encountered a demon of terrible might and was forcefully driven by it this way and that. And so, wailing inconsolably, he came to the tomb of the saint. And although the demon attacked him terribly there and was unwilling to be driven out of that place, by prayer to this <saint> he attained salvation <from the demon>.

From: "Life of St. Thomaïs of Lesbos," Paul Halsall, transl., in Alice-Mary Maffry, Talbot, *Holy women of Byzantium: ten saints' lives in English translation* (Washington, DC: Dumbarton Oaks Research Library and Collection, 1996), pp. 297–322.

QUESTIONS:

1. As a saint, St. Thomaïs is by definition unusual. What can you infer about the lives of other Byzantine women from the lessons of her life? In what ways was her life ordinary? How did she stand out? Why was she holy rather than dangerous?
2. What qualities about St. Thomaïs showed her holiness? What kind of screen image of holiness does the hagiographer project in this narration of St. Thomaïs' life?

6.4: *The Farmer's Law* (c. 700)

The *Farmer's Law* is from a period when the Byzantine state had to scrape together the financial and manpower resources that it needed to defend itself against the armies of the far larger and richer Arab Caliphate. Regular Arab invasions were hard on the rural population, and many regions contained abandoned settlements that the government then attempted to repopulate with migrants. The *Farmer's Law* regulated the organization of such new settlements. The *Law* is not a comprehensive regulation for all rural classes and types of communities. Most significantly, large landowners do not appear in the *Law* except tangentially in c. 9 and c. 10 as "the grantor" (that is, the person making a land grant in exchange for a fixed rent and set of labor services). This *Law* regulated communities of small, independent farmers who held a status barely above slavery and whose lack of freedom reflects their importance to the state as its primary source of tax income for supporting armies. Note that several provisions refer to the fact that the tax burden fell on the community as a whole: if a farmer fled his homestead, the rest of the community had to make up his share of the common tax burden.

1. The farmer who is working his own field must be just and must not encroach on his neighbor's furrows. If a farmer persists in encroaching and docks a neighboring lot—if he did this in plowing-time, he loses his plowing; if it was in sowing-time that he made this encroachment, he loses his seed and his husbandry and his crop—the farmer who encroached.

2. If a farmer without the landowner's cognizance enters and plows or sows, let him not receive either wages for his plowing or the crop for his sowing—no, not even the seed that has been cast.

3. If two farmers agree one with the other before two or three witnesses to exchange lands and they agreed for all time, let their determination and their exchange remain firm and secure and unassailable.

4. If two farmers, A and B, agree to exchange their lands for the season of sowing and A draws back, then, if the seed was cast, they may not drawback; but if the seed was not cast they may draw back; but if A did not plow while B did, A also shall plow.

5. If two farmers exchange lands either for a season or for all time, and one plot is found deficient as compared with the other, and this was not their agreement, let him who has more give an equivalent in land to him who has less; but if this was their agreement, let them give nothing in addition.

6. If a farmer who has a claim on a field enters against the sower's will and reaps, then, if he had a just claim, let him take nothing from it; but if his claim was baseless, let him provide twice over the crops that were reaped.

7. If two territories contend about a boundary or a field, let the judges consider it and they shall decide in favor of the territory which had the longer possession; but if there is an ancient landmark, let the ancient determination remain unassailed.

8. If a division wronged people in their lots or lands, let them have license to undo the division.

9. If a farmer on shares reaps without the grantor's consent and robs him of his sheaves, as a thief shall he be deprived of all his crop.

10. A shareholder's portion is nine bundles, the grantor's [rich absentee landlord's] one: he who divides outside these limits is accursed.

11. If a man takes land from an indigent farmer and agrees to plow only and to divide, let their agreement prevail; if they also agreed on sowing, let it prevail according to their agreement.

12. If a farmer takes from some indigent farmer his vineyard to work on a half-share and does not prune it as is fitting and dig it and fence it and dig it over, let him receive nothing from the produce.

13. If a farmer takes land to sow on a half-share, and when the season requires it does not plow but throws the seed on the surface, let him receive nothing from the produce because he played false and mocked the land-owner.

14. If he who takes on a half-share the field of an indigent farmer who is abroad changes his mind and does not work the field, let him restore the produce twice over.

15. If he who takes on a half-share changes his mind before the season of working and gives notice to the landowner that he has not the strength and the landowner pays no attention, let the man who took on a half-share go harmless.

16. If a farmer takes over the farming of a vineyard or piece of land and agrees with the owner and takes earnest-money and starts and then draws back and gives it up, let him give the just value of the field and let the owner have the field.

17. If a farmer enters and works another farmer's woodland, for three years he shall take its profits for himself and then give the land back again to its owner.

18. If a farmer who is too poor to work his own vineyard takes flight and goes abroad, let those from whom claims are made by the public treasury gather in the grapes, and the farmer if he returns

shall not be entitled to mulct them [demand forfeiture from them] in the wine.

19. If a farmer who runs away from his own field pays every year the extraordinary taxes of the public treasury, let those who gather in the grapes and occupy the field be mulcted [fined] twofold.

20. If a man cuts another's wood without its owner's cognizance and works and sows it, let him have nothing from the produce.

21. If a farmer builds a house or plants a vineyard in another's field or plot and after a time there come the owners of the plot, they are not entitled to pull down the house or root up the vines, but they may take an equivalent in land. If the man who built or planted on the field that was not his own stoutly refuses to give an equivalent, the owner of the plot is entitled to pull up the vines and pull down the house.

22. If a farmer at digging-time steals a spade or a hoe, and is afterwards recognized, let him pay its daily hire twelve folles; the same rule applies to him who steals a pruning-knife at pruning-time, or a scythe at reaping-time, or an axe at wood-cutting time.

Concerning Herdsmen

23. If a neatherd [cow herder] in the morning receives an ox from a farmer and mixes it with the herd, and it happens that the ox is destroyed by a wolf, let him explain the accident to its master and he himself shall go harmless.

25. If a herdsman receives an ox from a farmer in the morning and goes off and the ox gets separated from the mass of oxen and goes off and goes into cultivated plots or vineyards and does harm, let him not lose his wages, but let him make good the harm done.

26. If a herdsman in the morning receives an ox from a farmer and the ox disappears, let him swear in the Lord's name that he has not himself played foul and that he had no part in the loss of the ox and let him go harmless.

28. If a herdsman on occasion of the loss of an ox or its wounding or blinding makes oath and is afterwards by good evidence proved a perjurer, let his tongue be cut out and let him make good the damage to the owner of the ox.

30. If a marl cuts a bell from an ox or a sheep and is recognized as the thief, let him be whipped; and if the animal disappears, let him make it good who stole the bell.

31. If a tree stands on a lot, if the neighboring lot is a garden and is overshadowed by the tree, the owner of the garden may trim its branches; but if there is no garden, the branches are not to be trimmed.

33. If a guardian of fruit is found stealing in the place which he guards, let him lose his wages and be well beaten.

34. If a hired shepherd is found milking his flock without the owner's knowledge and selling them, let him be beaten and lose his wages.

36. If a man takes an ox or an ass or any beast without its owner's knowledge and goes off on business, let him give its hire twice over; and if it dies on the road, he shall give two for one, whatever it may be.

38. If a man finds an ox doing harm in a vineyard or in a field or in another place, and does not give it back to its owner, on the terms of recovering from him all the destruction of his crops, but kills or wounds it, let him give ox for ox, ass for ass, or sheep for sheep.

42. If while a man is trying to steal one ox from a herd, the herd is put to flight and eaten by wild beasts, let him be blinded.

45. If a slave kills one ox or ass or ram in a wood, his master shall make it good.

46. If a slave, while trying to steal by night, drives the sheep away from the flock in chasing them out of the fold, and they are lost or eaten by wild beasts, let him be hanged as a murderer.

47. If a man's slave often steals beasts at night, or often drives away flocks, his master shall make good what is lost on the ground that he

knew his slave's guilt, but let the slave himself be hanged.

49. If a man finds a pig doing harm or a sheep or a dog, he shall deliver it in the first place to its master; when he has delivered it a second time, he shall give notice to its master; the third time he may cut its tail or its ear or shoot it without incurring liability.

55. If a man kills a sheepdog and does not make confession but there is an inroad of wild beasts into the sheepfold, and afterwards he who killed the dog is recognized, let him give the whole flock of sheep together with the value of the dog.

64. Let those who set fire to a threshing-floor or stacks of corn by way of vengeance on their enemies be burnt.

81. If a man who is dwelling in a district ascertains that a piece of common ground is suitable for the erection of a mill and appropriates and then, after the completion of the building, if the commonalty of the district complain of the owner of the building as having appropriated common ground, let them give him all the expenditure that is due to him for the completion of the building and let them share it in common with its builder.

82. If after the land of the district has been divided, a man finds in his own lot a place which is suitable for the erection of a mill and sets about it, the farmers of the other lots are not entitled to say anything about the mill.

83. If the water which comes to the mill leaves dry cultivated plots or vineyards, let him make the damage good; if not, let the mill be idle.

84. If the owners of the cultivated plots are not willing that the water go through their plots, let them be entitled to prevent it.

From: Walter Ashburner, *The Journal of Hellenic Studies*, vol. 32, (1912), pp. 68–95.

QUESTIONS:

1. Based on the provisions of this *Law*, describe rural life in Byzantium during the seventh to ninth centuries. What features stand out to you?
2. What sorts of disputes and problems arose in a community of small farmers such as this? What concerns on the part of the farmers do these problems reflect?

6.5: *Land Reform in Song China*

These two documents give us a piece of a debate with a long history in China. As in Byzantium, the fiscal health of the government depended on the existence of a large class of independent farmers. But the power of great landowners periodically threatened both the livelihoods of independent farmers and state tax revenues. When this happened, proposals for land reform surfaced, that is, proposals for some scheme by which to redistribute land away from the rich and to the poor. The Song Dynasty faced this problem in the late eleventh century. In the first source, an official named Su Hsün (1009–66) defends the Song government against charges of overtaxation and attempts to prove that the "well field system" was infeasible. (The "well field system" was an ancient plan for equitable land distribution.) The second source is by Wang An-shih (1021–86), the Prime Minister of China under the Emperor Shen-tsung (r. 1068–85). He instituted a wide-ranging set of reforms of landholding and tax assessment. In the edict presented here he proposes to expand an experimental reform measure that the government had already tried in one province. Although he took his inspiration from the Confucian classics, his interpretation of Confucianism aroused significant opposition among other Confucian scholars as well as among the people whose interests came under attack. Eventually, almost all of his reform measures were repealed.

6.5a: *The Land System–A Dissenting View* (Su Hsün, eleventh century CE)

At the height of the Chou dynasty the heaviest taxes ran to as much as one part in four [that is, a tax of 25% of the harvest], the next heaviest to one part in five, and then on down to rates as low as one part in ten or below. Taxes today, though never as low as one part in ten, likewise do not exceed one part in four or one in five, provided that the local magistrate is not rapacious and grasping. Thus there is not a great difference in the rate of taxation between Chou times and our own. . . .

However, during the Chou dynasty the people of the empire sang, danced, and rejoiced in the benevolence of their rulers, whereas our people are unhappy, as if they were extracting their very muscles and peeling off their very skins to meet the needs of the state. The Chou tax was so much, and our tax is likewise so much. Why, then is there such a great difference between the people's sadness today and their happiness then? There must be a reason for this.

During Chou times, the well-field system was employed. Since the well-field system was abolished, the land no longer belongs to the cultivators, and those who own the land do not cultivate. Those who do cultivate depend for their land upon the rich people. The rich families possess much land and extensive properties; the paths linking their fields run on and on. They call in the migratory workers and assign each a piece of their land to till, whipping and driving them to work, and treating them as slaves. Sitting there comfortably, they look around, give commands, and demand services. In the summer the people hoe for them, in the fall they harvest for them. No one disobeys their commands. The landowner amuses himself and yet draws half the income of the land, while the other half goes to the cultivator. For every landowner there are ten cultivators. Thus the landowner accumulates his half share day by day and so becomes rich and powerful; the cultivators eat their half share day by day and so become poor and hungry, without means of appeal. . . .

Alas, the poor cultivate and yet are not free from hunger. The rich sit with full stomachs and amuse themselves and yet are not free from resentment over taxes. All these evils arise from the abolition of the well-fields. If the well-fields were restored, the poor would have land to till, and not having to share their grain and rice with the rich, they would be free from hunger. The rich, not being allowed to hold so much land, could not hold down the poor. Under these circumstances those who did not till would not be able to get food. Besides, having the whole product of the land out of which to pay their taxes to the local magistrate, they would not be resentful. For this reason all the scholars of the empire outdo themselves calling for the restoration of the well-fields. And some people say: "If the land of the rich were taken away and given to those who own no land, the rich would not acquiesce in it, and this would-lead to rebellion. After such a great cataclysm, when the people were decimated and vast lands lay unused, it would be propitious for instituting the well-field system at once. When Emperor Kao of Han overthrew the Ch'in dynasty or when Emperor Kuang-wu succeeded the Former Han, it could have been done and yet was not. This is indeed to be regretted!"

I do not agree with any of this. Now even if all the rich people offered to turn their lands over to the public, asking that they be turned into well-fields, it still could not be done. Why?

[Su Hsun proceeds to describe in detail the system of land organization, irrigation, and local administration associated with the well-field system as it is set forth in the Rites of Chou. He concludes that such an intricate system could never be reproduced under existing conditions.]

When the well-fields are established, [a corresponding system of] ditches and canals would have to be provided. . . . This could not be done without filling up all the ravines and valleys, leveling the hills and mountains, destroying the graves, tearing down the houses, removing the cities, and changing the boundaries of the land. Even if it were possible to get possession of all the plains and vast wildernesses and then lay them out according to plan, still we would have to drive all the people of the empire, exhaust all the grain of the empire, and devote all our energy to this alone for several hundred years, without attending to anything else, if we were ever to see all the land of the empire turned into well-fields and provided with ditches and canals. Then it would be necessary to build houses within the well-fields for the people to settle down and live in peace. Alas, this is out of the question. By the time the well-fields were established, the people would have died and their bones would have rotted away. . . .

Although the well-field [system] cannot be put into effect, nevertheless, it actually would offer certain advantages in the present situation. Now if there were something approximating the well-field [system], which could be adopted, we might still be able to relieve the distress of the people.

[At this point Su reviews the proposals made in the Han dynasty for a direct limitation of land ownership, and the reasons for their failure.]

I want to limit somewhat the amount of land which one is allowed to hold, and yet not restrict immediately those whose land is already in excess of my limit, but only make it so that future generations would not try to occupy land beyond that limit. In short, either the descendants of the rich would be unable to preserve their holdings after several generations and would become poor, while the land held in excess of my limit would be dispersed and come into the possession of others; or else as the descendants of the rich came along they would divide up the land into several portions. In this way, the land occupied by the rich would decrease and the surplus land would increase. With surplus land in abundance, the poor would find it easy to acquire land as a basis for their family livelihood. They would not have to render service to others, but each would reap the full fruit of the land himself. Not having to share his produce with others, he would be pleased to contribute taxes to the government. Now just by sitting at court and promulgating the order throughout the empire, without frightening the people, without mobilizing the public, without adopting the well-field system, still all the advantages of the well-fields would be obtained. Even with the well-fields of the Chou, how could we hope to do better than this?

6.5b: *Memorial on the Crop Loans Measure* (Wang An-shih, eleventh century CE)

In the second year of Hsi-ning [1069], the Commission to Coordinate Fiscal Administration presented a memorial as follows:

The cash and grain stored in the Ever-Normal and the Liberal-Charity granaries of the various circuits, counting roughly in strings of cash and bushels of grain, amount to more than 15,000,000. Their collection and distribution are not handled properly, however, and therefore we do not derive full benefit from them. Now we propose that the present amount of grain in storage should be sold at a price lower than the market price when the latter is high; and that when the market price is low, the grain in the market should be purchased at a rate higher than the market price. We also propose that our reserves be made interchangeable with the proceeds of the land tax and the cash and grain held by the Fiscal Intendants, so that conversion of cash and grain may be permitted whenever convenient.

With the cash at hand, we propose to follow the example set by the crop loan system in Shensi province. Farmers desirous of borrowing money before the harvest should be granted loans, to be repaid at the same time as they pay their tax, half with the summer payment and half with the autumn payment. They are free to repay either in kind or in cash, should they prefer to do so if the price of grain is high at the time of repayment. In the event disaster strikes, they should be allowed to defer payment until the date when the next harvest payment would be due. In this way not only would we be prepared to meet the distress of famine, but, since the people would receive loans from the government, it would be impossible for the monopolistic houses to exploit the gap between harvests by charging interest at twice the normal rate.

Under the system of Ever-Normal and Liberal-Charity granaries, it has been the practice to keep grain in storage and sell it only when the harvest is poor and the price of grain is high. Those who benefit from this are only the idle people in the cities.

Now we propose to survey the situation in regard to surpluses and shortages in each circuit as a whole, to sell when grain is dear and buy when it is cheap, in order to increase the accumulation in government storage and to stabilize the prices of commodities. This will make it possible for the farmers to go ahead with their work at the proper season, while the monopolists will no longer be able to take advantage of their temporary stringency. All this is proposed in the interests of the people, and the government derives no advantage therefrom. Moreover, it accords with the idea of the ancient kings who bestowed blessings upon all impartially and promoted whatever was of benefit by way of encouraging the cultivation and accumulation of grain.

This proposal was adopted by the emperor, and put into effect first in [certain provinces], as suggested by the Commission to Coordinate Fiscal Administration. The results obtained were later considered to justify extension of the system to other areas.

From: De Bary, William Theodore, *Sources of Chinese Tradition* (New York: Columbia University Press, 1960), pp. 406–8, 420–21.

QUESTIONS:

1. From the somewhat indirect evidence of these sources, what can you surmise about life in the Chinese countryside under the Song? How does it compare to life in eighth-century Byzantium?
2. What are the key issues for these reformers? Do they seem motivated more by concern for the welfare of the people, or by fears for the fiscal health of the state? What implicit frame values guide the thinking of both of these writers, even when they disagree about details or practicality?

CHAPTER 7

The Salvation Religions: 200 to 900

INTRODUCTION

The sources in this chapter illustrate the rise and spread of the salvation religions, the most important cultural development since the philosophical and religious thought of the Axial Age. The sources give us some of the basic beliefs and characteristics of two older religions that underwent transformation in this period, Mahayana Buddhism and Devotional Hinduism, and of two religions that emerged as major belief systems at this time, Christianity and Islam, both of which had roots in Judaism. They also show some of the mechanisms the religions deployed to gain new converts and the accommodations they made to the cultures of new converts.

7.1: *Mahayana Buddhism: The Lotus Sutra* (c. first century CE)

Buddhism began to change after the conversion of Ashoka (see Chapter 5). A new form of Buddhism emerged, described by its practitioners as Mahayana, or the Greater Vehicle, meaning that this sect promised to carry far more people to salvation than the older version could. It was Mahayana Buddhism that spread all over central and East Asia. Early Buddhism was nontheistic and the search for Enlightenment was a matter of individual practice and achievement, as laid out in the Four Noble Truths and the Noble Eightfold Path (see Chapter 4). But in Mahayana belief, the Buddha became a godlike being and was joined by bodhisattvas, or Wise Beings, essentially people who had reached the edge of nirvana (release from the cycle of death and rebirth) only to compassionately turn back to help others cross over into bliss. Nirvana itself then became a heavenly paradise. One of the most popular of the bodhisattvas was Avalokitesvara, or "Perceiver of the World's Sounds," who first shows up in a book called The *Lotus Sutra*, one of the earliest and most influential of the sacred texts of Mahayana Buddhism.

7.1a: *The Lotus Sutra*

At that time the Bodhisattva Inexhaustible Intent immediately rose from his seat, bared his right shoulder, pressed his palms together and, facing the Buddha, spoke these words: "World Honored One, this Bodhisattva Perceiver of the World's Sounds—why is he called Perceiver of the World's Sounds?"

The Buddha said to Bodhisattva Inexhaustible Intent: "Good man, suppose there are immeasurable hundreds, thousands, ten thousands, millions of living beings who are undergoing various trials and suffering. If they hear of this Bodhisattva Perceiver of the Word's Sounds and single-mindedly call his name, then at once he will perceive the sound of their voices and they will all gain deliverance from their trials.

If someone, holding fast to the name of Bodhisattva Perceiver of the World's Sounds, should enter a great fire, the fire could not burn him. This would come about because of this bodhisattva's authority and supernatural power. If one were washed away by a great flood and call upon his name, one would immediately find himself in a shallow place.

"Suppose there were a hundred, a thousand, ten thousand, a million living beings who, seeking for gold, silver, lapis lazuli, seashell, agate, coral, amber, pearls, and other treasures, set out on the great sea. and suppose a fierce wind should blow their ship off course and it drifted to the land of rakshasas [evil but pretective beings] demons. If among those people there is even just one who calls the name of Bodhisattva Perceiver of the World's sounds, then all those people will be delivered from their troubles with the rakshasas. This is why he is called Perceiver of the World's Sounds.

"If a person who faces imminent threat of attack should call the name of Bodhisattva Perceiver of the World's sounds, then the swords and staves wielded by his attackers would instantly shatter into so many pieces and he would be delivered.

"Though enough yakshas and rakshasas to fill all the thousand-million-fold world should try to come and torment a person, if they hear him calling the name of Bodhisattva Perceiver of the World's Sounds, then these evil demons will not even be able to look at him with their evil eyes, much less do him harm.

"Suppose, in a place filled with all the evil-hearted bandits of the thousand-million-fold world, there is a merchant leader who is guiding a band of merchants carrying valuable treasures over a steep and dangerous road, and that one man shouts out these words: 'Good men, do not be afraid! You must single-mindedly call on the name of Bodhisattva Perceiver of the World's Sounds. This bodhisattva can grant fearlessness to living beings. If you call his name, you will be delivered from these evil-hearted bandits!' When the band if merchants hear this, they all together raise their voices, saying, 'Hail to the Bodhisattva Perceiver of the World's Sounds!' And because they call his name, they are at once able to gain deliverance. Inexhaustible Intent, the authority and supernatural power of the Bodhisattva Perceiver of the World's Sounds are as mighty as this!

"If there should be living beings beset by numerous lusts and cravings, let them think with constant reverence of Bodhisattva Perceiver of the World's Sounds and then they can shed their desires. If they have great wrath and ire, let them think with constant reverence of Bodhisattva Perceiver of the World's Sounds and then they can shed their ire. If they have great ignorance and stupidity, let them think with constant reverence of Bodhisattva Perceiver of the World's Sounds and they can rid themselves of stupidity.

"Inexhaustible Intent, the Bodhisattva Perceiver of the World's Sounds possesses great authority and supernatural powers, as I have described, and can confer many benefits. For this reason, living beings should constantly keep the thought of him in mind.

"If a woman wishes to give birth to a male child, she should offer obeisance and alms to Bodhisattva Perceiver of the World's Sounds and then she will bear a son blessed with merit, virtue, and wisdom. And if she wishes to bear a daughter, she will bear one with all the marks of comeliness, one who in the past planted the roots of virtue and is loved and respected by many persons.

"Inexhaustible Intent, suppose there is a person who accepts and upholds the names of as many bodhisattvas as there are sands in sixty-two million Ganges, and for as long as his present body lasts, he offers them alms in the form of food and drink, clothing, bedding and medicines. What is your opinion? Would this good man or good woman gain many benefits or would he not?"

Inexhaustible Intent replied, "They would be very many, World-Honored One."

The Buddha said: "Suppose also that there is a person who accepts and upholds the name of Bodhisattva Perceiver of the World's Sounds and even just once offers him obeisance and alms. The good fortune gained by these two persons would be exactly equal and without difference. . . . Inexhaustible Intent, if one accepts and upholds the name of Bodhisattva Perceiver of the World's Sounds, he will gain the benefit of merit and virtue that is as immeasurable and boundless as this!"

Bodhisattva Inexhaustible Intent said to the Buddha, "World-Honored One, Bodhisattva Perceiver of the World's Sounds—how does he come and go in this world? How does he preach the Law for the sake of living beings? How does the power of expedient means apply in this case?"

The Buddha said to Bodhisattva Inexhaustible Intent: "Good man, if there are living beings in the land who need someone in the body of a Buddha in order to be saved, Bodhisattva Perceiver of the World's Sounds immediately manifests himself in a Buddha body and preaches the Law for them. If they need someone in a pratyekabuddha's [Buddhist sage] body in order to be saved, immediately he manifests a pratyekabuddha's body and preaches the Law to them. If they need a voice-hearer to be saved, immediately he becomes a voice-hearer and preaches the Law for them. If they need King Brahma to be saved, immediately he becomes King Brahma [Hindu god of creation] and preaches the Law for them. If they need the lord Shakra [Indra, Hindu god of thunder] to be saved, immediately he becomes the lord Shakra and preaches the Law for them. If they need the heavenly being Freedom to be saved, immediately he becomes the heavenly being Freedom and preaches the Law for them. If they need a great general of heaven to be saved, immediately he becomes a great general of heaven and preaches the Law for them. . . . If they need a petty king to be saved, immediately he becomes a petty king and preaches the law for them.

If they need a rich man to be saved, immediately he becomes a rich man and preaches the Law for them. If they need a householder to be saved, immediately he becomes a householder and preaches the Law for them. If they need a chief minister to be saved, immediately he becomes a chief minister and preaches the Law for them. If they need a Brahman to be saved, immediately he becomes a Brahman and preaches the Law for them. If they need a monk, a nun, a layman believer, or a laywoman believer and preaches the Law for them. If they need the wife of a rich man, of a householder, a chief minister, or a Brahman to be saved, immediately he becomes those wives and preaches the Law for them. If they need a young boy or a young girl and preaches the Law for them. If they need a heavenly being, a dragon, . . . he becomes all of these and preaches the Law for them. . . .

"Inexhaustible Intent, this Bodhisattva Perceiver of the World's Sounds has succeeded in acquiring benefits such as these. Taking on a variety of different forms, goes about among the lands saving living beings. For this reason you and the others should single-mindedly offer alms to Bodhisattva Perceiver of the World's Sounds can bestow fearlessness on those who are in fearful, pressing or difficult circumstances. That is why in this saha world everyone calls him Bestower of Fearlessness."

"Bodhisattva Inexhaustible Intent said to the Buddha, "World-Honored One, now I must offer alms to Bodhisattva Perceiver of the World's Sounds."

Then he took from his neck a necklace adorned with numerous precious gems, worth a hundred or a thousand taels of gold, and presented it to [the bodhisattva], saying, "Sir, please accept this necklace of precious gems as a gift in the Dharma."

At that time Bodhisattva Perceiver of the World's Sounds was unwilling to accept the gift.

Inexhaustible Intent spoke once more to Bodhisattva Perceiver of the World's Sounds, saying, "Sir, out of compassion for us, please accept this necklace."

Then the Buddha said to Bodhisattva Perceiver of the World's Sounds, "Out of compassion for this Bodhisattva Inexhaustible Intent and for the four kinds of believers, the heavenly kings, . . . human and nonhuman beings, you should accept this necklace."

Thereupon Bodhisattva Perceiver of the World's Sounds, having compassion for the four kinds of believers and the heavenly beings, dragons, human and nonhuman beings and the others, accepted the necklace and, dividing it into two parts, presented one part to Shakyamuni Buddha and presented the other to the tower of the Buddha Many Treasures.

At that time Bodhisattva Inexhaustible Intent posed this question in verse form:

World-Honored One replete with wonderful features,
I now ask you once again
for what reason that Buddha's son
is named Bodhisattva Perceiver of the World's Sounds?
The honored One endowed with wonderful features
replied to Inexhaustible Intent in verse:
Listen to the actions of the Perceiver of Sounds,
how aptly he responds in various quarters.
He has attended many thousands and millions of Buddhas,
setting forth his great pure vow.
I will describe him in outline for you-listen to his name, observe his body,
bear him in mind, not passing the time vainly,
for he can wipe out the pains of existence.
Suppose you are surrounded by evil-hearted bandits,
each brandishing a knife to wound you.
Think on the power of that Perceiver of Sounds
and at once all will be swayed by compassion!
If living beings encounter weariness or peril,
immeasurable suffering pressing them down,
the power of the Perceiver of Sounds' wonderful wisdom
can save them from the sufferings of the world.
He sends down the sweet dew, the Dharma rain,
to quench the flames of earthly desires.
Endowed with all benefits,
he views living beings with compassionate eyes.

At that time the Bodhisattva Earth Holder immediately rose from his seat, advanced, and said to the Buddha, "World-Honored One, if there are living beings who hear this chapter on Bodhisattva Perceiver of the World's Sounds, on the freedom of his actions, his manifestation of a universal gateway, and his transcendental powers, it should be known that the benefits these persons gain are not few!"

From: The Lotus Sutra, Burton Watson, transl. (Columbia UP, 1993), pp. 298–303.

QUESTIONS:

1. How does someone get help from the "Perceiver of the World's Sounds"? How difficult is it to get this help? Are the tasks required of worshipper personal or communal?
2. What strikes you as the central message of Mahayana Buddhism? What screen image of Buddhism does the *Lotus Sutra* project? What is the appeal of that image?

7.1b: *The Disposition of Error* (Mou Tzu, c. fifth century CE)

Mahayana Buddhism spread from its homeland in northern India along the trade routes of central Asia known as the Silk Road. When Buddhism reached China it encountered an already established civilization with canonical literature and deeply rooted intellectual traditions whose scholarly elite were somewhat hostile to "foreign" influence. By the 400s Buddhism had become established widely enough to cause concern among traditionalist Chinese, especially among the Confucian scholarly elite, to provoke counterattacks, both in the form of government persecution in the North and of political tracts attacking the new faith in the South. This text, whose author(s) and exact date of composition are unknown, takes the form of an answer to some of the common lines of attack contained in such tracts. It therefore probably comes from southern China during the fifth century CE. The author argues that the practice of Buddhism is compatible with traditional Chinese values and that the ideas in Buddhist texts are similar to those in the Chinese classics, complementing and extending rather than contradicting them.

The questioner said: If the way of the Buddha is the greatest and most venerable of ways, why did Yao, Shun, the Duke of Chou, and Confucius not practice it?. . . . You, sir, are fond of the Book of Odes and the Book of History, and you take pleasure in rites and music. Why, then, so you love the way of Buddha and rejoice in outlandish arts? Can they exceed the Classics and commentaries and beautify the accomplishments of the sages?

Mou Tzu said: All written works need not necessarily be the words of Confucius, and all medicine does not necessarily consist of the formulae of [the famous physician] P'ien-ch'üeh. What accords with principle is to be followed, what heals the sick is good. The gentleman-scholar draws widely on all forms of good, and thereby benefits his character. . . . [Other sages are not mentioned in the Five Classics, yet are accepted.] How much less, then, may one reject the Buddha, whose distinguishing marks are extraordinary and whose superhuman powers know no bounds! How may one reject him and refuse to learn from him? . . .

The questioner said: Now of felicities there is none greater than the continuation of one's line, of unfilial conduct there is none worse than childlessness. The monks forsake wife and children, reject property and wealth. Some do not marry all their lives. How opposed this conduct is to felicity and filial piety! . . .

Mou Tzu said: Wives, children, and property are the luxuries of the world, but simple living and inaction are the wonders of the Way. Lao Tzu has said, "Of reputation and life, which is dearer? Of life and property, which is worth more?" . . . The monk practices the way and substitutes that for the pleasures of disporting himself in the world. He accumulates goodness and wisdom in exchange for the joys of wife and children.

The questioner said: The Buddhists say that after a man dies he will be reborn. I do not believe in the truth of these words. . . .

Mou Tzu said: . . . The spirit never perishes. Only the body decays. The body is like the roots and leaves of the five grains, the spirit is like the seeds and kernels of the five grains. When the roots and leaves come forth they inevitably die. But do the seeds and kernels perish? Only the body of one who has achieved the Way perishes. . . .

Someone said: If one follows the Way one dies. If one does not follow the Way one dies. What difference is there?

Mou Tzu said: You are the sort of person who, having not a single day of goodness, yet seeks a lifetime of fame. If one has the Way, even if one dies one's soul goes to an abode of happiness. If one does not have the Way, when one is dead one's soul suffers misfortune.

The questioner said: . . . You, sir, at the age of twenty learned the way of Yao, Shun, Confucius, and the Duke of Chou. But now you have rejected them, and instead have taken up the arts of the barbarians. Is this not a great error?

Mou Tzu said: . . . According to the Buddhist scriptures, above, below, and all around, all beings containing blood belong to the Buddha-clan. Therefore I revere and study these scriptures. Why should I reject the Way of Yao, Shun, Confucius, and the Duke of Chou? Gold and jade do not harm each other, crystal and amber do not cheapen each other. . . .

The questioner said: Of those who live in the world, there is none who does not love wealth and position and hate poverty and baseness, none who does not enjoy pleasure and idleness and shrink from labor and fatigue. . . . But now the monks wear red cloth, they eat one meal a day, they bottle up the six emotions, and thus they live out their lives. What value is there in such an existence?

Mou Tzu said: "Wealth and rank are what a man desires, but if he cannot obtain them in a moral way, he should not enjoy them. Poverty and meanness are what a man hates, but if he can only avoid them by departing from the Way, he should not avoid them." Lao Tzu has said, "The five colors make men's eyes blind, the five sounds make men's ears deaf, the five flavors dull the palate, chasing about and hunting make men's minds mad, possessions difficult to acquire bring men's conduct to an impasse. The sage acts for his belly, not for his eyes." Can these words possibly be in vain? . . .

The questioner said: You , sir, say that the scriptures are like the rivers and the sea, their phrases like the brocade and embroidery. Why, then, do you not draw on the Buddhist scriptures to answer my questions? Why instead do you refer to the books of Odes and History, joining together things that are different to make them appear the same?

Mou Tzu said: . . . I have quoted those things, sir, which I knew you would understand. Had I preached the words of the Buddhist scriptures or discussed the essence of nonaction, it would have been like speaking to a blind man of the five colors or playing the five sounds to a deaf man.

The questioner said: The Taoists say that Yao, Shun, the Dike of Chou, and Confucius and his seventy two disciples did not die, but became immortals. The Buddhists say that men must all die, and that none can escape. What does this mean?

Mou Tzu said: Talk of immortality is superstitious and unfounded; it is not the word of the sages. Lao Tzu says, "Even Heaven and earth cannot be eternal. How much the less can man!" Confucius says, "The wise man leaves the world, but humanity and filial piety last forever." . . . I make the Classics and the commentaries my authorities and find my proof in the world of men. To speak of immortality, is this not a great error?

From: De Bary, William Theodore, *Sources of Chinese tradition* (New York: Columbia University Press, 1960), pp. 274–80.

QUESTIONS:

1. What characteristics of Buddhism does Mou Tzu emphasize in order to make it appear acceptable to Chinese scholars? What connections does he make between Buddhist beliefs and traditional Chinese values?

2. What can you infer about Chinese literate culture in this time from the objections to Buddhism named in *The Disposition of Error*? How would you characterize the objections to Buddhism? Are they intellectually coherent and consistent, or are they more a grab bag of hostile reactions?

7.2: *Devotional Hinduism: The Vishnu Purana* (c. second century CE)

Hinduism adapted to Mahayana Buddhism's popularity in India by developing a form of worship called *bhakti*, or devotion, meaning unconditional devotion to a god. Devotional Hinduism built on the yoga, or discipline, of devotion in the *Bhagavad Gita* (see Chapter 4). Accompanying the development of the new practice of devotionalism was the rise, between 100 and 300 CE, of a new body of sacred literature that explained and promoted that practice. These works, known as puranas, are compilations of myth, folklore, simplified teachings, and other stories aimed at popular audiences—they were probably meant to be read or recited aloud as much as read—whose central message was that unconditional devotion to the worship of a single god would bring salvation. They are long, sometimes disjointed, but full of colorful images and easy to grasp ideas. There are eighteen major puranas; the Vishnu Purana, which recounts the ten incarnations of the great Vishnu, is one of (if not the) oldest and most important of the set. It probably dates to as early as the second century CE.

BOOK VI, CHAP. VIII

I have related to you this Purana, which is equal to the Vedas in sanctity, and by hearing which all faults and sins whatever are expiated. In this have been described to you the primary and secondary creation . . .; the distinctions of the four castes, and the actions of the most eminent amongst men; holy places on the earth, holy rivers and oceans, sacred mountains, and legends of the truly wise; the duties of the different tribes, and the observances enjoined by the Vedas. By hearing this, all sins are at once obliterated. In this also the glorious Hari [Vishnu] has been revealed, the cause of the creation, preservation, and destruction of the world; the soul of all things, and himself all things: by the repetition of whose name man is undoubtedly liberated from all sins, which fly like wolves that are frightened by a lion. The repetition of his name with devout faith is the best remover of all sins, destroying them as fire purifies the metal from the dross. The stain of the Kali age, which ensures to men sharp punishments in hell, is at once effaced by a single invocation of Hari. He who is all that is, the whole egg of Brahmá, with . . . men, Brahmans and the rest, animals tame and wild, insects, birds, ghosts and goblins, trees, mountains, woods, rivers, oceans, the subterrene legions, the divisions of the earth, and all perceptible objects—he who is all things, who knoweth all things, who is the form of all things, being without form himself, and of whom whatever is, from mount Meru to an atom, all consists—he, the glorious Vishńu, the destroyer of all sin—is described in this Puráńa. By hearing this Puráńa an equal recompense is obtained to that which is derived from the performance of an Aśwamedha sacrifice, or from fasting at the holy places Prayága, Pushkara, Kurukshetra, or Arbuda. Hearing this Puráńa but once is as efficacious as the offering of oblations in a perpetual fire for a year . . . . The man who bathes in the waters of the Yamuná on the twelfth lunation of the light fortnight of the month in which the moon is in the mansion Jyeshťhá, and who fasts and worships Achyuta [Vishnu] in the city of Mathurá, receives the reward of an uninterrupted Aśwamedha. . . . A man of good extraction will present obsequial cakes to his fortunate ancestors in the Yamuná, having worshipped Janárddana in the light fortnight of Jyeshťha. But the same degree of merit that a man reaps front adoring Janárddana at that season with a devoted heart, and from bathing in the Yamuná, and effecting the liberation of his progenitors by offering to them on such an occasion obsequial cakes, he derives also from hearing with equal devotion a section of this Puráńa. This Puráńa is the best of all preservatives for those who are afraid of worldly existence, a certain alleviation of the sufferings of men, and remover of all imperfections.

This Puráńa, originally composed by the Rishi . . . Through the blessing of Vaśishťha it came to my knowledge, and I have now, Maitreya, faithfully imparted it to you. You will teach it. . . . Whoever hears this great mystery, which removes the contamination of the Kali, shall be freed from all his sins. He who hears this every day acquits himself of his daily obligations to ancestors, gods, and men. The great and rarely attainable merit that a man acquires by the gift of a brown cow, he derives from hearing ten chapters of this Puráńa. He who hears the entire Puráńa, contemplating in his mind Achyuta, who is all things, and of whom all things are made; who is the stay of the whole world, the receptacle of spirit; who is knowledge, and that which is to be known; who is without beginning or end, and the benefactor of the gods—obtains assuredly the reward that attends the uninterrupted celebration of the Aśwamedha rite. He who reads and retains with faith this Puráńa, in the beginning, middle, and end of which is described the glorious Achyuta, the lord of the universe in every stage, the master of all that is stationary or moveable, composed of spiritual knowledge, acquires such purity as exists not in any world, the eternal state of perfection, which is Hari. The man who fixes his mind on Vishńu goes not to hell: he who meditates upon him regards heavenly enjoyment only as an impediment: and he whose mind and soul are penetrated by him thinks little of the world of Brahmá; for when present in the minds of those whose intellects are free from soil, he confers upon them eternal freedom. What marvel therefore is it that the sins of one who repeats the name of Achyuta should be wiped away? Should not that Hari be heard of, whom those devoted to acts worship with sacrifices continually as the god of sacrifice; whom those devoted to meditation contemplate as primary and secondary, composed of spirit; by obtaining whom man is not born, nor nourished, nor subjected to death; who is all that is, and that is not (or both cause and of effect); who, as the progenitors, receives the libations made to them; who, as the gods, accepts the offerings addressed to them; the glorious being who is without beginning or end; whose name is both Swáhá and Swadhá; who is the abode of all spiritual power; in whom the limits of finite things cannot be measured; and who, when he enters the ear, destroys all sin?

I adore him, that first of gods, Purushottama, who is without end and without beginning, without growth, without decay, without death; who is substance that knows not change. I adore that ever inexhaustible spirit; who assumed sensible qualities; who, though one, became many; who, though pure, became as if impure, by appearing in many and various shapes; who is endowed with divine wisdom, and is the author of the preservation of all creatures. I adore him, who is the one conjoined essence and object of both meditative wisdom and active virtue; who is watchful in providing for human enjoyments; who is one with the three qualities; who, without undergoing change, is the cause of the evolution of the world; who exists of his own essence, ever exempt from decay. I constantly adore him, who is entitled heaven, air, fire, water, earth, and ether; who is the bestower of all the objects which give gratification to the senses; who benefits mankind with the instruments of fruition; who is perceptible, who is subtile, who is imperceptible. May that unborn, eternal Hari, whose form is manifold, and whose essence is composed of both nature and spirit, bestow upon all mankind that blessed state which knows neither birth nor decay!

From: Wilson, H. H., *The Vishńu Puráńa: a system of Hindu mythology and tradition* (London: J. Murray, 1840), Bk. VI, Ch. VIII, pp. 660–65.

QUESTIONS:

1. What must a worshipper do to receive the blessings of Vishnu? How difficult is it to get these blessings? Are the things a worshipper must do personal or communal?
2. What strikes you a the central message of Devotional Hinduism? What screen image of Hinduism does the Vishnu Purana project? What is the appeal of that image?

7.3a: Christianity: *The New Testament*

Joshua of Nazareth, or Jesus in Greek, (c. 4 BCE–c. 30 CE) was a prophet in the tradition of Second Isaiah (Chapter 4), who preached the coming of a spiritual Messiah who would lead not just Jews but all of mankind to the promised land of salvation and heavenly reward. The teachings of Jesus himself formed the basis of a new religion, Christianity. But because Jesus left no writings of his own, Christianity was also shaped by a Jew named Saul (3 BCE–64 or 67 CE) who underwent a sudden conversion experience, changed his name to Paul, and became early Christianity's most influential missionary and teacher. His letter to a group of Christians in Rome is his fullest, most complete statement of the tenets of the new religion, and came to be part of the New Testament of the Bible. A section of this Epistle is the first reading here. The foundation of the New Testament were accounts of Jesus's life and teachings, known as Gospels. Four came to be considered canonical, with pride of place taken by that of Matthew, a second generation Christian writing around 80 CE. Included here is the section of the Gospel of Matthew known as the Sermon on the Mount, which almost certainly represents not a faithful transcription of a single speech, but Matthew's summary of Jesus's key teachings.

7.3a: from *The New Testament*

ROMANS 1

1Paul, a servant of Christ Jesus, called to be an apostle and set apart for the gospel of God.

. . .

7To all in Rome who are loved by God and called to be saints:

Grace and peace to you from God our Father and from the Lord Jesus Christ.

11I long to see you so that I may impart to you some spiritual gift to make you strong—12that is, that you and I may be mutually encouraged by each other's faith. . . .

14I am obligated both to Greeks and non-Greeks, both to the wise and the foolish. 15That is why I am so eager to preach the gospel also to you who are at Rome.

16I am not ashamed of the gospel, because it is the power of God for the salvation of everyone who believes: first for the Jew, then for the Gentile. 17For in the gospel a righteousness from God is revealed, a righteousness that is by faith from first to last, just as it is written: "The righteous will live by faith."

ROMANS 5

1Therefore, since we have been justified through faith, we have peace with God through our Lord Jesus Christ, 2through whom we have gained access by faith into this grace in which we now stand. And we rejoice in the hope of the glory of God. 3Not only so, but we also rejoice in our sufferings, because we know that suffering produces perseverance; [4]perseverance, character; and character, hope. [5]And hope does not disappoint us, because God has poured out his love into our hearts by the Holy Spirit, whom he has given us.

[6]You see, at just the right time, when we were still powerless, Christ died for the ungodly. [7]Very rarely will anyone die for a righteous man, though for a good man someone might possibly dare to die. [8]But God demonstrates his own love for us in this: While we were still sinners, Christ died for us.

[9]Since we have now been justified by his blood, how much more shall we be saved from God's wrath through him! [10]For if, when we were God's enemies, we were reconciled to him through the death of his Son, how much more, having been reconciled, shall we be saved through his life! [11]Not only is this so, but we also rejoice in God through our Lord Jesus Christ, through whom we have now received reconciliation.

ROMANS 10

"The word is near you; it is in your mouth and in your heart," that is, the word of faith we are proclaiming: [9]That if you confess with your mouth, "Jesus is Lord," and believe in your heart that God raised him from the dead, you will be saved. [10]For it is with your heart that you believe and are justified, and it is with your mouth that you confess and are saved. [11]As the Scripture says, "Anyone who trusts in him will never be put to shame."[5] [12]For there is no difference between Jew and Gentile—the same Lord is Lord of all and richly blesses all who call on him, [13]for, "Everyone who calls on the name of the Lord will be saved."[6]

[14]How, then, can they call on the one they have not believed in? And how can they believe in the one of whom they have not heard? And how can they hear without someone preaching to them? [15]And how can they preach unless they are sent? As it is written, "How beautiful are the feet of those who bring good news!"

MATTHEW 5

[1]Now when he saw the crowds, he went up on a mountainside and sat down. His disciples came to him, [2]and he began to teach them saying:

[3]"Blessed are the poor in spirit,
for theirs is the kingdom of heaven.
[4]"Blessed are those who mourn,
for they will be comforted.
[5]"Blessed are the meek,
for they will inherit the earth.
[6]"Blessed are those who hunger and thirst for righteousness, for they will be filled.
[7]"Blessed are the merciful,
for they will be shown mercy.
[8]"Blessed are the pure in heart,
for they will see God.
[9]"Blessed are the peacemakers,
for they will be called sons of God.
[10]"Blessed are those who are persecuted because of righteousness,
for theirs is the kingdom of heaven.

[11]"Blessed are you when people insult you, persecute you and falsely say all kinds of evil against you because of me. [12]Rejoice and be glad, because great is your reward in heaven, for in the same way they persecuted the prophets who were before you.

[13]"You are the salt of the earth. But if the salt loses its saltiness, how can it be made salty again? It is no longer good for anything, except to be thrown out and trampled by men.

[14]"You are the light of the world. A city on a hill cannot be hidden. [15]Neither do people light a lamp and put it under a bowl. Instead they put it on its stand, and it gives light to everyone in the house. [16]In the same way, let your light shine before men, that they may see your good deeds and praise your Father in heaven.

[17]"Do not think that I have come to abolish the Law or the Prophets; I have not come to abolish them but to fulfill them. [18]I tell you the truth, until heaven and earth disappear, not the smallest letter, not the least stroke of a pen, will by any means

disappear from the Law until everything is accomplished. [19]Anyone who breaks one of the least of these commandments and teaches others to do the same will be called least in the kingdom of heaven, but whoever practices and teaches these commands will be called great in the kingdom of heaven. [20]For I tell you that unless your righteousness surpasses that of the Pharisees and the teachers of the law, you will certainly not enter the kingdom of heaven.

[21]"You have heard that it was said to the people long ago, 'Do not murder, and anyone who murders will be subject to judgment.' [22]But I tell you that anyone who is angry with his brother will be subject to judgment. . . .

[33]"Again, you have heard that it was said to the people long ago, 'Do not break your oath, but keep the oaths you have made to the Lord.' [34]But I tell you, Do not swear at all: either by heaven, for it is God's throne; [35]or by the earth, for it is his footstool; or by Jerusalem, for it is the city of the Great King. [36]And do not swear by your head, for you cannot make even one hair white or black. [37]Simply let your 'Yes' be 'Yes, and your 'No,' 'No'; anything beyond this comes from the evil one.

[38]"You have heard that it was said, 'Eye for eye, and tooth for tooth.' [39]But I tell you, Do not resist an evil person. If someone strikes you on the right cheek, turn to him the other also. [40]And if someone wants to sue you and take your tunic, let him have your cloak as well. [41]If someone forces you to go one mile, go with him two miles. [42]Give to the one who asks you, and do not turn away from the one who wants to borrow from you.

[43]"You have heard that it was said, 'Love your neighbor and hate your enemy.' [44]But I tell you: Love your enemies and pray for those who persecute you, [45]that you may be sons of your Father in heaven. He causes his sun to rise on the evil and the good, and sends rain on the righteous and the unrighteous. [46]If you love those who love you, what reward will you get? Are not even the tax collectors doing that? [47]And if you greet only your brothers, what are you doing more than others? Do not even pagans do that? [48]Be perfect, therefore, as your heavenly Father is perfect.

MATTHEW 6

[1]Be careful not to do your 'acts of righteousness' before men, to be seen by them. If you do, you will have no reward from your Father in heaven.

[2]So when you give to the needy, do not announce it with trumpets, as the hypocrites do in the synagogues and on the streets, to be honored by men. I tell you the truth, they have received their reward in full. [3]But when you give to the needy, do not let your left hand know what your right hand is doing, [4]so that your giving may be in secret. Then your Father, who sees what is done in secret, will reward you.

[5]And when you pray, do not be like the hypocrites, for they love to pray standing in the synagogues and on the street corners to be seen by men. I tell you the truth, they have received their reward in full. [6]But when you pray, go into your room, close the door and pray to your Father, who is unseen. Then your Father, who sees what is done in secret, will reward you. [7]And when you pray, do not keep on babbling like pagans, for they think they will be heard because of their many words. [8]Do not be like them, for your Father knows what you need before you ask him.

[9]This, then, is how you should pray:

"Our Father in heaven, hallowed be your name,

[10]your kingdom come,
your will be done
on earth as it is in heaven.
[11]Give us today our daily bread.
[12]Forgive us our debts,
as we also have forgiven our debtors.
[13]And lead us not into temptation,
but deliver us from the evil one.

[14]For if you forgive men when they sin against you, your heavenly Father will also forgive you.

15But if you do not forgive men their sins, your
Father will not forgive your sins.

19"Do not store up for yourselves treasures on
earth, where moth and rust destroy, and where
thieves break in and steal. 20But store up for yourselves treasures in heaven, where moth and rust do
not destroy, and where thieves do not break in and
steal. 21For where your treasure is, there your heart
will be also.

22"The eye is the lamp of the body. If your eyes
are good, your whole body will be full of light.
23But if your eyes are bad, your whole body will be
full of darkness. If then the light within you is darkness, how great is that darkness!

24"No one can serve two masters. Either he will
hate the one and love the other, or he will be devoted to the one and despise the other. You cannot
serve both God and Money.

25"Therefore I tell you, do not worry about
your life, what you will eat or drink; or about your
body, what you will wear. Is not life more important than food, and the body more important than
clothes? 26Look at the birds of the air; they do not
sow or reap or store away in barns, and yet your
heavenly Father feeds them. Are you not much
more valuable than they? 27Who of you by worrying can add a single hour to his life?

28And why do you worry about clothes?
See how the lilies of the field grow. They do
not labor or spin. 29Yet I tell you that not even
Solomon in all his splendor was dressed like one
of these. 30If that is how God clothes the grass
of the field, which is here today and tomorrow
is thrown into the fire, will he not much more
clothe you, O you of little faith? 31So do not
worry, saying, "What shall we eat?" or "What
shall we drink?" or "What shall we wear?" 32For
the pagans run after all these things, and your
heavenly Father knows that you need them. 33But
seek first his kingdom and his righteousness, and
all these things will be given to you as well.
34Therefore do not worry about tomorrow, for
tomorrow will worry about itself. Each day has
enough trouble of its own.

From: Holy Bible, RSE.

QUESTIONS:

1. What must a worshipper do to receive the blessings of Christ? How difficult is it to receive these blessings? Are the things a worshipper must do personal or communal?
2. What strikes you as the central message of Christianity? What screen image of Christianity does the New Testament project? What is the appeal of that image?

7.3b: *History of the Franks* (Gregory of Tours, c. 590 CE)

Gregory, bishop of Tours (c. 538–94), was a Gallo-Roman aristocrat and writer whose *History of the Franks* is the major source for the history of the Merovingian period (c. 450–750) in what would become France. Although he almost certainly had a classical education, he wrote his history in the form of Latin spoken in France at the time (called "Vulgar"), probably to reach a wider audience. Broader circulation was important because his *History* told the story of the conversion of the Franks, the most powerful "barbarian" confederation in the Roman west, to the Roman Catholic form of Christianity. This ensured the triumph in the region of that form of Christianity over others, which the Roman Catholic Church then declared heretical. The conversion of king Clovis, told in this excerpt, was the key episode in that story.

As Clovis often sent embassies to Burgundy, the maiden Clotilda was found by his envoys. And when they saw that she was of good bearing and wise, and learned that she was of the family of the king, they reported this to King Clovis, and he sent an embassy to [the Burgundian king] without delay asking her hand in marriage. And [the Burgundian king] was afraid to refuse, and surrendered her to the men, and they took the girl and brought her swiftly to the king. The king was very glad when he saw her, and married her. . . .

He had a first-born son by Queen Clotilda, and as his wife wished to consecrate him in baptism, she tried unceasingly to persuade her husband, saying: "The gods you worship are nothing, and they will be unable to help themselves or any one else. For the names you have given them are names of men and not of gods, as Saturn, who is declared to have fled in fear of being banished from his kingdom by his son; as Jove himself, the fould perpetrator of all shameful crimes, committing incest with men, mocking at his kinswomen, not able to refrain from intercourse with his own sister. . . . What could Mars or Mercury do? They are endowed rather with the magic arts than with the power of the divine name. But he ought to be worshipped who created by his word heaven and earth, the sea and all that is in them out of a state of nothingness, who made the sun shine, and adorned the heavens with stars, who filled the waters with creeping things, the earth with living things and the air with creatures that fly, at whose nod the earth is decked with growing crops, the trees with fruit, the vines with grapes, by whose hand mankind was created, by whose generosity all that creation serves and helps man whom he created as his own." But though the queen said this the spirit of the king was by no means moved to belief, and he said: "It was at the command of our gods that all things were created and came forth, and it is plain that your God has no power and, what is more, he is proven not to belong to the family of the gods." Meantime the faithful queen made her son ready for baptism; she gave command to adorn the church with hangings and curtains, in order that he who could not be moved by persuasion might be urged to belief by this mystery. The boy, whom they named Ingomer, died after being baptized, still wearing the white garments in which he became regenerate. At this the king was violently angry, and reproached the queen harshly, saying: "If the boy had been dedicated in the name of my gods he would certainly have lived; but as it is, since he was baptized in the name of your God, he could not live at all." To this the queen said: "I give thanks to the omnipotent God, creator of all, who has judged me not wholly unworthy, that he should deign to take to his kingdom one born from my womb. My soul is not stricken with grief for his sake, because I know that, summoned from this world as he was in his baptismal garments, he will be fed by the vision of God."

After this she bore another son, whom she named Chlodomer at baptism; and when he fell sick, the king said: "It is impossible that anything else should happen to him than happened to his brother, namely, that being baptized in the name of your Christ, he should die at once." But through the prayers of his mother, and the Lord's command, he became well.

The queen did not cease to urge him to recognize the true God and cease worshipping idols. But he could not be influenced in any way to this belief, until at last a was arose with the Alamanni, in which he was driven by necessity to confess what before he had of his free will denied. It came about that as the two armies were fighting fiercely, there was much slaughter, and Clovis' army began to be in danger of destruction. He saw it and raised his eyes to heaven, and with remorse in his heart he burst into tears and cried: "Jesus Christ, whom Clotilda asserts to be the son of the living God, who art said to give aid to those in distress, and to bestow victory on those who hope in thee, I beseech the glory of thy aid, with the vow that if thou wilt grant me victory over these enemies, and I shall know that power which she says that people dedicated in thy name have had from thee, I will believe in thee and be baptized in thy name. For I have invoked my own gods, but, as I find, they have withdrawn from aiding me; and therefore I believe that they possess no power, since they do not help those who obey them. I now call upon thee, I desire to believe thee, only let me be rescued from my adversaries." And when he said this, the Alamanni turned their backs, and began to disperse in flight. And when they saw that their king was killed, they submitted to the dominion of Clovis, saying: "Let not the people perish further, we pray; we are yours now." And he stopped the fighting, and after encouraging his men, retired in peace and told the queen how he had merit to win the victory by calling on the name of Christ. This happened in the fifteenth year of his reign.

Then the queen asked Remi, bishop of Rheims, to summon Clovis secretly, urging him to introduce the king to the word of salvation. And the bishop sent for him secretly and began to urge him to believe in the true God, maker of heaven and earth, and to cease worshipping idols, which could help neither themselves nor anyone else. But the king said: "I gladly hear you, most holy father; but there remains one thing: the people who follow me cannot endure to abandon their gods; but I shall go and speak to them according to your words." He met with his followers, but before he could speak the power of God anticipated him, and all the people cried out together: "O pious king, we reject our mortal gods, and we are ready to follow the immortal God whom Remi preaches." This was reported to the bishop, who was greatly rejoiced, and bade them get ready the baptismal font. The squares were shaded with tapestried canopies, the churches adorned with white curtains, the baptistery set in order, the aroma of incense spread, candles of fragrant odor burned brightly, and the whole shrine of the baptistery was filled with a divine fragrance: and the Lord gave such grace to those who stood by that they thought they were placed amid the odors of paradise. And the king was the first to ask to be baptized by the bishop. Another Constantine advanced to the baptismal font. . . . And of his army more than 3000 were baptized.

From: Gregory Bishop of Tours, *History of the Franks*, Ernest Brehaut, transl. (New York: Columbia University Press, 1969), pp. 38–41.

QUESTIONS:

1. What factors influenced Clovis's decision to convert to Christianity? What do you think the relative importance of those factors were? Was his decision a religious one?
2. How do you think Gregory shaped his story to present a persuasive screen image of Clovis and Christianity? At what audience do you think he is aiming his image?

7.4a: Islam: *The Quran* (seventh century CE)

Muhammad (c. 570–632) became the prophet of a new Arab creed and, according to Muslim belief, he was the last of the line of prophets running from Abraham and Moses through Isaiah and Jesus and finally to him. Just as Christians consider the New Testament to be the sacred word of God, Islamic tradition holds that the verses of the *Qur'an* are unchangingly perfect and that Muhammad was Allah's mouthpiece. Like Jesus, Muhammad did not write down his own teachings. Unlike early Christianity, which had a single voice in Paul to define much of its doctrine, Islam emerged from a much broader, more communal (and contested) recording, reordering, and refining of the words of the Prophet until about eighty years or after his death. The developed doctrines of Islam from that time have remained the core of Islamic belief to this day. Islam means "submission"; a Muslim is one who submits to the will of Allah.

THE COW

In the name of Allah, the Beneficent, the Merciful.

[2.1] Alif Lam Mim.

[2.2] This Book, there is no doubt in it, is a guide to those who guard (against evil).

[2.3] Those who believe in the unseen and keep up prayer and spend out of what We have given them.

[2.4] And who believe in that which has been revealed to you and that which was revealed before you and they are sure of the hereafter.

[2.5] These are on a right course from their Lord and these it is that shall be successful.

[2.6] Surely those who disbelieve, it being alike to them whether you warn them, or do not warn them, will not believe.

[2.21] O men! serve your Lord Who created you and those before you so that you may guard (against evil).

[2.22] Who made the earth a resting place for you and the heaven a canopy and (Who) sends down rain from the cloud then brings forth with it subsistence for you of the fruits; therefore do not set up rivals to Allah while you know.

[2.23] And if you are in doubt as to that which We have revealed to Our servant, then produce a chapter like it and call on your witnesses besides Allah if you are truthful.

[2.25] And convey good news to those who believe and do good deeds, that they shall have gardens in which rivers flow; whenever they shall be given a portion of the fruit thereof, they shall say: This is what was given to us before; and they shall be given the like of it, and they shall have pure mates in them, and in them, they shall abide.

[2.28] How do you deny Allah and you were dead and He gave you life? Again He will cause you to die and again bring you to life, then you shall be brought back to Him.

[2.30] And when your Lord said to the angels, I am going to place in the earth a khalif, they said: What! wilt Thou place in it such as shall make mischief in it and shed blood, and we celebrate Thy praise and extol Thy holiness? He said: Surely I know what you do not know.

[2.40] O children of Israel! call to mind My favor which I bestowed on you and be faithful to (your) covenant with Me, I will fulfill (My) covenant with you; and of Me, Me alone, should you be afraid.

[2.43] And keep up prayer and pay the poor-rate and bow down with those who bow down.

[2.44] What! do you enjoin men to be good and neglect your own souls while you read the Book; have you then no sense?

[2.45] And seek assistance through patience and prayer, and most surely it is a hard thing except for the humble ones,

[2.46] Who know that they shall meet their Lord and that they shall return to Him.

[2.62] Surely those who believe, and those who are Jews, and the Christians, and the Sabians, whoever believes in Allah and the Last day and does good, they shall have their reward from their Lord, and there is no fear for them, nor shall they grieve.

[2.79] Woe, then, to those who write the book with their hands and then say: This is from Allah, so that they may take for it a small price; therefore woe to them for what their hands have written and woe to them for what they earn.

[2.82] And (as for) those who believe and do good deeds, these are the dwellers of the garden; in it they shall abide.

[2.87] And most certainly We gave Musa the Book and We sent apostles after him one after another; and We gave Isa, the son of Marium, clear arguments and strengthened him with the holy spirit, What! whenever then an apostle came to you with that which your souls did not desire, you were insolent so you called some liars and some you slew.

[2.105] Those who disbelieve from among the followers of the Book do not like, nor do the polytheists, that the good should be sent down to you from your Lord, and Allah chooses especially whom He pleases for His mercy, and Allah is the Lord of mighty grace.

[2.106] Whatever communications We abrogate or cause to be forgotten, We bring one better than it or like it. Do you not know that Allah has power over all things?

[2.107] Do you not know that Allah's is the kingdom of the heavens and the earth, and that besides Allah you have no guardian or helper?

[2.110] And keep up prayer and pay the poor-rate and whatever good you send before for yourselves, you shall find it with Allah; surely Allah sees what you do.

[2.112] Yes! whoever submits himself entirely to Allah and he is the doer of good (to others) he has his reward from his Lord, and there is no fear for him nor shall he grieve.

[2.115] And Allah's is the East and the West, therefore, whither you turn, thither is Allah's purpose; surely Allah is Amplegiving, Knowing.

[2.119] Surely We have sent you with the truth as a bearer of good news and as a warner, ...

[2.125] And when We made the House a pilgrimage for men and a (place of) security, and: Appoint for yourselves a place of prayer on the standing-place of Ibrahim. And We enjoined Ibrahim and Ismail saying: Purify My House for those who visit (it) and those who abide (in it) for devotion and those who bow down (and) those who prostrate themselves.

[2.129] Our Lord! and raise up in them an Apostle from among them who shall recite to them Thy communications and teach them the Book and the wisdom, and purify them; surely Thou art the Mighty, the Wise.

[2.130] And who forsakes the religion of Ibrahim but he who makes himself a fool, and most certainly We chose him in this world, and in the hereafter he is most surely among the righteous.

[2.131] When his Lord said to him, Be a Muslim, he said: I submit myself to the Lord of the worlds.

[2.147] The truth is from your Lord, therefore you should not be of the doubters.

[2.148] And every one has a direction to which he should turn, therefore hasten to (do) good works; wherever you are, Allah will bring you all together; surely Allah has power over all things.

[2.149] And from whatsoever place you come forth, turn your face towards the Sacred Mosque; and surely it is the very truth from your Lord, and Allah is not at all heedless of what you do.

[2.150] And from whatsoever place you come forth, turn your face towards the Sacred Mosque; and wherever you are turn your faces towards it, so that people shall have no accusation against you, except such of them as are unjust; so do not fear them, and fear Me, that I may complete My favor on you and that you may walk on the right course.

[2.151] Even as We have sent among you an Apostle from among you who recites to you Our communications and purifies you and teaches you the Book and the wisdom and teaches you that which you did not know.

[2.152] Therefore remember Me, I will remember you, and be thankful to Me, and do not be ungrateful to Me.

[2.153] O you who believe! seek assistance through patience and prayer; surely Allah is with the patient.

[2.154] And do not speak of those who are slain in Allah's way as dead; nay, (they are) alive, but you do not perceive.

[2.155] And We will most certainly try you with somewhat of fear and hunger and loss of property and lives and fruits; and give good news to the patient,

[2.156] Who, when a misfortune befalls them, say: Surely we are Allah's and to Him we shall surely return.

[2.157] Those are they on whom are blessings and mercy from their Lord, and those are the followers of the right course.

[2.158] Surely the . . . whoever makes a pilgrimage to the House or pays a visit (to it), there is no blame on him if he goes round them both; and whoever does good spontaneously, then surely Allah is Grateful, Knowing.

[2.190] And fight in the way of Allah with those who fight with you, and do not exceed the limits, surely Allah does not love those who exceed the limits.

[2.191] And kill them wherever you find them, and drive them out from whence they drove you out, and persecution is severer than slaughter, and do not fight with them at the Sacred Mosque until they fight with you in it, but if they do fight you, then slay them; such is the recompense of the unbelievers.

[2.192] But if they desist, then surely Allah is Forgiving, Merciful.

[2.193] And fight with them until there is no persecution, and religion should be only for Allah, but if they desist, then there should be no hostility except against the oppressors.

[2.196] And accomplish the pilgrimage and the visit for Allah, but if, you are prevented, (send) whatever offering is easy to obtain, and do not shave your heads until the offering reaches its destination; but whoever among you is sick or has an ailment of the head, he (should effect) a compensation by fasting or alms or sacrificing, then when you are secure, whoever profits by combining the visit with the pilgrimage (should take) what offering is easy to obtain; but he who cannot find (any offering) should fast for three days during the pilgrimage and for seven days when you return; these (make) ten (days) complete; this is for him whose family is not present in the Sacred Mosque, and be careful (of your duty) to Allah, and know that Allah is severe in requiting (evil).

[2.263] Kind speech and forgiveness is better than charity followed by injury; and Allah is Self-sufficient, Forbearing.

[2.270] And whatever alms you give or (whatever) vow you vow, surely Allah knows it; and the unjust shall have no helpers.

[2.271] If you give alms openly, it is well, and if you hide it and give it to the poor, it is better for you; and this will do away with some of your evil deeds; and Allah is aware of what you do.

[2.277] Surely they who believe and do good deeds and keep up prayer and pay the poor-rate they shall have their reward from their Lord, and they shall have no fear, nor shall they grieve.

[2.284] Whatever is in the heavens and whatever is in the earth is Allah's; and whether you manifest what is in your minds or hide it, Allah will call you to account according to it; then He will forgive whom He pleases and chastise whom He pleases, and Allah has power over all things.

ALMS

In the name of Allah, the Beneficent, the Merciful.

[107.1] Have you considered him who calls the judgment a lie?

[107.2] That is the one who treats the orphan with harshness,

[107.3] And does not urge (others) to feed the poor.

[107.4] So woe to the praying ones,

[107.5] Who are unmindful of their prayers,

[107.6] Who do (good) to be seen,

[107.7] And withhold the necessaries of life.

From: The Holy Qur'an, M. H. Shakir, transl. (Tahrike Tarsile Qur'an, Inc., 1983).

QUESTIONS:

1. What are the key duties that a Muslim must perform to receive the blessing of Allah? How difficult are they? Are they communal or personal?
2. What strikes you as the central message of Islam? Put another way, what screen image of Islam does the *Qur'an* project? What is the appeal of that message?

7.4b: *The Pact of Umar* (Umar I, c. 637 CE)

After the rapid expansion of the Muslim dominion in the seventh century, Muslims leaders were required to work out a way of dealing with non-Muslims, who remained in the majority in many areas for centuries. The solution was to develop the notion of *dhimma* or contract of protection for non-Muslim "People of the Book," including Christian and Jews (and later people of some other religions). A *dhimmī*, such a protected non-Muslim, is required to pay a special tax, but is allowed to live in peace. This was far more tolerant than the treatment meted out to non-Christians in Christian Europe. The *Pact of Umar* is supposed to have been the peace accord offered by the Caliph Umar to the Christians of Syria (it is in fact a later forgery, but represents accurately the practice that emerged), a "pact" which formed the pattern of later interaction.

We heard from ʻAbd al-Rahman ibn Ghanam [died 78/697] as follows: When Umar ibn al-Khattab, may God be pleased with him, accorded a peace to the Christians of Syria, we wrote to him as follows:

In the name of God, the Merciful and Compassionate. This is a letter to the servant of God Umar [ibn al-Khattab], Commander of the Faithful, from the Christians of such-and-such a city. When you came against us, we asked you for safe-conduct (aman) for ourselves, our descendants, our property, and the people of our community, and we undertook the following obligations toward you:

We shall not build, in our cities or in their neighborhood, new monasteries, Churches, convents, or monks' cells, nor shall we repair, by day or by night, such of them as fall in ruins or are situated in the quarters of the Muslims.

We shall keep our gates wide open for passersby and travelers. We shall give board and lodging to all Muslims who pass our way for three days.

We shall not give shelter in our churches or in our dwellings to any spy, nor bide him from the Muslims.

We shall not teach the Qur'an to our children.

We shall not manifest our religion publicly nor convert anyone to it. We shall not prevent any of our kin from entering Islam if they wish it.

We shall show respect toward the Muslims, and we shall rise from our seats when they wish to sit.

We shall not seek to resemble the Muslims by imitating any of their garments, the qalansuwa, the turban, footwear, or the parting of the hair. We shall not speak as they do, nor shall we adopt their kunyas.

We shall not mount on saddles, nor shall we gird swords nor bear any kind of arms nor carry them on our- persons.

We shall not engrave Arabic inscriptions on our seals.

We shall not sell fermented drinks.

We shall clip the fronts of our heads.

We shall always dress in the same way wherever we may be, and we shall bind the zunar round our waists.

We shall not display our crosses or our books in the roads or markets of the Muslims. We shall use only clappers in our churches very softly. We shall not raise our voices when following our dead. We shall not show lights on any of the roads of the

Muslims or in their markets. We shall not bury our dead near the Muslims.

We shall not take slaves who have been allotted to Muslims.

We shall not build houses overtopping the houses of the Muslims.

(When I brought the letter to Umar, may God be pleased with him, he added, "We shall not strike a Muslim.")

We accept these conditions for ourselves and for the people of our community, and in return we receive safe-conduct.

If we in any way violate these undertakings for which we ourselves stand surety, we forfeit our covenant [dhimma], and we become liable to the penalties for contumacy and sedition.

Umar ibn al-Khittab replied: Sign what they ask, but add two clauses and impose them in addition to those which they have undertaken. They are: "They shall not buy anyone made prisoner by the Muslims," and "Whoever strikes a Muslim with deliberate intent shall forfeit the protection of this pact."

From: Lewis, Bernard, *Islam, from the Prophet Muhammad to the capture of Constantinople* (New York: Walker, 1976), vol. 2, pp. 217–19.

QUESTIONS:

1. What conditions does the *Pact* impose on non-Muslim populations? How harsh do the conditions seem?
2. Does the *Pact* seem to encourage conversion to Islam? What kind of screen image of Muslims is the author of the *Pact* projecting?

CHAPTER 8

Contested Intersections: Networks, Hierarchies, and Traditional Worlds to 1500

INTRODUCTION

In this chapter we examine the operations of the Afro-Eurasian network. We begin with two sources that show us instances of intersection between network activity and hierarchies, where the different cultural values of the two kinds of structures met. We then see sources that illuminate the three major kinds of people who worked in the network: *wise practitioners*, the merchants and other specialists who generated most network activity; *informed officials*, the people who managed network activity on behalf of hierarchies; and *worldly travelers*, the people who made a living from the dynamics of the network.

INTERSECTIONS

8.1a: *The Revolt of the Laon commune* (Guibert of Nogent, 1115)

Guibert of Nogent (c. 1064–1125) was a Benedictine monk, the abbot of the small abbey of Nogent-sous-Coucy in northern France, and a writer of history, theology, and autobiography. His best known works are a history of the First Crusade and the autobiographical *De vita sua*, from which this excerpt on the revolt of the commune of Laon is taken. Communes were merchant-centered pacts for urban self-governance with the approval (at a price) of the king or lord of the town, and they reflected the network-based interests of the townspeople. They came into conflict with the traditional, hierarchical privileges of the nobles and church barons who controlled the towns and the surrounding lands. Bishop Gaudry of Laon objected strongly when Laon formed a commune in his absence, bought back the support of King Louis VI, and sparked the revolt that Guibert narrates. Guibert views the revolt from the perspective of a traditional religious elite, misunderstanding the mechanisms of trade and the sort of people engaged in the revolt, but he has little sympathy for Bishop Gaudry, either, whom he considers oppressive and vain.

CHAPTER 7

Some time after the bishop had set out for England to extract money from the English king, whom he had served and who had been his friend, the archdeacons Gautier and Guy and the nobles of the city devised the following plan. Since ancient times it had been the misfortune of the city of Laon that neither God nor any lord was feared there, but, according to each man's power and desire, the public authority was involved in rapine and murder. To begin with the source of the plague, whenever the king, who ought to have exacted respect for himself with royal severity, happened to visit the city, he was himself first shamefully fined on his own property. When his horses were led out to water in the morning or evening, his grooms were beaten and the horses seized. Also, it was known that the clergy themselves were held in such contempt that neither their persons nor their goods were spared, but the situation then followed the text "As it is with the people, so with the priest." What then shall I say about the lower classes? None of the peasants came into the city (no one who did not have the best guaranteed safe-conduct even approached it) who was not thrown into prison and held for ransom, or, if the opportunity occurred, was not drawn into some lawless lawsuit. . . .

The clergy and the archdeacons and the nobles, taking account of these conditions and looking out for ways of exacting money from the people, offered them through their agents the opportunity to have authorization to create a commune, if they would offer an appropriate sum of money. Now, "commune" is a new and evil name for an arrangement for them all to pay the customary head tax, which they owe their lords as a servile due, in a lump sum once a year, and if anyone commits a crime, he shall pay a fine set by law, and all other financial exactions which are customarily imposed on serfs are completely abolished. Seizing on this opportunity for commuting their dues, the people gathered huge sums of money to fill the gaping purses of so many greedy men. Pleased with the shower of income poured upon them, those men established their good faith by proffering oaths that they would keep their word in this matter.

After this sworn association of mutual aid among the clergy, nobles, and people had been established, the bishop returned with much wealth from England. Angered at those responsible for this innovation, for a long time he kept away from the city. . . .

Although he said that he was moved by relentless wrath against those who had sworn an oath to the association and those who were the principals in the transaction, in the end his high-sounding words were suddenly quieted by the offer of a great heap of silver and gold. Then he swore that he would maintain the rights of the commune, following the terms of the charters of the city of Noyon and the town of Saint-Quentin. The king, too, was induced to confirm the same thing by oath with a bribe from the people.

O my God, who can describe the controversy that broke out when, after accepting so many gifts from the people, they then took oaths to overturn what they had sworn; that is, when they tried to return the serfs to their former condition after once freeing them from the yoke of their exactions? The hatred of the bishop and the nobles for the burghers was indeed implacable, and as he was not strong enough to crush the freedom of the French, following the fashion of Normandy and England, the pastor remained inactive, forgetful of his sacred calling through his insatiable greed. Whenever one of the people was brought into a court of law, he was judged not on his condition in the eyes of God but, if I may put it this way, on his bargaining power, and he was drained of his substance to the last penny.

Since the taking of gifts is commonly attended by the subversion of all justice, the coiners of the currency, knowing that if they did wrong in their office they could save themselves by paying money, corrupted the coinage with so much base metal that because of this many people were reduced to poverty. As they made their coins of the cheapest bronze, which in a moment by certain dishonest practices they made brighter than silver, the attention of the foolish people was shamefully deceived, and, giving up their goods of great or little value, they got in exchange nothing but the most debased dross. The lord bishop's acceptance of this practice was well rewarded, and thus not only within the diocese of Laon but in all directions the ruin of many was hastened. When he was deservedly powerless to uphold or improve the value of his own currency, which he had wickedly debased, he instituted halfpence of Amiens, also very debased, to be current in the city for some time. And when he could by no means keep them going, he struck a contemporary impression on which he had stamped a pastoral staff to represent himself. This was received with such secret laughter and scorn that it had even less value than the debased coinage.

However, since on the issue of each of these new coins a proclamation was made that no one should laugh at the dreadful designs, there were a great many opportunities to accuse the people of speaking evil of the bishop's ordinances, and hence they could exact all sorts of heavy fines. Moreover, a monk named Thierry, who had the most shameful reputation in every respect, imported very large quantities of silver from Flanders and from Tournai, of which he was native. Bring it all down to the very debased money of Laon, he scattered it all over the surrounding province. By appealing to the greed of the rich people of the province with his hateful presents and by bringing in lies, perjury, and poverty, he robbed the country of truth, justice, and wealth. No enemy action, no plundering, no burning has ever hurt the province more since the Roman walls contained the ancient and thoroughly respected mint of the city. . . .

Calling together the nobles and certain of the clergy in the last days of Lent in the most holy Passiontide of Our Lord, the bishop determined to attack the commune, to which he had sworn and had with presents induced the king to swear. He had summoned the king to that pious duty, and on the day before Good Friday—that is, on Maundy Thursday—he instructed the king and all his people to break their oaths, after first placing his own neck in that noose. As I said before, this was the day on which his predecessor Bishop Ascelin had betrayed his king. On the very day when he should have performed that most glorious of all episcopal duties, the consecration of the oil and the absolution of the people from their sins, he was not even seen to enter the church. He was intriguing with the king's courtiers so that after the sworn association was destroyed the king would restore the laws of the city to their former state. But the burghers, fearing their overthrow, promised the king and his courtiers four hundred pounds, and possibly more. In reply, the bishop begged the nobles to go with him to interview the king, and they promised on their part seven hundred pounds. King Louis, Philippe's son, was a remarkable person who seemed well-suited for royal majesty, mighty in arms, intolerant toward sloth in business, of dauntless courage in adversity; although in other respects he was a good man, in this matter he was most unjust and paid too much attention to worthless persons debased by greed. This redounded to his own great loss and blame and the ruin of many, which certainly happened here and elsewhere.

When the king's desire was turned, as I said, toward the larger promise and he ruled against God, the oaths of the bishop and the nobles were voided without any regard for honor or the sacred season. Because of the turmoil with which he had so unjustly struck the people, that night the king was afraid to sleep outside the bishop's palace, although he had the right to compulsory lodging elsewhere. Very early the next morning the king departed, and the bishop promised the nobles they need have no fear about the agreement to pay so much money, informing them that he would himself pay whatever they had promised. "And if I do not fulfill my promise," he said, "hand me over to the king's prison until I pay it off."

After the bonds of the association were broken, such rage, such amazement seized the burghers that all the craftsmen abandoned their jobs, and the stalls of the tanners and cobblers were closed and nothing was exposed for sale by the innkeepers and chapmen, who expected to have nothing left when the lords began plundering. For at once the property of such individuals was calculated by the bishop and nobles, and the amount any man was known to have given to establish the commune was demanded of him to pay for its annulment.

These events took place on the Parasceve, which means preparation. On Holy Saturday, when they should have been preparing to receive the Body and Blood of the Lord, they were actually preparing only for murder and perjury. To be brief, all the efforts of the bishop and the nobles in these days were reserved for fleecing their inferiors. But those inferiors were no longer merely angry, but were goaded into an animal rage. Binding themselves by mutual oaths, they conspired for the death, or rather the murder, of the bishop and his accomplices. They say that forty took the oath. Their great undertaking could not be kept completely secret, and when it came to the attention of Master Anselm toward evening of Holy Saturday, he sent word to the bishop, who was retiring to rest, not to go out to the service of matins, knowing that if he did he would be killed. With excessive pride the bishop stupidly said, "Nonsense, I'm not likely to die at the hands of such people." But although he scorned them orally, he did not dare to go out for matins and to enter the church.

The next day, as he followed the clergy in procession, he ordered the people of his household and all the knights to come behind him carrying short swords under their garments. During this procession when a little disorder began to arise, as often happens in a crowd, one of the burghers came out of the church and thought the time had come for the murder to which they were sworn. He then began to cry out in a loud voice, as if he were signaling, "Commune, Commune!" over and over again. Because it was a feast day, this was easily stopped, yet it brought suspicion on the opposition. And so, when the service of the mass was over, the bishop summoned a great number of peasants from the episcopal manors and manned the towers of the cathedral and ordered them to guard his palace, although they hated him almost as much, since they knew that the piles of money which he had promised the king must be drained from their own purses.

On Easter Monday it is the custom for the clergy to assemble at the abbey of Saint-Vincent. Since the conspirators knew they had been anticipated the day before, they had decided to act on this day, and they would have done so if they had not seen that all the nobles were with the bishop. They did find one of the nobles in the outskirts of the city, a harmless man who had recently married a young cousin of mine, a girl of modest character. But they were unwilling to attack him, fearing to put others on their guard. Coming through to Tuesday and feeling more secure, the bishop dismissed those men whom he had put in the towers and palace to protect him and whom he had to feed there from his own resources. On Wednesday I went to him because through his disorders he had robbed me of my grain supply and of some legs of pork, called *bacons* in French. When I requested him to relieve the city of these great disturbances, he replied, "What do you think they can do with their riots? If Jean, my moor, were to take by the nose the most powerful man among them, he would not even dare to grunt. For just now I have compelled them to renounce what they call their commune for as long as I live." I said something, and then, seeing the man was overcome with arrogance, I stopped. But before I left the city, because of his instability we quarreled with mutual recriminations. Although he was warned by many of the imminent peril, he took no notice of anyone.

CHAPTER 8

The next day—that is, on Thursday—when the bishop and Archdeacon Gautier were engaged after the noon offices in collecting money, suddenly there arose throughout the city the tumult of men shouting, "Commune!" Then through the nave of the cathedral of Notre-Dame . . . , a great crowd of burghers attacked the episcopal palace, armed with rapiers, double-edged swords, bows, and axes, and carrying clubs and lances. As soon as this sudden attack was discovered, the nobles rallied from all sides to the bishop, having sworn to give him aid against such an assault if it should occur. In this rally Guimar the castellan, an older nobleman of handsome presence and guiltless character, armed only with a shield and spear, ran through the church. Just as he entered the bishop's hall, he was the first to fall, struck on the back of the head with a sword by a man named Raimbert, who had been his close friend. Immediately afterward that Renier of whom I spoke before as married to my cousin, rushing to enter the palace, was struck from behind with a spear when he tried to duck under it while poised on the porch of the bishop's chapel. Struck to the ground there, he was soon consumed by the fire of the palace from his groin downward. Adon the *vidame*, sharp in small matters and even keener in important ones, separated from the rest and able to do little by himself among so many, encountered the full force of the attack as he was striving to reach the bishop's palace. With his spear and sword he made such a stand that in a moment he struck down three of those who rushed at him. Then he mounted the dining table in the hall, where he was wounded in the knees and other parts of the body. At last, falling on his knees and striking at his assailants all round him, he kept them off for a long time, until someone pierced his exhausted body with a javelin. After a little he was burned to ashes by the fire in that house.

While the insolent mob was attacking the bishop and howling before the walls of his palace, the bishop and the people who were aiding him fought them off as best they could by hurling stones and shooting arrows. Now, as at all times, he showed great spirit as a fighter; but because he had wrongly and in vain taken up that other sword, he perished by the sword. Unable to resist the reckless assaults of the people, he put on the clothes of one of his servants and fled into the warehouse of the church, where he hid himself in a container. When the cover had been fastened on by a faithful follower, he thought himself safely hidden. As those looking for him ran hither and thither, they did not call out for the bishop but for a felon. They seized one of his pages, but he remained faithful and they could get nothing out of him. Laying hands on another, they learned from the traitor's nod where to look for him. Entering the warehouse and searching everywhere, at last they found him. . . .

From: Guibert, and John F. Benton, *Self and society in Medieval France: the memoirs of Abbot Guibert of Nogent* (1064?–c. 1125) (New York: Harper & Row, 1970), pp. 165–74.

QUESTIONS:

1. Guibert does not have much praise for anyone in this story, it seems. What character flaws does he attribute to the townspeople? What character flaws does he see in the nobles and clergy? Do they differ? What virtues does Guibert value, if only by implication?
2. What aspects of Guibert's story show the potentially disruptive impact of network operations on the world Guibert is used to and the values he holds to be important?

8.1b: *Guild Regulations of the Guild Merchant of Southampton* (twelfth century)

The guild merchant of Southampton was typical of early (eleventh and twelfth century) guilds, which were dominated by major merchants. (Craft guilds were a later development.) The merchants organized themselves for a variety of reasons, and the guild often assumed many of the functions of city government, sometimes in the form of a commune. Guilds of merchants emerged as a self-protective response to how medieval European elites viewed merchant activity—with a combination of neglect, hostility, and avaricious self-interest.

. . . In the first place, there shall be elected from the gild merchant, and established, an alderman, a steward, a chaplain, four skevins, and an usher. And it is to be known that whosoever shall be alderman shall receive from each one entering into the gild fourpence; the steward, twopence; the chaplain, twopence; and the usher, one penny. And the gild shall meet twice a year: that is to say, on the Sunday next after St. John the Baptist's day, and on the Sunday next after St. Mary's day.

And when the gild shall be sitting no one of the gild is to bring in any stranger, except when required by the alderman or steward. And the alderman shall have a sergeant to serve before him, the steward another sergeant, and the chaplain shall have his clerk.

And when the gild shall sit, the alderman is to have, each night, so long as the gild sits, two gallons of wine and two candles, and the steward the same; and the four skevins and the chaplain, each of them one gallon of wine and one candle, and the usher one gallon of wine.

And when the gild shall sit, the lepers of La Madeleine shall have of the alms of the gild, two sesters (approximately eight gallons) of ale, and the sick of God's House and of St. Julian shall have two sesters of ale. And the Friars Minors shall have two sesters of ale and one sester of wine. And four sesters of ale shall be given to the poor wherever the gild shall meet.

And when the gild is sitting, no one who is of the gild shall go outside the town for any business, without the permission of the steward. And if any does so, let him be fined two shillings, and pay them.

And when the gild sits, and any gildsman is outside of the city so that he does not know when it will happen, he shall have a gallon of wine, if his servants come to get it. And if a gildsman is ill and is in the city, wine shall be sent to him, two loaves of bread and a gallon of wine and a dish from the kitchen; and two approved men of the gild shall go to visit him and look after his condition.

And when a gildsman dies, all those who are of the gild and are in the city shall attend the service of the dead, and the gildsmen shall bear the body and bring it to the place of burial. And whoever will not do this shall pay according to his oath, two pence, to be given to the poor. And those of the ward where the dead man shall be ought to find a man to watch over the body the night that the dead shall lie in his house. And so long as the service of the dead shall last, that is to say the vigil and the mass, there ought to burn four candles of the gild, each candle of two pounds weight or more, until the body is buried. And these four candles shall remain in the keeping of the steward of the gild.

And when a gildsman dies, his eldest son or his next heir shall have the seat of his father, or of his uncle, if his father was not a gildsman, and of no other one; and he shall give nothing for his seat. No husband can have a seat in the gild by right of his wife, nor demand a seat by right of his wife's ancestors.

And no one of the city of Southampton shall buy anything to sell again in the same city, unless he is of the gild merchant or of the franchise. And if anyone shall do so and is convicted of it, all which he has so bought shall be forfeited to the king; and no one shall be quit of custom unless he proves that he is in the gild or in the franchise, and this from year to year.

And no one shall buy honey, fat, salt herrings, or any kind of oil, or millstones, or fresh hides, or any kind of fresh skins, unless he is a gildsman: nor keep a tavern for wine, nor sell cloth at retail, except in market or fair days; nor keep grain in his granary beyond five quarters, to sell at retail, if he is not a gildsman; and whoever shall do this and be convicted, shall forfeit all to the king.

If any gildsman falls into poverty and has not the wherewithal to live, and is not able to work or to provide for himself, he shall have one mark from the gild to relieve his condition when the gild shall sit. No one of the gild nor of the franchise shall avow another's goods for his by which the custom of the city shall be injured. And if any one does so and is convicted, he shall lose the gild and the franchise; and the merchandise so avowed shall be forfeited to the king.

And no private man nor stranger shall bargain for or buy any kind of merchandise coming into the city before a burgess of the gild merchant, so long as the gildsman is present and wishes to bargain for and buy this merchandise; and if anyone does so and is convicted, that which he buys shall be forfeited to the king.

The common chest shall be in the house of the chief alderman or of the steward, and the three keys of it shall be lodged with three discreet men of the aforesaid twelve sworn men, or with three of the skevins, who shall loyally take care of the common seal, and the charters and of the treasure of the town, and the standards, and other muniments of the town; and no letter shall be sealed with the common seal, nor any charter taken out of the common-chest but in the presence of six or twelve sworn men, and of the alderman or steward; and nobody shall sell by any kind of measure or weight that is not sealed, under forfeiture of two shillings.

No one shall go out to meet a ship bringing wine or other merchandise coming to the town, in order to buy anything, before the ship be arrived and come to anchor for unlading; and if any one does so and is convicted, the merchandise which he shall have bought shall be forfeited to the king.

From: Tierney, Brian, *The Middle Ages*, (New York: Knopf, 1983), pp. 188–90.

QUESTIONS:

1. Based on these regulations, what was the function (or what were the functions) of the guild merchant?
2. What screen image of themselves do the merchants of Southampton project to themselves through these regulations? What underlying frame values do the regulations express?

8.2: Wise Practitioners: *The Arabian Nights* (c. 1000)

The Arabian Nights is a collection of various types of folk tales. The narrative device that holds them together is a story in itself that need not be detailed here. The collection seems to have come into existence by around 1000, but it continued to evolve after that and so has no one author. The story presented here tells about a Baghdad merchant, Ali Cogia, who goes on a pilgrimage to Mecca and, on his return home, must undertake a search for justice. It is the tale of a wise practitioner, wise not just in the ways of the network from which he makes his living but in the relationship of his network activities to the Muslim hierarchy in which he also lives. Islam was friendlier to merchant activity than most other Agrarian cultures at the time, and the story reflects the world of the 'Abbasid Caliphate at the height of its power and prestige under Caliph Harun Al-Rashid (786–809).

THE STORY OF ALI COGIA, A MERCHANT OF BAGDAD

In reign of the caliph Haroun Al-Rashid, there lived at Bagdad a merchant, whose name was Ali Cogia, that was neither one of the richest nor meanest sort. . . .

As a good Muslim, he knew he was obliged to undertake a pilgrimage; . . . to be able to go that year, he sold off his household goods, his shop, and with it the greatest part of his merchandizes; reserving only some which he thought might turn to a better account at Mecca; and meeting with a tenant for his house, let that also.

Things being thus disposed, he was ready to go when the Bagdad caravan set out for Mecca; the only thing he had to do, was to secure a sum of a thousand pieces of gold, which would be troublesome to carry along with him, besides the money he had set apart to defray his expenses. To this end he made choice of a jar, of a proportionable size, put the thousand pieces of gold into it, and covered them over with olives. When he had closed the mouth of the jar, he carried it to a merchant, a particular friend of his, and said to him, You know, brother, that in two or three days time I set out with the caravan on my pilgrimage to Mecca; and I beg the favour of you, that you would take upon you the charge of keeping a jar of olives for me till I return. The merchant promised him he would, and in an obliging manner said, Here, take the key of my warehouse, and set your jar where you please; I promise you shall find it there when you come again.

On the day the caravan was to set out, Ali Cogia added himself to it, with a camel, (loaded with what merchandizes he thought fit to carry along with him,) which served him to ride on, and arrived safe at Mecca, where he visited, along with other pilgrims, the temple so much celebrated and frequented by all Muslims every year, who come from all parts of the world, and observe religiously the ceremonies prescribed them; and when he had acquitted himself of the duties of his pilgrimage, he exposed the merchandizes he had brought with him, to sell or exchange them.

Two merchants passing by, and seeing Ali Cogia's goods, thought them so fine and choice, that they stopped some time to look at them, though they had no occasion for them; and when they had satisfied their curiosity, one of them said to the other, as they were going away, If this merchant knew to what profit these goods would turn at Cairo, he would carry them thither, and not sell them here, though this is a good market.

Ali Cogia heard these words; and as he had often heard talk of the beauties of Egypt, he was resolved to take the opportunity of seeing them, and take a journey thither; therefore, after having packed up his goods again, instead of returning to Bagdad, he set out for Egypt with a caravan of Cairo; and when he came thither, he found his account in his journey, and in a few days sold all his goods to a greater advantage than he hoped for. [Using his profits to buy goods for sale back in Baghdad, he journeys homeward, but is lured into visiting other places by curiosity and business opportunity. Hence, he is gone from Baghdad for many years.] . . .

All this time, his friend, with whom he had left his jar of olives, neither thought of him nor them; but . . . one evening, when this merchant was supping at home with his family, and the discourse happening to fall upon olives, his wife was desirous to eat some, saying, that she had not tasted any for a long while. Now you talk of olives, said the merchant, you put me in mind of a jar which Ali Cogia left with me seven years ago, when he went to Mecca, and put it himself in my warehouse, for me to keep it for him against he returned; and what is become of him I know not; though, when the caravan came back, they told me he was gone for Egypt. Certainly he must be dead, since he has not returned in all this time; and we may eat the olives, if they prove good. Lend me a plate and a candle, and I will go and fetch some of them, and we will see. . . .

When he came into the warehouse, he opened the jar, and found the olives all mouldy; but, to see if they were all so at the bottom, he turned the jar topsy-turvy upon the plate; and by shaking the jar, some of the gold tumbled out.

At the sight of the gold, the merchant, who was naturally covetous, looked into the jar, and perceived that he had shaked out almost all the olives, and what remained was gold coin fast wedged in: he immediately put the olives into the jar again. . . .

The next morning he went and bought some olives of that year, took out the old, with the gold, and filled the jar with the new, covered it up, and put it in the same place.

About a month after the merchant had committed so base an action, (for which he ought to pay dear,) Ali Cogia arrived at Bagdad; and, as he had let his house, he alighted at an inn, choosing to stay there till he gave his tenant warning, that he might provide himself of another house.

The next morning, Ali Cogia went to pay a visit to the merchant his friend, who received him in the most obliging manner imaginable, and expressed a great deal of joy at his return, after so many years absence; telling him that he had begun to lose all hopes of ever seeing him again.

After the usual compliments on such a meeting, Ali Cogia desired the merchant to return him the jar of olives which he had left with him, and to excuse the liberty he had taken in giving him so much trouble.

My dear friend, Ali Cogia, replied the merchant, you are to blame to make all these apologies on such an occasion; I should have made as free with you; there, take the key of the warehouse, go and take it; you will find it in the same place where you left it.

Ali Cogia went into the merchant's warehouse, took his jar, and after having returned him the key, and thanks for the favour he had done, returned with it to the khan where he lodged; and opening the jar, and putting his hand down to the bottom, to see for his gold, was very much surprised to find none. At first he thought he might perhaps be mistaken; and, to discover the truth, poured out all the olives, without so much as finding one single piece of money. His astonishment was so great, that he then stood for some time motionless: lifting up his hands and eyes to heaven, he cried out, Is it possible that a man whom I took for my very good friend, should be guilty of so base an action?

Ali Cogia . . . returned immediately to the merchant.

[Ali Cogia accuses the merchant of theft, which the merchant denies.]

You bring it upon yourself, said Ali Cogia, taking him by the arm; but since you use me so basely, I cite you according to the law of God: Let us see whether you will have the assurance to say the same thing before the qadi [Islamic judge].

The merchant could not refuse this summons, which every good Muslim is bound to observe, or be declared a rebel against his religion; but said, With all my heart, we shall soon see who is in the wrong.

Ali Cogia carried the merchant before the qadi, before whom he accused him of cheating him of a thousand pieces of gold, which he had left with him. The qadi asked him if he had any witnesses; to which he replied that he had not taken that necessary precaution, because he believed the person he trusted his money with, to be his friend, and always took him for an honest man.

The merchant made the same defence he had done before the merchants his neighbours, offering to make oath that he never had the money he was accused of, and that he did not so much as know there was such a sum; upon which the qadi took his oath, and afterwards dismissed him.

[Ali Cogia submits an appeal to the caliph] . . .

The same evening, the caliph, the grand visier Giafar, and Mesrour, the chief of the eunuchs, went all disguised through the town . . .; and passing through a street, the caliph heard a noise, and mending his pace, he came to a gate which led into a little court, where, through a hole, he perceived ten or twelve children placing by moon-light.

The caliph, who was curious to know at what play these children played, sat down upon a bench which he found just by; and still looking through the hole, he heard one of the briskest and liveliest of the children say, Come, let us play at the qadi. I will be qadi; bring Ali Cogia and the merchant who cheated him of the thousand pieces of gold before me.

These words of the child put the caliph in mind of the petition Ali Cogia had given him that day, and made him redouble his attention. As Ali Cogia's affairs and the merchant's made a great noise, and were in every body's mouth in Bagdad, it had not escaped the children, who all accepted the proposition with joy, and agreed on the parts each was to act; not one of them refused him that made the proposal to be qadi; and when he had taken his seat, which he did with all the seeming gravity of a qadi, another, as an officer of the court, presented two before him; one as Ali Cogia, and the other as the merchant against whom he complained.

Then the pretended qadi, directing his discourse to the feigned Ali Cogia, asked him what he had to say to that merchant's charge?

Ali Cogia, after a low bow, informed the young qadi of the fact, and related every particular, and afterwards begged that he would use his authority, that he might not lose so considerable a sum of money.

Then the qadi, turning about to the merchant, asked him why he did not return the money which Ali Cogia demanded of him?

The young merchant alleged the same reasons as the real merchant had done before the qadi himself, and proffered to confirm it by an oath, that what he had said was truth.

Not so fast, replied the pretended qadi; before you come to your oath, I should be glad to see the jar of olives. Ali Cogia, said he, addressing himself to the lad who acted that part, have you brought the jar? No, replied he: Then go and fetch it immediately.

The pretended Ali Cogia went immediately, and returning as soon, feigned to bring a jar before the qadi, telling him, that it was the same he left with the accused person, and took away again. But to omit no part of the formality, the supposed qadi asked the merchant if it was the same; and as, by his silence, he seemed not to deny it, he ordered it to be opened. He that represented Ali Cogia, seemed to take off the cover, and the pretended qadi made as if he looked into it. They are fine olives, said he; let me taste them; and then pretending to eat of them, added, they are excellent: But, continued he, I cannot think that olives will keep seven years, and be so good: Send for two olive merchants, and let me hear what is their opinion. Then the two boys, as olive merchants, presented themselves. Are you olive merchants, said the sham qadi? Tell me how long olives will keep to be fit to eat.

Sir, replied the two merchants, let us take what care we can, they will hardly be worth any thing at the third year; for they have neither taste nor colour. If it be so, answered the qadi, look into that jar, and tell me how old those olives are?

The two merchants pretended to examine and to taste the olives, and told the qadi they were new and good. You are deceived, said the young qadi; there is Ali Cogia, who says they were put into the jar seven years ago.

Sir, replied the merchants, we can assure you they are of this year's growth; and we will maintain, there is not a merchant in Bagdad but will say the same.

The sham merchant that was accused would fain have objected against the evidence of the olive merchants; but the qadi would not suffer him. Hold your tongue, said he; you are a rogue, and ought to be hanged. Then the children put an end to their play, by clapping their hands with a great deal of joy, and seizing the criminal, to carry him to execution.

I cannot express how much the caliph Haroun Al-Rashid admired the wisdom and sense of the boy who had passed so just a sentence, in an affair which was to be pleaded before him the next day; and rising up off the bench he sat on, he asked the grand visier, who heard all that passed, what he thought of it? Indeed, Commander of the True Believers, answered the grand visier Giafar, I am surprised to find so much sense in one so young.

But, answered the caliph, dost thou know one thing? I am to pronounce sentence in this very cause tomorrow, and that the true Ali Cogia presented his petition to me today: And do you think, continued he, that I can judge better? I think not, answered the visier, if the case is as the children represented it. Take notice then of this house, said the caliph, and bring the boy to me tomorrow, that he may judge of this affair in my presence; and also order the qadi who acquitted the roguish merchant to attend, to take example by a child: Besides, take care to bid Ali Cogia bring his jar of olives with him, and let two olive merchants be present. After this charge, he pursued his rounds, without meeting with any thing worth his attention.

[The boy and the parties appear the next day.] . . .

Then the caliph set [the boy] on the throne by him, and asked for the two parties. When they were called, they came and prostrated themselves before the throne, bowing their heads quite down to the tapestry. Afterwards, the caliph said to them, Plead both of you your causes before this child, who shall do you both justice; and if he be at any loss, I will rectify it.

Ali Cogia and the merchant pleaded one after the other, as before; but when the merchant proposed his oath, the child said, It is too soon; it is proper that we should see the jar of olives.

At these words, Ali Cogia presented the jar, placed it at the caliph's feet, and opened it. The caliph looked upon the olives, and took one, and tasted of it. Afterwards the merchants were called, who examined the olives, and reported that they were good, and of that year. The boy told them, that Ali Cogia assured him that it was seven years since he put them up; and they returned the same answer as the children who represented them the night before.

Though the merchant who was accused saw plainly that these merchants' opinion would condemn him, yet he would say something in his own justification: When the child, instead of ordering him to be hanged, looked upon the caliph, and said, Commander of the Faithful, this is no jesting matter; it is your majesty that must condemn him to death, and not me, though I did it yesterday in my play.

The caliph, fully satisfied of the merchant's villany, gave him into the hands of the ministers of justice, to be hanged; which sentence was executed upon him, after he had confessed where he had hid the thousand pieces of gold, which were restored to Ali Cogia. Then the monarch, who was all just and equitable, turning to the qadi, bid him learn of the child how to acquit himself of his duty; and embracing the boy, sent him home with a purse of an hundred pieces of gold, as a token of his liberality.

From: Mack, Robert L., *Arabian nights' entertainments* (Oxford: Oxford University Press, 1995), pp. 787–96.

QUESTIONS:

1. What does the story tell us about merchant practices and network operations in the heart of Islamic civilization? What seems to be the status of merchants in this society? What values guide merchant activity?
2. What does the judgment in Ali Cogia's court case tell us about the relationship between the Islamic hierarchy on one hand and merchants and network activity on the other? Do state officials and merchants seem to share a common cultural frame?

8.3: Informed Officials: *Description of the Barbarous Peoples* (Zhao Rugua, early twelfth century CE)

Zhao Rugua (1170–1228) was a customs official who served the Southern Song Dynasty at the port city of Quanzhou. He wrote his two volume *Description of the Barbarous Peoples* around 1225, as his career and life were coming to a close. He relied on reports from merchants as well as on an earlier description of lands and trade goods written around 1178 by the geographer Zhou Qufei. The first volume of Zhao's work describes different lands and peoples, detailing their customs and the sorts of goods available they trade; the second volume describes in some detail many of those goods. This selection includes a description of the Chola kingdom from the first volume and descriptions of two trade goods, asafetida (a spice) and rhinoceros horn (still believed today in Chinese culture to have medicinal properties), from the second volume. Zhao's work is representative of the knowledge generated by network connections and often gathered by informed officials such as Zhao.

THE CHOLA (CHU-LIÉN) DOMINION

The Kingdom of Chu-lién is the Southern Yin-tu of the west [of India].

This country had not from olden times carried on trade (with China). By water one comes to Ts'üan-chóu after some 411,400 *li*.

If you wish to go to this kingdom, then you must change ships at Ku-lin to go there. Some say that one can go there by way of the kingdom of P'u-kan.

In this kingdom there is a city with a seven-fold wall, seven feet high, and extending twelve *li* from north to south and seven *li* from east to west. The different walls are one hundred paces distant from each other. Four of these walls are of brick, two of mud, and the one in the centre of wood. There are flowers, fruit trees, and other trees planted (on them).

The first and second walls enclose the dwellings of the people, — they are surrounded by small ditches; the third and fourth walls (surround) the dwellings of the court officers; within the fifth dwell the king's four sons; 13 within the sixth are the Buddhist monasteries where the priests dwell; the seventh wall encloses over four hundred buildings forming the royal palace.

. . .

When any one among the people is guilty of an offense, one of the Court Ministers punishes him; if the offense is light, the culprit tied to a wooden frame and given fifty, seventy, or up to an hundred blows, with a stick. Heinous crimes are punished with decapitation or by being trampled to death by an elephant.

At state banquets both the Prince and the four Court Ministers salaam [bow] at the foot of the throne, then the whole (company present) break into music, song and dancing. He (the Prince) does not drink wine, but he eats meat, and, as is the native custom, dresses in cotton clothing and eats flour-cakes. For his table and escort he employs fully a myriad dancing-girls, three thousand of whom are in attendance daily in rotations. When contracting marriage, they send, in the first place, a female go-between with a gold (or) silver finger-ring to the girl's home. Three days afterwards there is a meeting of the man's family to decide upon the amount of land, cotton, betel nuts, wine and the like to be given as marriage portion. The girl's family sends in return (a) gold or silver finger-ring, *yüe-no* cloth and brocaded clothing to be worn by the bride to the (intended) son-in-law. Should the man wish to withdraw from the engagement, he would not dare reclaim the marriage gifts; if the girl should wish to reject the man she must pay back double.

As the taxes and imposts of the kingdom are numerous and heavy, traders rarely go there.

This country is at war with the kingdoms of the west (of India?). The government owns sixty thousand war-elephants, every one seven or eight feet high. When fighting these elephants carry on their backs houses, and these houses are full of soldiers who shoot arrows at long range, and fight with spears at close quarters. When victorious, the elephants are granted honorary names to signalize their merit.

The inhabitants are hot-tempered and reckless of life; nay, in the presence of the king they will fight man to man with swords and die without regret.

Father and son, elder and younger brother, have their meals cooked in separate kettles and served in separate dishes; yet they are deeply alive to family duties.

The native products comprise pearls, elephants' tusks, coral, transparent glass, betel nuts, cardamoms, opaque glass, cotton stuffs with coloured silk threads, and cotton stuffs.

Of quadrupeds they have goats and domestic cattle; of birds, pheasants and parrots; of fruits, the *yü-kan,* the *t'ong-lo,* Persian dates, cocoanuts, the *kan-lo,* the *k'un-lun* plum, and the *po-lo-mi* (jack-fruit).

Of flowers, they have the white jasmine, the *san-ssï,* the *shö-ts'i-sang,* the *li-ts'iu,* the blue, yellow and green *p'o-lo,* the *yau-lién-ch'an,* the red canna.

Of grain they have green and black beans, wheat and rice; the bamboo is indigenous.

In former times they did not send tribute to our court, but in the eighth year of the *ta-chung* and *siang-fu* periods [1015 CE], its sovereign sent a mission with pearls and like articles as tribute. The interpreters, in translating their speech, said they wished to evince the respect of a distant nation for [Chinese] civilization. They were ordered by Imperial decree to remain in waiting at the side gate of the Palace, and to be entertained at a banquet by the Associates in the College of Court Annalists. By Imperial favor they were ranked with the envoys of *K'iu-tz'ï.* It happened to be the Emperor's birthday, and the envoys had a fine opportunity to witness the congratulations in the Sacred Enclosure.

In the tenth year *si-ning* [1077] they again sent tribute of native produce. The Emperor Shün-tsung sent an officer of the Inner Department to bid them welcome.

. . .

ASA-FOETIDA [A SPICE]

A-weï comes from the country of Mu-kü-lan Ta-shï country. The tree is not a very high or large one, but the resin exudes freely from its bark. The natives wind a piece of string round a twig, remove its tip, and cover it with a bamboo tube which fills with resin. This bamboo tube is broken up in the winter, when the resin is gathered and packed in skin bags.

Some say that this resin is so poisonous that people do not dare to come near it themselves, but, when the drug has to be gathered, tie up a sheep at the foot of the tree and shoot arrows at it from a distance. The poison of the resin then drops upon the sheep, which dies of it, and its decayed flesh turns into asafetida. I do not know which of the two accounts is correct; meanwhile they are both placed here on record.

. . .

RHINOCEROS HORNS

The *si,* or rhinoceros, resembles the domestic cattle, but it has only one horn. Its skin is black and its hair scanty; its tongue is like the burr of a chestnut. Fierce and violent in its temper, this animal runs so quickly that you may imagine it is flying. Its food consists solely of bamboo and other woods. Since he rips up a man with his horn, none dare come near him, but hunters shoot him with a stiff arrow from a good distance, after which they remove the horn, which in this state is called a fresh horn, whereas, if the animal has died a natural death the horn obtained from it is called a dropped-in-the-hills horn. The horn bears marks like bubbles; the horns which are more white than black are the best.

From: Chao, Ju-Kua, Friedrich Hirth, and William Woodville Rockhill, *Chau Ju-Kua: his work on the Chinese and Arab trade in the twelfth and thirteenth centuries, entitled Chu-fan-chï* (St. Petersburg: Imperial Academy of Sciences, 1911), pp. 93–96, 233.

QUESTIONS:

1. Judging from what Zhao describes in these selections, what was the purpose of the *Description?* Why do you think he wrote it, and for what audience? Does the fact that he wrote it at the end of his career influence your answer?
2. What Song Chinese frame values can you infer from what Zhao finds remarkable about his topics or how he writes about them? For example, what might you infer from his including two different descriptions of how asafoetida is gathered?

8.4: Worldly Travelers: from *Travels* (Ibn Battuta, c. 1355)

Ibn Battuta (1304–69) is the quintessential worldly traveler of the High Agrarian Era. Born in Tangiers, Morocco, to a Berber family of legal scholars, he studied law in the family tradition. At the age of twenty one he set off on a pilgrimage to Mecca. He would not return to Tangiers for twenty four years: his life as a traveler had begun. He visited a vast range of places across the Islamic world and even beyond, traveling more than three times as far as Marco Polo. His travels included West Africa, Egypt, India, China, southern Russia, and eastern Europe, among other places. He recorded his observations around 1355 in a book whose short title is *Rihla* ("Journey"), but which is usually referred to as the *Travels* and whose full title is *A Gift to Those Who Contemplate the Wonders of Cities and the Marvels of Travelling,* a title that reflects the culture of reciprocity in which Ibn Battuta lived. In this selection, he describes his visit to the Somali coastal city of Mogadishu, part of the East African circuit of the Indian Ocean network of exchange.

. . . I lodged in ʻAdan with a merchant called Nāṣir al-Dīn al-Fa'rī. There used to come to his table every night about twenty of the merchants, and he had slaves and servants in still larger numbers. Yet with all this, they are men of piety, humility, uprightness and generous qualities, doing good to the stranger, giving liberally to the poor brother, and paying God's due in tithes as the Law commands. I met [also] in this city its pious qāḍī Sālim b. ʻAbdallāh al-Hindī; the father of this man had been a slave, employed as a porter, but the son devoted himself to learning and became a master and leader [in the religious sciences]. He is one of the best and worthiest of qāḍīs. I stayed as his guest for some days. . . .

We sailed on from there for fifteen nights and came to Maqdashaw, which is a town of enormous size. Its inhabitants are merchants possessed of vast resources; they own large numbers of camels, | of which they slaughter hundreds every day [for food], and also have quantities of sheep. In this place are manufactured the woven fabrics called after it, which are unequalled and exported from it to Egypt and elsewhere. It is the custom of the people of this town that, when a vessel reaches the anchorage, the *sumbuqs,* which are small boats, come out to it. In each *sumbuq* there are a number of young men of the town, each one of whom brings a covered platter containing food and presents it to one of the merchants on the ship saying 'This is my guest,' and each of the others does the same. The merchant, on disembarking, goes only to the house of his host among the young men, except those of them who have made frequent journeys to the town and have gained some acquaintance with its inhabitants; these lodge where they please. When he takes up residence with his host, the latter sells his goods for him | and buys for him; and if anyone buys anything from him at too low a price or sells to him in the absence of his host, that sale is held invalid by them. This practice is a profitable one for them.

When the young men came on board the vessel in which I was, one of them came up to me. My companions said to him 'This man is not a merchant, but a doctor of the law,' where-upon he called out to his friends and said to them 'This is the guest of the qāḍī.' There was among them one of the qāḍī's men, who informed him of this, and he came down to the beach with a number of students and sent one of them to me. I then disembarked with my companions and saluted him and his party. He said to me 'In the name of God, let us go to salute the Shaikh.' And who is the Shaikh?' I said, and he answered, 'The Sultan,' for it is their custom to call the sultan 'the Shaikh'. Then I said to him 'When I am lodged, I shall go to him,' but he said to me, 'It is the custom that whenever there comes a jurist I or a sharif or a man of religion, he must first see the sultan before taking a lodging.' So I went with him to the sultan, as they asked.

Account of the Sultan of Maqdashaw. The sultan of Maqdashaw is, as we have mentioned, called only by the title of 'the Shaikh'. His name is Abū Bakr, son of the shaikh 'Omar; he is by origin of the Barbara and he speaks in Maqdishī, but knows the Arabic language. One of his customs is that, when a vessel arrives, the sultan's *sumbuq* goes out to it, and enquiries are made as to the ship, whence it has come, who is its owner and its *rubbān* (that is, its captain), what is its cargo, and who has come on it of merchants and others. When all of this information has been collected, it is presented to the sultan, and if there are any persons [of such quality] that the sultan should assign a lodging to him as his guest, he does so.

When I arrived with the qāḍī I have mentioned, who was called Ibn al-Burhān, an Egyptian | by origin, at the sultan's residence, one of the serving-boys came out and saluted the qāḍī, who said to him 'Take word to the intendant's office and inform the Shaikh that this man has come from the land of al-Hijāz.' So he took the message, then returned bringing a plate on which were some leaves of betel and areca nuts. He gave me ten leaves along with a few of the nuts, the same to the qāḍī and what was left on the plate to my companions and the qāḍī's students. He brought also a jug of rose-water of Damascus, which he poured over me and over the qāḍī [i.e. over our hands], and said 'Our master commands that he be lodged in the students' house,' this being a building equipped for the entertainment of students of religion. The qāḍī took me by the hand and we went to this house, which is in the vicinity of the Shaikh's residence, and furnished with carpets and all necessary appointments. Later on [the serving boy] brought food from the Shaikh's residence. With him came one of his viziers, who was responsible for [the care of] the guests, and who said 'Our master greets you and says to you that you are heartily welcome.' He then set down the food and we ate. Their food is rice cooked with ghee, which they put into a large wooden platter, and on top of this they set platters of *kūshān*. This is the seasoning, made of chickens, fleshmeat, fish and vegetables. They cook unripe bananas in fresh milk and put this in one dish, and in another dish they put curdled milk, on which they place [pieces of] pickled lemon, bunches of pickled pepper steeped in vinegar and salted, green ginger, and mangoes. These resemble apples, but have a stone; when ripe they are exceedingly sweet and are eaten like [other] fruit, but before ripening they are acid like lemons, and they pickle them in vinegar. When they take a mouthful of rice, they eat some of these salted and vinegar conserves after it. A single person of the people of Maqdashaw eats as much as a whole company of us would eat, as a matter of habit, | and they are corpulent and fat in the extreme.

After we had eaten, the qāḍī took leave of us. We stayed there three days, food being brought to us three times a day, following their custom.

On the fourth day, which was a Friday, the qāḍī and students and one of the Shaikh's viziers came to me, bringing a set of robes; these [official] robes of theirs consist of a silk wrapper which one ties round his waist in place of drawers (for they have no acquaintance with these), a tunic of Egyptian linen with an embroidered border, a furred mantle of Jerusalem stuff, and an Egyptian turban with an embroidered edge. They also brought robes for my companions suitable to their position. We went to the congregational mosque and made our prayers behind the *maqṣūra*. When the Shaikh came out of the door of the *maqṣūra* I saluted him along with the qāḍī; he said a word of greeting, spoke in their tongue with the qāḍī, and then said in Arabic 'You are heartily | welcome, and you have honoured our land and given us pleasure.' He went out to the court of the mosque and stood by the grave of his father, who is buried there, then recited some verses from the Qur'ān and said a prayer. After this the viziers, amīrs, and officers of the troops came up and saluted him. Their manner of salutation is the same as the custom of the people of al-Yaman; one puts his forefinger to the ground, then raises it to his head and says 'May God prolong thy majesty.' The Shaikh then went out of the gate of the mosque, put on his sandals, ordered the qāḍī to put on his sandals and me to do likewise, and set out on foot for his residence, which is close to the mosque. All the [rest of the] people walked barefoot. Over his head were carried four canopies of coloured silk, with the figure of a bird in gold on top of each canopy. His garments on that day were a large green mantle of Jerusalem stuff, with fine robes of Egyptian stuffs with their appendages (?) underneath it, and he was girt with a waist-wrapper | of silk and turbaned with a large turban. In front of him were sounded drums and trumpets and fifes, and before and behind him were the commanders of the troops, while the qāḍī, the doctors of the law and the sharīfs walked alongside him. He entered his audience-hall in this disposition, and the viziers, amīrs and officers of the troops sat down in a gallery there. For the qāḍī there was spread a rug, on which no one may sit but he, and beside him were the jurists and sharīfs. They remained there until the hour of the afternoon prayer, and after they had prayed it, the whole body of troops came and stood in rows in order of their ranks. Thereafter the drums, fifes, trumpets and flutes are sounded; while they play no person moves or stirs from his place, and anyone who is walking stands still, moving neither backwards nor forwards. When the playing of the drum-band comes to an end, they salute I with their fingers as | we have described and withdraw. This is a custom of theirs on every Friday.

On the Saturday, the population comes to the Shaikh's gate and they sit in porticoes outside his residence. The qāḍī, jurists, sharīfs, men of religion, shaikhs and those who have made the Pilgrimage go in to the second audience-hall, where they sit on platforms prepared for that purpose. The qāḍī will be on a platform by himself, and each class of persons on the platform proper to them, which is shared by no others. The Shaikh then takes his seat in his hall and sends for the qāḍī, who sits down on his left ; thereafter the jurists enter, and the principal men amongst them sit down in front of the Shaikh, while the remainder salute and withdraw. Next the sharīfs come in, their principal men sit down in front of him, and the remainder salute and withdraw. If they are guests, they sit on the Shaikh's right. Next the shaikhs and pilgrims come in, and their principal men sit, and the rest salute and withdraw. Then come | the viziers, then the amīrs, then the officers of the troops, group after group, and they salute and withdraw. Food is brought in; the qāḍī and sharīfs and all those who are sitting in the hall eat in the presence of the Shaikh, and he eats with them. If he wishes to honour one of his principal amīrs, he sends for him, and the latter eats with them. The rest of the people eat in the dining-hall, and the order of eating is the same as their order of entry into the Shaikh's presence. The Shaikh then goes into his residence, and the qāḍī, with the viziers, the private secretary, and four of the principal amīrs, sits for deciding cases among the population and petitioners. Every case that is concerned with the rulings of the Divine Law is decided by the qāḍī, and all cases other than those are decided by the members of the council, that is to say, the viziers and amīrs. If any case calls for consultation of the sultan, they write to him about it, and he sends out the reply to them immediately on the reverse of the document as I determined by his judgement. And this too is their fixed custom. . . .

From: Ibn Battuta, C. Defremery, B. R. Sanguinetti, H. A. R. Gibb, C. F. Beckingham, and A. D. H. Bivar. 1958. *The travels of Ibn Battuta, A.D. 1325–1354.* London: Hakluyt Society. Vol. 2, pp. 372–378.

QUESTIONS:

1. Judging from Ibn Battuta's descriptions, what are some important elements of success for merchants operating in this part of the world? If someone wanted to become a merchant there, who or what would they need to know?
2. Ibn Battuta receives a welcome in Mogadishu as a "Doctor of Law". Why does this make him valuable to his hosts? What does his reception tell us about the unity of the Islamic world and about the variety within it?

CHAPTER 9

Traditional Worlds I: Inner Circuit Eurasia, 400 to 1100

INTRODUCTION

This chapter presents sources from the worlds of Inner Circuit Eurasia. These included the steppes themselves and the sedentary societies that surrounded them. The world of the central Asian steppes was home to the nomadic pastoralists whose armies of horse archers proved so formidable for millennia. The core sedentary societies that surrounded the steppes included China, north India, Islam, and Byzantium, with its newly emerging outpost in Russia. Since the steppe nomads themselves left almost no written sources down through 1100, we must view them through the eyes of their sedentary neighbors, who are usually hostile witnesses, reflecting the deep cultural divide between pastoralists and farming societies.

THE STEPPES

9.1a: *Descriptions of the Xiongnu* (Ban Biao, Ban Gu, Ban Zhao: *Han Shu,* first century CE)

The *Han Shu,* or Book of Han, is a history of the Former Han dynasty (206 BCE–25 CE) started by the court historian Ban Biao and continued by his son Ban Gu and his daughter Ban Zhao, China's first female court historian. This selection describes the early Han dealings with the Xiongnu, the dominant steppe people on China's northwestern frontier at the time. The selections describe a period in Han relations with the Xiongnu that can be described as conciliatory: the Chinese paid tribute to the Xiongnu (though the Chinese sources tend to call the goods gifts) and used diplomatic marriages and other techniques designed to acculturate the "barbarians" to Chinese ways. Later, under the martial emperor Han Wudi (140 BCE–87 BCE), the Han adopted a more aggressive policy of expansion and control. This worked for a time, but proved unsustainably expensive. Chinese policy under subsequent dynasties tended to oscillate between the poles of conciliation or passive defense and proactive management of the frontier (via aggression and at times conquest).

THE CUSTOMS OF THE XIONGNU

Previous to the time of Yao and Shun [legendary early Chinese rulers] we hear of a race called the mountain Jung. These were the Xiongnu, who inhabited the northern regions, and removed from place to place, according to the pasturage for their flocks and herds. The bulk of their stock consisted of horses, oxen and sheep; but in smaller numbers they bred likewise camels, asses, mules, horse-ass hybrids, wild horses and hybrids of the same. Removing their herds to find water and pasturage, they had no fixed cities, but dwelt on their rural patrimonies, each family having its allotted portion of land. They had no written characters, but performed oral contracts. The children rode on sheep, and shot birds and squirrels with the bow and arrow. When a little bigger, they shot foxes and hares, the flesh of which they ate. On reaching manhood, when able to bend a bow, they were fully equipped and mounted on horseback. In time of peace they hunted for their living; but when harassed by war, they cultivated martial exercises, to fit them for invasion or attack, which was agreeable to their disposition. The taller troops were armed with bows and arrows; the shorter with swords and spears. When successful in the contest, they pressed forward; but on meeting with a reverse, they retreated, and thought it no shame to run away. On gaining a victory they showed no regard to propriety or equity. From the king downwards all ate the flesh of domestic animals, and clothed themselves with the skins, wearing a fur covering over all. The able-bodied ate the fat and choice portions, while the aged ate and drank what was left. The strong and robust were held in esteem, while the old and feeble were treated with contempt. When a father died, they married their widowed mother; and when a brother died, it was customary to marry his widow. Their names were not transmitted to their descendants.

According to their laws, he who drew a sword a foot in length against another was put to death; anyone guilty of highway robbery was deprived of his family possessions. Small crimes were punished with the rack; and greater crimes with death. The longest imprisonment did not amount to ten days; and all the prisoners in the country only numbered a few individuals.

Early in the morning the Shen-yu [the chief of the Xiongnu] went outside the camp to worship the rising sun, and in the evening he worshipped the moon. . . . In funerals they used coffins and cases containing gold, silver and clothing; but they had no grave-mound, trees or mourning apparel. Several tens or even hundreds of near dependants and concubines were accustomed to follow their master's funeral.

In undertaking any military enterprise, they were always guided by the moon. When the moon was about full, they would engage in battle; but when on the wane, they withdrew from the contest. When one beheaded a captive in battle, he received a goblet of wine, and was allowed to retain the booty. Captives were given as slaves to their captors; so that in war, every man was struggling for personal profit. They were clever at leading the enemy into an ambuscade, and then surrounding them. The eagerness of the scramble was like birds flocking to the prey; but when calamity overtook them, they were dispersed like scattered tiles or passing clouds. Any one bringing home the body of a man slain in battle, got the property of the deceased.

DIPLOMACY ACROSS THE FRONTIER

[Xiongnu raids were] a cause of much anxiety to the Chinese, and eventually led the Emperor to adopt the notable expedient of sending a princess of the imperial house to Maou-tun [the first Xiongnu leader] for his consort.

The lady Ung-choo was selected, and conveyed to the home of her new lord by Liw King. It was hoped that the issue of this union might be more imbued with Chinese susceptibilities and tendencies, and thus be the more easily brought under control. In pursuance of the same policy, the Chinese sent yearly presents of raw and woven silk, wine, and food, thus aiming to cultivate Chinese tastes among them; and on each occasion the fraternal bond of peace and amity was renewed, so that for a time there was a cessation of Maou-tun's incursions. . . .

[In the year 176 BCE] Shen-yu resolved on a dispatch to the Emperor, to the following effect: "The Great Shen-yu, by the will of God ruler of the Xiongnu nation, respectfully salutes the Emperor of China. Formerly your Majesty was pleased to express your gratification on the conclusion of a treaty of peace and amity. In the same spirit the Right Sage prince bore without complaint the menacing insults of the Chinese officials on the border; till the matter assumed such dimensions, that it became a question of deliberation . . . how to avoid a breach of the treaty and maintain the fraternal relations. Once and again letters of remonstrance were received from Your Majesty; but when I dispatched an envoy with a reply, he did not return, nor was there any messenger from Your Majesty, while the case was treated by you as a cause for war. Now in consequence of a slight breach of the treaty by some petty officials, you pursued the Right Sage prince, till he was driven westward into the territories of the Yue-te. There, however, heaven favored our cause: our officers and troops were loyal and true; our horses were strong and spirited; and by slaughter, decapitation, subjugation and pacification, our army effected the complete reduction of the Yue-te; while Lou-lan, Wu-sun, Hoo-kee and the adjacent kingdoms, to the number of twenty-six in all, without exception, submitted to the Xiongnu; and thus all the bowmen nations are united as one family. Having also tranquillized the northern lands, we are now desirous that there should be a cessation of hostilities, and that the troops should send their horses to pasture. Let the past be forgotten and the treaty renewed; that the people on the borders may enjoy peace as it was in the days of old; and so the young may attain to maturity; the aged may live unmolested, and uninterrupted happiness prevail from age to age."

About the same time, the Chinese Emperor would seem to have been troubled with some suspicions regarding the Xiongnu, and dispatched the commissioner Ke Hoo-tseen with a letter, in which he requested Shen-yu to send him a camel, two riding horses and two studs of carriage horses. Uneasy about the approach of the Xiongnu to the stockades, he ordered all the officials and people dwelling on the borders to remove their habitations to a considerable distance. Shen-yu on his part complied with the Emperor's request, and sent forward the offerings with the above epistle. On the arrival of the missive at the Chinese court, during the summer of 175, a consultation was held to discuss the expediency of attacking the Xiongnu or renewing the treaty of peace with them. Peaceful counsels prevailed; it was the general opinion that Shen-yu having just acquired the prestige of victory over the Yue-te, it would be impolitic to make an attack on them then. Besides it was argued by some that the conquest of the Xiongnu territory would be of little advantage to China; the waters were salt and the country uninhabitable; so that the far wiser method would be to renew the treaty. The Emperor acceded to the suggestion.

Consequent on these deliberations, the following year an envoy was dispatched to the Xiongnu. The envoy carried a letter to the effect: "The Emperor of China respectfully salutes the Shen-yu of the Xiongnu. . . . [I]n recognition of your arduous achievements, I now beg to present you with a light figured lining imperial embroidered robe, a light long embroidered tunic, and a light variegated gown; also a golden hair comb, a gold ornamented waist-belt, and a buffalo-horn belt fastening; also ten pieces of twilled silk, thirty pieces of variegated silk, and forty pieces each of carnation satin and green silk." These articles were then handed over to the proper functionary, who caused them to be conveyed to the Shen-yu.

CHINESE AND XIONGNU CUSTOMS

In the 10th month of this year, Maou-tun died, and was succeeded by his son Ke-yuh, who assumed the title of "Venerable high" Shen-yu. On his accession, the Emperor Wan-te, following up the example and policy of his ancestor, sent a princess of the imperial house for a consort to the newly-elevated chieftain, and appointed the eunuch Chung-hing Yue to escort her to her new home. Yue would fain have excused himself, but the monarch overruled all his objections. "If I am compelled to go," he said, "it will be an unfortunate day for the house of Han." On reaching the Xiongnu camp, Yue, having resolved to make good his words, tendered his submission to the Shen-yu, who became much attached to him. The confidence thus established ensured to Yue a certain liberty of speech; and when he saw the Shen-yu giving way to a fondness for the dress and the food of China, he did not fail to raise a warning voice, and thus addressed his chief: "The entire Xiongnu population is not equal to that of one Chinese province; but one cause of their strength is the simplicity of their dress and food, in which they are independent of China. Now should your Highness change the national customs, and introduce a taste for Chinese luxuries, while the supply of these are only sufficient to meet about one fifth of the requirements, the Xiongnu will all go over to the Chinese. Suppose your people were clothed in Chinese silk, in riding about among the thorns and brush-wood their robes and tunics would be unavoidably torn and destroyed; and it is evident that for strength and durability they are not to be compared to good skin garments. It will be wise also to give up Chinese table delicacies, which are neither so convenient nor so wholesome as good milk and cream." Yue also instructed the officers of the Shen-yu in the art of keeping records, in order that they might preserve a register of the people and the cattle.

When the Emperor of China sent a letter eleven inches in length, inscribed "The Emperor respectfully salutes the Shen-yu of the Xiongnu," with presents and complimentary expressions, Chung-hing Yue induced the Shen-yu to send a return letter twelve inches long, with a larger and longer seal, and audaciously worded "The great Shen-yu of the Xiongnu, the offspring of heaven and earth, ordained by the sun and moon, respectfully salutes the Emperor of the Han," with the usual presents and complimentary expressions. When the Chinese envoy disparagingly remarked that the Xiongnu were wanting in their duty towards the aged, Chung-hing Yue replied, "You Chinese employ agricultural troops to defend the borders; but when they are sent on a military expedition, so miserably are they found in necessaries, is it not a fact that their aged parents deprive themselves of their warm clothing and comforts to supply their sons with requisite food during the campaign?" The envoy assented, and Yue continued, "The Xiongnu make war the business of life. The aged and infirm being unable to fight, the choice food is given to the healthy and robust, that they may be able to stand the fatigues of the camp. Thus father and sons are helpful to each other. How then can you say that the Xiongnu are wanting in their duty towards the aged?" Continuing the discussion, the envoy remarked, "Among the Xiongnu, father and son sleep in the same cabin. When the father dies, the son takes the mother to wife. When a brother dies, his widow is taken by a surviving brother. They neither wear cap nor sash, and know nothing of the rites of the entrance-hall or the guest-chamber." "As to that," replied Yue, "the Xiongnu live on their flocks and herds, and clothe themselves with the skins. The flocks being dependent on the herbage and water, it is necessary, from time to time, to remove to fresh localities. Hence, in time of danger, the men practice equestrian archery; and in the seasons of security, they live at ease and free from care. They have few restraints, and are unembarrassed by conventional forms.

The intercourse of prince and subject is simple and durable; and the government of the nation is consolidated as that of a single body. When a father or elder brother dies, the son or younger brother takes the widow to wife, as they abhor the mixture of families. Hence although there are disorders among the Xiongnu, yet they preserve the family stem untainted. Now in China, though they do not openly take the widows of their fathers and brothers to wife, yet while matrimonial etiquette requires more distant alliances, this is a fruitful source of murders; and even the change of the surname frequently arises from this custom. Then as to defects in the rites, the ill-feeling that is generated by stringency in the intercourse between superiors and inferiors is such that it may be said, by the time the edifice reaches the summit, the strength of the builders is utterly exhausted. The husbandman spends his force in the labors of tillage and mulberry culture, to procure a supply of food and clothing; and you build cities and outposts for self-defense. But in time of danger the people are not trained to warlike exercises; and in time of peace every one is taken up with his own business. Pshaw! People living in mud huts, with but half a costume and scarcely the power of intelligible speech, what have they to do with caps!" After that when the envoy wished to discuss the merits of Chinese civilization, Yue abruptly cut him short, saying, "Let not the Han envoy spend his words. The presentation of silks and grain from the Han to the Xiongnu is merely a clever device to estimate their numbers. Nor are these gifts in themselves without their drawbacks. On the contrary, when the grain is ripe, it is trodden down by mounted troops, and there is an end of their harvest, much misery and distress being the natural result."

From: Han Shu, A. Wylie, transl., in *Journal of the Anthropological Institute of Great Britain and Ireland,* vol. 3 (1874), 401–450.

QUESTIONS:

1. How do the Chinese and Xiongnu see each other? That is, what screen images does each project to the other? Are they projecting mutually comprehensible images? What allows them to do so?
2. What sources of information did the Chinese have about the Xiongnu? How accurate do you think the reports in these histories are? Was there an incentive to accuracy on the Chinese side? What was the purpose of these histories?

9.1b: "On the Huns" from *Res Gestae* (Ammianus Marcellinus, late fourth century CE)

Ammianus Marcellinus (c .325–c. 395) was a Greek officer in the Roman army. In retirement he wrote copiously on the history and politics of the Empire he knew. His *Res Gestae* also describes the various enemies Rome faced beyond (and increasingly within) its borders. Among these were the Huns, nomadic steppe peoples related to the Xiongnu known to the Chinese. Their appearance in the Roman world was the end result of a series of westward migrations initiated when Emperor Han Wudi reversed the conciliatory policy described in the *Han Shu* and expanded Chinese influence aggressively into the steppes. Ammianus's description, while exhibiting the prejudice of Romans (and sedentary people in general) against "uncivilized" nomads, is by Roman standards reasonably fair and, to the extent that it can be checked against archaeological records, seems to be pretty accurate.

1. However, the seed and origin of all the ruin and various disasters that the wrath of Mars [god of war] aroused, putting in turmoil all places with unwonted fires, we have found to be this. The people of the Huns, but little known from ancient records, dwelling beyond the Maeotic Sea near the ice-bound ocean, exceed every degree of savagery.

2. Since there the cheeks of the children are so deeply furrowed with the steel from their very birth, in order that the growth of hair, when it appears at the proper time, may be checked by the wrinkled scars, they grow old without beards and without any beauty, like eunuchs. They all have compact, strong limbs and thick necks, and are so monstrously ugly and misshapen, that one might take them for two-legged beasts or for the stumps, rough-hewn into images, that are used in putting sides to bridges.

3. But although they have the form of men, however ugly, they are so hardy in their mode of life that they have no need of fire nor of savory food, but eat the roots of wild plants and the half-raw flesh of any kind of animal whatever, which they put between their thighs and the backs of their horses, and thus warm it a little.

4. Never sheltering themselves with roofed houses, they avoid them as people avoid sepulchers as not fit for common use. Not even a cabin thatched with reeds is to be found among them; but they wander, traveling through mountains and woods, and accustom themselves to put up with frost and hunger and thirst from the cradle. These wanderers do not live under roofs unless under the greatest necessity, for they do not count their safety to be under roofs. . . .

6. They cover their heads with round caps and protect their hairy legs with goatskins; their shoes are formed upon no lasts, and so prevent their walking with free step. For this reason they are not at all adapted to battles on foot, but they are almost glued to their horses, which are hardy, it is true, but ugly, and sometimes they sit them women-fashion and thus perform their ordinary tasks. From their horses by night or day every one of that nation buys and sells, eats and drinks, and bowed over the narrow neck of the animal relaxes into a sleep so deep as to be accompanied by many dreams.

7. And when deliberation is called for about weighty matters, they all consult as a common body in that fashion. They are subject to no royal restraint, but they are content with the disorderly government of their important men, and led by them they force their way through every obstacle.

8. They also sometimes fight when provoked, and then they enter the battle drawn up in wedge-shaped masses, while their medley of voices makes a savage noise. And as they are lightly equipped for swift motion, and unexpected in action, they purposely divide suddenly into scattered bands and attack, rushing about in disorder here and there, dealing terrific slaughter; and because of their extraordinary rapidity of movement they are never seen to attack a rampart or pillage an enemy's camp.

9. And on this account you would not hesitate to call them the most terrible of all warriors, because they fight from a distance with missiles having sharp bone, instead of their usual points, joined to the shafts with wonderful skill; then they gallop over the intervening spaces and fight hand to hand with swords, regardless of their own lives; and while the enemy are guarding against wounds from the sabre-thrusts, they throw strips of cloth plaited into nooses over their opponents and so entangle them that they fetter their limbs and take from them the power of riding or walking.

10. None of them plow nor even touch a plow handle, for they live without settled abode, but constantly wander without home, law or stable source of food, with the wagons in which they live, like people always fleeing. . . .

From: Ammianus Marcellinus, *Res Gestae* 31.2 (available at http://www.thelatinlibrary.com/ammianus/31.shtml); Stephen Morillo, transl.

QUESTIONS:

1. Ammianus often describes the Huns in terms of negatives: "they do not have X; they do not do Y". What does this sort of description tell you about Ammianus and his frame values? Given this style of negative description, what do you think Ammianus might have missed in describing the Huns?
2. How does Ammianus's description of the Huns compare to the *Han Shu's* description of the Xiongnu? Are there common elements that might reflect something accurate about steppe pastoralist peoples?

CHINA

9.2a: *Poems* (Du Fu, 759, 766)

Du Fu (712–70) wanted to be a civil servant—a Confucian scholar-official—under the Tang dynasty, but circumstance and his own temperament prevented his ever attaining this goal except in minor posts for brief periods. Instead, he spent his life as a poet, writing on a vast variety of subjects in an equally wide range of styles. Along with his older contemporary Li Bo, he is considered one of China's greatest poets. He was an acute and sympathetic observer of the lives of those around him, perhaps because he shared in the hardships of the time. The last twenty years of his life were affected by chronic ill-health and even more by the devastating effects of the An-Lushan Rebellion (755–63), in which millions of Chinese died or were displaced. The first poem included here reflects these times. The second is more personal, showing something of the impulsive but thoughtful character of the poet himself.

Official at Stone Moat Village

At dusk, I stopped to rest at Stone Moat village,
An officer came that night to capture men.
The old man escaped by climbing over the wall,
The old wife went to look outside the door.
How angrily the officer now shouted,
How bitterly the wife did weep out loud!
I heard the words the wife was sending forth:
"Three sons of mine were sent to defend Yecheng.
From one of my sons, a letter has arrived,
The other two have recently died in battle.
The one who survived has kept alive for now,
The dead ones though have met their final end.
Inside this house, there are no people left,
There's just a grandson suckling on the breast.
The grandson's mother also cannot go,
She goes about without a skirt intact.
Although I'm an old woman with failing strength,
I ask you to take me with you tonight.
If you should need workers at Heyang,
I can prepare the morning meal for you."
Her voice then died away into the night,
I seemed to hear her sob and whimper still.
At dawn, before I set upon the road,
It's only from the old man that I part.

Many People Come to Visit and Bring Wine after I Fell Off My Horse, Drunk

I, Du Fu, the duke's elderly guest,
Finished my wine, drunkenly sang, and waved a golden halberd.
I mounted my horse and suddenly remembered the days of my youth,
The flying hooves sent stones pouring down into Qutang gorge.
Baidicheng's city gates are beyond the water's clouds,

Bending over, I plunged straight down eight thousand feet.
Whitewashed battlements passed like lightning, the purple reins were loose,
Then east, I reached the level ridge, out past heaven's cliff.
River villages and country halls vied to enter my eyes,
The whip hung down, the bridle drooped, I reached the crimson road.
All the ten thousand people amazed by my silver head,
I trusted to the riding and shooting skills of my rosy-cheeked youth.
How could I know that bursting its chest, hooves chasing the wind,
That racing horse, red with sweat, breathing spurts of jade,
Would unexpectedly take a tumble and end up injuring me?
In human life, taking pleasure often leads to shame.
That's why I'm feeling sad, lying on quilts and pillows,
Being in the sunset of my life only adds to the bother.
When I knew you'd come to visit, I wanted to hide my face,
With a bramble stick I manage to rise, leaning on a servant.
Then, after we've finished talking, we open our mouths and laugh,
Giving me support, you help to sweep by the clear stream's bend.
Wine and meat are piled up like mountains once again,
The feast starts: sad strings and brave bamboo sound out.
Together, we point to the western sun, not to be granted us long,
Noise and exclamations, then we tip the cup of clear wine.
Why did you have to hurry your horses, coming to ask after me?
Don't you remember Xi Kang, who nourished life and got killed?

From: http://www.chinese-poems.com/d12.html, http://www.chinese-poems.com/d47.html.

QUESTIONS:

1. What (if anything) connects the Chinese state to its people in Du Fu's first poem? If Du Fu had been a high Confucian official when he witnessed this scene, what might he have done?
2. Based on the second poem, what screen image of himself does Du Fu project? What frame values of Chinese culture make sense of that projection?

9.2b: *Further Reflections on the Things at Hand* (Chu Hsi, later twelfth century)

Chu Hsi (1130–1200) was the son of a local official in Song China, during a time of barbarian threats on the northern frontier, but also of economic growth and intellectual ferment. Chu showed early promise as a scholar, attaining the rough equivalent of a doctorate at eighteen when most at that level were at least thirty-five. He served off and on as an official himself, gaining a reputation for scrupulous honesty that at times earned him enemies. As a result, he refused public appointments and the factional politics that went with them for large portions of his career, devoting himself instead to writing. He built on the work of a group of scholars known as the Neo-Confucian School, whose main project was to respond to the challenge of Buddhism and Taoism. His synthesis of Neo-Confucianism became the standard version of this dominant philosophy thereafter. In these selections, he applies his philosophy to governance.

GOVERNING THE STATE

2. Master Chu said: It is only the sage who completes human relations, and it is only the ideal monarch who completes the rules of government. Certainly the common people do not reach up to this. However, in establishing the root of the mind, those who have completed them should be taken as a model, but those who do not complete them should not be taken as a standard.

3. Master Chu said: World affairs involve both ordinary and urgent matters, and court government concerns both ordinary and urgent events. If you handle ordinary matters as urgent everything becomes unduly critical and relentlessly faultfinding with no means of preserving the overall organization, while at court the atmosphere becomes very strained. But if you treat urgent affairs as ordinary you will become lax and negligent with no way of attending to critical matters, while world affairs daily grow worse. By balancing them, both problems will be gone.

4. Master Chu said: The senior officers determine the moral qualities and intellectual capabilities of those recommended to the ruler to carry out the affairs of state. They should not become sympathetic or friendly, but rather be completely objective about them. Their only concern is the nation, and in no way must they inject their own ideas lest they be unable to assist in this undertaking.

5. Master Chu said: Even though all things in the world are always inconstant and chainging, they are imbued with innumerable implications, still there is nothing that is not the ruler's concern.

The ruler's august person lies deep within the palace. Though the inner workings of his mind are not to be known, the results become manifest. They are like "what all eyes see and what all fingers point to," and can never be concealed.

This is why in ancient times the former sages and kings were cautious and wary and kept a firm grip on themselves. Whether they were in turbulent and unstable times, or in isolated and far-away places, they would focus and concentrate their mind, conquer and recover it. Like facing the spirits or approaching a steep precipice, there was not the slightest negligence.

6. Master Chu said: World order was not established by itself. The calculations of the ruler must be fair and just, impartial and unbiased, and only then will this order become interconnected and secure. Nor can the monarch correct it himself. He must be close to good and wise statesmen but keep distant from mean and selfish characters. By clearly explaining the attributes of rectitude and principle, and by blocking the road to selfishness and perversity, all of this can be realized and made right. . . .

9. Master Chu said: Anyone who is to be prime minister must prepare his one heart and two eyes. When the eyes are clear then one can know the honest and the dishonest. When the heart is impartial then one can advance the honest and retire the dishonest.

10. Someone asked about the comment that in the art of ruling one should know the essentials.

Master Chu said: Just so. If one is to manage a district or a county he should punish those who expose secrets, root out thieves and brigands, promote agriculture and sericulture [the raising of silkworms], and restrict the lower professions. If one attends court he must be open to the people, be familiar with the feelings of the people, and eliminate special interest groups and cliques. If one is going to be a senior official he must recruit wise and talented men, get rid of corrupt bureaucrats, remove extortion, and equally distribute power and labor. All of these measures follow an established form and should be handled in this way. If one is to be a close advisor to the emperor he should be outspoken and direct, as well as composed and taciturn. If one is going to administer a town or a village, he should be confidential and exercise self-control, and be personally incorrupt and reserved. But if you still move forward and do things [arrogance and pride] will injure the essentials. . . .

12. Master Chu said: The art of governing does not lie in exerting one's own strengths, but rather values the empire's excellence.

13. Master Chu said: The ruler should concentrate on the truth of intelligence and not seek merely the name of intelligence. Trusting senior officials, daily planning affairs, constantly analyzing arguments, all in order to determine the most appropriate line of action: this is the truth of intelligence. Being inattentive to one's advisors and unquestioningly accepting their words: this is the name of intelligence. . . .

16. Master Chu said: When it comes to the affairs of state there is not one man with the intelligence and ability who can execute them single handedly. This is why the ancient exemplars, even though their moral undertakings and resourceful methods were enough to do the job, still drew widely from the abilities of others in order to benefit. But before they used this acquired ability they gathered together their disciples to encourage and commend their accomplishments to build a large pool of them. So when the time came to use them they recommended their achievements, and displayed their abilities, and there was nothing that was not done.

17. Master Chu said: The most urgent aim of all the ancient exemplary individuals was nothing other than to gather throughout the world wise and virtuous men. The reason why they so urgently sought such wise and virtuous ones was not simply a desire to have their works compiled and edited by them, or to have their services to mankind praised just for appearance's sake. But it was in order to broaden their knowledge and thinking to heights never before reached, and to extend their thinking further than ever before. There were some who had not perfected goodness who used [the worthies] to correct it. Therefore, search for them as widely as possible, respect them as magnanimously as possible, and treat them as sincerely as possible. They had to have the worthies of the empire, known and unknown, all gladly come before them to correct their mistakes. After that, in their moral achievements, they never felt remorse about some hidden indignity. Rather, they were completely immersed in greatness. . . .

28. Master Chu said: In ancient times the learning of sage emperors and enlightened kings always began with pursuing the principles of things to the furthest extent and perfecting knowledge to the highest degree. If you make moral principles completely clear without even a hair of darkness, then naturally your intentions will be sincere and your mind upright, and they will respond to the affairs of the empire.

LAWS AND REGULATIONS

1. Master Chu said: Systems the world over are neither completely beneficial nor completely harmful, and so we must determine to what extent they are so.

2. Master Chu said: If we fail to observe whether someone is good or evil, or loyal or corrupt, but simply concerned with sectarian affairs, then the petty conniver will come up with schemes which are meant only to cover up his deeds. On the other hand, the gentleman relies only on impartiality and straight dealing, and is never devious. Frequently, however, there may be some discrimination and factionalism. Such cases that have occurred in the

Han and Tang, and even in our own era, are not all that distant.

3. Master Chu said: Systems are easily talked about, but where is there anyone to make them work?

4. Master Chu said: The gentleman should at all costs refrain from being excessively angry or spiteful with the mean man, but neither is there any reason to engage in close relations. . . .

20. Some students were discussing the demerits of the local government and feudal systems. Master Chu said: Generally speaking, any law must have its drawbacks. No law is perfect. The important thing lies in having the right men. If there are the right men, even though the laws are no good, there are still many benefits. But if there are the wrong men, there may be excellent laws, but of what benefit would they be? . . .

From: Chu Hsi, *Further Reflections of Things at Hand,* translation and commentary by Allen Wittenborn (Lanham, MD: University Press of America, 1991), 60–66, 129–134, 138.

QUESTIONS:

1. What audience does Chu Hsi seem to be writing for? Who does he seem to be arguing against? How practical does his advice sound?
2. What frame values shape Chu Hsi's principles of good government? What does he assume about government without even defending the assumptions?

9.3: Islam: *The Merits of the Turks* (Al-Jahiz, mid-ninth century)

Abū 'Uthman 'Amr ibn Baḥr al-Kinānī al-Baṣrī (776–869), known as al-Jāḥiẓ, was an Arabic writer under the Abbasid Caliphate. A scholar his entire life, he wrote on politics (which prompted an invitation from the Caliph to move from his home town of Basra to Baghdad to join the scholarly community there), religion, and biology, among many other topics—he wrote over two hundred books in the course of his career. He developed a theory of biological evolution that posited natural variability within species, environmental influences on the struggle for survival and reproduction, and resulting speciation. His view of environmental influences extended to cultural differences among human societies, as these selections show. The first explains why the Turks had come to dominate Islamic armed forces; the second discusses the cultural characteristics of different peoples. Moving back to Basra after more than fifty years in Baghdad, Al-Jāḥiẓ died at the age of ninety-three. Popular legend has it that he was killed instantly in his study when one of his piles of books fell on him.

. . . If the Turk's daily life were to be reckoned up in detail, he would be found to spend more time in the saddle than on the ground.

The Turk sometimes rides a stallion, sometimes a brood mare. Whether he is going to war, on a journey, out hunting or on any other errand, the brood mare follows behind with her foals. If he gets tired of hunting the enemy he hunts waterfowl. If he gets hungry, jogging up and down in the saddle, he has only to lay hands on one of his animals. If he gets thirsty, he milks one of his brood mares. If he needs to rest his mount, he vaults on to another without so much as putting his feet to the ground.

Of all living creatures he is the only one whose body can adapt itself to eating nothing but meat. As for his steed, leaves and shoots are all it needs; he gives it no shelter from the sun and no covering against the cold.

As regards ability to stand trotting, if the stamina of the border fighters, the posthorse outriders, the

Khārijites and the eunuchs were all combined in one man, they would not equal a Turk.

The Turk demands so much of his mount that only the toughest of his horses is equal to the task; even one that he had ridden to exhaustion, so as to be useless for his expeditions, would outdo a Khārijite's horse in staying-power, and no Ṭukhārī pony could compare with it.

The Turk is at one and the same time herdsman, groom, trainer, horse-dealer, farrier and rider: in short, a one-man team.

When the Turk travels with horsemen of other races, he covers twenty miles to their ten, leaving them and circling around to right and left, up on to the high ground and down to the bottom of the gullies, and shooting all the while at anything that runs, crawls, flies or stands still. The Turk never travels like the rest of the band, and never rides straight ahead. On a long, hard ride, when it is noon and the halting-place is still afar off, all are silent, oppressed with fatigue and overwhelmed with weariness. Their misery leaves no room for conversation. Everything round them crackles in the intense heat, or perhaps is frozen hard. As the journey drags on, even the toughest and most resolute begin to wish that the ground would open under their feet. At the sight of a mirage or a marker post on a ridge they are transported with joy, supposing it to be the halting-place. When at last they reach it, the horsemen all drop from the saddle and stagger about bandy-legged like children who have been given an enema, groaning like sick men, yawning to refresh themselves and stretching luxuriously to overcome their stiffness. But your Turk, though he has covered twice the distance and dislocated his shoulders with shooting, only to catch sight of a gazelle or an onager near the halting-place, or put up a fox or a hare, and he is off again at a gallop as though he had only just mounted. It might have been someone else who had done that long ride and endured all that weariness.

. . . Know that every nation, people, generation or tribe that shows itself outstanding in craftsmanship or pre-eminent in eloquence, the various branches of learning, the establishment of empires or the art of war, only attains the peak of perfection because God has steered it in that direction and given it the means and the special aptitudes appropriate to those activities. Peoples of varying habits of thought, different opinions and dissimilar characters cannot attain perfection unless they fulfil the conditions needed to carry on an activity, and have a natural aptitude for it. Good examples are the Chinese in craftsmanship, the Greeks in philosophy and literature, the Arabs in fields that we mean to deal with in their proper place, the Sāsānians in imperial administration, and the Turks in the art of war. Do you not see that the Greeks, who studied theory, were not merchants, artisans, sowers, farmers, builders, fruit-farmers, hoarders of treasure or men bent on making money by hard work? Their rulers absolved them from the necessity to work by providing for their needs; and hence they were free to engage in research, and (thanks to their single-mindedness, ingenuity and imaginativeness) to invent machines, tools and musical instruments—music which brings peace to the soul, relaxation after travail, and blessed balm for the ulcer of anxiety. They built for men's profit and edification scales, balances, astrolabes, hourglasses and other [instruments], and invented medicine, mathematics, geometry, music and engines of war such as the mangonel, etc. They were thinkers, not doers: they designed the machine, made a template and drew a model of the tool, but could not use it; they confined themselves to giving directions about instruments, without handling them themselves. They loved science, but shrank from its application.

The Chinese for their part are specialists in smelting, casting and metalworking, in fine colours, in sculpture, weaving and drawing; they are very skilful with their hands, whatever the medium, the technique or the cost of the materials. The Greeks are theoreticians rather than practitioners, while the Chinese are practitioners rather than theoreticians; the former are thinkers, the latter doers.

The Arabs, again, were not merchants, artisans, physicians, farmers—for that would have degraded them—mathematicians or fruit-farmers—for they wished to escape the humiliation of the tax; nor were they out to earn or amass money, hoard possessions or lay hands on other people's; they were not of those who make their living with a pair of scales, or [by giving short measure] in dried foods, and knew neither the *qīrāṭ* nor the *dānaq*; they were not poor enough to be indifferent to learning, pursued neither wealth, that breeds foolishness, nor good fortune, that begets apathy, and never tolerated humiliation, which was dishonour and death to their souls. They dwelt in the plains, and grew up in contemplation of the desert. They knew neither damp nor rising mist, neither fog nor foul air, nor a horizon bounded by walls. When these keen minds and clear brains turned to poetry, fine language, eloquence and oratory, to physiognomy and astrology, genealogy, navigation by the stars and by marks on the ground, and knowledge of *anwā'*, to horse-breeding, weaponry and engines of war, to memorizing all that they heard, pondering on everything that caught their attention and discriminating between the glories and the shames of their tribes, they achieved perfection beyond the wildest dreams. Certain of these activities broadened their minds and exalted their aspirations, so that of all nations they are now the most glorious and the most given to recalling their past splendours.

It is the same with the Turks who dwell in tents in the desert and keep hers: they are the Bedouins of the non-Arabs . . . Uninterested in craftsmanship or commerce, medicine, geometry, fruit-farming, building, digging canals or collecting taxes, they care only about raiding, hunting, horsemanship, skirmishing with rival chieftains, taking booty and invading other countries. Their efforts are all directed towards these activities, and they devote all their energies to these occupations. In this way they have acquired a mastery of these skills, which for them take the place of craftsmanship and commerce and constitute their only pleasure, their glory and the subject of all their conversation. Thus have they become in the realm of warfare what the Greeks are in philosophy, the Chinese in craftsmanship, and the Arabs in the fields we have enumerated.

From: Jahiẓ, and Charles Pellat, *The life and works of Jaḥiẓ* (Berkeley: University of California Press, 1969), pp. 93–97.

QUESTIONS:

1. Al-Jāḥiẓ projects vivid and specific images of various peoples of Inner Circuit Eurasia. What traits do the Arabs share with the non-Arabs according to al-Jāḥiẓ? What kind of screen image of the Arabs, the founders of the Islamic world, does al-Jāḥiẓ project?
2. What does al-Jāḥiẓ's knowledge of other peoples tell us about the network connections among Inner Circuit Eurasian hierarchies?

9.4: India: *A History of India* (Abū al-Rayhān al-Bīrūnī, c. 1030)

Abū al-Rayhān Muhammad ibn Ahmad al-Bīrūnī (973–1048) was a Persian Muslim scholar who spent most of his life in Ghzni (modern Afghanistan). Expert in multiple sciences, history, and linguistics (he knew at least eight languages), in 1017 he traveled to India and became the most important interpreter of Indian science and culture to the Islamic world. This selection gives his assessment of Hindu learning in his own time.

Before entering on our exposition, we must form an adequate idea of that which renders it so particularly difficult to penetrate to the essential nature of any Indian subject. The knowledge of these difficulties will either facilitate the progress of our work, or serve as an apology for any shortcomings of ours. For the reader must always bear in mind that the Hindus entirely differ from us in every respect, many a subject appearing intricate and obscure which would be perfectly clear if there were more connection between us. The barriers which separate Muslims and Hindus rest on different causes.

First, they differ from us in everything which other nations have in common. And here we first mention the language, although the difference of language also exists between other nations. . . .

Secondly, they totally differ from us in religion, as we believe in nothing in which they believe, and vice versa. On the whole, there is very little disputing about theological topics among themselves; at the utmost, they fight with words, but they will never stake their soul or body or their property on religious controversy. On the contrary, all their fanaticism is directed against those who do not belong to them—against all foreigners. They call them impure, and forbid having any connection with them, be it by intermarriage or any other kind of relation ship, or by sitting, eating, and drinking with them, because thereby, they think, they would be polluted. They consider as impure anything which touches the fire and the water of a foreigner; and no household can exist without these two elements. Besides, they never desire that a thing which once has been polluted should be purified and thus recovered, as, under ordinary circumstances, if anybody or anything has become unclean, he or it would strive to regain the state of purity. They are not allowed to receive anybody who does not belong to them, even if he wished it, or was inclined to their religion. This, too, renders any connection with them quite impossible, and constitutes the widest gulf between us and them.

In the third place, in all manners and usages they differ from us to such a degree as to frighten their children with us, with our dress, and our ways and customs, and as to declare us to be devil's breed, and our doings as the very opposite of all that is good and proper. By the way, we must confess in order to be just, that a similar depreciation of foreigners not only prevails among us and the Hindus, but is common to all nations towards each other. . . .

But then came Islam; the Persian empire perished, and the repugnance of the Hindus against foreigners increased more and more when the Muslims began to make their inroads into their country; for Muhammad Ibn al-Qasim entered Sind . . . and conquered the cities of Bahmanwa and Mulasthana, the former of which he called Al-mansura the latter Al-mamura. He entered India proper, and penetrated even as far as Kanauj, marched through the country of Gandhara, and on his way back, through the confines of Kashmir, sometimes fighting sword in hand, sometimes gaining his ends by treaties, leaving to the people their ancient belief, except in the case of those who wanted to become Muslims. All these events planted a deeply rooted hatred in their hearts.

Now in the following times no Muslim conqueror passed beyond the frontier of Kabul and the river Sind until the days of the Turks, when they seized the power in Ghazna under the Samani dynasty, and the supreme power fell to the lot of Sabuktagin. This prince chose the holy war as his calling, and therefore called himself al-Ghazi. In the interest of his successors he constructed, in order to weaken the Indian frontier, those roads on which afterwards his son Mahmud marched into India during a period of thirty years and more. God be merciful to both father and son! Mahmud utterly ruined the prosperity of the country, and performed there wonderful exploits, by which the Hindus became like atoms of dust scattered in all directions, and like a tale of old in the mouth of the people. Their scattered remains cherish, of course, the most inveterate aversion towards all Muslims. This is the reason, too, why Hindu sciences have retired far away from those parts of the country conquered by us, and have fled to places which our hand cannot yet reach, to Kashmir, Benares, and other places. And there the antagonism between them and all foreigners receives more and more nourishment both from political and religious sources.

In the fifth place, there are other causes, the mentioning of which sounds like satire—peculiarities of their national character, deeply rooted in them, but manifest to everybody. We can only say, folly is an illness for which there is no medicine, and the Hindus believe that there is no country but theirs, no nation like theirs, no kings like theirs, no religion like theirs, no science like theirs. They are haughty, foolishly vain, self-conceited, and stolid. They are by nature niggardly in communicating that which they know, and they take the greatest possible care to withhold it from men of another caste among their own people, still much more, of course, from any foreigner. According to their belief, there is no other country on earth but theirs, no other race of man but theirs, and no created beings besides them have any knowledge of science whatsoever. . . . If they traveled and mixed with other nations, they would soon change their mind, for their ancestors were not as narrow-minded as the present generation is. One of their scholars, Varahamihira, in a passage where he calls on the people to honor the Brahmins, says: "The Greeks, though impure, must be honored, since they were trained in sciences and therein excelled others. What, then, are we to say of a Brahmin, if he combines with his purity the height of science?" In former times, the Hindus used to acknowledge that the progress of science due to the Greeks is much more important than that which is due to themselves. But from this passage of Varahamihira alone you see what a self-lauding man he is, while he gives himself airs as doing justice to others. . . .

The heathen Greeks, before the rise of Christianity, held much the same opinions as the Hindus; their educated classes thought much the same as those of the Hindus; their common people held the same idolatrous views as those of the Hindus. Therefore I like to confront the theories of the one nation with those of the other simply on account of their close relationship, not in order to correct them. For that which is not the truth does not admit of any correction and all heathenism, whether Greek or Indian, is in its heart and soul one and the same belief, because it is only a deviation from the truth. The Greeks, however, had philosophers who, living in their country, discovered and worked out for them the elements of science, not of popular superstition, for it is the object of the upper classes to be guided by the results of science, while the common crowd will always be inclined to plunge into wrong-headed wrangling, as long as they are not kept down by fear of punishment. Think of Socrates when he opposed the crowd of his nation as to their idolatry and did not want to call the stars gods! At once eleven of the twelve judges of the Athenians agreed on a sentence of death, and Socrates died faithful to the truth.

The Hindus had no men of this stamp both capable and willing to bring sciences to a classical perfection. Therefore you mostly find that even the so-called scientific theorems of the Hindus are in a state of utter confusion, devoid of any logical order, and in the last instance always mixed up with the silly notions of the crowd, e.g. immense numbers, enormous spaces of time, and all kinds of religious dogmas, which the vulgar belief does not admit of being called into question. . . . I can only compare their mathematical and astronomical literature, as far as I know it, to a mixture of pearl shells and sour dates, or of pearls and dung, or of costly crystals and common pebbles. Both kinds of things are equal in their eyes, since they cannot raise themselves to the methods of a strictly scientific deduction.

From: Bīrūnī, Muḥammad ibn Aḥmad, and Eduard Sachau, *Alberuni's India an account of the religion, philosophy, literature, geography, chronology, astronomy, customs, laws and astrology of India about A.D. 1030* (London: K. Paul, Trench, Trübner, 1910).

QUESTIONS:

1. Al-Bīrūnī's fifth reason for the hostility between Hindus and Muslims sounds, as he says, like satire, or perhaps like an unfair polemic. But it follows four other reasons that sound sympathetic to the Hindus, or at the least objective. How believable is his fifth reason in light of the first four?
2. Al-Bīrūnī's report on India, including its sections comparing the Hindus with the Greeks of Socrates' time, was widely disseminated and influential. What does this tell us about the spread of his and other people's knowledge—of both contemporary and historical events—across the Afro-Eurasian network and about the audiences for such a work?

BYZANTIUM

9.5a: *Digenes Akritas* (c. twelfth century CE)

The epic poem *Digenes Akritas,* or the tale of Basil the "Two-Blooded Border Lord", is the best known of a set of oral epic songs or poems that originated in the Byzantine Empire between the seventh and eleventh centuries. This version of the poem was written down in the late eleventh or early twelfth century. Its hero, Basil, is the son of a Syrian Muslim emir and a Greek mother—thus the "Two Blooded". After kidnapping Basil's mother, the emir marries her and converts to Christianity. Basil grows up to be an heroic *akritas,* or border warrior. As a work of popular culture, the poem therefore gives us a valuable look at Byzantine provincial life and values; most Byzantine literature came from the scholarly elite in Constantinople.

. . . Record not Homer; nor Achilles' tales,
Nor Hector's; they are false. And Alexander
The Macedonian, mighty in purpose,
Was master of the world with God's assistance.
For with firm purpose he acknowledged God
From whom he had his valor and his daring.
But of old Philopappos, Ioannakes,
Or Kinnamos there's nothing worth the telling,
For they just boasted, but accomplished nothing.
But this man's deeds are true and well attested:
Ambron his grandsire, Karoës his uncle.
They gave three thousand chosen lancers to him;
He quelled all Syria and captured Kufah,
Then came to places in Romania,
Seized castles in the land of Heracles,
And plundered Charizané and Cappadocia.
He carried off the Ducas' charming daughter
Because of her great beauty and fine figure,
Denying everything, both faith and fame,
Becoming Orthodox, a Christian, for her;
The one-time foe appeared the slave of Romans.
To them a really lovely child was born
Who was named Basil from his very birth
And also Two-Blood from his parentage,
A pagan father and a Roman mother.
He became fearsome, as this tale will show,
And was named Border Lord from conquering borders.
Antakinos, one of the Kinnamades,
His grandsire, died, exiled by the Emperor,
Basil the Blesséd, mighty Border Lord.
His future had been bright, his fame immense;
All thought he was an excellent general.
His grandam was the General's wife, a Ducas;

His uncles were his mother's wondrous brothers
Who fought in single combat for their sister
Against the marvelous Emir, his father.
Thus he sprang from a race of noble Romans,
And was admired for his bravery.
So let us now begin to tell his deeds.
This Basil, then, the wonderful Border Lord,
Was given by his father to a teacher
In childhood, spending three whole years in lessons,
And, with his sharp mind he acquired much learning.
Then, wanting horsemanship and also hunting,
He spent each day on these things with his father.
And so one day he said this to his father:
"The wish, master and father, is in my soul
To test myself in warring with the beasts.
So, if you really love Basil, your son,
Let us go out some place where there are beasts,
And you'll quite see the thought that's troubling me."
. . .
The next morning he took his brother-in-law,
The one born latest, golden Constantine.
And took his son, the noble Border Lord,
And certain horsemen too from his Companions,
And went straight from the marsh up to the woods
Where from afar they saw ferocious bears;
There were a male, a female and two cubs.
His uncle cried, "Now Basil, let me watch you!
Take nothing but your club; carry no sword,
For fighting bears with swords is not commended."
It was a strange and awesome sight to see,
For when he heard his uncle's voice, the boy
Dismounted right away, loosened his belt,
Took off his tunic, for the heart was great,
Fastened his skirts up firmly to his belt,
Put a camel's hair cap upon his head,
And then like lightning jumped out of his cuirass,
Carrying nothing but a simple staff.
He had great strength, and speed to go with it.
Now when they had approached close to the bears,
The female, jealous of her cubs, met him,
And loudly bellowing, came out towards him,
He inexperienced in fighting beasts,
Did not swing back so he could use his club,
But attacked quickly, caught her by the middle,
And squeezing with his arms, he strangled her
So that her entrails all came out of her mouth.
The male ran out again into the marsh.
His uncle called, "Don't let him get away, son!"
In his great hurry he had dropped his club,
So, flying like an eagle, he caught the beast.
The bear turned on him, opened its mouth wide,
And rushed to gobble down the youngster's head.
But the boy quickly seized it by the jowl,
Shook the beast, killed it, threw it on the ground,
Twisting its neck so that he broke its spine,
And straightway it expired in the young man's hands. . . .

[Basil meets and secretly marries the daughter of a prominent General. He announces the deed and rides off with her, pursued by an army of the General's men.]

. . . Just as the light of day was growing bright,
They overtook them down in the dark plains.
The lovely maiden saw them from afar,
For she was looking back, and watching keenly
While held close in the arms of her belovéd,
And spoke these words to him, clutching him tightly:
"Exert yourself, dear, lest they separate us;
And whip the black horse on with all your strength.
Look, our pursuers are about to catch us!"
When he heard this, that marvelous young man
Was filled with courage, and turning from the road,
He found a double tree which had two branches,
And set the girl down in between the branches.
"Sit there, my lovely one, and watch your darling,"
And then straightway he armed himself completely.
Then said the sun-born maiden to the boy,
"Take care you do no injury to my brothers!"
Then a strange thing was shown to those there present:
All by himself he dared encounter thousands,
And in a short time slaughtered countless soldiers,
All fully armed and mounted, trained for war.
He first advised them to turn back again,
And not to undertake to test his valor,
But they, ashamed to have one man defeat them,
Preferred to die instead of being shamed.
He started forward, drawing out his sword-club,
And, ere the General came, not one was left.
Then, finally finished with his war, the boy
Came back, a victor, to the girl, rejoicing,
Got off his horse, and kissed her countless times:
"Delightful girl, you've proof of deeds in me."
The maid herself admiring him still more,
Accepted with delight his noisy kisses,
And spoke to the boy quietly as follows:
"Don't injure my own brothers, dearest soul;
For those whom you see coming towards us now
I judge to be my brothers, from their horses;
The third man who is with them is my father.
Return them to me safe; keep them unharmed."
"It shall be as you wish," he told the girl,
"Unless some unexpected thing occurs,
For he who spares his foes in time of war
Is often slain unfeelingly by them."
Saying these words he leaped upon his horse,
And fell on those around the General.
The brothers of the maiden, filled with zeal,
Told their companions that they should destroy him,
Planning that other hands should murder him.
The boy observed his dearest one's behest,
Attacked with skill, and wisely killed them all.
The brothers charged down on him furiously.
He circled them, and threw them from their horses
So neatly that he did not harm nor wound them.
Then turning toward the General, he dismounted,
Clasped his hands tight, and bowing low to him,

Began to speak to him with a bold look:
"Forgive me, master. Do not censure me.
Your troops are clods the way they strike and parry,
And therefore most of them have gone to Hell.
But I'm not of ignoble, coward stock,
And so if you will bid me do you service,
You'll be assured about your son-in-law.
And if you'll test me strictly by my deeds,
You'll often bless yourself for your good fortune."
At once the General raised his hands on high,
And looking towards the east, gave thanks to God:
"Glory to Thee, God; all that profits us
Thou orderest with inexpressible wisdom.
For I'm vouchsafed the son-in-law I wished,
Handsome and well born, temperate and brave,
Such as none ever found in the whole world."
. . . And once again there was a grand arrival.
Then, since the youth had shown that he was worthy,
And had become renowned for his exploits,
For he'd made good in almost all the world,
He chose to live alone upon the border,
And took his girl and his own servants with him.
He had an endless longing to live alone,
And walk around alone with no one with him.
In fact, where he had gone he had his own tent
In which he and the girl lived all alone.
Her two maidservants had another tent,
The Border Lord's Companions still another,
And each was a great distance from the others.
Now many of the outlaws heard about this,
And hatched a plot to carry off the girl.
He overcame them, and he slew them all
Just as he conquered all of Babylon,
Tarsus, Baghdad, the Mavrochionites,
And other parts of the dread Ethiops' land.
On hearing of these deeds, the Emperor
Who at that time was governing the Romans,
Basil the Blesséd, the great trophy winner,
Whose imperial fame was buried with him,
Chanced to be on campaign against the Persians
In those same places where the boy was living,
And when he heard about it was amazed.
So wishing greatly he might see the youth,
He sent a letter to him with these words:
"We've learned the stories of your many exploits,
My son, and we have much rejoiced in them,
And offered thanks to God who works with you.
Our purpose is to see you with our own eyes,
And give requital worthy of your deeds.
Come to us gladly, without hesitation,
And don't suspect you'll suffer hurt from us."
When he received this, he returned an answer:
"I am your majesty's most abject slave;
Indeed, I have no right to your good things.
Master, what deed of mine do you admire,
Who am so humble, base, and quite undaring?
Still, he who trusts in God can do all things.
Therefore, since you desire to see your servant,
Be by the Euphrates after a little while.
You'll see me all you wish, my sacred master.
Don't think that I refuse to come before you,
But you have certain inexperienced soldiers,

And if perhaps they say something they shouldn't,
I certainly would deprive you of such men,
For such things, master, happen to the young."
The Emperor read his letter word by word,
Admired the humbleness of the boy's statement,
And understood with pleasure his high courage.
Since he wished strongly to behold the youth,
He took along with him a hundred soldiers,
Some spearmen too, and went to the Euphrates,
Ordering all on no account to utter
A word offensive to the Border Lord.
Those posted to keep watch on his account
Shortly announced the Emperor's arrival
To the marvelous Two-Blood Border Lord.
The Two-Blood came out all alone to meet him,
And bowed his head down to the ground, and said,
"Hail, you who take imperial power from God,
And rule us all because of the heathen's sins.
Why has it happened that the whole world's master
Comes before me, who am of no account?"
The Emperor, astonished when he saw him,
Forgot the burden of his majesty,
Advanced a little from his throne, embraced him,
Joyfully kissed him, and admired his stature,
And the great promise of his well-formed beauty.
"My son," he said, "you've proof of all your deeds;
The way you're put together shows your courage.
Would that Romania had four such men!
So speak, my son, freely and openly,
And then take anything you wish from us."
"Keep everything, my lord," the boy replied,
"Because your love alone is enough for me.
It's not more blesséd to receive than give;
You have immense expenses in your army.
So I beseech your glorious majesty:
Love him who is obedient, pity the poor,
Deliver the oppressed from malefactors,
Forgive those who unwittingly make blunders,
And heed no slanders, nor accept injustice,
Sweep heretics out, confirm the orthodox.
These, master, are the arms of righteousness
With which you can prevail over all foes.
To rule and reign are not part of that power
Which God and His right hand alone can give.
Vile as I am, I grant your majesty
To take what you once gave Iconium
As tribute, and as much again, from them.
Master, I'll make you carefree about this
Until my soul shakes off this mortal coil."
The Emperor was delighted at these words.
"O marvelous and excellent young man,"
He said, "we name you a patrician now,
And grant you all your grandfather's estates;
We give to you the power to rule the borders,
And will confirm this with a golden bull,
And furnish you with rich imperial raiment."
So spoke the Emperor. The youth at once
Ordered one of his wild, unbroken horses
Brought before them, hobbled in iron chains.
He told his boys to release it: "Let it run!"
Fastened his skirts up firmly to his belt,
Then started running after it to catch it,
And in a little space he grasped its mane,
And turned the big, wild beast around backwards,
Kicking and plunging, trying to escape.
When the boy came before the Emperor,
He threw it down, spread flat upon the ground.
All were astonished at the marvelous sight.

He wished to leave. A lion from the grove
Came out, and startled those there present
with him
(For there were many lions in that place),
And even the Emperor had turned to flee.
The boy ran up at once toward the lion,
And seizing it by one of its hind legs,
He shook it hard, and dashed it to the ground,
Displaying it quite dead while all were
watching.
Then in his hand, held like a hare, he
brought it
Before the Emperor, and said, "Accept
The game your servant hunted for you,
master."
All were astonished and began to tremble;
They recognized his strength was super-
human.
The Emperor, with his hands stretched
toward heaven,
Said, "Glory to Thee, Master, Maker of all
things,
Who made me worthy to see such a man,
Strong above all the present generation!"
He ordered the lion's skin to be picked up,
And made the boy a lot of promises.
They embraced each other, and at once
withdrew,
One to his troops, the other to his girl.
Thenceforth the story was confirmed by all:
The boy was called Basil the Border Lord
From the gold bull that he should rule the
borders.
. . .

From: Hull, Denison Bingham, *Digenis Akritas; the two-blood border lord. The Grottaferrata version* (Athens: Ohio University Press, 1972), pp. 33–63.

QUESTIONS:

1. What characteristics make Basil heroic? Does his Christianity play a major role in his heroic identity?
2. What relationship between the border provinces and the Emperor in Constantinople does the poem portray?

9.5b: *The Russian Primary Chronicle* (c. 1113)

The Russian *Primary Chronicle* is a history of Kievan Rus from the mid-800s to 1110, written in Kiev shortly after its end date. It is the crucial source for the early history of the Eastern Slavs and their rulers, who came from Scandinavian Viking heritage. It is in many ways similar to Gregory of Tours' *History of the Franks,* as it presents the tale of a pagan people who convert to Christianity and construct a collective identity. The excerpts presented here tell two stories. First is the account of how the brothers Constantine (Cyril) and Methodius invented the Cyrillic alphabet so that the Gospels could be translated into Slavic. Second is the story of the conversion of the Slavs under their ruler Vladimir.

There was at the time but one Slavic race including the Slavs who settled along the Danube and were subjugated by the Magyars, as well as the Moravians, the Czechs, the Lyakhs, and the Polyanians, the last of whom are now called Rus'. It was for these Moravians that Slavic books were first written, and this writing prevails also in Rus' and among the Danubian Bulgarians. When the Moravian Slavs and their princes were living in baptism, the Princes Rostislav, Svyatopolk, and Kotsel sent messengers to the Emperor Michael, saying, "Our nation is baptized, and yet we have no teacher to direct and instruct us and interpret the sacred scriptures. We understand neither Greek nor Latin. Some teach us one thing and some another. Furthermore, we do not understand written characters nor their meaning.

Therefore send us teachers who can make known to us the words of the scriptures and their sense." The Emperor Michael, upon hearing their request, called together all the scholars, and reported to them the message of the Slavic princes. The scholars suggested that there was a man in Salonika, by name Leo, who had two sons familiar with the Slavic tongue, being learned men as well. When the Emperor was thus informed, he immediately summoned the sons of Leo from Salonika, directing him to send to court forthwith his sons Methodius and Constantine [who later took the name Cyril]. . . . The Emperor prevailed upon them to undertake the mission, and sent them into the Slavic country to Rostislav, Svyatopolk, and Kotsel. When they arrived, they undertook to compose a Slavic alphabet, and translated the Acts and the Gospel. The Slavs rejoiced to hear the greatness of God extolled in their native tongue. The apostles afterward translated the Psalter, the Oktoechos, and other books.

Now some zealots began to condemn the Slavic books, contending that it was not right for any other nation to have its own alphabet apart from the Hebrews, the Greeks, and the Latins, according to Pilate's superscription, which he composed for the Lord's Cross. When the Pope at Rome heard of this situation, he rebuked those who murmured against the Slavic books, saying, "Let the word of the Scripture be fulfilled that 'all nations shall praise God' (Ps. lxxi, 17), and likewise that 'all nations shall declare the majesty of God according as the Holy Spirit shall grant them to speak' (cf. Acts, ii, 4). Whosoever condemns the Slavic writing shall be excluded from the Church until he mend his ways. For such men are not sheep but wolves; by their fruits ye shall know them and guard against them. Children of God, hearken unto his teachings, and depart not from the ecclesiastical rule which Methodius your teacher has appointed unto you." Constantine then returned again, and went to instruct the people of Bulgaria; but Methodius remained in Moravia.

Prince Kotsel appointed Methodius Bishop of Pannonia in the see of St. Andronicus, one of the Seventy, a disciple of the holy Apostle Paul. Methodius chose two priests who were very rapid writers, and translated the whole Scriptures in full from Greek into Slavic in six months between March and the twenty-sixth day of October. After completing the task, he appropriately rendered praise and honor to God. . . .

6495 (987). Vladimir summoned together his boyars and the city-elders, and said to them, "Behold, the Bulgars came before me urging me to accept their religion. Then came the Germans and praised their own faith; and after them came the Jews. Finally the Greeks appeared, criticizing all other faiths but commending their own, and they spoke at length, telling the history of the whole world from its beginning. Their words were artful, and it was wondrous to listen and pleasant to hear them. They preach the existence of another world. 'Whoever adopts our religion and then dies shall arise and live forever. But whosoever embraces another faith, shall be consumed with fire in the next world.' What is your opinion on this subject, and what do you answer?" The boyars and the elders replied, "You know, oh Prince, that no man condemns his own possessions, but praises them instead. If you desire to make certain, you have servants at your disposal. Send them to inquire about the ritual of each and how he worships God."

Their counsel pleased the prince and all the people, so that they chose good and wise men to the number of ten, and directed them to go first among the Bulgars and inspect their faith. The emissaries went their way, and when they arrived at their destination they beheld the disgraceful actions of the Bulgars and their worship in the mosque; then they returned to their country. Vladimir then instructed them to go likewise among the Germans, and examine their faith, and finally to visit the Greeks. They thus went into Germany, and after viewing the German ceremonial, they proceeded to Tsargrad, where they appeared before the Emperor. He inquired on what mission they had come, and they reported to him all that had occurred. When the Emperor heard their words, he rejoiced, and did them great honor on that very day.

On the morrow, the Emperor sent a message to the Patriarch to inform him that a Rus' delegation had arrived to examine the Greek faith, and directed him to prepare the church and the clergy, and to array himself in his sacerdotal robes, so that the Rus' might behold the glory of the God of the Greeks. When the Patriarch received these commands, he bade the clergy assemble, and they performed the customary rites. They burned incense, and the choirs sang hymns. The Emperor accompanied the Rus' to the church, and placed them in a wide space, calling their attention to the beauty of the edifice, the chanting, and the pontifical services and the ministry of the deacons, while he explained to them the worship of his God. The Rus' were astonished, and in their wonder praised the Greek ceremonial. Then the Emperors Basil and Constantine invited the envoys to their presence, and said, "Go hence to your native country," and dismissed them with valuable presents and great honor.

Thus they returned to their own country, and the Prince called together his boyars and the elders. Vladimir then announced the return of the envoys who had been sent out, and suggested that their report be heard. . . . The envoys reported, "When we journeyed among the Bulgars, we beheld how they worship in their temple, called a mosque, while they stand ungirt. The Bulgar bows, sits down, looks hither and thither like one possessed, and there is no happiness among them, but instead only sorrow and a dreadful stench. Their religion is not good. Then we went among the Germans, and saw them performing many ceremonies in their temples; but we beheld no glory there. Then we went to Greece, and the Greeks led us to the edifices where they worship their God, and we knew not whether we were in heaven or on earth. For on earth there is no such splendor or such beauty, and we are at a loss how to describe it. We only know that God dwells there among men, and their service is fairer than the ceremonies of other nations. For we cannot forget that beauty. Every man, after tasting something sweet, is afterward unwilling to accept that which is bitter, and therefore we cannot dwell longer here." Then the boyars spoke and said, "If the Greek faith were evil, it would not have been adopted by your grandmother Olga who was wiser than all other men." Vladimir then inquired where they should all accept baptism, and they replied that the decision rested with him.

After a year had passed, in 6496 (988), Vladimir proceeded with an armed force against Kherson, a Greek city, and the people of Kherson barricaded themselves therein. . . . Then a man of Kherson, Anastasius by name, shot into the Rus' camp an arrow on which he had written, "There are springs behind you to the east, from which water flows in pipes. Dig down and cut them off." When Vladimir received this information, he raised his eyes to heaven and vowed that if this hope was realized, he would be baptized. He gave orders straightway to dig down above the pipes, and the water-supply was thus cut off. The inhabitants were accordingly overcome by thirst, and surrendered.

Vladimir and his retinue entered the city, and he sent messages to the Emperors Basil and Constantine, saying, "Behold, I have captured your glorious city. I have also heard that you have an unwedded sister. Unless you give her to me to wife, I shall deal with your own city as I have with Kherson." When the Emperors heard this message they were troubled, and replied, "It is not meet for Christians to give in marriage to pagans. If you are baptized, you shall have her to wife, inherit the kingdom of God, and be our companion in the faith. Unless you do so, however, we cannot give you our sister in marriage." When Vladimir learned their response, he directed the envoys of the Emperors to report to the latter that he was willing to accept baptism, having already given some study to their religion, and that the Greek faith and ritual, as described by the emissaries sent to examine it, had pleased him well. When the Emperors heard this report, they rejoiced, and persuaded their sister Anna to consent to the match. They then requested Vladimir to submit to baptism before they should send their sister to him, but Vladimir desired that the Princess should herself bring priests to baptize him. The Emperors complied with his request, and sent forth their sister, accompanied by some dignitaries and priests. Anna, however, departed with reluctance. "It is as if I were setting out into captivity," she lamented; "better were it for me to die at home." But her brothers protested, "Through your agency God turns the land of Rus' to repentance, and you will relieve Greece from the danger of grievous war. Do you not see how much harm the Rus' have already brought upon the Greeks? If you do not set out, they may bring on us the same misfortunes." It was thus that they overcame her hesitation only with great difficulty. The Princess embarked upon a ship, and after tearfully embracing her kinfolk, she set forth across the sea and arrived at Kherson. The natives came forth to greet her, and conducted her into the city, where they settled her in the palace.

By divine agency, Vladimir was suffering at that moment from a disease of the eyes, and could see nothing, being in great distress. The Princess declared to him that if he desired to be relieved of this disease, he should be baptized with all speed, otherwise it could not be cured. When Vladimir heard her message, he said, "If this proves true, then of a surety is the God of the Christians great," and gave order that he should be baptized. The Bishop of Kherson, together with the Princess's priests, after announcing the tidings, baptized Vladimir, and as the Bishop laid his hand upon him, he straightway received his sight. Upon experiencing this miraculous cure, Vladimir glorified God, saying, "I have now perceived the one true God." When his followers beheld this miracle, many of them were also baptized.

From: Nestor, Samuel H. Cross, and Olgerd P. Sherbowitz-Wetzor, *The Russian Primary chronicle Laurentian text* (Cambridge, MA: Mediaeval Academy of America, 1953), pp. 62–63, 110–13.

QUESTIONS:

1. What does the invention of a new alphabet and the translation of the Gospels tell you about the audiences that Constantine and Methodius thought they would reach and the social structure of the society they were trying to convert?
2. What factors led Vladimir and the Rus to convert to Orthodox Christianity? What are the similarities and differences between Vladimir's and Clovis's conversions?

CHAPTER 10

Traditional Worlds II: Outer Circuit Afro-Eurasia, 400 to 1100

INTRODUCTION

This chapter presents sources from the worlds of Outer Circuit Afro-Eurasia. Buffered from the threat of the steppes by the core Inner Circuit worlds of Chapter 9, which provided cultural models for many Outer Circuit societies, these societies developed their own cultural trajectories. The sources presented here reflect at least two themes that tended to arise for such societies: the tension between imitating the core worlds versus establishing a distinct identity; and the prominent role of warrior elites in many of these societies.

10.1: *The Tale of Genji* (Murasaki Shikubu, 1021)

Murasaki Shikubu (c. 973–c. 1031) was the daughter of a minor court official and member of a secondary line of the Fujiwara clan, the family that dominated Japanese in the Heian period through their close marriage ties to the imperial family. Widowed when she was still young, she became the tutor of the young empress and a close observer of the stylized but fiercely competitive sexual politics of the aristocratic Heian court. She wove her observations into *The Tale of Genji,* a book often and justifiably referred to as the world's first novel. It is a story of Genji, the talented but illegitimate son of an emperor. The outline of the story follows Genji from his youth as a star of the court to his mature understanding, in good Buddhist fashion, of the ephemeral nature of the physical world. In this selection Genji takes part in a celebration, the centerpiece of which is a ceremonial dance Genji performs with his friend and court rival Tō-no-Chūjō. The other characters we meet are the Fujitsubo lady, Genji's lover and the current wife of Genji's father, the emperor; and Lady Murasaki, a ten-year-old girl Genji has adopted and who will eventually be his wife. Welcome to Heian soap opera!

A CELEBRATION AMID AUTUMN LEAVES

The emperor's visit to the Suzakuin was to take place soon after the tenth of the tenth month. Since it promised to be much more interesting than the usual imperial excursion, the consorts were upset about missing the spectacle. The emperor himself felt that something would be lacking if the Fujitsubo lady were not able to see the dances, and he arranged for a rehearsal in the courtyard outside his private residence.

Genji danced "The Waves of the Blue Sea." His partner, Tō-no-chūjō, was extraordinarily handsome and confident, but he was like a nondescript mountain tree alongside a blossoming cherry. It was a moment of absorbing interest, the music especially beautiful in the glittering rays of the setting sun; and Genji's dancing and demeanor seemed to belong to another realm of existence, familiar though the piece was. When he chanted the Chinese lines, it was like hearing the voice of a *kalaviṇka* bird in paradise. The emperor wiped away tears of admiration, and all the senior nobles and princes wept.

When Genji straightened his sleeves at the end of the chant, the waiting musicians resumed in a tempo so spirited that he flushed and looked even more radiant than usual. "His is the kind of face a heavenly spirit might take a notion to carry off. I call it creepy," said the crown prince's mother, ill-pleased by the brilliance of the performance. Her young attendants considered the remark distasteful.

The Fujitsubo lady thought that she might have enjoyed his dancing more if her mind had not been tormented by the heinous impropriety of their relationship, which seemed more dream than reality. She spent the night with the emperor.

"It seemed to me that 'The Waves of the Blue Sea' swept the board in the rehearsal today," the emperor said to her. "What did you think of it?"

Conscious of a strange awkwardness, she replied merely, "It was remarkable."

"Tō-no-chūjō wasn't at all bad, either," he said. "There's something distinctive about the way the son of a good house moves and gestures. Our famous professionals are highly accomplished, of course, but they can't create the same effect of fresh, youthful charm. After such a dazzling rehearsal, I'm afraid the real event under the autumn foliage may be an anticlimax, but I arranged this because I wanted you to see it."

Early the next morning, the lady received a letter from Genii. "How did the performance strike you? I've never felt as agitated as I did during my dance." [His poem:]

Did you understand
the sentiments of the one
who fluttered his sleeves,
all but unable to dance
for the burden of grief he bore?

"But I ought not to write this way."

She sent an answer, apparently unable to let the message pass in silence while the beauty of his face and figure was still vivid in her mind:

Though I know not why
a man of Cathay might have wished
to flutter his sleeves,
I watched every movement
with the deepest feeling.

"I was exceptionally impressed."

For Genji, it was the most precious of gifts. "She's even a connoisseur of dance, and she's already talking like an empress with that reference to ancient China," he thought, an unconscious smile on his lips. He sat gazing at the letter, which he had spread with as much care as if it had been his special sutra.

The emperor was attended on his excursion by the entire court, princes and all. The crown prince also made the journey. The musicians' boats moved across the lake as usual, and there were innumerable dances, both Chinese and Korean. The sounds of instruments and the throbbing of drums filled the air. After having watched Genji in the late sunlight on the day of the rehearsal, the emperor had felt uneasy enough to commission sutra recitations at various temples, a precaution that received sympathetic approval from all who heard of it—all, that is, except the crown prince's disapproving mother, who considered it excessive. Nobody who was not a recognized expert had been selected for the flutists' circle, which included both courtiers and men of lower rank. The two groups of dances, those of the left and those of the right, were under the supervision of two consultants, Saemon-no-kami and

Uemon-no-kami. The performers had been rehearsing in the seclusion of their homes, with the finest dancing masters as coaches.

The wind in the pines, a veritable mountain gale, gusted in concert with the strains of the flutes, which were played with indescribable beauty by forty men standing in a circle under the tall maple trees; and the spectacle was almost frightening to behold when Genji emerged from among the swirling colored leaves, dancing "The Waves of the Blue Sea" with dazzling brilliance. Upon observing that most of the leaves had fallen from the maple twig in his headdress, making it a poor match for his glowing face, the major captain of the left picked some chrysanthemums from the garden as a substitute. A few scattered raindrops fell in the waning light, as though the very heavens had been moved to admiration. Genii danced that day as never before, his beauty enhanced by the delightful hues of the fading chrysanthemums, and his performance of the withdrawal was chilling in its perfection, a thing not of this world. Even among the menials who watched from behind trees, rocks, and piles of leaves—people who could scarcely have been expected to appreciate what they saw—those who possessed a modicum of taste were moved to tears.

Second only to "The Waves of the Blue Sea" was "The Song of the Autumn Wind," danced by the emperor's fourth son (the offspring of the Shōkyōden lady), who was still a child. The two performances exhausted the spectators' capacity for enjoyment. The other numbers attracted little attention, and actually seemed to detract from the occasion.

That night, Genji was granted senior third rank, and Tō-no-chūjō received senior fourth lower rank. All the eligible senior nobles also enjoyed suitable promotions, thanks to their association with Genji's triumph. One wondered what deed in a previous life might have enabled him to both astonish people's eyes and delight their hearts. . . .

Sweet, pretty, and innocent, young Murasaki grew ever more attached to Genji as she came to know him better. For the time being, he resolved to let nobody know who she was, not even the members of his household. He kept her in the isolated wing, which he had furnished with incomparable splendor, and devoted much of his time to her education. As he prepared calligraphy models and set her to writing, it seemed to him quite as though he had welcomed home a daughter who had lived elsewhere. To the bafflement of everyone but Koremitsu, he safeguarded her position by providing her with an independent administrative office, stewards, and other functionaries. Meanwhile, her father had been unable to find out anything about her.

There were still many times when the child remembered the past and missed her grandmother. She had other things to distract her while Genji was there, and he spent an occasional night at home. But more often, he would prepare to leave at dusk, bound for one of his usual destinations, and then she would sometimes protest his departure in a manner that he found tremendously appealing. Whenever he spent two or three days on duty and went straight from the palace to his father-in-law's house, she would lapse into deep gloom, and he would feel like a man with a pathetic motherless child. He no longer found it possible to pursue casual amours in a carefree spirit.

From: McCullough, Helen Craig, and Murasaki Shikibu, *Genji and Heike: selections from The Tale of Genji and The Tale of the Heike* (Stanford, CA: Stanford University, 1994), pp. 113–16.

QUESTIONS:

1. The author presents this celebration centered on Genji's dance as both artistic entertainment and competition. What values are celebrated? What aesthetic traits are projected as admirable? In what sense is this a competition within a hierarchical structure?

2. The author is a woman, many of the key characters are women, and the sexual politics of the Heian court gave women unusual prominence and power. The *Frameworks* model connects loosened gender power with heightened class power. What evidence does this selection provide of very strong class divisions and attitudes?

10.2: *The Book of Routes and Realms* (Al-Bakri, 1068)

Abū 'Ubayd 'Abd Allāh ibn 'Abd al-'Azīz al-Bakrī (c. 1014–94) was a Muslim from al-Andalus, or Muslim Iberia. His father was the ruler of a small province that lost its independence when al-Bakri's father was deposed and killed. Al-Bakri moved to Cordoba, studied geography and history, and spent the rest of his life in al-Andalus, mostly in Seville. Thus, he never visited the lands in North Africa, including the Sahara and its trade caravans and the Kingdom of Ghana, that he describes in *The Book of Routes and Realms* (which has also been translated as *The Book of Highways and Kingdoms,* and which we might call *The Book of Networks and Hierarchies*). Instead, he relied on previous literature and the reports of Muslim and Jewish merchants. His reports have an air of objectivity and are considered generally reliable, and so his book is one of the key sources for African history in this period.

Zawīla is like the town of Ajdābiya. It is a town without walls and situated in the midst of the desert. It is the first point of the land of the Sūdān. It has a cathedral mosque, a bath, and markets. Caravans meet there from all directions and from there the ways of those setting out radiate. There are palm groves and cultivated areas which are irrigated by means of camels.

Between Zawīla and the town of Ajdābiya there are fourteen stages. The inhabitants of Zawīla use a very ingenious method of guarding their town. He whose turn it is to stand watch takes a beast of burden (*dābba*) and ties to it a large faggot of palm-fronds so that their ends trail on the ground, and then goes round the town. The next morning the watchman, accompanied by his subordinates, goes on a saddle-camel around the town. If they see footprints coming out of the town they follow them until they overtake whomever has made them, in whatever direction he has gone, whether thief, runaway slave or slave-woman, or camel.

Zawīla lies between the *maghrib* and the *qibla* from Aṭrābulus. From there slaves are exported to Ifrīqiya and other neighbouring regions. They are bought for short pieces of red cloth (*thiyāb qiṣār ḥumr*). Between Zawīla and the region of the Kānim is 40 stages. The Kānimīs live beyond the desert of Zawīla and scarcely anyone reaches them. They are pagan Sūdān. Some assert that there is a people there descended from the Banū Umayya, who found their way there during their persecution by the Abbasids. They still preserve the dress and customs of the Arabs.

It is said that there are great sands there, known as al-Jazā'ir "the Islands", which have many palm trees and springs but no habitations nor human beings, and that the whistling of the *jinn* is heard there all the time. Sometimes Sūdān raiders and robbers stay there to waylay Muslims. The dates pile up there for years without anybody coming far enough to come across them until people come foraging for them in years of famine or when they have an urgent need.

From Bādīs to Qayṭūn Bayāḍa, which is the beginning of the land of Sumāṭa, and from which the route diverges to the land of the Sūdān, to Aṭrābulus and to Qayrawān.

The town of Sijilmāsa was built in the year 140/757–8. Its growth caused the depopulation of the town of Targha, which is two days distant. It caused too the depopulation of the town of Zīz.

The town of Sijilmāsa is situated on a plain the soil of which is salty. Around the town are numerous suburbs with lofty mansions and other splendid buildings. There are also many gardens. The lower section of the wall surrounding the town is made of stone, but the upper one is of brick. This wall was built by al-Yasa 'Abū Manṣūr b. Abī' l-Qāsim at his own expense, without anyone else sharing the cost. He expended on it [the value of] 1,000 *mudy* of wheat. There are twelve gates, eight of which are of iron. Al-Yasa' built the wall in the year 199/814–5 and in 200 he moved into the town, which he divided among the tribes, as it still continues till this day. The inhabitants wear the face *veil (niqā b)*, and if one of them uncovers his face none of his relatives can recognize him.

Sijilmāsa stands on two rivers, whose source, in the place called Ijlaf, is fed by many springs. On approaching Sijilmāsa this stream divides into two branches which flow to the east and west of the town.

The cathedral mosque of the town is strongly built. It was constructed by al-Yasa' who did it excellently. The baths, however, are of poor construction and bad workmanship. The water in the town is brackish as it is in all the wells of Sijilmāsa. The cultivated land is irrigated with water from the river collected in basins like those used for watering gardens. There are many date-palms, grapes, and all sorts of fruit. The grapes grown on trellises which the sun does not reach do not turn into raisins except in the shade, and for this reason they are known as *ẓillī* "shady", but those which the sun does reach become raisins in the sun.

The town of Sijilmāsa is situated at the beginning of the desert and no inhabited places are known to the west and south of it. There are no flies in Sijilmāsa and none of the inhabitants falls ill with leprosy *(judhām)*. When anyone suffering from this complaint enters the town his illness does not develop further. The inhabitants of Sijilmāsa fatten dogs and eat them, as do the people of the towns of Qafṣa and Qasṭīliya. They eat grain (*zar'*) when it puts forth its shoots, and this they regard as a delicacy. The lepers *(mujadhdham* "suffering from judh*ā m*") there are occupied as scavengers (*kannā f*) and their masons are Jews, whom they restrict to this trade alone.

From the town of Sijilmāsa you may travel to the land of the Sūdān, namely to the town of Ghāna. From Sijilmāsa to Ghāna is a distance of two months' travelling through deserts inhabited only by nomads who do not stay anywhere permanently. They are the Banū Masūfa of the Ṣanhāja, who have no town to which they may resort save Wādī Dar'a. Between Sijilmāsa and Wādī Dar'a is five days' journey.

They sow in the land of Sijilmāsa in one year and they harvest from that sowing for three years. The reason for this is that it is an extremely hot country with severe summer heat, so when the grain is dry it gets scattered during harvesting, and as the ground is cracked the scattered grain falls into those cracks. In the second year they plough without sowing, and so in the third year. Their wheat has a small grain and is *ṣīnī* "chinese" *[sic]; a* Prophet's *mudd* contains 75,000 grains. Their *mudy* contains twelve *qanqals*, the *qanqal* contains eight *zalā fas*, and the *zalā fa* eight Prophet's *mudds*.

A strange thing is that gold, with the Sijilmāsīs, is bought or sold *juzā f* i.e. by number, not by weight, whereas leeks *(kurrāth)* are sold by weight, not number. . . .

GHĀNA AND THE CUSTOMS OF ITS INHABITANTS

Ghāna is a title given to their kings; the name of the region is Awkār, and their king today, namely in the year 460/1067–8, is Tunkā Manīn. He ascended the throne in 455/1063. The name of his predecessor was Basī and he became their ruler at the age of 85. He led a praiseworthy life on account of his love of justice and friendship for the Muslims. At the end of his life he became blind, but he concealed this from his subjects and pretended that he could see. When something was put before him he said: "This is good" or "This is bad". His ministers deceived the people by indicating to the king in cryptic words what he should say, so that the commoners could not understand. Basī was a maternal uncle of Tunkā Manīn. This is their custom and their habit, that the kingship is inherited only by the son of the king's sister. He has no doubt that his successor is a son of his sister, while he is not certain that his son is in fact his own, and he is not convinced of the genuineness of his relationship to him. This Tunkā Manīn is powerful, rules an enormous kingdom, and possesses great authority.

The city of Ghāna consists of two towns situated on a plain. One of these towns, which is inhabited by Muslims, is large and possesses twelve mosques, in one of which they assemble for the Friday prayer. There are salaried imams and muezzins, as well as jurists and scholars. In the environs are wells with sweet water, from which they drink and with which they grow vegetables. The king's town is six miles distant from this one and bears the name of Al-Ghāba. Between these two towns there are continuous habitations. The houses of the inhabitants are of stone and acacia (*sunṭ*) wood. The king has a palace and a number of domed dwellings all surrounded with an enclosure like a city wall (*sūr*). In the king's town, and not far from his court of justice, is a mosque where the Muslims who arrive at his court (*yafid'alayh*) pray. Around the king's town are domed buildings and groves and thickets where the sorcerers of these people, men in charge of the religious cult, live. In them too are their idols and the tombs of their kings. These woods are guarded and none may enter them and know what is there. In them also are the king's prisons. If somebody is imprisoned there no news of him is ever heard. The king's interpreters, the official in charge of his treasury and the majority of his ministers are Muslims. Among the people who follow the king's religion only he and his heir apparent (who is the son of his sister) may wear sewn clothes. All other people wear robes of cotton, silk, or brocade, according to their means. All of them shave their beards, and women shave their heads. The *king* adorns himself like a woman [wearing necklaces] round his neck and [bracelets] on his forearms, and he puts on a high cap (*ṭarṭūr*) decorated with gold and wrapped in a turban of fine cotton. He sits in audience or to hear grievances against officials (*maẓālim*) in a domed pavilion around which stand ten horses covered with gold-embroidered materials. Behind the king stand ten pages holding shields and swords decorated with gold, and on his right are the sons of the [vassal] kings of his country wearing splendid garments and their hair plaited with gold. The governor of the city sits on the ground before the king and around him are ministers seated likewise. At the door of the pavilion are dogs of excellent pedigree who hardly ever leave the place where the king is, guarding him. Round their necks they wear collars of gold and silver studded with a number of balls of the same metals. The audience is announced by the beating of a drum which they call *dubā*, made from a long hollow log. When the people who profess the same religion as the king approach him they fall on their knees and sprinkle dust on their heads, for this is their way of greeting him. As for the Muslims, they greet him only by clapping their hands.

Their religion is paganism and the worship of idols (*dakākīr*). When their king dies they construct over the place where his tomb will be an enormous dome of *sāj* wood. Then they bring him on a bed covered with a few carpets and cushions and place him beside the dome. At his side they place his ornaments, his weapons, and the vessels from which he used to eat and drink, filled with various kinds of food and beverages. They place there too the men who used to serve his meals. They close the door of the dome and cover it with mats and furnishings. Then the people assemble, who heap earth upon it until it becomes like a big hillock and dig a ditch around it until the mound can be reached at only one place.

They make sacrifices to their dead and make offerings of intoxicating drinks.

On every donkey-load of salt when it is brought into the country their king levies one golden dinar, and two dinars when it is sent out. From a load of copper the king's due is five mithqals, and from a load of other goods ten mithqals. The best gold found in his land comes from the town of Ghiyārū, which is eighteen days' travelling distant from the king's town over a country inhabited by tribes of the Sūdān whose dwellings are continuous.

The nuggets (*nadra*) found in all the mines of his country are reserved for the king, only this gold dust (*al-tibr al-daqīq*) being left for the people. But for this the people would accumulate gold until it lost its value. The nuggets may weigh from an ounce (*ūqiyya*) to a pound (*raṭl*). It is related that the king owns a nugget as large as a big stone. . . .

The countryside of Ghāna is unhealthy and not populous, and it is almost impossible to avoid falling ill there during the time their crops are ripening. There is mortality among strangers at the time of harvest.

The king of Ghāna, when he calls up his army, can put 200,000 men into the field, more than 40,000 of them archers. The horses in Ghāna are very small. Excellent black-and-white-veined (*mujazzaʿ*) ebony grows there. The inhabitants sow their crops twice yearly, the first time in the moist earth (*tharā*) during the season of the Nīl flood, and later in the earth [that has preserved its humidity].

West of Ghiyārū, on the Nīl, is the town of Yarisnā, inhabited by Muslims surrounded by polytheists. In Yarisnā is a species of small goat. When a goat gives birth to a male it is slaughtered, only females being allowed to live. In this country is a certain tree against which the goats rub themselves and become fecundated by the wood without the medium of the male. This fact is well known to them; none of them deny it and it has been related by many trustworthy Muslims. From Yarisnā the Sūdān who speak an unintelligible language (*aʿjam*, pl. *ʿujm*) called the Banū Naghmārata, who are merchants, export gold to other countries.

From: Hopkins, J. F. P., and Nehemia Levtzion, *Corpus of early Arabic sources for West African history* (Cambridge, UK: Cambridge University Press, 1981), pp. 62–66, 79–83.

QUESTIONS:

1. From al-Bakri's descriptions, how important was trade to Zawīla? To Ghana? How does trade affect the religious life of the kingdom, and how does it affect the geography of Ghana's capital city?
2. What are the key elements of Ghana as a hierarchy? What do you think the hierarchy diagram of Ghana should look like?

10.3: *The Gesta Guillelmi* (William of Poitiers, after 1066)

William of Poitiers (c. 1020–90) was a Norman French priest who came from an influential Norman family and originally trained as a knight before entering the Church. His military training proved valuable when he became chaplain to William the Bastard, Duke of Normandy, who in 1066 earned a new nickname—the Conqueror—by defeating Harold Godwinson of England at the Battle of Hastings and becoming king himself. William of Poitiers wrote about the Duke's life in his *Gesta Guillelmi* (*Deeds of William*), celebrating in particular the great battle. It is a panegyric—a book of praise—as much as a history, and William took as his model Julius Caesar's account of his invasion of Britain, comparing the Duke favorably to the Roman commander in many ways. It is nonetheless a reasonably accurate account whose biases for William and against Harold are obvious enough that the careful reader can discount them. This selection focuses on the battle.

14. Meanwhile experienced knights, who had been sent out scouting, reported that the enemy would soon be there. For the furious king was hastening his march all the more because he had heard that the lands near to the Norman camp were being laid waste. He thought that in a night or surprise attack he might defeat them unawares; and, in case they should try to escape, he had laid a naval ambush for them with an armed fleet of up to 700 ships. The duke hastily ordered all who could be found in the camp (for a large number of his companions had gone off foraging) to arm themselves. . . .

15. We do not doubt that the exhortation, brief because of the circumstances, with which he added still greater ardour to the valour of his troops, was outstanding, even though it has not been transmitted to us in all its distinction. He reminded the Normans that in many and great dangers they had always come out victorious under his leadership. He reminded them all of their fatherland, of their noble exploits and their great fame. Now they were to prove with their arms with what strength they were endowed, with what valour they were inspired. Now the question was not who should live and rule, but who should escape alive from imminent danger. If they fought like men they would have victory, honour, and wealth. If not, they would let themselves either be slaughtered, or captured to be mocked by the most cruel enemies—not to mention that they would bring on themselves perpetual ignominy. No way was open to flight, since their way was barred on one side by armed forces and a hostile and unknown country, and on the other by the sea and armed forces. It was not seemly for men to be terrified by numbers. . . .

16. Now this is the well-planned order in which he advanced behind the banner which the pope had sent him. He placed foot-soldiers in front, armed with arrows and cross-bows; likewise foot-soldiers in the second rank, but more powerful and wearing hauberks; finally the squadrons of mounted knights, in the middle of which he himself rode with the strongest force, so that he could direct operations on all sides with hand and voice. If any author of antiquity had been writing of Harold's line of march he would have recorded that in his passage rivers were dried up and forests laid flat. For huge forces of English had assembled from all the shires. Some showed zeal for Harold, and all showed love of their country, which they wished to defend against invaders even though their cause was unjust. . . . However, not daring to fight with William on equal terms, for they thought him more formidable than the king of the Norwegians, they took their stand on higher ground, on a hill near to the wood through which they had come. At once dismounting from their horses, they lined up all on foot in a dense formation. Undeterred by the roughness of the ground, the duke with his men climbed slowly up the steep slope.

17. The harsh bray of trumpets gave the signal for battle on both sides. The Normans swiftly and boldly took the initiative in the fray. Similarly, when orators are engaged in a lawsuit about theft, he who prosecutes the crime makes the first speech. So the Norman foot-soldiers closed to attack the English, killing and maiming many with their missiles. The English for their part resisted bravely each one by any means he could devise. They threw javelins and missiles of various kinds, murderous axes and stones tied to sticks. You might imagine that our men would have been crushed at once by them, as by a death-dealing mass. The knights came to their rescue, and those who had been in the rear advanced to the fore. Disdaining to fight from a distance, they attacked boldly with their swords. The loud shouting, here Norman, there foreign, was drowned by the clash of weapons and the groans of the dying. So for a time both sides fought with all their might. The English were greatly helped by the advantage of the higher ground, which they held in serried ranks without sallying forward, and also by their great numbers and densely-packed mass, and moreover by their

weapons of war, which easily penetrated shields and other protections. So they strongly held or drove back those who dared to attack them with drawn swords. They even wounded those who flung javelins at them from a distance. So, terrified by this ferocity, both the footsoldiers and the Breton knights and other auxiliaries on the left wing turned tail; almost the whole of the duke's battle line gave way, if such a thing may be said of the unconquered people of the Normans. The army of the Roman empire, containing royal contingents and accustomed to victory on land and sea, fled occasionally, when it knew or believed its leader to have been killed. The Normans believed that their duke and lord had fallen, so it was not too shameful to give way to flight; least of all was it to be deplored, since it helped them greatly.

18. For the leader, seeing a great part of the opposing force springing forward to pursue his men, rushed towards them, met them as they fled and halted them, striking out and threatening with his spear. Baring his head and lifting his helmet, he cried, 'Look at me. I am alive, and with God's help I will conquer. What madness is persuading you to flee? What way is open to escape? You could slaughter like cattle the men who are pursuing and killing you. You are abandoning victory and imperishable fame, and hurrying to disaster and perpetual ignominy. Not one of you will escape death by flight.' At these words they recovered their courage. He rushed forward at their head, brandishing his sword, and mowed down the hostile people who deserved death for rebelling against him, their king. Full of zeal the Normans surrounded some thousands who had pursued them and destroyed them in a moment, so that not a single one survived.

19. Emboldened by this, they launched an attack with greater determination on the main body of the army, which in spite of the heavy losses it had suffered seemed not to be diminished. The English fought confidently with all their might, striving particularly to prevent a gap being opened by their attackers. They were so tightly packed together that there was hardly room for the slain to fall. However paths were cut through them in several places by the weapons of the most valiant knights. Pressing home the attack were men of Maine, Frenchmen, Bretons, Aquitanians, above all Normans, whose valour was outstanding. . . .

20. When the Normans and the troops allied to them saw that they could not conquer such a solidly massed enemy force without heavy loss, they wheeled round and deliberately feigned flight. They remembered how, a little while before, their flight had brought about the result they desired. There was jubilation among the foreigners, who hoped for a great victory. Encouraging each other with joyful shouts, they heaped curses on our men and threatened to destroy them all forthwith. As before, some thousands of them dared to rush, almost as if they were winged, in pursuit of those they believed to be fleeing. The Normans, suddenly wheeling round their horses, checked and encircled them, and slaughtered them to the last man.

21. Having used this trick twice with the same result, they attacked the remainder with greater determination: up to now the enemy line had been bristling with weapons and most difficult to encircle. So a combat of an unusual kind began, with one side attacking in different ways and the other standing firmly as if fixed to the ground. The English grew weaker, and endured punishment as though confessing their guilt by their defeat. The Normans shot arrows, smote and pierced; the dead by falling seemed to move more than the living. It was not possible for the lightly wounded to escape, for they were crushed to death by the serried ranks of their companions. So fortune turned for William, hastening his triumph.

. . . William, their duke, deserves to be placed above certain of the ancient generals of the Greeks and Romans, who are so much praised in their writings, and to be compared with others. He led his men nobly, checking flight, giving encouragement, courting danger, more often calling on them to follow than ordering them to go ahead. From this it is plain to see that his valour in the van opened the way for his followers and gave them courage. No small part of the enemy lost heart without being injured at the sight of this astounding and redoubtable mounted warrior. Three horses were killed under him and fell. Three times he sprang to the ground undaunted, and avenged without delay the loss of his steed. Here his speed, here his physical strength and courage could be seen. With his angry blade he tirelessly pierced shields, helmets, and hauberks; with his buckler he threw back many. Marvelling at seeing him fight on foot his knights, many of them smitten with wounds, took heart again. Some even, 'weakened by loss of blood', leant on their shields and fought on courageously; others, incapable of more, encouraged their companions by word and gesture, to follow the duke without fear, so that victory should not slip through their hands. He himself helped and saved many of them. . . .

23. Towards the end of the day the English army realized that there was no hope of resisting the Normans any longer. They knew that they had been weakened by the loss of many troops; that the king himself and his brothers and not a few of the nobles of the kingdom had perished; that all who remained were almost at the end of their strength, and that they could hope for no relief. They saw that the Normans were not greatly weakened by the loss of those who had fallen and, seeming to have found new strength as they fought, were pressing on more eagerly than at first. They saw that the duke in his ferocity spared no opponent; and that nothing but victory could quench his ardour. So they turned to escape as quickly as possible by flight, some on horses they had seized, some on foot; some along roads, others through untrodden wastes. Some lay helplessly in their own blood, others who struggled up were too weak to escape. The passionate wish to escape death gave strength to some. Many left their corpses in deep woods, many who had collapsed on the routes blocked the way for those who came after. The Normans, though strangers to the district, pursued them relentlessly, slashing their guilty backs and putting the last touches. . . .

25. So, after completing the victory, William returned to the battlefield and discovered the extent of the slaughter, surveying it not without pity, even though it had been inflicted on impious men, and even though it is just and glorious and praiseworthy to kill a tyrant. . . .

From: R. H. C. Davis, and Marjorie Chibnall, *The Gesta Guillelmi of William of Poitiers* (Oxford, UK: Clarendon Press, 1998), pp. 123–39.

QUESTIONS:

1. What screen image of William the Conqueror does William of Poitiers project? What are the Duke's most admirable characteristics? What are his most heroic deeds? What does this image tell you about political leadership in eleventh century Europe?
2. What evidence does this account of the Battle of Hastings present for the medieval view that battles were trials in which the judgment of God was revealed in the outcome? Is this evidence of an underlying frame value?

10.4: *Epic of Sundiata* (oral tale with origins in the thirteenth century)

Sundiata is an oral epic, a tale told in many versions ever since the early fourteenth century by griots, professional storytellers who have semiofficial status as historians, advisors to rulers, and preservers of cultural traditions. The "official" version from which this selection comes was recorded by a griot in 1960. The epic tells the story of Sundiata Keita (c. 1217–c. 1255), a historical king and founder of the Empire of Mali. As an oral epic, it mixes echoes of historical events with elements of fantasy and magic. In this selection Sundiata, son of a previous king and his ugly second wife Songolon, begins his final campaign against the evil sorcerer king Soumaoro Kanté of Sosso, who has conquered Sundiata's father's kingdom. Note the central role of smiths—iron workers—in the political, military, and magical exercise of power in this story.

Every man to his own land! If it is foretold that your destiny should be fulfilled in such and such a land, men can do nothing against it. Mansa Tounkara could not keep Sundiata back because the destiny of Sogolon's son was bound up with that of Mali. Neither the jealousy of a cruel stepmother, nor her wickedness, could alter for a moment the course of great destiny.

The snake, man's enemy, is not long-lived, yet the serpent that lives hidden will surely die old. Djata was strong enough now to face his enemies. At the age of eighteen he had the stateliness of the lion and the strength of the buffalo. His voice carried authority, his eyes were live coals, his arm was iron, he was the husband of power.

Moussa Tounkara, king of Mema, gave Sundiata half of his army. The most valiant came forward of their own free will to follow Sundiata in the great adventure. The cavalry of Mema, which he had fashioned himself, formed his iron squadron. Sundiata, dressed in the Muslim fashion of Mema, left the town at the head of his small but redoubtable army. The whole population sent their best wishes with him. He was surrounded by five messengers from Mali and Manding Bory rode proudly at the side of his brother. The horsemen of Mema formed behind Djata a bristling iron squadron. The troop took the direction of Wagadou, for Djata did not have enough troops to confront Soumaoro directly, and so the king of Mema advised him to go to Wagadou and take half of the men of the king, Soumaba Cissé. A swift messenger had been sent there and so the king of Wagadou came out in person to meet Sundiata and his troops. He gave Sundiata half of his cavalry and blessed the weapons. Then Manding Bory said to his brother, 'Djata, do you think yourself able to face Soumaoro now?'

'No matter how small a forest may be, you can always find there sufficient fibres to tie up a man. Numbers mean nothing; it is worth that counts. With my cavalry I shall clear myself a path to Mali.'

Djata gave out his orders. They would head south, skirting Soumaoro's kingdom. The first objective to be reached was Tabon, the iron-gated town in the midst of the mountains, for Sundiata had promised Fran Kamara that he would pass by Tabon before returning to Mali. He hoped to find that his childhood companion had become king. It was a forced march and during the halts the divines, Singbin Mara Cissé and Mandjan Bérété, related to Sundiata the history of Alexander the Great and several other heroes, but of all of them Sundiata preferred Alexander, the king of gold and silver, who crossed the world from west to east. He wanted to outdo his prototype both in the extent of his territory and the wealth of his treasury.

However, Soumaoro Kanté, being a great sorcerer, knew that the son of Sogolon had set out and that he was coming to lay claim to Mali. The soothsayers told him to forestall this calamity by attacking Sundiata, but good fortune makes men blind. . . .

Soumaoro sent a detachment under his son Sosso Balla to block Sundiata's route to Tabon.

Sosso Balla was about the same age as Sundiata. He promptly deployed his troops at the entrance to the mountains to oppose Sundiata's advance to Tabon.

In the evening, after a long day's march, Sundiata arrived at the head of the great valley which led to Tabon. The valley was quite black with men, for Sosso Balla had deployed his men everywhere in the valley, and some were positioned on the heights which dominated the way through. When Djata saw the layout of Sosso Balla's men he turned to his generals laughing.

'Why are you laughing, brother, you can see that the road is blocked.'

'Yes, but no mere infantrymen can halt my course towards Mali,' replied Sundiata.

The troops stopped. All the war chiefs were of the opinion that they should wait until the next day to give battle because, they said, the men were tired.

'The battle will not last long,' said Sundiata, 'and the men will have time to rest. We must not allow Soumaoro the time to attack Tabon.'

Sundiata was immovable, so the orders were given and the war drums began to beat. On his proud horse Sundiata turned to right and left in front of his troops. He entrusted the rearguard, composed of a part of the Wagadou cavalry, to his younger brother Manding Bory. Having drawn his sword, Sundiata led the charge, shouting his war cry.

The Sossos were surprised by this sudden attack for they all thought that the battle would be joined the next day. The lightning that flashes across the sky is slower, the thunderbolts less frightening and floodwaters less surprising than Sundiata swooping down on Sosso Balla and his smiths. In a trice, Sundiata was in the middle of the Sossos like a lion in the sheepfold. The Sossos, trampled under the hooves of his fiery charger, cried out. When he turned to the right the smiths of Soumaoro fell in their tens, and when he turned to the left his sword made heads fall as when someone shakes a tree of ripe fruit. The horsemen of Mema wrought a frightful slaughter and their long lances pierced flesh like a knife sunk into a paw-paw. Charging ever forwards, Sundiata looked for Sosso Balla; he caught sight of him and like a lion bounded towards the son of Soumaoro, his sword held aloft. His arm came sweeping down but at that moment a Sosso warrior came between Djata and Sosso Balla and was sliced like a calabash. Sosso Balla did not wait and disappeared from amidst his smiths. Seeing their chief in flight, the Sossos gave way and fell into a terrible rout. Before the sun disappeared behind the mountains there were only Djata and his men left in the valley. Manding Bory, who was keeping an eye on the men perched on the heights, seeing that his brother had got the upper hand, dispatched some horsemen across the mountains to dislodge the Sossos. The Sossos were pursued until nightfall and several of them were taken prisoner. . . .

The son of Sogolon had already decided on his plan of campaign—to beat Soumaoro, destroy Sosso and return triumphantly to Niani. He now had five army corps at his disposal, namely, the cavalry and infantry of Mema, those of Wagadou and the three tribes forming the army of Tabon Wana Fran Kamara. He must assume the offensive as soon as possible.

Soumaoro marched out to meet Sundiata. The meeting took place at Neguéboria in the Bouré country. As usual, the son of Sogolon wanted to join battle straight away. Soumaoro thought to draw Sundiata into the plain, but Sundiata did not allow him the time to do it. Compelled to give battle, the king of Sosso drew up his men across the narrow valley of Neguéboria, the wings of his army occupying the slopes. Sundiata adopted a very original form of deployment. He formed a tight square with all his cavalry in the front line. The archers of Wagadou and Tabon were stationed at the back. Soumaoro was on one of the hills dominating the valley and he could be distinguished by his height and his helmet bristling with horns. Under an overpowering sun the trumpets sounded, on both sides the drums and bolons echoed and courage entered the hearts of the Sofas. Sundiata charged at the gallop and the valley soon disappeared in a cloud of red dust kicked up by thousands of feet and hooves. Without giving an inch, the smiths of Soumaoro stopped the wave.

As though detached from the battle, Soumaoro Kanté watched from the top of his hill. Sundiata and the king of Tabon were laying about them with mighty blows. Sundiata could be distinguished by his white turban and Soumaoro could see the breach he was opening up in the middle of his troops. The centre was about to cave in under the crushing pressure of Djata.

Soumaoro made a sign and from the hills came smiths swooping down into the bottom of the valley to encircle Sundiata. Then, without the slightest order from Sundiata, who was in the thick of the struggle, his square stretched and elongated itself into a great rectangle. Everything had been foreseen. The change was so quick that Soumaoro's men, halted in their mad career, could not use their weapons. In Djata's rear the archers of Wagadou and those of Tabon, on one knee, shot arrows into the sky, which fell thickly, like a rain of iron, on the ranks of Soumaoro. Like a stretching piece of elastic, Djata's line ascended to attack the hills. Djata caught sight of Sosso Balla and bore down on him, but the latter slipped away and the warriors of the buffalo woman's son raised a huzza of triumph. Soumaoro rushed up and his presence in the centre revived the courage of the Sossos. Sundiata caught sight of him and tried to cut a passage through to him. He struck to the right and struck to the left and trampled underfoot. The murderous hooves of his 'Daffeké' dug into the chests of the Sossos. Soumaoro was now within spear range and Sundiata reared up his horse and hurled his weapon. It whistled away and bounced off Soumaoro's chest as off a rock and fell to the ground. Sogolon's son bent his bow but with a motion of the hand Soumaoro caught the arrow in flight and showed it to Sundiata as if to say 'Look, I am invulnerable.'

Furious, Sundiata snatched up his spear and with his head bent charged at Soumaoro, but as he raised his arm to strike his enemy he noticed that Soumaoro had disappeared. Manding Bory riding at his side pointed to the hill and said, 'Look, brother.'

Sundiata saw Soumaoro on the hill, sitting on his black-coated horse. How could he have done it, he who was only two paces from Sundiata? By what power had he spirited himself away on to the hill? The son of Sogolon stopped fighting to watch the king of Sosso. The sun was already very low and Soumaoro's smiths gave way but Sundiata did not give the order to pursue the enemy. Suddenly, Soumaoro disappeared!

How can I vanquish a man capable of disappearing and reappearing where and when he likes? How can I affect a man invulnerable to iron? Such were the questions which Sogolon's son asked himself. He had been told many things about Sosso Soumaoro but he had given little credence to so much gossip. Didn't people say that Soumaoro could assume sixty-nine different shapes to escape his enemies? According to some, he could transform himself into a fly in the middle of the battle and come and torment his opponent; he could melt into the wind when his enemies encircled him too closely—and many other things.

The battle of Neguéboria showed Djata, if he needed to be shown, that to beat the king of Sosso other weapons were necessary. . . .

'How was he able to escape me? Why did neither my spear nor my arrow wound him?' he wondered. 'What is the jinn that protects Soumaoro? What is the mystery of his power?' . . .

He did not sleep that night.

From: Niane, Djibril Tamsir, David W. Chappell, and Jim Jones, *Sundiata: an epic of old Mali* (Harlow, England: Pearson Longman, 2006), pp. 38–40, 47–54.

QUESTIONS:

1. What screen image of Sundiata does the epic project? To the extent that we can read this projection back into historical king's time (which is a bit uncertain), what does this image say about rulership in thirteenth century Mali? What virtues are valued? How does the image of Sundiata compare to the image of William of Normandy?
2. What might the central role of magic in this story say about politics and the exercise of power in the Empire of Mali?

CHAPTER 11

Traditional Worlds III: Separate Circuits, 400 to 1500

INTRODUCTION

This chapter presents sources from the isolated worlds beyond the Afro-Eurasian network. More accurately, this chapter presents sources from the American subset of isolated societies. More accurately still, this chapter presents sources that almost entirely postdate the connection of American societies with the Afro-Eurasian network, but that are about as good as we can do at getting written sources from precontact times. This reflects the paucity of sources generated by societies many of which were preliterate, a reminder of historians' dependence on the survival of evidence for creating a complete picture of the past.

11.1: *Popol Vuh* (c. 1560)

Our first source comes from Mayan society. The Classical Era of Mayan history runs from around 600 to 800 CE. Mayan civilization seems to have been influenced by the earlier Olmec culture, and it definitely influenced in its own turn the Aztec civilization encountered by the Spanish in 1519. The Mayan's developed intricate calendar computations based on a sophisticated knowledge of astronomy. The foundation for their view of time is the sacred Mayan story known as the *Popol Vuh*, or the *Council Book*. It has ancient origins, but the version that we have was produced by a Mayan around 1560, after the Spanish Conquest and the forced Christianization that accompanied it. The passages included here tell of the gods' first efforts at creating proper worshippers, creatures capable of properly reading and observing the days. The creation process required some trial and error.

This is the account, here it is:

Now it still ripples, now it still murmurs, ripples, it still sighs, still hums, and it is empty under the sky.

Here follow the first words, the first eloquence:

There is not yet one person, one animal, bird, fish, crab, tree, rock, hollow, canyon, meadow, forest. Only the sky alone is there; the face of the earth is not clear. Only the sea alone is pooled under all the sky; there is nothing whatever gathered together. It is at rest; not a single thing stirs. It is held back, kept at rest under the sky.

Whatever there is that might be is simply not there: only the pooled water, only the calm sea, only it alone is pooled.

Whatever might be is simply not there: only murmurs, ripples, in the dark, in the night. Only the Maker, Modeler alone, Sovereign Plumed Serpent, the Bearers, Begetters are in the water, a glittering light. They are there, they are enclosed in quetzal feathers, in blue-green.

Thus the name, "Plumed Serpent." They are great knowers, great thinkers in their very being.

And of course there is the sky, and there is also the Heart of Sky. This is the name of the god, as it is spoken.

And then came his word, he came here to the Sovereign Plumed Serpent, here in the blackness, in the early dawn. He spoke with the Sovereign Plumed Serpent, and they talked, then they thought, then they worried. They agreed with each other, they joined their words, their thoughts. Then it was clear, then they reached accord in the light, and then humanity was clear, when they conceived the growth, the generation of trees, of bushes, and the growth of life, of humankind, in the blackness, in the early dawn, all because of the Heart of Sky, named Hurricane. Thunderbolt Hurricane comes first, the second is Newborn Thunderbolt, and the third is Raw Thunderbolt.

So, there were three of them, as Heart of Sky, who came to the Sovereign Plumed Serpent, when the dawn of life was conceived:

"How should it be sown, how should it dawn? Who is to be the provider, nurturer?"

"Let it be this way, think about it: this water should be removed, emptied out for the formation of the earth's own plate and platform, then comes the sowing, the dawning of the sky-earth. But there will be no high days and no bright praise for our work, our design, until the rise of the human work, the human design," they said.

And then the earth arose because of them, it was simply their word that brought it forth. For the forming of the earth they said "Earth." It arose suddenly, just like a cloud, like a mist, now forming, unfolding. Then the mountains were separated from the water, all at once the great mountains came forth. By their genius alone, by their cutting edge alone they carried out the conception of the mountain-plain, whose face grew instant groves of cypress and pine.

And the Plumed Serpent was pleased with this:

"It was good that you came, Heart of Sky, Hurricane, and Newborn Thunderbolt, Raw Thunderbolt. Our work, our design will turn out well," they said.

. . .

A Bearer, Begetter speaks:

"Why this pointless humming? Why should there merely be rustling beneath the trees and bushes?"

"Indeed, they had better have guardians," the others replied. As soon as they thought it and said it, deer and birds came forth.

. . .

And then the deer and birds were told by the Maker, Modeler, Bearer, Begetter:

"Talk, speak out. Don't moan, don't cry out. Please talk, each to each, within each kind, within each group," they were told—the deer, birds, puma, jaguar, serpent.

"Name now our names, praise us. We are your mother, we are your father. Speak now:

'Hurricane,
Newborn Thunderbolt, Raw Thunderbolt,
Heart of Sky, Heart of Earth,
Maker, Modeler,
Bearer, Begetter,'

speak, pray to us, keep our days," they were told. But it didn't turn out that they spoke like people: they just squawked, they just chattered, they just howled. It wasn't apparent what language they spoke; each one gave a different cry. When the Maker, Modeler heard this:

"It hasn't turned out well, they haven't spoken," they said among themselves. "It hasn't turned out that our names have been named. Since we are their mason and sculptor, this will not do," the Bearers and Begetters said among themselves. So they told them:

"You will simply have to be transformed. Since it hasn't turned out well and you haven't spoken, we have changed our word:

"What you feed on, what you eat, the places where you sleep, the places where you stay, whatever is yours will remain in the canyons, the forests. Although it turned out that our days were not kept, nor did you pray to us, there may yet be strength in the keeper of days, the giver of praise whom we have yet to make. Just accept your service, just let your flesh be eaten.

. . .

Again there comes an experiment with the human work, the human design, by the Maker, Modeler, Bearer, Begetter:

"It must simply be tried again. The time for the planting and dawning is nearing. For this we must make a provider and nurturer. How else can we be invoked and remembered on the face of the earth? We have already made our first try at our work and design, but it turned out that they didn't keep our days, nor did they glorify us.

"So now let's try to make a giver of praise, giver of respect, provider, nurturer," they said

. . .

"There is yet to find, yet to discover how we are to model a person, construct a person again, a provider, nurturer, so that we are called upon and we are recognized: our recompense is in words. . . ."

. . .

This was the peopling of the face of the earth:

They came into being, they multiplied, they had daughters, they had sons, these manikins, wood-carvings. But there was nothing in their hearts and nothing in their minds, no memory of their mason and builder. They just went and walked wherever they wanted. Now they did not remember the Heart of Sky.

And so they fell, just an experiment and just a cutout for humankind. They were talking at first but their faces were dry. They were not yet developed in the legs and arms. They had no blood, no lymph. They had no sweat, no fat. Their complexions were dry, their faces were crusty. They flailed their legs and arms, their bodies were deformed.

And so they accomplished nothing before the Maker, Modeler who gave them birth, gave them heart. They became the first numerous people here on the face of the earth.

Again there comes a humiliation, destruction, and demolition. The manikins, wood-carvings were killed when the Heart of Sky devised a flood for them. A great flood was made; it came down on the heads of the manikins, wood-carvings. The man's body was carved from the wood of the coral tree by the Maker, Modeler. And as for the woman, the Maker, Modeler needed the pith of reeds for the woman's body. They were not competent, nor did they speak before the builder and sculptor who made them and brought them forth, and so they were killed, done in by a flood:

There came a rain of resin from the sky.
There came the one named Gouger of
    Faces: he gouged out their eyeballs.
There came Sudden Bloodletter: he snapped
    off their heads.
There came Crunching Jaguar: he ate their
    flesh.
There came Tearing Jaguar: he tore them
    open.

They were pounded down to the bones and tendons, smashed and pulverized even to the bones. Their faces were smashed because they were incompetent before their mother and their father, the Heart of Sky, named Hurricane. The earth was blackened because of this; the black rainstorm began, rain all day and rain all night. Into their houses came the animals, small and great. Their faces were crushed by things of wood and stone. Everything spoke: their water jars, their tortilla griddles, their plates, their cooking pots, their dogs, their grinding stones, each and every thing crushed their faces. Their dogs and turkeys told them:

"You caused us pain, you ate us, but now it is *you* whom *we* shall eat." . . .

Such was the scattering of the human work, the human design. The people were ground down, overthrown. The mouths and faces of all of them were destroyed and crushed. And it used to be said that the monkeys in the forests today are a sign of this. They were left as a sign because wood alone was used for their flesh by the builder and sculptor.

So this is why monkeys look like people: they are a sign of a previous human work, human design—mere manikins, mere wood-carvings.

From: Popol Vuh: The Definitive Edition of the Mayan Book of the Dawn of life and the Glories of the Gods and Kings, Dennis Tedlock, transl. (New York: Simon and Schuster, 1985), pp. 72–86.

QUESTIONS:

1. What is the implied relationship between man and nature presented in *Popol Vuh*? What does *Popol Vuh* tell us about proper human behavior?
2. What can we discern about the nature of the divine (the gods) in the Mayan belief system from *Popol Vuh*?

11.2: *General History of New Spain* (Bernard de Sahagún, 1545-90)

Bernard de Sahagún (c. 1499–1590) was a Spanish Franciscan friar, missionary, and remarkable student of the Aztec people among whom he worked starting in 1529. His *General History of New Spain* presents information gathered from his Aztec informants about their culture, beliefs, and history, including the Spanish invasion and conquest of the Aztec Empire. The manuscript is in facing pages of Spanish and Nahuatl, the Aztec language, and contains over two thousand drawings by Aztec artists of the events the text describes. The *General History* is therefore one of the best Aztec account of Aztec culture that we have.

The first bad omen: Ten years before the Spaniards first came here, a bad omen appeared in the sky. It was like a flaming ear of corn, or a fiery signal, or the blaze of daybreak; it seemed to bleed fire, drop by drop, like a wound in the sky. It was wide at the base and narrow at the peak, and it shone in the very heart of the heavens.

This is how it appeared: it shone in the eastern sky in the middle of the night. It appeared at midnight and burned till the break of day, but it vanished at the rising of the sun. The time during which it appeared to us was a full year, beginning in the year 12-House.

When it first appeared, there was great outcry and confusion. The people clapped their hands against their mouths; they were amazed and frightened, and asked themselves what it could mean.

The second bad omen: The temple of Huitzilopochtli burst into flames. It is thought that no one set it afire, that it burned down of its own accord. The name of its divine site was Tlacateccan [House of Authority].

And now it is burning, the wooden columns are burning! The flames, the tongues of fire shoot out, the bursts of fire shoot up into the sky!

The flames swiftly destroyed all the woodwork of the temple. When the fire was first seen, the people shouted: "Mexicanos, come running! We can put it out! Bring your water jars . . .!" But when they threw water on the blaze it only flamed higher. They could not put it out, and the temple burned to the ground.

The third bad omen: A temple was damaged by a lightning-bolt. This was the temple of Xiuhtecuhtli, which was built of straw, in the place known as Tzonmolco. It was raining that day, but it was only a light rain or a drizzle, and no thunder was heard. Therefore the lightning-bolt was taken as an omen. The people said: "The temple was struck by a blow from the sun."

The fourth bad omen: Fire streamed through the sky while the sun was still shining. It was divided into three parts. It flashed out from where the sun sets and raced straight to where the sun rises, giving off a shower of sparks like a red-hot coal. When the people saw its long train streaming through the heavens, there was a great outcry and confusion, as if they were shaking a thousand little bells.

The fifth bad omen: The wind lashed the water until it boiled. It was as if it were boiling with rage, as if it were shattering itself in its frenzy. It began from far off, rose high in the air and dashed against the walls of the houses. The flooded houses collapsed into the water. This was in the lake that is next to us.

The sixth bad omen: The people heard a weeping woman night after night. She passed by in the middle of the night, wailing and crying out in a loud voice: "My children, we must flee far away from this city!" At other times she cried: "My children, where shall I take you?"

The seventh bad omen: A strange creature was captured in the nets. The men who fish the lakes caught a bird the color of ashes, a bird resembling a crane. They brought it to Motecuhzoma in the Black House.

This bird wore a strange mirror in the crown of its head. The mirror was pierced in the center like a spindle whorl, and the night sky could be seen in its face. The hour was noon, but the stars and the *mamalhuaztli* could be seen in the face of that mirror. Motecuhzoma took it as a great and bad omen when he saw the stars and the *mamalhuaztli*.

But when he looked at the mirror a second time, he saw a distant plain. People were moving across it, spread out in ranks and coming forward in great haste. They made war against each other and rode on the backs of animals resembling deer.

Motecuhzoma called for his magicians and wise men and asked them: "Can you explain what I have seen? Creatures like human beings, running and fighting . . . !" But when they looked into the mirror to answer him, all had vanished away, and they saw nothing.

The eighth bad omen: Monstrous beings appeared in the streets of the city: deformed men with two heads but only one body. They were taken to the Black House and shown to Motecuhzoma; but the moment he saw them, they all vanished away.

. . .

A few days later a *macehual* [common man] came to the city from Mictlancuauhtla. No one had sent him, none of the officials; he came of his own accord. He went directly to the palace of Motecuhzoma and said to him: "Our lord and king, forgive my boldness. I am from Mictlancuauhtla. When I went to the shores of the great sea, there was a mountain range or small mountain floating in the midst of the water, and moving here and there without touching the shore. My lord, we have never seen the like of this, although we guard the coast and are always on watch."

Motecuhzoma thanked him and said: "You may rest now." The man who brought this news had no ears, for they had been cut off, and no toes, for they had also been cut off.

Motecuhzoma said to his *petlacalcatl*: "Take him to the prison, and guard him well." Then he called for a *teuctlamacazqui* [priest] and appointed him his grand emissary. He said to him: "Go to Cuetlaxtlan, and tell the official in charge of the village that it is true, strange things have appeared on the great sea. Tell him to investigate these things himself, so as to learn what they may signify. Tell him to do this as quickly as he can, and take the ambassador Cuitlalpitoc with you."

When they arrived in Cuetlaxtlan, the envoys spoke with the official in charge there, a man named Pinotl. He listened to them with great attention and then said: "My lords, rest here with me, and send your attendants out to the shore." The attendants went out and came back in great haste to report that it was true: they had seen two towers or small mountains floating on the waves of the sea. The grand emissary said to Pinotl: "I wish to see these things in person, in order to learn what they are, for I must testify to our lord as an eyewitness. I will be satisfied with this and will report to him exactly what I see." Therefore he went out to the shore with Cuitlalpitoc, and they saw what was floating there, beyond the edge of the water. They also saw that seven or eight of the strangers had left it in a small boat and were fishing with hooks and lines.

The grand emissary and Cuitlalpitoc climbed up into a broad-limbed tree. From there they saw how the strangers were catching fish and how, when they were done, they returned to the ship in their small boat. The grand emissary said: "Come, Cuitlalpitoc." They climbed down from the tree and went back to the village, where they took hasty leave of Pinotl. They returned as swiftly as possible to the great city of Tenochtitlan, to report to Motecuhzoma what they had observed.

When they reached the city, they went directly to the king's palace and spoke to him with all due reverence and humility: "Our lord and king, it is true that strange people have come to the shores of the great sea. They were fishing from a small boat, some with rods and others with a net. They fished until late and then they went back to their two great towers and climbed up into them. There were about fifteen of these people, some with blue jackets, others with red, others with black or green, and still others with jackets of a soiled color, very ugly, like our *ichtilmatli*. There were also a few without jackets. On their heads they wore red kerchiefs, or bonnets of a fine scarlet color, and some wore large round hats like small *comales*, which must have been sunshades. They have very light skin, much lighter than ours. They all have long beards, and their hair comes only to their ears."

Motecuhzoma was downcast when he heard this report, and did not speak a word.

After a long silence, Motecuhzoma finally spoke: "You are the chiefs of my own house and palace and I can place more faith and credit in you than in anyone else because you have always told me the truth. Go with the *petlacalcatl* and bring me the man who is locked up in the jail, the *macehual* who came as a messenger from the coast." They went to the jail, but when they opened the doors, they could not find him anywhere. They hurried back to tell Motecuhzoma, who was even more astonished and terrified than they were. He said: "It is a natural thing, for almost everyone is a magician. But hear what I tell you now, and if you reveal anything of what I am about to command, I will bury you under my halls, and your wives and children will be killed, and your property seized. Your houses will be destroyed to the bottom of their foundations, until the water seeps up, and your parents and all your kin will be put to death. Now bring me in secret two of the best artists among the silversmiths, and two lapidaries who are skillful at working emeralds."

They went and returned and said to him: "Our lord, here are the craftsmen you commanded us to bring you." Motecuhzoma said: "Tell them to enter." They entered, and he said to them: "Come here to me, my fathers. You are to know that I have called for you to have you make certain objects. But take care that you do not reveal this to anyone, for if you do, it will mean the ruin of your houses to their foundations, and the loss of your goods, and death to yourselves, your wives, your children and your kin, for all shall die. Each of you is to make two objects, and you are to make them in my presence, here in secret in this palace."

He told one craftsman: "Make a throat-band or chain of gold, with links four fingers wide and very thin, and let each piece and medallion bear rich emeralds in the center and at the sides, like earrings, two by two. Then make a pair of gold bracelets, with chains of gold hanging from them. And do this with all the haste in the world."

He ordered the other craftsman to make two great fans with rich feathers, in the center of one side a half-moon of gold, on the other a gold sun, both well burnished so that they would shine from far away. He also told him to make two gold armlets rich with feathers. And he ordered each of the lapidaries to make two double bracelets—that is, for both wrists and both ankles—of gold set with fine emeralds.

Then he ordered his *petlacalcatl* to bring in secret many *canutos* of gold, and plumage of the noblest sort, and many emeralds and other rich stones of the finest quality. All of this was given to the artisans and in a few days they had finished their work. One morning, after the king had risen, they sent a palace hunchback to the king Motecuhzoma, to beg him to come to their workroom.

When he entered, they showed him great reverence and said: "Our lord, the work is finished. Please inspect it." Motecuhzoma saw that the work was excellent, and he told them that all had been done to his satisfaction and pleasure. He called for his *petlacalcatl* and said: "Give each of these, my grandfathers, a portion of various rich cloths; and huipiles and skirts for my grandmothers; and cotton, chiles, corn, squash seeds and beans, the same amount to each." And with this the craftsmen returned to their homes contented. . . .

From: León Portilla, Miguel, *The broken spears: the Aztec account of the Conquest of Mexico* (Boston: Beacon Press, 2006), pp. 3–6, 16–19.

QUESTIONS:

1. What do we learn about pre-Conquest Aztec beliefs, lives, society, and culture from this account of the first arrival of the Spaniards into Mexico?
2. Even though the account comes from Aztec informants, they must see the events they describe through the lens of fifty years of conquest, Christianization, and massive socioeconomic change. What passages show evidence of the Aztec informants' hindsight on events?

11.3: *The Book of Gods and Rites* (Diego Durán, c. 1574–76)

The other great source for pre-Conquest Aztec culture is *The Book of Gods and Rites,* written by the Dominican friar Diego Durán in the 1570s. A missionary like Bernard de Sahagún, Durán became fluent in Nahuatl and interviewed many Aztecs about their pre-Conquest culture. Though his Christian perspective is clear, he is a sympathetic chronicler.

Just as this Mexican nation had male gods, it also worshiped female deities, honored in the most solemn and elaborate festivities.

[Perhaps] some of these goddesses originated through qualities or graces or took the name of the rugged mountain where each was worshiped or of some idol to whom sacrifice was offered or of some place where there was a dark cave for the offering of sacrifice or of a place which gave birth to furious showers and thunderstorms, places called by the names of gods and goddesses. . . .

. . . The main goddess was called Cihuacoatl, deity of the people of Xochimilco; and though she was the special goddess of Xochimilco, she was revered and greatly exalted in Mexico, Tetzcoco, and all the land.

The goddess Cihuacoatl was made of stone. She had a huge, open mouth and ferocious teeth. The hair on her head was long and bulky, and she was clad in womanly garb—skirt, blouse, and mantle—all white. . . . This was the usual habit in which she was kept in her lofty and sumptuous temples, especially in that of Xochimilco, whose patroness she was. It *was* not quite as elaborate in Mexico or Tetzcoco. But even in these cities at the top of the steps [of the temple] stood a large chamber some sixty or seventy feet in length and thirty in width. This hall was elaborately decorated, and the goddess stood upon an altar no less ornate than the rest. This room was always pitch-black. It had no small openings, no windows, no main door save for a small one through which one could barely crawl. This door was always hidden by a sort of lid so that no one would see it and enter the chamber except for the priests who served the goddess. These were elders who performed the usual ceremonies. This room was called Tlillan, which means Blackness or the Place [of Blackness]. Next to the walls of this temple stood all the gods of the land, some large, some small. They were called Tecuacuiltin, which means Image of Stone or In the Round. All these idols were attired with paper scapulars striped with rubber (a gum we call *batel* [rubber], very common in the native offerings). These idols also wore paper headdresses or miters painted and striped with the same rubber.

The idols were taken out whenever it was necessary to perform a special feast for them or when their day arrived or when their help was needed. They were carried out in a procession to the woods, to the mountains, or to the caves from which they had taken their names. There, in that cave or in that forest, they were presented with the usual offerings and sacrifices, and the mountain was invoked for some special need—lack of water, a plague or famine, or a future war. When the ceremony had ended, [the image] was returned to the hall, to the place where it always stood.

The celebration of this goddess was held on the eighteenth of July according to our calendar, and according to theirs it was the festivity known as the Feast of Huey Tecuilhuitl, which was the eighth festivity of the calendar. Besides being the day of the commemoration of the goddess, it was a solemn day among the feasts of the calendar. . . .

Huey Tecuilhuitl means the Great Feast of the Lords, and was celebrated by the lords in a lordly way. Twenty days before the date this was done: a female slave was bought, purified, and dressed in the same manner as the stone idol—all in white with her white mantle. Thus dressed, she represented the goddess and received the honors and courtly attentions [the goddess herself] would have received had she been alive. She was taken from one feast to another, from one banquet to the next; she was led to all the market places and was regaled with every known type of gaiety and merriment. She was always kept drunk, tipsy, inebriated, out of her wits. Some say that this was done with wine; others say that, besides drinking wine, she was bewitched in one manner or another. This was done so that she would always walk about gaily, forgetting that she was to be slain. At night she slept in a cage, for they feared she might try to escape. The woman was named Xilonen.

Thus it went, from the day of her purification to that of her death.

First of all, on the day of her feast, one hour before dawn, the four captives were slain, and their bodies were cast upon the ground close together. The woman was thrown upon them, and her throat was slit. Her blood was then gathered in a bowl, and her heart was torn out. The stone goddess was touched with it and sprinkled with blood. The entire chamber and the idols were also sprinkled, and the bodies were given back to their owners for the banquet. All this was done early, one hour before dawn. The bodies of these four men were called the Dais of the Captives of the Goddess. It should be remarked, however, that the goddess was offered the same fire sacrifice as that offered to Xocotl, according to what some tell me and according to a picture I saw, dedicated to this deity. I wish here to tell some particulars about this and relate the method and manner used in sacrificing—a frightful thing.

Four days before the principal feast day of this goddess a fire was prepared in a great hearth within a room in front of the goddess's chamber; for four days and nights they never ceased feeding oakwood to that brazier, or hearth. The brazier, which was in the floor of the chamber, was made of finely carved stone and was called Teotlecuilli, which means Divine Brazier or Divine Hearth. This hearth was so stuffed with the live coals of oakwood that it burned like a furnace, furiously. On the same day, before the sacrifice of the woman who represented the goddess was performed, she was made to sit in the chamber in front of the fire and was greatly revered and honored. In her presence, in the place of the goddess, the sacrifice was offered [Plate 21]. The sacrifice was performed before this live woman and not before the stone one because the stone goddess was kept concealed within the dark chamber. No one was ever allowed to enter or leave that place unless he was [a person] of great importance and majesty. She was kept within that sacred place, and no priest, no other person, dared touch the statue. . . .

REGARDING THE COUNT OF THE PASSING OF THE YEARS USED BY THE NATIVES AND THE NUMBERS [OF DAYS] IN EACH WEEK AND THE IMAGES WITH WHICH THEY WERE REPRESENTED.

The curious reader interested in discovering what this circular design means will understand and easily comprehend what the characters and symbols signify. . . . It simply teaches us to understand the way in which the years were counted by the natives in olden times. Within this circle, it must be understood, we shall find fifty-two squares, and each signifies a year. So it is that in this circle are shown fifty-two years. These fifty-two years were called a hebdomadary by the natives. At the end of the cycle a solemn feast was held. This was called Nexiuhilpiliztli, which means Completion, or Binding, of a Perfect Circle of Years. At this time this round circle reached the end of its cycle and returned to its starting point again, terminating the complete number of fifty-two years. As I have described, a great solemnity and feast was held—it was in many ways similar to the manner in which the Jews under the Old Law commemorated the year of the jubilee every fifty years.

The round circle was divided into four parts, each part containing thirteen years. The first part belonged to the East, the second to the North, the third to the West, and the fourth to the South. The first part, belonging to the East, was called the Thirteen Years of the Reeds, and so it was that each square of the thirteen contained a picture of a reed and the number of the year in the same way that we reckon the day of this present year, as in December, 1579, we say, "Such and such a thing happened in this year."

So it was that the natives said: "On the year One Reed or Two or Three Reeds a certain thing took place."

. . .

The fifth month of the Mexica year fell upon May 20 according to our own calendar [Plate 42]. On this first day of the month, just as on the first days of the other months, was held a solemn feast called Toxcatl, one of the most ostentatious and imposing known to the Indians. I have dealt with this festivity in Chapter VIII [IV], when I referred to the solemnization of Tezcatlipoca, one of the most revered of all the native gods. The day was held to be so important that it excelled even that of Huitzilopochtli, as I have narrated in the above-mentioned chapter. There I explained that the festival, merrymaking, dance, farces, and representations can be compared to those of Corpus Christi, which usually falls around this time. Cursed be the Evil Adversary who planned it thus and brought this water to the mill so that his wheel would keep turning! And his mill grinds out the ceremonies, rites, and hellish sacrifices we have described.

Aside from being the day of the feast we have mentioned, this was one of the festivities counted by twenties, one of those which occurred at the beginning of the month. It was called Toxcatl. Though I had studied this name at length, I had been unable to decipher it because of the obscurity of the term. At long last I realized that it meant Dry Thing and that it symbolized drought. I finally understood it through a word uttered by a native informant. He told me that around this time of the year rain was scarce and was greatly desired. The people begged it of the god whose feast they were keeping, similar to the way we say "as welcome as rain in May." The Indians also had a proverb, *titotoxcahuia,* which means "to dry up with thirst," and so it is that Toxcatl means Drought and Lack of Rain. I am going to refer to some of the things which took place upon this day other than what I have said regarding the solemnization of this idol.

The priests performed a superstitious ceremony in every part of each town. Early in the morning the minor priests from the wards went from home to home with incense burners in their hands, and even though the master of the house was most humble, [the priest] would incense the entire house all the way from the threshold to the last corner. Having done this, he then went on to the furnishings of the home; he incensed the hearth, then the grinding stone, then the tortilla griddle, the pots, small vessels and jugs, the plates, bowls, weaving instruments, the agricultural implements, storage bins, and the artisans' tools. In this way everything received incense—even the little baskets in which were kept spinning and weaving instruments and those used for tortillas. The house owners were obliged to give alms to these priests. This was done in return for having performed the ceremony and having favored the house by incensing and blessing it. The ministers were given as many ears of corn as objects they had blessed. These priests went about in this way because of the alms which were given to them, since, as I have said, they lived on alms and in poverty. It was like Spain, where the acolytes go from door to door to sprinkle holy water with the hope that they will be given alms in the form of flour or firewood. Thus these priests ate nothing but that which was given to them as alms. They begged for it, and it was offered to them in the doorways, just as the fathers of Saint Francis do today. Because of this I think the Indians are especially fond of them.

On this day a great and solemn dance took place. All crowned themselves with headdresses or miters made up of small painted wreaths, beautifully adorned like latticework. In the small spaces between reed and reed hung little figures of gold or stone or many other finely worked things, for all those who danced were lords or chieftains. This feast was called Toxcanetotiliztli, which means Dance of Toxcatl. These crowns of headdresses were called tzatzaztli, which means "something wrought like a lattice." Since it was a great feast, the usual foods on this day were birds of different types and human flesh; this was the flesh of the numerous sacrificial victims on this occasion.

The purpose of this feast was to pray for rain. The people invoked the clouds when the water had ceased to fall in May, so that that which they requested would be granted. On this day there was a general invocation of the main gods: Huitzilopochtli and Tezcatlipoca, the Sun, and the goddess Cihuacoatl. All of these were remembered on that day. When the people of each town heard the piping of the flutes which were played on that day, everyone ate earth and prostrated himself on the ground.

Owing to their heathen customs, the natives of all this land ate toasted burst corn on this day. These grains of corn were like sweets. Besides eating them, the people made necklaces of the corn to adorn their idols and wore them around their necks while dancing. At this time men and women took part in the same dance, and each woman had to be a maiden. These maidens adorned their legs with red feathers up to the knee and on their arms as far down as the elbow. This superstition was usual at weddings: all those who were marriageable, as long as they were unwed maidens, were feathered on their legs and arms with red plumes. On this feast they were the singers who began the chanting, and the lords, who formed a circle about them, responded while the maidens danced around the drum.

From: Durán, Diego, *Book of the gods and rites and The ancient calendar,* Fernando Horcasitas and Doris Heyden, transl. (Norman: University of Oklahoma Press, 1971), pp. 210–13, 388–89, 426–28.

QUESTIONS:

1. What social functions did the festivals of gods and goddesses play? How, in other words, did Aztec religion make society function?
2. What advantages were there for Aztec society to structuring the year so meticulously according to a ritual calendar?

11.4: *Chronicles* (Pedro Cieza de León, before 1554)

Pedro de Cieza de León (c. 1520–54) was a Spanish conquistador who left home at the age of thirteen. Arriving in Peru at sixteen, in 1536, he spent the next fifteen years traveling and gathering information. Returning to Spain in 1551, he married and wrote his *Chronicles of Peru* in four parts. Though nominally a history of the Spanish conquest of the Inca Empire, his work is important for his detailed descriptions of the pre-Conquest peoples, cultures, flora, and fauna of the region. He published the first part of his book in 1553 but died the next year. The rest was only published in pieces in the last 140 years. This selection details Incan methods of taxation and record keeping.

THE MANNER IN WHICH THE PROVINCES WERE TAXED, AND THE EQUITABLE FASHION IN WHICH THIS WAS DONE

As in the previous chapter I described the way in which the Incas carried out their conquests, in this it would be well to tell how the different nations were taxed, and how the returns of this taxation were handled in Cuzco. For as is well known to all, not a single village of the highlands or the plains failed to pay the tribute levied on it by those who were in charge of these matters. There were even provinces where, when the natives alleged that they were unable to pay their tribute, the Inca ordered that each inhabitant should be obliged to turn in every four months a large quill full of live lice, which was the Inca's way of teaching and accustoming them to pay tribute. We know that for a time they paid their tax in lice until, after they had been given flocks and had raised them, and made clothing, they were able to pay tribute henceforth.

According to the *Orejones* of Cuzco and the other native rulers of the land, the system of taxing was said to be this: . . . when the Lord-Inca wished to learn what all the provinces between Cuzco and Chile, such a vast extension, were to contribute, he sent out, . . . , persons who enjoyed his confidence, who went from village to village observing the attire of the natives and their state of prosperity, and the fertility of the land, and whether they had flocks, or metals, or stores of food, or the other things which they valued and prized. After they had made a careful survey, they returned to report to the Inca about all this. He then called a general assembly of the principal men of the kingdom, and when the chieftains of the different provinces that were to be taxed had gathered, he addressed them with affectionate words, saying that inasmuch as they accepted him as sole sovereign and monarch of so many and such great lands, they would agree, without being distressed thereby, to give him the tribute due his royal person, which he wanted to be moderate and so unvexing that they could easily pay it. And when he had been answered to his satisfaction, certain of the *Orejones* set out with the native lords to fix the tribute they were to pay. In some regions this was more than that now paid to the Spaniards, but the system the Incas employed was so good that the people did not feel it, and prospered; but with the disorder and greed of the Spaniards the number of the people has fallen off to such a degree that most of them have disappeared, and they will be wiped out completely as a result of the covetousness and greed of most, or all of us here, . . .

On these visits of the envoys of the Incas to the provinces, as soon as they arrived they could tell from the quipus the number of people, men and women, old folks and children, and gold or silver miners, and they ordered that so many thousand Indians be put to work in the mines, to dig the amount of those metals that had been set to be turned over to the inspectors assigned for that purpose. And as during the time the Indians appointed to work the mines were doing this they could not cultivate their fields, the Incas ordered those from other provinces to come and plant the crops at the proper season in lieu of tribute, so that they [the fields] would not lie fallow. If the province was a large one, it furnished Indians both to mine the metals and to sow and work the land. If one of the Indians working in the mines got sick, he was allowed to return home at once, and another came to take his place; but none was assigned to the mines unless he was married so that his wives could look after his food and drink, and, aside from this, it was seen to it that they were supplied with food in abundance. With this way of doing things, none of them considered it hard work even if they spent their whole life in the mines, and none of them died from overwork. Besides, they were permitted to stop work several days in the month for their feasts and recreation; and the same Indians were not continuously in the mines, but every so often they were sent away and others came in their place.

So well had the Incas organized this that the amount of gold and silver mined throughout the kingdom was so great that there must have been years when they took out over fifty thousand arrobas of silver, and over fifteen thousand of gold, and all this metal was for their use. . . .

To know how and in what way the tributes were paid and the other taxes collected, each *huata,* which is the word for year, they sent out certain *Orejones* as supervisory magistrates, for they had no authority beyond visiting the provinces and notifying the inhabitants that if any of them had a complaint, he should state it, so that the one who had done him a wrong could be punished. And when the complaints were heard, if there were any, or it was learned that somewhere a debt was pending, they returned to Cuzco, from which another set out with authority to punish the culprits. In addition to this, there was another important provision, which was that from time to time the headmen of the provinces appeared on the day appointed for each nation to speak to bring to the knowledge of the Inca the state of the province and the shortage or abundance that existed in it, and whether the tribute was too large or too small, and whether they could pay it or not. After which they were sent away satisfied, for the Inca rulers were certain they were not lying but telling the truth. For if there was any attempt at deceit, stern punishment followed and the tribute was increased. Of the women given by the provinces, some of them were brought to Cuzco to become the possession of the Lord-Incas, and some of them were sent to the temple of the sun.

. . . When the Incas came to rule the natives of Peru, as this fashion and manner of living seemed bad to them, they ordered them, sometimes with flattery, other times with threats, and always with gifts they made them, to give up living like savages and behave like people of reason, establishing their villages with the houses beside one another on the plains and hillsides in keeping with the lay of the land. Thus these Indians, leaving the *pucarás* fortified strongholds they had first had, constructed their villages in comely fashion, both in the valleys of the savannah and in the highlands and plains of the Colla. . . .

Realizing how difficult it would be to travel the great distances of their land where every league and at every turn a different language was spoken, and how bothersome it would be to have to employ interpreters to understand them, these rulers, as the best measure, ordered and decreed, with severe punishment for failure to obey, that all the natives of their empire should know and understand the language of Cuzco, both they and their women. This was so strictly enforced that an infant had not yet left its mother's breast before they began to teach it the language it had to know. And although at the beginning this was difficult and many stubbornly refused to learn any language but their own, the Incas were so forceful that they accomplished what they had proposed, and all had to do their bidding. This was carried out so faithfully that in the space of a few years a single tongue was known and used in an extension of more than 1,200 leagues; yet, even though this language was employed, they all spoke their own [languages], which were so numerous that if I were to list them it would not be credited.

When a captain set out from Cuzco, or one of the *Orejones* went to check the accounts or make a report, or act as judge, or on some errand with which he had been entrusted, wherever he went he spoke no other language than that of Cuzco [i.e., Quechua], nor did those of the different provinces to him. It is a very good tongue, succinct, easily grasped, and rich in words and so clear that in the few days I gave to it, I knew enough to ask many things wherever I went. The word for man in this language is *runa;* woman, *huarmi;* father, *yaya;* brother, *huayqui;* sister, *nana;* the moon, *quilla,* which is also the word for month; year, *huata;* day, *pinche;* night, *tuta;* the head is called *uma,* and the ears, *rinri;* the eyes, *ñaui;* the nose, *senkka;* the teeth, *quiru;* the arms, *rillra;* and the legs, *chaqui.*

I include these words in this chronicle only because I now see that with regard to the ancient language of Spain, there are differences of opinion, and some say one thing, and some another. In times to come, God alone knows what things may happen; therefore, in case something should occur to bury or cause to be forgotten this language which was so widespread and used by so many people, there will be no doubt about which was the first or general, or where it came from, or whatever else may be sought to know. It was a great advantage for the Spaniards that there was this language, for with it they could go everywhere, and in some places it is already [i.e., 1549] disappearing. . . .

Of how they had chroniclers to keep record of their deeds, and the use of the quipus, and what we see of them now.

. . . [The Indians] had a method of knowing how the tributes of food supplies should be levied on the provinces when the Lord-Inca came through with his army, or was visiting the kingdom; or, when nothing of this sort was taking place, what came into the storehouses and what was issued to the subjects, so nobody could be unduly burdened, that was so good and clever that it surpasses the *carastes* used by the Mexicans for their accounts and dealings. This involved the quipus, which are long strands of knotted strings, and those who were the accountants and understood the meaning of these knots could reckon by them expenditures or other things that had taken place many years before. By these knots they counted from one to ten and from ten to a hundred, and from a hundred to a thousand. On one of these strands there is the account of one thing, and on the other of another, in such a way that what to us is a strange, meaningless account is clear to them. In the capital of each province there were accountants whom they called *quipu-camayocs,* and by these knots they kept the account of the tribute to be paid by the natives of that district in silver, gold, clothing, flocks, down to wood and other more insignificant things, and by these same quipus at the end of a year, or ten, or twenty years, they gave a report to the one whose duty it was to check the account so exact that not even a pair of sandals was missing.

I was dubious about this accounting, and even though I was assured that it was so done, I considered it for the most part a fable. But when I was in the province of Jauja, in what they call Marcavillca, I asked the cacique Huacara-pora to explain the system to me in such a way that I could understand it and make sure that it was exact and dependable. Whereupon he sent his servants to fetch the quipus, and as this man is of goodly understanding and reason, for all he is an Indian, he readily satisfied my request. He told me, so that I would better understand, that I should observe that all he had given to the Spaniards from the time of the entry of Governor Francisco Pizarro in the valley [1533] was recorded there without a single omission; and in this I saw the account of the gold, silver, and clothing that had been given, the llamas and other things, and I was amazed thereby. And there is another thing which I firmly believe: the wars, cruelties, pillaging, and tyranny of the Spaniards have been such that if these Indians had not been so accustomed to order and providence they would all have perished and been wiped out. But being very prudent and sensible, and trained by such wise princes, they all decided that if an army of Spaniards passed through any of the provinces, unless the harm was irreparable, such as destroying the crops and robbing the houses and doing other still greater damage, as all the regions along the highway by which our men passed had their accountants, these would give out all the supplies the people could furnish so as to avoid the destruction of everything, and thus they were provided. And after they had passed through, the chieftains came together with the keepers of the quipus, and if one had expended more than another, those who had given less made up the difference, so they were all on an equal footing. . . .

From: Cieza de León, Pedro de, Harriet De Onís, and Victor Wolfgang Von Hagen, *The Incas* (Norman: University of Oklahoma Press, 1959), pp. 161–75, passim.

QUESTIONS:

1. How sophisticated were Incan taxation and record keeping, according to this account? Does the author admire Incan administration?
2. Judging from what the author notices, how similar were the Incan and Spanish social structures? What were the key differences?

CHAPTER 12

War, States, Religions: 1100 to 1400

INTRODUCTION

This chapter presents sources that illustrate the increasing levels of cultural contact and conflict that characterized the period from 1100 to 1400. The intersection of warrior values with religious values, especially those associated with the salvation religions, featured prominently in many of these conflicts. The role of warrior elites in different societies often had implications for state building, a process illustrated in one particular form in our last source.

12.1: The First Crusade

12.1a: "The Siege of Antioch" from *The Chronicle, Book I* (Fulcher of Chartres, 1095–1100)

Fulcher of Chartres (c. 1059–1127?) was a French writer and priest who accompanied the army of the First Crusade and wrote a Latin prose chronicle of the events shortly afterwards—he probably started it shortly after the capture of Jerusalem in 1099. He became chaplain to Baldwin of Boulogne, one of the leaders of the crusade, at the siege of Antioch, which he describes in this excerpt. Baldwin became king of Jerusalem in 1100 and Fulcher probably lived in that city for the rest of his life. He disappears from any records after 1127, when he may have died in a plague that struck Jerusalem that year. His account of the Crusade is detailed and largely reliable (though not, of course, impartial) and was used as a primary source by many other twelfth-century Crusade historians.

1. In the month of October, after crossing the river which they call the Fernus or Orontes, the Franks came to Antioch in Syria, the city which Seleucus, son of Antiochus, founded and made the capital of Syria. It was formerly called Reblata. Tents were ordered to be pitched within the first milestone before the city, where later fierce encounters were often made by both sides. For when the Turks darted forth from that city, they killed many of our men. But retaliation having been made, they mourned for the men they had lost also.

2. Antioch is an extensive city, has a strong wall, and is well situated for defense. It could never be captured by outside enemies if the inhabitants, supplied with bread, wished to defend it long enough. . . .

4. The sea is about thirteen miles, I judge, from Antioch. Since the Fernus [Orontes] River happens to flow into the sea, boats loaded with all goods come from far distant parts almost to Antioch through the channel of this river. Thus the city, fortified by sea as well as by land, abounds in manifold riches.

5. When our princes had seen the great difficulty of overcoming it, they swore mutually by oath to work together in siege until, with God favoring, they would capture it either by force or by ruse.

6. They found some boats on the aforementioned river, which they seized, and out of them fashioned a bridge for themselves. They were able to cross over this to carry on their work, whereas before they had to wade over with difficulty.

7. When the Turks saw that they were besieged by such a great Christian multitude, they feared that they could in no way shake them off. After a plan was mutually formed, Aoxian, prince and emir of Antioch, sent his son, Sensadolus by name, to the Sultan, that is, the emperor, of Persia, to get his help most quickly, since they held hope for aid from no other except Mohammed, their advocate. Thus directed, he conducted this legation there very hastily.

. . .

8. Meanwhile, those who remained, awaiting the requested aid, guarded the city, and frequently plotted many kinds of harm to the Franks. Nevertheless the Franks resisted their cunning with all their power. . .

10. Alas! how many Christians, Greeks, Syrians, and Armenians, who lived in the city, were killed by the maddened Turks. With the Franks looking on, they threw outside the walls the heads of those killed, with their petrariae and slings. This especially grieved our people. Holding these Christians in hatred, the Turks feared lest by some chance they give the Franks information to their own detriment.

11. When the Franks had besieged the city for some time, and had pillaged the surrounding region for food necessary for themselves and had devastated it on all sides, bread could be bought nowhere, and they endured excessive hunger. As a result, everybody was especially desolate and many secretly considered withdrawal from the siege in flight, either by land or by sea.

12. They had no supplies on which they could live. It was with great fear that they sought food far away, in going distances of forty or fifty miles from the siege, that is, in the mountains, where they were often killed by the Turks lying in ambush.

13. We believed that these misfortunes befell the Franks, and that they not able for so long a time to take the city because of their sins. Not only dissipation, but also avarice or pride or rapaciousness corrupted them.

14. After holding council, they drove out the women from the army, both married and unmarried, lest they, stained by the defilement of dissipation, displease the Lord. Those women then found places to live in the neighboring camps.

. . .

1. In the year of the Lord 1098, after the region all around Antioch had been wholly devastated by the multitude of our people, the strong as well as the weak were more and more harassed by famine.

2. At that time, the famished ate the shoots of beanseeds growing in the fields and many kinds of herbs unseasoned with salt; also thistles, which, being not well cooked because of the deficiency of firewood, pricked the tongues of those eating them; also horses, asses, and camels, and dogs and rats. The poorer ones ate even the skins of the beasts and seeds of grain found in manure.

3. They endured winter's cold, summer's heat, and heavy rains for God. Their tents became old and torn and rotten from the continuation of rains. Because of this, many of them were covered by only the sky.

4. So like gold thrice proved and purified sevenfold by fire, long predestined by God, I believe, and weighed by such a great calamity, they were cleansed of their sins. . . .

8. The siege lasted continuously from this same month of October, as it was mentioned, through the following winter and spring until June. The Turks and Franks alternately staged many attacks and counter-attacks; they overcame and were overcome. Our men, however, triumphed more often than theirs. Once it happened that many of the fleeing Turks fell into the Fernus River, and being submerged in it, they drowned. On the near side of the river, and on the far side, both forces often waged war alternately.

XVII. THE SURRENDER OF THE CITY OF ANTIOCH

1. When it pleased God that the labor of His people should be consummated, perhaps pleased by the prayers of those who daily poured out supplications and entreaties to Him, out of His compassion He granted that through a fraud of the Turks the city be returned to the Christians in a secret surrender. Hear, therefore, of a fraud, and yet not a fraud.

2. Our Lord appeared to a certain Turk, chosen beforehand by His grace, and said to him: "Arise, thou who sleepest! I command thee to return the city to the Christians." The astonished man concealed that vision in silence.

3. However, a second time, the Lord appeared to him: "Return the city to the Christians," He said, "for I am Christ who command this of thee." Meditating what to do, he went away to his ruler, the prince of Antioch, and made that vision known to him. To him the ruler responded: "You do not wish to obey the phantom, do you, stupid?" Returning, he was afterwards silent.

4. The Lord again appeared to him, saying: "Why hast thou not fulfilled what I ordered thee? Thou must not hesitate, for I, who command this, am Lord of all." No longer doubting, he discreetly negotiated with our men, so that by his zealous plotting they might receive the city.

5. He finished speaking, and gave his son as hostage to Lord Bohemond, to whom he first directed that discourse, and whom he first persuaded. On a certain night, he sent twenty of our men over the wall by means of ladders made of ropes. Without delay, the gate was opened. The Franks, already prepared, entered the city. Forty of our soldiers, who had previously entered by ropes, killed sixty Turks found there, guards of the tower. In a loud voice, altogether the Franks shouted: "God wills it! God wills it!" For this was our signal cry, when we were about to press forward on any enterprise.

6. After hearing this, all the Turks were extremely terrified. Then, when the redness of dawn had paled, the Franks began to go forward to attack the city. When the Turks had first seen Bohemond's red banner on high, furling and unfurling, and the great tumult aroused on all sides, and the Franks running far and wide through the streets with their naked swords and wildly killing people, and had heard their horns sounding on the top of the wall, they began to flee here and there, bewildered. From this scene, many who were able fled into the citadel situated on a cliff.

7. Our rabble wildly seized everything that they found in the streets and houses. But the proved soldiers kept to warfare, in following and killing the Turks.

XVIII. THE FINDING OF THE LANCE

1. After the city was taken, it happened that a Lance was found by a certain man. When it was discovered in a pit in the ground of Saint Peter's Church, he asserted confidently that, according to the Scriptures, it was the one with which Longinus pierced Christ in the right side. He said that this had been revealed by Saint Andrew the Apostle.

2. When it had been found, and he himself had told this to the Bishop of Puy and to Count Raymond, the Bishop thought it was false, but the Count hoped it was true.

3. Upon hearing this, all the people, rejoicing, glorified God for it, and for almost a hundred days it was held in great veneration by all, and handled gloriously by Count Raymond, who guarded it. Then it happened that many of the clergy and the people hesitated, thinking it was not the Lord's Lance, but another one deceitfully found by that foolish man.

4. A plan was formed, and a three-day fast was fixed and executed with a supplication in prayer to God. After this, they set fire to a heap of wood in the middle of the plain before the town of

Archas. This was in the eighth month after the capture of Antioch. After an invocation asking for judgment was made over the fire by priests, the finder of the Lance spontaneously crossed quickly through the middle of the blazing pyre, as he himself had earnestly requested to prove his own truthfulness. After he crossed it, they saw him going forth from the flames as a culprit, burned on the skin, and they knew that he was mortally injured within, just as the end of the affair showed, for on the twelfth day, being burned, he died in anguish.

5. Since everybody had venerated that Lance for the honor and love of God, after judgment was thus accomplished, those who formerly appeared credulous of this culprit, now especially saddened, remained incredulous. Nevertheless, Count Raymond kept it for a long time after that.

XIX. THE SIEGE OF THE CHRISTIANS BY THE TURKS IN THE CITY OF ANTIOCH

1. On the day after Antioch had been taken, as has been told, an innumerable multitude of Turks surrounded the city in siege. The Sultan, that is, the King of the Persians, had been told by a legation that the Franks were besieging Antioch, and after collecting many people, immediately he sent an army against the Franks. Corbagath was the leader and commander of this people.

2. He had besieged the city of Edessa, which Lord Baldwin possessed at that time, for three weeks; but accomplishing nothing there, he hastened to Antioch to aid Prince Aoxian.

3. Seeing this army, the Franks were more desolate than ever, because punishment for their sins was doubled. For when they had entered the city, many of them had sought out unlawful women without delay.

4. Almost sixty thousand Turks entered by way of a fort on the top of a cliff. These exerted pressure on our men most fiercely in repeated attacks. There was not a pause; filled with great trembling, after leaving the city, they went forth to the siege. The Franks, shut in, remained unbelievably anxious.

. . .

XXI. THE BATTLE WHICH THE FRANKS ASKED OF THE TURKS

1. Meanwhile, after holding council, they announced to the Turks through a certain Peter the Hermit, that unless they peacefully evacuated the region which at one time belonged to the Christians, they would surely begin war against them on the following day. But if they wished it to be done otherwise, war could be waged by five or ten or twenty or by one hundred soldiers chosen from each side, so that with not all fighting at the same time, such a great multitude of people would not die, and the party which overcame the other would take the city and kingdom freely without controversy.

2. This was proposed, but not accepted by the Turks, who, confident in the large number of their people and in their courage, thought that they could overcome and destroy ours.

3. In number, they were estimated to be three hundred thousand altogether, both cavalry and infantry. They knew our knights had been forced to become footmen, weak and helpless.

4. After Peter, the ambassador, returned, the answer was given. After they heard it, the Franks prepared to fight, stopping at nothing, but placing their hope wholly in God.

5. There were many Turkish princes whom they called emirs present. These are Corbagath, Maleducat, Amisoliman, and many others whom it takes too long to name.

XXII. THE PREPARATION FOR BATTLE

1. The Frankish princes were: Hugh the Great, Robert, Count of the Normans, Robert, Count of Flanders, Duke Godfrey, Count Raymond, Bohemond, and others of lesser rank. May God bless the soul of Ademar, Bishop of Puy, an apostolic man, who always kindly comforted the people and strengthened them in the Lord.

2. Oh, pious circumstance! On the preceding evening, he ordered by heralds to all the soldiers of the army of God, that each one lay out as much grain as he could, considering the dearness of it, to supply his horse, so that those carrying the riders on the morrow might not become weak from hunger in the hour of battle. It was ordered, and it was done.

3. All having been thus prepared, they went forth to battle from the city in the early morning, which fell four days before the Kalends of July. The banners of the squadrons and lines, conveniently divided into troops and phalanges, went first. Among these were the priests clothed in white vestments, who, weeping for all the people, sang hymns to God, and poured out many prayers devoutly.

4. When a certain Turk, Amirdal by name, a well-proven soldier had seen our people with standards raised coming forth against them, he was exceedingly astonished. And when he had carefully regarded our nobles' standards, which he saw advancing one by one in order, he supposed that the battle would shortly ensue.

5. He had reconnoitred frequently in Antioch, where he had learned this about the Franks. He immediately hastened to Corbagath, and informed him what he had seen, saying: "Why do you amuse yourself with chess? Behold, the Franks are coming!" Corbagath responded to him: "Are they coming to fight?" Amirdal responded: "Up to the present time, I do not know, but wait a little while."

6. When Corbagath also saw the banners of our nobles carried before them in order and the divisions of men, properly ordered, following them, returning quickly, he said: "Behold, the Franks! What do you think?" Amirdal responded: "It is war, I believe, but it is still doubtful. I shall soon recognize to whom these standards, which I see, belong."

7. Looking more closely, he recognized the standard of the Bishop of Puy advancing in the third squadron. Without waiting any longer, he told Corbagath:

> "Behold, the Franks are coming; either flee now, or fight well; for I see the standard of the great Pope advancing. Today you may fear to be overcome by those whom you thought could be entirely annihilated."

8. Corbagath said: "I shall send word to the Franks, that what they asked of me yesterday, today I shall grant." Amirdal said, "You have spoken too late." Although he demanded it, he did not obtain what he asked. Amirdal presently

> Withdrawing from that place, drove his horse with spurs.
> He reflected whether or not to flee; yet he told his comrades
> That everybody should fight bravely and hurl arrows.

XXIII. THE BATTLE AND THE VICTORY OF THE CHRISTIANS AND THE FLIGHT OF THE TURKS

1. Behold, Hugh the Great and Count Robert the Norman, and also Robert, Count of Flanders, were stationed in the first line of battle for the attack. In the second, Duke Godfrey followed with the Germans and Lotharingians. After those marched the Bishop of Puy and the people of Count Raymond, Gascons and Provencals. Count Raymond himself remained in the city to guard it. Bohemond skilfully led the last division.

2. When the Turks saw that they were being fiercely attacked by the whole army of the Franks, they began to dart out in a scattered fashion, as was their custom, and to hurl arrows. But fear having been let loose from heaven against them, as if the whole world had fallen, all of them took to unrestrained flight, and the Franks chased them with all their might.

3. But because the Franks had few horses and these weak from hunger, they did not take as much booty as they should have. Nevertheless, all the

tents remained on the plains, and they found many kinds of things in them, such as gold, silver, coverlets, clothing, utensils, and many other things, which the Turks, in great flight, had left or flung away in their flight, namely, horses, mules, camels, asses, the best helmets, and bows and arrows with quivers.

4. Corbagath, who had slain the Franks many times with such cruel words and threats, fled more swiftly than a deer. But why did he, who had a people so great and so well equipped with horses, flee? Because he strove to fight against God, and the Lord seeing him afar, entirely broke his pomp and strength.

5. Because they had good and swift horses, they escaped, although the slower ones fell into the hands of the Franks. Many of them and of the Saracen infantry were killed. A few of ours were injured. When their women were found in the tents, the Franks did nothing evil to them except pierce their bellies with their lances.

6. Everybody, placed in such great need and distress, blessed and glorified God in a voice of exultation, God, who in the righteousness of His compassion liberated those trusting in Him from such savage enemies. He powerfully scattered them in defeat, after the Christians were almost conquered first. Made wealthy with the substance of those people, they returned pleased to the city.

From: Peters, Edward, *The First Crusade: the chronicle of Fulcher of Chartres and other source materials,* (Philadelphia: University of Pennsylvania Press, 1998), pp. 71–81.

QUESTIONS:

1. What conflicts do you see between the screen images the Crusaders have of themselves and their goal on one hand and their actions on the other? How do the central screen images affect the Crusaders' treatment of women and children, both Christian and Muslim?
2. How does Fulcher explain the victory of the Crusaders over the Turks that lifted the siege of Antioch?

12.1b: "The Siege of Antioch" from *The Perfect History* (Ibn al-Athīr, c. 1231)

Ibn al-Athīr (1160–1233) was an Arab or Kurdish historian best known for his *Complete History,* a world history written in Arabic. He lived, working as a scholar, for most of his life in Mosul, in northern Mesopotamia, as well as Damascus and Aleppo, and he made many visits to Baghdad. He spent some time traveling with the army of Saladin, the great Kurdish Muslim leader who dealt the Crusader States a near-fatal blow at the battle of Hattin in 1187. He is an excellent firsthand source for events from the late 1180s down to his death in 1233, including the first devastating Mongol invasion of the Islamic world (see Chapter 13). In this selection about the siege of Antioch, he draws on earlier Islamic historians and oral traditions to give the Muslim version of the events narrated in the previous source by Fulcher of Chartres.

In 490/1097 the Franks attacked Syria. This is how it all began: Baldwin, their King, a kinsman of Roger the Frank who had conquered Sicily, assembled a great army and sent word to Roger saying: 'I have assembled a great army and now I am on my way to you, to use your bases for my conquest of the African coast. Thus you and I shall become neighbours.'

Roger called together his companions and consulted them about these proposals. 'This will be a fine thing both for them and for us!' they declared, 'for by this means these lands will be converted to the Faith !' At this Roger raised one leg and farted loudly, and swore that it was of more use than their advice. 'Why?' 'Because if this army comes here it will need quantities of provisions and fleets of ships to transport it to Africa, as well as reinforcements from my own troops. Then, if the Franks succeed in conquering this territory they will take it over and will need provisioning from Sicily. This will cost me my annual profit from the harvest. If they fail they will return here and be an embarrassment to me here in my own domain. As well as all this Tamīm will say that I have broken faith with him and violated our treaty, and friendly relations and communications between us will be disrupted. As far as we are concerned, Africa is always there. When we are strong enough we will take it.'

He summoned Baldwin's messenger and said to him: 'If you have decided to make war on the Muslims your best course will be to free Jerusalem from their rule and thereby win great honour. I am bound by certain promises and treaties of allegiance with the rulers of Africa.' So the Franks made ready and set out to attack Syria.

. . .

When the Franks decided to attack Syria they marched east to Constantinople, so that they could cross the straits and advance into Muslim territory by the easier, land route. When they reached Constantinople, the Emperor of the East refused them permission to pass through his domains. He said: 'Unless you first promise me Antioch, I shall not allow you to cross into the Muslim empire.' His real intention was to incite them to attack the Muslims, for he was convinced that the Turks, whose invincible control over Asia Minor he had observed, would exterminate every one of them. They accepted his conditions and in 490/1097 they crossed the Bosphorus at Constantinople. Iconium and the rest of the area into which they now advanced belonged to Qilij Arslān ibn Sulaimān ibn Qutlumísh, who barred their way with his troops. They broke through in rajab 490/July 1097, crossed Cilicia, and finally reached Antioch, which they besieged.

When Yaghi Siyān, the ruler of Antioch, heard of their approach, he was not sure how the Christian people of the city would react, so he made the Muslims go outside the city on their own to dig trenches, and the next day sent the Christians out alone to continue the task. When they were ready to return home at the end of the day he refused to allow them. 'Antioch is yours,' he said, 'but you will have to leave it to me until I see what happens between us and the Franks.' 'Who will protect our children and our wives?' they said. 'I shall look after them for you.' So they resigned themselves to their fate, and lived in the Frankish camp for nine months, while the city was under siege.

Yaghi Siyān showed unparalleled courage and wisdom, strength and judgment. If all the Franks who died had survived they would have overrun all the lands of Islām. He protected the families of the Christians in Antioch and would not allow a hair of their heads to be touched.

After the siege had been going on for a long time the Franks made a deal with one of the men who were responsible for the towers. He was a cuirass-maker called Ruzbih whom they bribed with a fortune in money and lands. He worked in the tower that stood over the river-bed, where the river flowed out of the city into the valley. The Franks sealed their pact with the cuirass-maker, God damn him! and made their way to the water-gate. They opened it and entered the city. Another gang of them climbed the tower with ropes. At dawn, when more than 500 of them were in the city and the defenders were worn out after the night watch, they sounded their trumpets. Yaghi Siyān woke up and asked what the noise meant. He was told that trumpets had sounded from the citadel and that it must have been taken. In fact the sound came not from the citadel but from the tower. Panic seized Yaghi Siyān and he opened the city gates and fled in terror, with an escort of thirty pages. His army commander arrived, but when he discovered on enquiry that Yaghi Siyān had fled, he made his escape by another gate. This was of great help to the Franks, for if he had stood firm for an hour, they would have been wiped out. They entered the city by the gates and sacked it, slaughtering all the Muslims they found there. This happened in jumada I (491/April/May 1098). As for Yaghi Siyān, when the sun rose he recovered his self control and realized that his flight had taken him several *farsakh* from the city. He asked his companions where he was, and on hearing that he was four *farsakh* from Antioch he repented of having rushed to safety instead of staying to fight to the death. He began to groan and weep for his desertion of his household and children. Overcome by the violence of his grief he fell fainting from his horse. His companions tried to lift him back into the saddle, but they could not get him to sit up, and so left him for dead while they escaped. He was at his last gasp when an Armenian shepherd came past, killed him, cut off his head and took it to the Franks at Antioch.

The Franks had written to the rulers of Aleppo and Damascus to say that they had no interest in any cities but those that had once belonged to Byzantium. This was a piece of deceit calculated to dissuade these rulers from going to the help of Antioch.

. . .

When Qawām ad-Daula Kerbuqā heard that the Franks had taken Antioch he mustered his army and advanced into Syria, where he camped at Marj Dabiq. All the Turkish and Arab forces in Syria rallied to him except for the army from Aleppo. Among his supporters were Duqāq ibn Tutūsh, the Ata-beg Tughtikīn, Janāh ad-Daula of Hims, Arslān Tash of Sanjār, Sulaimān ibn Artūq and other less important amīrs. When the Franks heard of this they were alarmed and afraid, for their troops were weak and short of food. The Muslims advanced and came face to face with the Franks in front of Antioch. Kerbuqā, thinking that the present crisis would force the Muslims to remain loyal to him, alienated them by his pride and ill-treatment of them. They plotted in secret anger to betray him and desert him in the heat of battle.

After taking Antioch the Franks camped there for twelve days without food. The wealthy ate their horses and the poor ate carrion and leaves from the trees. Their leaders, faced with this situation, wrote to Kerbuqā to ask for safe-conduct through his territory but he refused, saying 'You will have to fight your way out.' Among the Frankish leaders were Baldwin, Saint-Gilles, Godfrey of Bouillon, the future Count of Edessa, and their leader Bohemond of Antioch. There was also a holy man who had great influence over them, a man of low cunning, who proclaimed that the Messiah had a lance buried in the Qusyān, a great building in Antioch: 'And if you find it you will be victorious and if you fail you will surely die.' Before saying this he had buried a lance in a certain spot and concealed all trace of it. He exhorted them to fast and repent for three days, and on the fourth day he led them all to the spot with their soldiers and workmen, who dug everywhere and found the lance as he had told them. Whereupon he cried 'Rejoice ! For victory is secure.' So on the fifth day they left the city in groups of five or six. The Muslims said to Kerbuqā: 'You should go up to the city and kill them one by one as they come out; it is easy to pick them off now that they have split up.' He replied: 'No, wait until they have all come out and then we will kill them.' He would not allow them to attack the enemy and when some Muslims killed a group of Franks, he went himself to forbid such behaviour and prevent its recurrence. When all the Franks had come out and not one was left in Antioch, they began to attack strongly, and the Muslims turned and fled. This was Kerbuqā's fault, first because he had treated the Muslims with such contempt and scorn, and second because he had prevented their killing the Franks. The Muslims were completely routed without striking a single blow or firing a single arrow. The last to flee were Suqmān ibn Artūq and Janāh ad-Daula, who had been sent to set an ambush. Kerbuqā escaped with them. When the Franks saw this they were afraid that a trap was being set for them, for there had not even been any fighting to flee from, so they dared not follow them. The only Muslims to stand firm were a detachment of warriors from the Holy Land, who fought to acquire merit in God's eyes and to seek martyrdom. The Franks killed them by the thousand and stripped their camp of food and possessions, equipment, horses and arms, with which they re-equipped themselves.

From: Gabrieli, Francesco, *Arab historians of the Crusades* (Berkeley, CA: University of California Press, 1984), pp. 3–12.

QUESTIONS:

1. What screen image of the Crusaders does the author project? How does it compare to the Crusaders' self-image?
2. What points of agreement are there between this account of the First Crusade and Fulcher's? What disagreements? Are the agreements more about events or attitudes? For example, how does the author account for the Turkish defeat that ended the siege?

12.2: *The Conquest of Constantinople* (Geoffroy Villehardouin, 1207)

Geoffrey de Villehardouin (c. 1160–c. 1212) was a French knight who participated in the infamous Fourth Crusade, including the capture of Constantinople in 1204. Starting around 1207, he wrote an account of the expedition, *The Conquest of Constantinople,* in French, the earliest French prose history to survive to the present day. Villehardouin was an interested chronicler, as he held important positions in the Crusading army and benefited from the division of spoils and land that followed the conquest of the city. But other contemporary accounts of the crusade show that while he has his own perspective, he is not inaccurate about the main events.

SECOND SIEGE OF CONSTANTINOPLE

February–April 1204

I will now leave this subject and return to the troops before Constantinople. These had put all their machines in working order, set up their petraries and mangonels and every other device of use in taking a city on their warships and transports, and raised scaling ladders so high on the lateen yards that it was a sight to wonder at.

The Greeks, for their part, seeing these preparations in hand, had begun to strengthen the defences of the city, which was already well entrenched behind high walls and towers. There was, however, no tower so high that they did not add two or three wooden storeys to it to heighten it still more. No city, in fact, had ever been so well fortified. In this way both Greeks and Franks had employed their time, working continuously during the greater part of Lent.

The barons now held a conference to discuss what plan of action to adopt. Plenty of different suggestions were put forward, but in the end the following decisions were taken: if, by God's grace, they effected an entry by force into the city, they would have all the booty collected in one place, and fairly and properly shared out among the troops; if in addition, they gained complete control of the city, they would choose six men from the French army, and six from among the Venetians, who would each be required to swear on the Holy Gospels that they would elect as Emperor the man whom they considered most fitted to rule in the best interests of the state. Whoever was thus elected Emperor would have as his share one quarter of all the booty, whether within the city or without, and would also be given possession of the palaces of Bucoleon and Blachemae. The remaining three-quarters of the booty would be divided into two equal parts, one to be allotted to the Venetians and the other to the French. After this they would select twelve of the wisest and most capable men in the French army, and twelve equally qualified

Venetians, who would be responsible for allotting fiefs and offices and arranging what services were to be rendered to the Emperor for such honours.

This compact was confirmed by oath on the part of French and Venetians alike, with the provision that at the end of March in the following year anyone who wished to leave would be free to go where he pleased. Those who remained, however, would come under the jurisdiction of the Emperor to perform such service for him as he required. To complete the compact a final clause was added to the effect that anyone failing to observe its terms would do so on pain of excommunication.

The fleet was now well equipped and armed, and all the provisions the Crusaders would need had been put aboard. On the Thursday after mid-Lent Sunday all the troops embarked on the warships, and the horses were put into the transports. Each division had its own ships, ranged one beside the other, the warships alternating with galleys and transports. It was, I can assure you, a marvellous sight to see the fleet drawn up in battle-formation, in a line extending well over half a French league.

On the Friday morning the warships, galleys, and other vessels approached the city in due order, and began to deliver a fierce and determined assault. In many places the Crusaders landed and advanced right up to the walls; in many others the scaling ladders on the ships came so close to the battlements that those on the walls and the towers crossed lances hand to hand with their assailants. The assault continued, fast and fierce and furious, in more than a hundred places, till round about three o'clock in the afternoon.

But, for our sins, our troops were repulsed in that attack, and those that had landed from the galleys and transports were forcibly driven back aboard. I must admit that on that day our army lost more men than the Greeks, and the latter were greatly delighted. Some of our people withdrew from the assault, taking their ships right out of the battle; others let their vessels ride at anchor so near the walls of the city that each side was able to launch stones from petraries and mangonels at the other.

That evening, towards six o'clock, the barons and the Doge of Venice assembled for a conference in a church on the further side of the harbour, close to where they had been encamped. Many different points of view were exchanged at that meeting; the French, in particular, were greatly distressed by the reverse they had suffered that day. Many of those present advised an attack on the city from another side, at a place where the defences were weaker. The Venetians, who had more experience of the sea, pointed out that if they went to that side, the current would carry them down the straits, and they would be unable to stop their ships. There were, I might say, certain people in the company who would have been only too pleased if the current had borne them down the straits, or the wind had done so; they did not care where they went, so long as they left that land behind and went on their way. Nor was that to be wondered at, for we were in very grave danger at the time.

After much discussion, it was finally decided to spend the next day, which was a Saturday, and the whole of Sunday, repairing the damage done to the ships and the equipment, and to renew the assault on the Monday. This time they would have the ships that carried the scaling ladders bound together, two by two, so that each pair could make a combined attack on one tower. This plan was adopted because, in that day's engagement, they had noticed that when only one ship had attacked each tower, the greater number of men on a tower than on a ladder had made it too heavy a task for a ship to undertake alone. It was therefore reasonable to assume that two ships together would do more effective damage than one. This plan of binding the ships in pairs was carried out while the troops were standing by on the Saturday and the Sunday.

Meanwhile the Emperor Murzuphlus had come to encamp with all his forces on an open space directly opposite our lines, and had pitched his scarlet tents there. Thus matters remained till the Monday morning, when all the men on the various ships got their arms and equipment ready. The citizens of Constantinople were now much less afraid of our troops than at the time of our first assault. They were, in fact, in such a confident mood that all along the walls and towers there was nothing to be seen but people. Then began a fierce and magnificent assault, as each ship steered a straight course forward. The shouts that rose from the battle created such a din that it seemed as if the whole earth were crumbling to pieces.

The assault had been going on for a considerable time when our Lord raised for us a wind called Boreas, which drove the ships still further on to the shore. Two of the ships which were bound together – the one called the *Pilgrim* and the other the *Paradise* – approached so close to a tower, one of them on one side and one on the other, as God and the wind drove them onwards, that the ladder of the *Pilgrim* made contact with it. Immediately a Venetian, in company with a French knight named André Durboise, forced their way in. Other men began to follow them, and in the end the defenders were routed and driven out.

The moment the knights aboard the transports saw this happen, they landed, and raising their ladders against the wall, climbed to the top, and took four more towers. Then all the rest of the troops started to leap out of warships, galleys, and transports, helter-skelter, each as fast as he could. They broke down about three of the gates and entered the city. The horses were then taken out of the transports; the knights mounted and rode straight towards the place where the Emperor Murzuphlus had his camp. He had his battalions drawn up in front of the tents; but as soon as his men saw the knights charging towards them on horseback, they retreated in disorder. The Emperor himself fled through the streets of the city to the castle of Bucoleon.

Then followed a scene of massacre and pillage: on every hand the Greeks were cut down, their horses, palfreys, mules, and other possessions snatched as booty. So great was the number of killed and wounded that no man could count them. A great part of the Greek nobles had fled towards the gate of Blachernae; but by this time it was past six o'clock, and our men had grown weary of fighting and slaughtering. The troops began to assemble in a great square inside Constantinople. Then, convinced that it would take them at least a month to subdue the whole city, with its great churches and palaces, and the people inside it, they decided to settle down near the walls and towers they had already captured.

. . .

Our troops, all utterly worn out and weary, rested quietly that night. But the Emperor Murzuphlus did not rest; instead, he assembled his forces and said he was going to attack the Franks. However he did not do as he had announced, but rode along certain streets as far away as possible from those occupied by our army, till he came to a gate called the Golden Gate through which he escaped, and so left the city. All the Greeks who could manage to do so followed him in his flight. But our army knew absolutely nothing of all this.

During that night, near the place where the Marquis de Montferrat had encamped, certain unknown persons, fearing the enemy might attack them, set fire to the buildings between themselves and the Greeks. The fire began to take hold on the city, which was soon blazing fiercely, and went on burning the whole of that night and all the next day till evening. This was the third fire there had been in Constantinople since the French and Venetians arrived in the land, and more houses had been burnt in that city than there are in any three of the greatest cities in the kingdom of France.

That night passed, and the next day came; it was a Tuesday. Early that morning all the troops, knights and sergeants alike, armed themselves, and each man went to join his division. They left their quarters thinking to meet with stronger resistance than they had encountered the day before, since they did not know that the Emperor had fled during the night. But they found no one to oppose them.

The Marquis de Montferrat rode straight along the shore to the palace of Bucoleon. As soon as he arrived there the place was surrendered to him, on condition that the lives of all the people in it should be spared. . . .

In the same way that the palace of Bucoleon was surrendered to the Marquis de Montferrat, so the palace of Blachernae was yielded to the Comte de Flandre's brother Henri, and on the same conditions. There too was found a great store of treasure, not less than there had been in the palace of Bucoleon. The Marquis de Montferrat and Henri de Flandre each garrisoned the castle surrendered to him, and set a guard over the treasure.

The rest of the army, scattered throughout the city, also gained much booty; so much, indeed, that no one could estimate its amount or its value. It included gold and silver, table-services and precious stones, satin and silk, mantles of squirrel fur, ermine and miniver, and every choicest thing to be found on this earth. Geoffroy de Villehardouin here declares that, to his knowledge, so much booty had never been gained in any city since the creation of the world.

Everyone took quarters where he pleased, and there was no lack of fine dwellings in that city. So the troops of the Crusaders and the Venetians were duly housed. They all rejoiced and gave thanks to our Lord for the honour and the victory He had granted them, so that those who had been poor now lived in wealth and luxury. Thus they celebrated Palm Sunday and the Easter Day following, with hearts full of joy for the benefits our Lord and Saviour had bestowed on them. And well might they praise Him; since the whole of their army numbered no more than twenty thousand men, and with His help they had conquered four hundred thousand, or more, and that in the greatest, most powerful, and most strongly fortified city in the world.

From: Geoffroi de Villehardouin, and Jean Joinville, *Chronicles of the Crusades* (Baltimore: Penguin Books, 1963), pp. 87–93.

QUESTIONS:

1. How does Villehardouin characterize the Greek elites? How does this characterization contribute to his justification of the attack on Constantinople?
2. What contrasts do you see between how Villehardouin characterizes the city of Constantinople itself and how he characterizes its inhabitants?

12.3: *The Poem of the Cid* (Anonymous, c. twelfth century)

Rodrigo Diaz de Vivar (c. 1040–99) was a Castilian nobleman whose military exploits inspired an epic poem known as *The Poem of the Cid.* ("Cid" is from a Muslim honorific world and means something like "Lord".) Rodrigo was exiled by the king of Castile in 1081 for political reasons, and he spent the next decade as a mercenary leader for Muslim and Christian rulers alike. By 1094 he had conquered for himself an independent principality based on Valencia. The *Poem,* which mixes historical fact and fiction freely, is difficult to date: it seems to originate with an anonymous literary composition of the 1130s, but survives only in a fourteenth century manuscript copy of a version copied in 1207. The selections here recount El Cid's preparations for going into exile and his capture of the city of Castejon.

1. Tears streamed from his eyes as he turned his head and stood looking at them. He saw doors left open and gates unlocked, empty pegs without fur tunics or cloaks, perches without falcons or moulted hawks. The Cid sighed, for he was weighed down with heavy cares. Then he said, with dignity and restraint: 'I give Thee thanks, O God, our Father in Heaven. My wicked enemies have contrived this plot against me.'

2. They made ready for the journey and slackened their reins. As they left Vivar a crow flew on the right, and as they entered Burgos they saw it on the left. The Cid shrugged his shoulders and nodded his head: 'Good cheer, Álvar Fáñez, for we are banished from this land.'

3. Ruy Díaz entered Burgos with his company of sixty knights. Men and women came out to see him pass, while the burghers and their wives stood at their windows, sorrowfully weeping. With one accord they all said, 'What a good vassal. If only he had a good lord!'

4. They would have offered him hospitality, but no one dared to do so for fear of the King's anger. The King's despatch had arrived the night before, laying down severe conditions and heavily sealed: . . . All these Christian people were overcome with grief; they hid from the Cid and dared not speak to him. The Campeador made his way to the house where he hoped to lodge, but when he arrived there he found the door locked fast. They had all agreed on this: for fear of King Alfonso, if the Cid did not break in the door, nobody would open it to him. His followers called loudly, but those within returned no answer. The Cid spurred his horse, rode up to the door and, drawing his foot from the stirrup, gave it a kick, but the door did not open, for it was securely locked. A little nine-year-old girl appeared (and said): 'Campeador, you were knighted in a fortunate hour. The King has forbidden us (to receive you); his letter came last night, with harsh conditions and heavy seals. We could not possibly dare to open the door or ask you to come in. If we did, we should lose our money and our houses and even the sight of our eyes. Cid, you have nothing to gain by our misfortune. May the Creator protect you with all his holy powers.' When the little girl had finished speaking she turned and went back into her house. Then the Cid saw that he had lost the King's favour. He turned away from the door and rode through Burgos. When he came to the Church of Santa María he alighted from his horse, knelt down and prayed from his heart. When his prayer was ended the Cid remounted, rode out by the city gate and crossed the river Arlanzón. Beside the town (of Burgos) he had his tent pitched on the sandy shore and then dismounted. The Cid Ruy Díaz, knighted in a fortunate hour, encamped on the river bank, since no one would give him lodging in his house; with his good band of followers around him he settled there as if he were out in the woods. He had been forbidden to buy any food at all in the town of Burgos, and they did not dare to sell him as much as a pennyworth.

5. Martín Antolínez, worthy citizen of Burgos, provided the Cid and his companions with bread and wine; he did not buy them, for he had them already. He supplied them lavishly with provisions for the journey, and the Cid and all those who served him were very well satisfied. Martín Antolínez spoke, and you will hear what he said: 'Campeador, born in a fortunate hour, let us rest here tonight and take our departure in the morning, for I shall be accused of having helped you and shall incur the King's anger. If I escape safe and sound with you, sooner or later the King will want me for a friend. Whether or not, I don't care a fig for all that I am leaving behind.'

6. The Cid spoke: 'Martín Antolínez, you are a brave and daring fighter. If I survive, I shall double your pay. I have spent the gold and all the silver. As you can very well see, I have no money with me and I shall need some to pay all my followers. I shall do this reluctantly, but otherwise I should have nothing. With your help I shall provide two chests: let us fill them with sand to make them very

heavy; they shall be covered with figured leather and finely studded.

7. The leather will be red and the studs will be fine golden ones. You must go in secret to Rachel and Vidas. (Say) that I am forbidden to trade in Burgos and that the King has banished me; I cannot carry my wealth about with me as it is too heavy, so I intend to pawn it for a reasonable sum. Let them take it away by night so that no one may see it. May the Creator and all His saints see it (and know) there is nothing else I can do, and I do it reluctantly.'

. . .

19 After having his supper, the Cid lay down and fell into a deep and pleasant sleep. When the Cid awoke he made the sign of the cross on his forehead and his lips. He crossed himself and commended himself to God, greatly pleased with his dream.

20 Next morning they mounted and rode on their way, for note that they had only one day left; they came to a halt at the Sierra de Miedes.

21 It was still daylight and the sun had not set when the Cid ordered a review of his men. Not counting the valiant foot soldiers he reckoned three hundred horsemen, each with a pennon on his lance.

22 '(Do not fail to) rise early to give fodder to the horses, as you hope for salvation. Any man who wishes to eat may do so; the rest (must) mount and ride on. We shall cross this wild and lofty mountain range and leave the land of King Alfonso tonight. After that anyone who wishes to join us will be able to find us.' They crossed the mountains by night and when morning came they began the descent into the valley. In the middle of a vast wood the Cid ordered a halt to be made to feed the horses. He told his followers that he wished to continue marching by night, and like good vassals they wholeheartedly agreed to obey his commands. So they mounted again before nightfall, for the Cid wished to avoid discovery. They travelled all night without resting, and at the place called Castejón de Henares the Cid went into ambush with the whole of his troops. The Cid lay all night in ambush. . . . Dawn was breaking; it was morning, and what a lovely sunrise it was! In Castejón the inhabitants got up, opened the gates and went out to inspect their estates and the farm-work in progress there. Everyone went out, leaving the gates open. Only a few were left in Castejón, for most of them were scattered about in the fields. The Campeador issued from his hiding place and harried Castejón, capturing many Moorish men and women with the cattle and sheep that were in the fields. Don Rodrigo marched up to the gate, and when those on guard there saw the sudden attack they took fright and left it undefended. The Cid went through the gate and, carrying his sword unsheathed in his hand, he overtook and killed fifteen Moors. In the capture of Castejón he won much gold and silver. His knights then arrived with the loot they had collected and handed it over to the Cid as if it meant nothing to them. Here you have the two hundred and three knights of the raiding party going relentlessly into the attack. Minaya's banner reached Alcalá, and back upstream his men returned with the spoils, along the river Henares and through Guadalajara. They carried away great quantities of booty in sheep and cattle, garments and other rich gains. Minaya's banner went forward, borne high, and no one dared to disturb the rearguard. His troops returned with all this wealth and presented themselves in Castejón, where the Campeador was already in possession. He left the fortress well guarded and rode out with his men to welcome them. He received Minaya with open arms (saying): 'Here you come, Álvar Fáñez, (like the) daring fighter that you are! Wherever I send you I expect to hear of victory. Putting the two lots of booty together I give you a fifth share of the whole, *if* you will accept it, Minaya.'

24 'I am most grateful to you, illustrious Campeador' (Minaya answered). 'King Alfonso of Castile would be well pleased with the fifth share you have assigned to me. I hand it back to you to have again freely, and I swear in God's name that

until, on my good horse, fighting Moors in the field, I use my lance and my sword till the blood drips down to my elbow in the presence of the great warrior Ruy Díaz, I shall not take a penny piece from you. Until I have won on your behalf some really valuable prize, I leave everything in your hands.'

25 When all the booty had been collected together the fortunate Cid, reflecting that King Alfonso might arrive with his army and seek to harm him and his vassals, ordered those charged with the task to distribute all this wealth, writing down every man's share. The gains were great, one hundred marks falling to the share of each knight and half that amount to each foot soldier, the Cid receiving his customary fifth share. He could not sell or give it away, and as he did not wish to take the men and women prisoners with him, he parleyed with the inhabitants of Castejón and sent word to those of Hita and Guadalajara, asking how much they would offer for his shareeven with what the Moors would give they would make a great gain. The Moors calculated the value of the property at three thousand silver marks, and the Cid was satisfied with this gift, which was paid in full on the third day. The Cid reckoned that he and his men should not remain in the fortress, for though he could indeed hold it, there would be no water there. 'The Moors' (he thought) 'are at peace, having a pact in writing, and King Alfonso might come after us with his entire army, so I shall leave Castejón.' (Then he said) 'Listen to me, my men, and Minaya ÁlvarFáñez.

26 Do not take in bad part what I am about to say. We cannot remain in Castejón, for King Alfonso is not far off and will come in search of us. I do not wish to destroy the fortress, so I shall set free one hundred Moorish men and their women, that they may not blame me for taking it from them. You are all well provided for and no one has been left unpaid. Let us ride away tomorrow morning, for I should not like to fight against my lord, King Alfonso.' The Cid's decision pleased them all. They went away from the fortress which they had taken with a rich booty and the blessings of the Moorish men and women. They rode at full speed up the river Henares, traversed the Alcarria and went pastthe caves of Anguita. There they crossed the river (Tajuña) and entered Campo Taranz, riding down through those lands as quickly as they could, taking great booty as they went. At length the Cid pitched his camp between Ariza and Cetina. The Moors were at a loss to know what his plan might be. The next day the Cid, the man from Vivar, struck camp, passed Alhama and went down the river bend and past Bubierca and Ateca, which is farther on. Then he encamped near Alcocer on a great rounded height. As the river Jalón ran past it their water could not be cut off, so the Cid made up his mind to take Alcocer.

. . .

31 Listen to me, Álvar Fáñez, and all my knights. We have gained great wealth in capturing this stronghold; many Moors lie dead and few remain alive. We shall not be able to sell our captives, whether men or women. We should gain nothing by cutting off their heads. Let us allow them to return to the town, for we are masters here. We shall occupy their houses and make them serve us.'

From: Hamilton, Rita, Janet H. Perry, and Ian Michael, *The Poem of the Cid* (Harmondsworth: Penguin, 1984), pp. 23–27, 43–55.

QUESTIONS:

1. The poem projects a screen image of El Cid that is heroic. What attributes of the El Cid contribute to this image, that is, what does this society value in a hero?
2. What motivates El Cid and his followers? How important does religion seem compared to material and other considerations?

12.4: *The Tale of the Heike* (from oral tradition, c. thirteenth century)

The Tale of the Heike is an epic war tale that tells the story of the Genpei War of 1180 to 1185, in which the forces of the Minamoto clan, led from Kamakura by Minamoto Yoritomo, defeat the ruling the Taira clan based in Kyoto, the capital and site of the imperial court. In a characteristic Japanese way, the losing Taira (also known as the Heike) are the tragic heroes of the tale, along with Minamoto Yoshitsune, a younger brother of Yoritomo who led the major Minamoto victories only to be falsely accused of treason by his politically ruthless brother. This tale of honorable losers emerged from an oral tradition of war tales sung by wandering Buddhist monks. The written version translated here dates to the fourteenth century. This selection tells the fates of two members of the Taira clan at the end of the decisive battle of the war.

9.15. THE CAPTURE OF SHIGEHIRA

Middle Captain Shigehira, the deputy commander at Ikuta-no-mori, had been deserted by all of his men but one. That day, he was wearing a dark blue tunic, embroidered with bright yellow plovers, and a suit of armor with purple-shaded lacing, and he was riding a famous charger named Dōji Kage [Child Deerskin]. His foster-brother, Morinaga, was wearing a tie-dyed tunic with white spots and a suit of armor with flame-red lacing, and he was riding Shigehira's prized horse Yomenashi Tsukige [Night-eyeless White].

Recognizing Shigehira as a commander-in-chief, Kajiwara Genda Kage-sue and Shō no Shirō Takaie pursued him with flailing whips and flapping stirrups. Too hard-pressed to escape to one of the many rescue vessels at the water's edge, Shigehira crossed the Minato and Karumo rivers, galloped between Hasu Pond on the right and Koma Woods on the left, passed Itayado and Suma, and fled westward. His splendid mount forged farther and farther ahead, until there seemed little chance that the battle-weary Genji horses could overtake him. But Kagesue stood in his stirrups, drew his bow to the full, and sent off an arrow, hoping for a lucky hit. The arrow sank shaft-deep into Dōji Kage's rump. When the horse faltered, Morinaga raised his whip and fled, possibly because he feared that Shigehira would take his horse.

"What are you doing, Morinaga? This isn't the way you always swore to act! Where will you go after you desert me?" Shigehira asked. Morinaga pretended not to hear. He got rid of his red armor-badge and rode away as fast as he could.

The enemy was approaching and the horse was weakening. Shigehira rode into the sea, but the water was shoaling, too shallow to drown in. He dismounted, slashed his belt, and unfastened his shoulder-cord. Then he took off his armor and helmet and got ready to cut open his belly.

Takaie came up ahead of Kagesue, galloping with flailing whip and flapping stirrups. He jumped down. "It would be a mistake to kill yourself," he said. "I'll attend you wherever you go." He mounted Shigehira on his own horse, tied him to the pommel, and escorted him back, riding a remount.

Thanks to his splendid, long-winded steed, Morinaga got away without any trouble. Later, he sought refuge with a Kumano monk, the Onaka Dharma Bridge. After the monk's death, he went to the capital with the widow, a nun who was prosecuting a lawsuit, and everybody recognized him as Shigehira's foster-brother. "He's a shameless rascal!" people said. "Shigehira thought the world of him, but he refused to face death at his master's side. Instead, the wretch turns up with a nun, of all things!" We are told that the criticism seems to have embarrassed even so dishonorable a man, and that Morinaga hid his face with a fan.

9.16. THE DEATH OF ATSUMORI

After the defeat of the Heike, Kumagae no Naozane walked his horse toward the beach. "The Taira nobles will be fleeing to the shore to get on board the rescue vessels," he thought. "I wish I could wrestle with one of their high-ranking commanders-in-chief!" Just then, he saw a lone rider splash into the sea, bound for a vessel offshore. The enemy was wearing a silk tunic embroidered with cranes, a suit of armor with shaded green lacing, and a horned helmet. At his waist, there was a sword with gilt bronze fittings; on his back, he carried a quiver containing arrows fledged with black-banded white eagle feathers. He held a rattan-wrapped bow and rode a white-dappled reddish horse, with a saddle trimmed in gold. When the horse had swum out a hundred and fifty or two hundred feet, Naozane beckoned with his fan.

"I see that you're a commander-in-chief! It's dishonorable to show your back to an enemy! Come on back!" he shouted.

The warrior came back. As he left the water, Naozane rode up beside him, gripped him as hard as he could, and crashed with him to the ground. Holding him motionless, he pushed aside his helmet, intending to cut off his head, and saw that he was only sixteen or seventeen years old, with a lightly powdered face and blackened teeth—a boy just the age of Naozane's own son Naoie, and so handsome that he could find no place to strike.

"Who are you? Announce your name. I'll spare you," Naozane said.

"Who are you?" the youth asked.

"Nobody of any special importance: Kumagae no Jirō Naozane of Musashi Province."

"Then I don't need to give you my name. I'm the kind of opponent you want. Ask about me after you take my head. Somebody will recognize me, even if I don't tell you."

"He's bound to be a commander-in-chief," Naozane thought. "Killing this one person won't change defeat into victory, and sparing him won't change victory into defeat. When I think of how I grieved when Naoie got just a little wound, it's easy to imagine how this young lord's father would feel if he heard that he'd been killed. I have a notion to let him go." Casting a swift glance to the rear, he discovered Sanehira and Kagetoki coming along with fifty riders.

"I'd like to spare you," he said, restraining tears, "but there are Genji warriors everywhere. You can't possibly escape. It will be better if I'm the one to kill you, because I'll offer prayers for you."

"Just take my head; don't waste time," the boy said.

Overwhelmed by compassion, Naozane could find no place to strike. His senses reeled, his brain seemed paralyzed, and he was scarcely conscious of his surroundings. But matters could not go on like that forever. In tears, he took the head.

"No life is as miserable as a warrior's. It's only because I was born into a military house that I've had this terrible experience. What a cruel thing I've done!" He pressed his sleeve to his face and wept.

But matters could not go on like that forever. He started to remove the youth's tunic, preparatory to wrapping the head in it, and found a flute in a brocade bag tucked in at the waist. "Poor fellow! He must have been one of the people I heard playing inside the stronghold just before dawn. There are tens of thousands of riders in our eastern armies, but I'd be willing to bet not one of them carried a flute to the battlefield. Those court nobles are men of refinement," he thought.

When Naozane's trophies were presented to Yoshitsune for inspection, they brought tears to everyone's eyes. It was learned later that the slain youth was Atsumori, aged seventeen, a son of Tsunemori, the head of the Palace Repairs Office.

After that, Naozane thought increasingly of becoming a monk.

The flute in question is supposed to have been a present from Retired Emperor Toba to Atsumori's grandfather Tadamori, who was an excellent musician. I believe I have heard that Tsunemori inherited it, and that he turned it over to Atsumori because the boy played so well. Saeda [Little Branch] was its name. It is deeply moving that music, a profane entertainment, should have led a warrior to a life of religion.

From: McCullough, Helen Craig, *Genji and Heike: selections from The tale of Genji and The tale of the Heike*. (Stanford, CA: Stanford University, 1994), pp. 392–97.

QUESTIONS:

1. Compare the differing behavior of Middle Captain Shigahira and Atsumori. What lesson about honorable behavior does the contrast between the episodes convey?
2. Why does Naozane consider joining a monastery? What values does he admire, what conflicts do they create for him, and how do these contribute to his emotional crisis?

12.5: The Investiture Controversy

The Investiture Controversy was the conflict between religious and secular authorities in medieval Europe that began to define separate spheres for "church" and "state," a peculiar division in Agrarian Era terms. It originated with the efforts of a series of popes to reform the Catholic Church, where "reform" meant free it from excessive influence by kings and the Holy Roman Emperor. Pope Gregory VII (r. 1073–85) initiated what became known as the Gregorian Reforms by issuing the "Dictates of the Pope" in 1075. These prohibited kings from investing bishops with their symbols of office, in effect removing the appointment of bishops from royal control. This threatened one of the bases of royal power, so rulers including the German Emperor Henry IV (r. 1084–1105) fought back against the pope, as Henry's letter to Gregory illustrates.

12.5a: *Dictatus Papae* (Pope Gregory VII, 1075)

1. That the Roman church was founded by God alone.
2. That the Roman pontiff alone can with right be called universal.
3. That he alone can depose or reinstate bishops.
4. That, in a council, his legate, even if a lower grade, is above all bishops, and can pass sentence of deposition against them.
5. That the pope may depose the absent.
6. That, among other things, we ought not to remain in the same house with those excommunicated by him.
7. That for him alone is it lawful, according to the needs of the time, to make new laws, to assemble together new congregations, to make an abbey of a canonry; and, on the other hand, to divide a rich bishopric and unite the poor ones.
8. That he alone may use the imperial insignia.
9. That of the pope alone all princes shall kiss the feet.
10. That his name alone shall be spoken in the churches.
11. That this is the only name in the world.
12. That it may be permitted to him to depose emperors.
13. That he may be permitted to transfer bishops if need be.
14. That he has power to ordain a clerk of any church he may wish.
15. That he who is ordained by him may *preside* over another church, but may not hold a subordinate position; and that such a one may not receive a higher grade from any bishop.
16. That no synod shall be called a general one without his order.
17. That no chapter and no book shall be considered canonical without his authority.
18. That a sentence passed by him may be retracted by no one; and that he himself, alone of all, may retract it.

19. That he himself may be judged by no one.
20. That no one shall dare to condemn one who appeals to the apostolic chair.
21. That to the latter should be referred the more important cases of every church.
22. That the Roman church has never erred; nor will it err to all eternity, the Scripture bearing witness.
23. That the Roman pontiff, if he have been canonically ordained, is undoubtedly made a saint by the merits of St. Peter; St. Ennodius, bishop of Pavia, bearing witness, and many holy fathers agreeing with him. As is contained in the decrees of St. Symmachus the pope.
24. That, by his command and consent, it may be lawful for subordinates to bring accusations.
25. That he may depose and reinstate bishops without assembling a synod.
26. That he who is not at peace with the Roman church shall not be considered catholic.
27. That he may absolve subjects from their fealty to wicked men.

. . .

Inasmuch as we have learned that, contrary to the establishments of the holy fathers, the investiture with churches is, in many places, performed by lay persons; and that from this case many disturbances arise in the church by which the Christian religion is trodden under foot: we decree that no one of the clergy shall receive the investiture with a bishopric or abbey or church from the hand of an emperor or king or of any lay person, male or female. But if he shall presume to do so he shall clearly know that such investiture is bereft of apostolic authority, and that he himself shall lie under excommunication until fitting satisfaction shall have been rendered.

12.5b: *Letter of Henry IV to Gregory VII* (1075)

Henry, king not through usurpation but through the holy ordination of God, to Hildebrand, at present not pope but false monk. Such greeting as this hast thou merited through thy disturbances, inasmuch as there is no grade in the church which thou hast omitted to make a partaker not of honour but of confusion, not of benediction but of malediction. For, to mention few and especial cases out of many, not only hast thou not feared to lay hands upon the rulers of the holy church, the anointed of the Lord—the archbishops, namely, bishops and priests—but thou hast trodden them under foot like slaves ignorant of what their master is doing. Thou hast won favour from the common herd by crushing them; thou hast looked upon all of them as knowing nothing, upon thy sole self, moreover, as knowing all things. This knowledge, however, thou hast used not for edification but for destruction; so that with reason we believe that St. Gregory, whose name thou hast usurped for thyself, was prophesying concerning thee when he said: "The pride of him who is in power increases the more, the greater the number of those subject to him; and he thinks that he himself can do more than all." And we, indeed, have endured all this, being eager to guard the honour of the apostolic see; thou, however, has understood our humility to be fear, and hast not, accordingly, shunned to rise up against the royal power conferred upon us by God, daring to threaten to divest us of it. As if we had received our kingdom from thee! As if the kingdom and the empire were in thine and not in God's hand! And this although our Lord Jesus Christ did call us to the kingdom, did not, however, call thee to the priesthood. For thou has ascended by the following steps. By wiles, namely, which the profession of monk abhors, thou hast achieved money; by money, favour; by the sword, the throne of peace. And from the throne of peace thou hast disturbed peace, inasmuch as thou hast armed subjects against those in authority over them; inasmuch as thou, who wert not called, hast taught that our bishops called of God are to be despised; inasmuch as thou hast usurped for laymen the ministry over their priests, allowing them to depose or condemn those whom they themselves had received as teachers from the hand of God through the laying on of hands of the bishops. On me also who, although unworthy to be among the anointed, have nevertheless been anointed to the kingdom, thou hast lain thy hand; me who—as the tradition of the holy Fathers teaches, declaring that I am not to be deposed for any crime unless, which God forbid, I should have strayed from the faith—am subject to the judgment of God alone. For the wisdom of the holy fathers committed even Julian the apostate not to themselves, but to God alone, to be judged and to be deposed. For himself the true pope, Peter, also exclaims: "Fear God, honour the king." But thou who does not fear God, dost dishonour in me his appointed one. Wherefore St. Paul, when he has not spared an angel of Heaven if he shall have preached otherwise, has not excepted thee also who dost teach otherwise upon earth. For he says: "If any one, either I or an angel from Heaven, should preach a gospel other than that which has been preached to you, he shall be damned." Thou, therefore, damned by this curse and by the judgment of all our bishops and by our own, descend and relinquish the apostolic chair which thou hast usurped. Let another ascend the throne of St. Peter, who shall not practise violence under the cloak of religion, but shall teach the sound doctrine of St. Peter. I Henry, king by the grace of God, do say unto thee, together with all our bishops: Descend, descend, to be damned throughout the ages.

From: Tierney, Brian, *Sources of medieval history* (New York: Knopf, 1983), pp. 142–43, 144–45.

QUESTIONS:

1. On what basis do Gregory and Henry claim authority for their actions? Is there any apparent way to judge between those claims?
2. What frame values surround this heated argument? That is, on what do the two sides presented here implicitly agree?

12.6: *Magna Carta* (1215)

Magna Carta, or The Great Charter, was a charter issued in 1215 by King John of England that guaranteed certain liberties to his subjects, in effect placing the law of England above the authority of the king. It is a milestone in the development of English constitutional government, but it achieved this status largely after the fact and mostly as an enduring screen image. John was forced to issue the charter by a group of rebellious nobles who resented John's apparantly arbitrary (and somewhat incompetent) exercise of royal power. He renounced it shortly afterwards (and had the Pope annul it as having been compelled under duress). But John died in 1217, leaving the kingdom to his infant son and a noble regency, who had the young Henry III resissue the Charter in 1225. It was subsequently reissued regularly. By this route, the principles and some of the specific provisions in the Charter (including habeas corpus) became embedded in English governance.

JOHN, by the grace of God King of England, Lord of Ireland, Duke of Normandy and Aquitaine, and Count of Anjou, to his archbishops, bishops, abbots, earls, barons, justices, foresters, sheriffs, stewards, servants, and to all his officials and loyal subjects, Greeting.

KNOW THAT BEFORE GOD, for the health of our soul and those of our ancestors and heirs, to the honour of God, the exaltation of the holy Church, and the better ordering of our kingdom, at the advice of [list of barons and churchmen]:

(1) FIRST, THAT WE HAVE GRANTED TO GOD, and by this present charter have confirmed for us and our heirs in perpetuity, that the English Church shall be free, and shall have its rights undiminished, and its liberties unimpaired. That we wish this so to be observed, appears from the fact that of our own free will, before the outbreak of the present dispute between us and our barons, we granted and confirmed by charter the freedom of the Church's elections—a right reckoned to be of the greatest necessity and importance to it—and caused this to be confirmed by Pope Innocent III. This freedom we shall observe ourselves, and desire to be observed in good faith by our heirs in perpetuity.

TO ALL FREE MEN OF OUR KINGDOM we have also granted, for us and our heirs for ever, all the liberties written out below, to have and to keep for them and their heirs, of us and our heirs:

(2) If any earl, baron, or other person that holds lands directly of the Crown, for military service, shall die, and at his death his heir shall be of full age and owe a 'relief,' the heir shall have his inheritance on payment of the ancient scale of 'relief'. That is to say, the heir or heirs of an earl shall pay £100 for the entire earl's barony, the heir or heirs of a knight 100s. at most for the entire knight's 'fee', and any man that owes less shall pay less, in accordance with the ancient usage of 'fees'.

(3) But if the heir of such a person is under age and a ward, when he comes of age he shall have his inheritance without 'relief' or fine.

(4) The guardian of the land of an heir who is under age shall take from it only reasonable revenues, customary dues, and feudal services. He shall do this without destruction or damage to men or property. If we have given the guardianship of the land to a sheriff, or to any person answerable to us for the revenues, and he commits destruction or damage, we will exact compensation from him, and the land shall be entrusted to two worthy and prudent men of the same 'fee', who shall be answerable to us for the revenues, or to the person to whom we have assigned them. If we have given or sold to anyone the guardianship of such land, and he causes destruction or damage, he shall lose the guardianship of it, and it shall be handed over to two worthy and prudent men of the same 'fee', who shall be similarly answerable to us.

(5) For so long as a guardian has guardianship of such land, he shall maintain the houses, parks, fish preserves, ponds, mills, and everything else pertaining to it, from the revenues of the land itself. When the heir comes of age, he shall restore the whole land to him, stocked with plough teams and such implements of husbandry as the season demands and the revenues from the land can reasonably bear.

(6) Heirs may be given in marriage, but not to someone of lower social standing. Before a marriage takes place, it shall be made known to the heir's next-of-kin.

(7) At her husband's death, a widow may have her marriage portion and inheritance at once and without trouble. She shall pay nothing for her dower, marriage portion, or any inheritance that she and her husband held jointly on the day of his death. She may remain in her husband's house for forty days after his death, and within this period her dower shall be assigned to her.

(8) No widow shall be compelled to marry, so long as she wishes to remain without a husband. But she must give security that she will not marry without royal consent, if she holds her lands of the Crown, or without the consent of whatever other lord she may hold them of.

(9) Neither we nor our officials will seize any land or rent in payment of a debt, so long as the debtor has movable goods sufficient to discharge the debt. . . .

(10) If anyone who has borrowed a sum of money from Jews dies before the debt has been repaid, his heir shall pay no interest on the debt for so long as he remains under age, irrespective of

whom he holds his lands. If such a debt falls into the hands of the Crown, it will take nothing except the principal sum specified in the bond.

(11) If a man dies owing money to Jews, his wife may have her dower and pay nothing towards the debt from it. . . . Debts owed to persons other than Jews are to be dealt with similarly.

(12) No 'scutage' [military tax] or 'aid' [general tax] may be levied in our kingdom without its general consent, unless it is for the ransom of our person, to make our eldest son a knight, and (once) to marry our eldest daughter. For these purposes only a reasonable 'aid' may be levied. 'Aids' from the city of London are to be treated similarly.

(13) The city of London shall enjoy all its ancient liberties and free customs, both by land and by water. We also will and grant that all other cities, boroughs, towns, and ports shall enjoy all their liberties and free customs.

(14) To obtain the general consent of the realm for the assessment of an 'aid'— except in the three cases specified above— or a 'scutage', we will cause the archbishops, bishops, abbots, earls, and greater barons to be summoned individually by letter. To those who hold lands directly of us we will cause a general summons to be issued, through the sheriffs and other officials, to come together on a fixed day (of which at least forty days notice shall be given) and at a fixed place. In all letters of summons, the cause of the summons will be stated. When a summons has been issued, the business appointed for the day shall go forward in accordance with the resolution of those present, even if not all those who were summoned have appeared.

(17) Ordinary lawsuits shall not follow the royal court around, but shall be held in a fixed place.

(18) Inquests [concerning landholding] . . . shall be taken only in their proper county court. We ourselves, or in our absence abroad our chief justice, will send two justices to each county four times a year, and these justices, with four knights of the county elected by the county itself, shall hold the assizes in the county court, on the day and in the place where the court meets.

(19) If any assizes cannot be taken on the day of the county court, as many knights and freeholders shall afterwards remain behind, of those who have attended the court, as will suffice for the administration of justice, having regard to the volume of business to be done.

(20) For a trivial offence, a free man shall be fined only in proportion to the degree of his offence, and for a serious offence correspondingly, but not so heavily as to deprive him of his livelihood. In the same way, a merchant shall be spared his merchandise, and a villein the implements of his husbandry, if they fall upon the mercy of a royal court. None of these fines shall be imposed except by the assessment on oath of reputable men of the neighbourhood.

(24) No sheriff, constable, coroners, or other royal officials are to hold lawsuits that should be held by the royal justices.

(27) If a free man dies intestate, his movable goods are to be distributed by his next-of-kin and friends, under the supervision of the Church. The rights of his debtors are to be preserved.

(28) No constable or other royal official shall take corn or other movable goods from any man without immediate payment, unless the seller voluntarily offers postponement of this. . . .

(35) There shall be standard measures of wine, ale, and corn (the London quarter), throughout the kingdom. . . . Weights are to be standardised similarly. . . .

(38) In future no official shall place a man on trial upon his own unsupported statement, without producing credible witnesses to the truth of it.

(39) No free man shall be seized or imprisoned, or stripped of his rights or possessions, or outlawed or exiled, or deprived of his standing in any other way, nor will we proceed with force against him, or send others to do so, except by the lawful judgement of his equals or by the law of the land.

(40) To no one will we sell, to no one deny or delay right or justice.

(41) All merchants may enter or leave England unharmed and without fear, and may stay or travel within it, by land or water, for purposes of trade, free from all illegal exactions, in accordance with ancient and lawful customs. This, however, does not apply in time of war to merchants from a country that is at war with us. Any such merchants found in our country at the outbreak of war shall be detained without injury to their persons or property, until we or our chief justice have discovered how our own merchants are being treated in the country at war with us. If our own merchants are safe they shall be safe too.

(45) We will appoint as justices, constables, sheriffs, or other officials, only men that know the law of the realm and are minded to keep it well.

(54) No one shall be arrested or imprisoned on the appeal of a woman for the death of any person except her husband.

(63) IT IS ACCORDINGLY OUR WISH AND COMMAND that the English Church shall be free, and that men in our kingdom shall have and keep all these liberties, rights, and concessions, well and peaceably in their fullness and entirety for them and their heirs, of us and our heirs, in all things and all places for ever.

Both we and the barons have sworn that all this shall be observed in good faith and without deceit. Witness the above-mentioned people and many others.

Given by our hand in the meadow that is called Runnymede, between Windsor and Staines, on the fifteenth day of June in the seventeenth year of our reign [i.e., 1215: the new regnal year began on 28 May].

From: http://www.bl.uk/treasures/magnacarta/translation/mc_trans.html, "The National Archives | Treasures from The National Archives | Magna Carta."

QUESTIONS:

1. What sort of action by an arbitrary monarch most concerned the drafters of Magna Carta? Consider the relative frequency of the words "heir" and "king": What does Magna Carta primarily address? Abstract rights or immediate circumstances?
2. What evidence in Magna Carta shows that this is a contract (that is, an agreement with mutual obligations and constraints) between the king and his subjects?

CHAPTER 13

The Crisis of the Mongol Age: 1200 to 1400

INTRODUCTION

In this chapter, we present sources from the age of the Mongols and the Eurasian bubonic plague pandemic that resulted from Mongol-era network connections. The first source gives us a virtually unique view of steppe nomadic societies from within, the second presents a more typical sedentary view of the terrors that steppe nomads (and the Mongols above all) brought to settled societies. Next, the chapter presents sources that show different reactions to the same plague, documenting how the same effects could be interpreted differently through different cultural frames. Finally, the last source reflects the appeal to traditional values that dominated reactions across Eurasia to the crises of Mongol invasions and plague.

THE MONGOLS

13.1a: *The Secret History of the Mongols* (Anonymous, c. 1240)

The *Secret History of the Mongols* is unique as the only Mongol-language account of the rise of the Mongol Empire, and indeed as one of the very few pieces of major literature from steppe nomadic societies. It was written in the Uighur script for the Mongol royal court in the generation after Chinngiz Khan's death in 1227, though it survives only in later translations into Chinese. It mixes historical accounts with folklore and prose with poetry, making it a valuable source for Mongol culture in both its form and its content. This selection tells the story of how Temujin (the future Chinngiz Khan), his brothers Qasar and Belgutei, and his allies To'oril and Jamuqa defeat the rival Three Meerkits confederation, who had earlier defeated Temujin and kidnapped his wife. The victory was a key episode in Temujin's rise to leadership of all the Mongols.

When they had finished talking, all three of them Temüjin, Qasar, and Belgütei—went to To'oril, the Ong Qan of the Kereyits, who was staying in the Qara Forest beside the Tu'ula River. They said: 'While we were [still] inexperienced [in such things,] the Three Merkits came and robbed me of my wife and of [my unborn] son. We have come to ask you, Qan my father, whether you can restore my wife and son to me.' To'oril Qan replied: 'Did I not say [as much] to you last year? When you brought the sable jacket to me you said that, in your father's time, I and your father swore brotherhood together, and that I am therefore as a father to you. When you placed the coat on me, I spoke these words:

In return for the black sable jacket
I will bring together
the people who abandoned you.
In return for the sable jacket,
I will unite your scattered people.

And I said:

[Let my thoughts]
be in the depths of my bowels
and in my ribcage.

Did I not say those words? Now I will stand by them.

In return for the sable jacket,
I will crush the Merkits
and rescue Lady Börte for you.
In return for the black sable jacket,
I will break all the Merkits into pieces
and bring back your qatan Börte.

Send a message to [your] younger brother Jamuqa, who is in the Qorqonaq Forest. I will set out from here with twenty thousand men to form the right flank. Tell [your] younger brother Jamuqa to take twenty thousand to form the left flank. Let Jamuqa decide the time and place [of our meeting].'

When Temüjin, Qasar, and Belgütei arrived at their yurt after visiting To'oril Qan, Temüjin told Qasar and Belgütei to take the following message to Jamuqa. 'Tell [my] sworn brother Jamuqa that the three Merkits

made my bed empty.
Are we not one family?
How can we gain vengeance?
My heart is broken.
Are we not blood relatives?
How can we take revenge?'

This was the message that he sent to [his] sworn brother Jamuqa. He also told [Qasar and Belgütei] to repeat to Jamuqa the words of To'oril, the qan of the Kereyits: 'In former days, your father, Yisügei Qan, helped me and did good by me; remember, [Temüjin], that I will be a companion to you. With twenty thousand men, I will form the right flank and do battle. I will set out from here with twenty thousand men to form the right flank. Tell [your] younger brother Jamuqa to take twenty thousand into battle. Let Jamuqa decide the time and place [of our meeting].' When these words [had been conveyed to] Jamuqa, Jamuqa said: Temüjin, [my] sworn brother,

my heart aches,
knowing that your bed is empty.
My liver aches,
knowing that your heart is broken.
Let us gain vengeance [by]
destroying the Uduyits and Uwas-Merkits.
Let us rescue our Lady Börte.
Let us avenge ourselves
by breaking the Qa'at-Merkits into pieces.
Let us restore our qatun Börte,
Let us bring her back and save her.

Now,

Toqto'a the Nervous,
takes the flapping of the saddle cloth
for the beating of drums.
[Toqto'a] must be on the Bu'ura Steppe.
When Dayir-usun the Treacherous
[sees] the swaying of the bow-nock and the quiver
[he flees].

Now [Toqto'a] must be on Talqun Island [between] the Orkhon and the Selengge.

When the tumbleweed blows,
Qa'atai-darmala the Disputer [flees]
into the dense forest.
Now he must be
on the Qaraji Steppe.
We must cut across the Kilqo River.

Let the sedges be abundant.
Binding up our rafts with them,
let us go.

That nervous Toqto'a—

we will strike through the smoke hole [of his yurt],
smash and knock down
his door frame,
rob and destroy
his wife and son,
break and knock down
his sacred door frame,
rob his entire people
until they are empty.

Again, Jamuqa said: 'Tell [my] sworn brother Temüjin and [my] elder brother To'oril the following: For my part,

I have made offerings
to the spear-tipped banner,
I have beaten the rumbling drum
made of the black bull's hide.
I have ridden my swift black [horse],
I have put on my strong clothing,
I have grasped my iron-tipped spear,
I have set my peach-bark arrow
[against the string].
Let us ride against the Qa'at-Merkits.

Tell [Temüjin] all this.

I have made offerings
to the long spear-tipped banner,
I have beaten the cow-hide drum
that sounds with a deep rumble,
I have ridden my swift grey [horse],
I have put on my leather-thonged armour,
I have grasped my hilted sword,
I have set my notched arrow [against the string].
Let us battle to the death against the Uduyit-Merkits.

Tell [Temüjin] all these things. When [my] older brother To'oril Qan sets forth, he [should] make his way to my sworn brother Temüjin by the south side of Burqan-qaldun and follow the Onon River to its source at Botoqan-bo'orji. Let us meet there. I will ascend the Onon River to where my sworn brother's people wait. The ten thousand [men] of [my] sworn brother's people and the ten thousand [of my own men] will constitute [a force of] twenty thousand. Following the Onon River to [its source at] Botoqan-bo'orji, the appointed place, we shall join forces.' So saying, he dispatched [this message].

Qasar and Belgütei returned and told Temüjin what Jamuqa had said. [Temüjin] then sent the message on to To'oril Qan. On hearing these words of Jamuqa, To'oril Qan set out at the head of twenty thousand [men]. 'When To'oril Qan sets out, he will come towards the Bürgi bank of the Kelüren on the south side of Burqan-qaldun,' thought Temüjin, who was on the Bürgi bank; 'and [I] am in his path.' So he yielded, and moved upstream along the Tünggelik to the Tana Stream on the south side of Burqanqaldun, where he set up camp. From there, Temüjin and his army set out. The ten thousand [men] under To'oril Qan and the ten thousand under To'oril Qan's younger brother, Jaqa-gambu, twenty thousand altogether, set up camp at Ayil-qaraqana on the Kimurqa Stream. At that point, [Temüjin] joined [them] and set up camp.

After joining forces, Temüjin, To'oril Qan, and Jaqagambu moved towards the source of the Onon River at Botoqan-bo'orji, Belgütei's mother was said to be in that [particular] yurt, so Belgütei went to rescue her. [However], when he entered the yurt through the right side of the doorway, his mother, in ragged sheepskin clothing, departed through the left door. Outside, she said to another person: 'I have been told that my sons have become qans, whereas I am joined with a common man. How can I look into the faces of my sons?' So saying, she ran off and slunk into the thick forest.

During his fruitless search for her, Belgütei-noyan fired horn-tipped arrows at the men of Merkit bone, saying: 'Bring back my mother.' The three hundred Merkits who had circled Burqan and their descendants' descendants were crushed and blown away like ashes. Those of the surviving wives who could be embraced were embraced [as concubines]; those of the surviving children who could be admitted through the door were admitted [as slaves].

Temüjin expressed his respectful thanks to both To'oril Qan and Jamuqa: 'After gaining the friendship of you, Qan, my father, and you, Jamuqa, [my] sworn brother, my power has been increased by Heaven and Earth.

Appointed by mighty Heaven
and escorted by Mother Earth,
we made man's enemy, the people of the Merkits,
empty their breasts
and tore their livers in half.
We emptied their beds
and destroyed [their] kinsmen.
Did we not also capture the survivors?

In this way, the Merkit people were demoralised. 'Let us [now] withdraw', [Temüjin and the others] said to one another.

While the Uduyit-Merkits were fleeing in panic, our soldiers found a boy who had been left behind in the camp. He was five years old, with fire in his eyes. His name was Küchü. He [wore] a hat of sable, boots made of the skin of a doe's forelegs, and a raiment sewn together from suede otter [skins]. The soldiers took him to Mother Hö'elün and gave him to her as a battle prize.

Temüjin, To'oril Qan, and Jamuqa came together and razed the bartering yurts and ravished the tall-hatted women of the Merkits. [After this,] they withdrew from Talqun Island between the Orqan and Selengge Rivers. Temüjin and Jamuqa, uniting, withdrew in the direction of the Qorqonaq Forest. To'oril Qan withdrew by way of the Hökörtü Foreston the northern side of Burqan-qaldun, the Qacha'uratu-sübchit [Pass], and the Huliyatu-sübchit [Pass], where he hunted wild beasts before heading for the Qara Forest on the Tu'ula [River].

Temüjin and Jamuqa pitched camp together in the Qorqonaq Forest. Recalling how they had sworn brotherhood with one another, they renewed their brotherhood, swearing to love one another. The first time that they had sworn brotherhood, Temüjin was eleven. Jamuqa had given Temüjin a roebuck's knucklebone and Temüjin had given Jamuqa a copper-[filled] knucklebone in exchange, and [so] they had sworn brotherhood. After agreeing to become brothers, they had played knucklebones on the ice of the Onon [River], calling each other sworn brother. The [following] spring, when they had competed against each other with pinewood bows, Jamuqa had given Temüjin a whistling arrow head that he had [made] by gluing [together] the horns of a two-year-old calf and boring holes into it to make it sing. In exchange, Temüjin had given Jamuqa a horn-tipped arrow with a butt of cypress wood and they had again become sworn brothers. This is how they renewed their brotherhood.

In earlier days, old men used to say: 'Men who are sworn brothers [share] one life. They do not abandon each other but become protectors of that life.' Thus [Temüjin and Jamuqa] loved each other. Renewing their bond of brotherhood, they said: 'Let us love one another.' While looting the Merkit Toqto'a, Temüjin had obtained a golden sash that he made his sworn brother Jamuqa wear. He [also] gave [Jamuqa] Toqto'a's horse, a fawn stallion with a black mane and tail. Jamuqa made his sworn brother Temüjin wear the golden sash that he had looted from Dayir-usun of the Uwas-Merkits and also gave him Dayirusun's horse to ride. It was white [like] a kid and had a horn. The [two men] swore their brotherhood and their love [for one another] at the Saqlaqar Tree on the southern side of the Quldaqar Cliff in the Qoronaq Forest. They enjoyed a feast, followed by more feasting. At night, they slept together under one quilt.

Temüjin and Jamuqa remained companions for one [whole] year and for half of the next year. . . .

From: Onon, Urgunge, *The secret history of the Mongols: the life and times of Chinggis Khan* (London: Routledge, 2011), pp. 247–53.

QUESTIONS:

1. How do Mongol leaders make alliances and cement diplomatic relationships? What motivates Mongol warfare?
2. What do the poetic passages add to the story? What values do they convey?

13.1b: *The Perfect History* (Ibn al-Athir, c. 1225)

Ibn al-Athīr (1160–1233) was an Arab or Kurdish historian best known for his *Complete History,* a world history written in Arabic, a selection from which we read in Chapter 12. He lived, working as a scholar, for most of his life in Mosul, in northern Mesopotamia, as well as Damascus and Aleppo, and made many visits to Baghdad. He spent some time travelling with the army of Saladin, the great Kurdish Muslim leader who dealt the Crusader States a near-fatal blow at the battle of Hattin in 1187, and is an excellent firsthand source for events from the late 1180s down to his death in 1233, including the first devastating Mongol invasion of the Islamic world. In this selection, he writes about the Mongol attacks in 1220–21 on the heart of the Muslim world. His view is personal, apocalyptic, and moralistic, and demonstrates very clearly the otherworldly character of the sudden eruption of the Mongols into the Islamic world.

THE HORROR

For some years I continued averse from mentioning this event, deeming it so horrible that I shrank from recording it, and ever withdrawing one foot as I advanced the other. To whom, indeed, can it be easy to write the announcement of the death-blow of Islam and the Muslims, or who is he on whom the remembrance thereof can weigh lightly? O would that my mother had not born me, or that I had died and become a forgotten thing ere this befell! Yet withal a number of my friends urged me to set it down in writing, and I hesitated long; but at last came to the conclusion that to omit this matter could serve no useful purpose. I say, therefore, that this thing involves the description of the greatest catastrophe and the most dire calamity (of the like of which days and nights are innocent) which befell all men generally, and the Muslims in particular; so that, should one say that the world, since God Almighty created Adam until now, hath not been afflicted with the like thereof, he would but speak the truth.

For indeed history doth not contain aught which approaches or comes nigh unto it. For of the most grievous calamities recorded was what Nebuchadnezzar inflicted on the children of Israel by his slaughter of them and his destruction of Jerusalem; and what was Jerusalem in comparison to the countries which these accursed miscreants destroyed, each city of which was double the size of Jerusalem? Or what were the children of Israel compared to those whom these slew? For verily those whom they massacred in a single city exceeded all the children of Israel. Nay, it is unlikely that mankind will see the like of this calamity, until the world comes to an end and perishes, except the final outbreak of Gog and Magog.

For even Antichrist will spare such as follow him, though he destroy those who oppose him; but these spared none, slaying women and men and children, ripping open pregnant women and killing unborn babes. Verily to God do we belong, and unto Him do we return, and there is no strength and no power save in God, the High, the Almighty, in face of this catastrophe, whereof the sparks flew far and wide, and the hurt was universal; and which passed over the lands like clouds driven by the wind.

THE MONGOL CONQUESTS

For these were a people who emerged from the confines of China, and attacked the cities of Turkistan, like Kashghar and Balasaghun, and thence advanced on the cities of Transoxiana, such as Samarqand, Bukhara and the like, taking possession of them, and treating their inhabitants in such wise as we shall mention; and of them one division then passed on into Khurasan, until they had made an end of taking possession, and destroying, and slaying, and plundering, and thence passing on to Ray, Hamadan and the Highlands, and the cities contained therein, even to the limits of Iraq, whence they marched on the towns of Adharbayjan and Arraniyya, destroying them and slaying most their inhabitants, of whom none escaped save a small remnant; and all this in less than a year; this is a thing whereof the like hath not been heard.

And when they had finished with Adharbayjan and Arraniyya, they passed on to Darband-i-Shirwan, and occupied its cities, none of which escaped save the fortress wherein was their King; wherefore they passed by it to the countries of the Lan and the Lakiz and the various nationalities which dwell in that region, and plundered, slew, and destroyed them to the full. And thence they made their way to the lands of Qipchaq, who are the most numerous of the Turks, and slew all such as withstood them, while the survivors fled to the fords and mountain-tops, and abandoned their country, which these Tartars overran. All this they did in the briefest space of time, remaining only for so long as their march required and no more.

Another division, distinct from that mentioned above, marched on Ghazna and its dependencies, and those parts of India, Sistan and Kirman which border thereon, and wrought therein deeds like unto the other, nay, yet more grievous.

Now this is a thing the like of which ear hath not heard; for Alexander, concerning whom historians agree that he conquered the world, did not do so with such swiftness, but only in the space of about ten years; neither did he slay, but was satisfied that men should be subject to him. But these Tartars conquered most of the habitable globe, and the best, the most flourishing and most populous part thereof, and that whereof the inhabitants were the most advanced in character and conduct, in about a year; nor did any country escape their devastations which did not fearfully expect them and dread their arrival. Moreover they need no commissariat, nor the conveyance of supplies, for they have with them sheep, cows, horses, and the like quadrupeds, the flesh of which they eat, [and] naught else. As for their beasts which they ride, these dig into the earth with their hoofs and eat the roots of plants, knowing naught of barley. And so, when they alight anywhere, they have need of nothing from without.

As for their religion, they worship the sun when it arises, and regard nothing as unlawful, for they eat all beasts, even dogs, pigs, and the like; nor do they recognize the marriage-tie, for several men are in marital relations with one woman, and if a child is born, it knows not who is its father.

Therefore Islam and the Muslims have been afflicted during this period with calamities wherewith no people hath been visited. These Tartars (may God confound them!) came from the East, and wrought deeds which horrify all who hear of them, and which thou shalt, please God, see set forth in full detail in their proper connection.

MUSLIM WEAKNESS

As for these Tartars, their achievements were only rendered possible by the absence of any effective obstacle; and the cause of this absence was that Muhammad Khwarazmshah [the ruler of Iran] had overrun the [other Muslim] lands, slaying and destroying their Kings, so that he remained alone ruling over all these countries; wherefore, when he was defeated by the Tartars, none was left in the lands to check those or protect these, that so God might accomplish a thing which was to be done.

It is now time for us to describe how they first burst forth into the lands. "Stories have been related to me," he says, "which the hearer can scarcely credit, as to the terror of them which God Almighty cast into men's hearts; so that it is said that a single one of them would enter a village or a quarter wherein were many people, and would continue to slay them one after another, none daring to stretch forth his hand against this horseman. And I have heard that one of them took a man captive, but had not with him any weapon wherewith to kill him; and he said to his prisoner, 'Lay your head on the ground and do not move'; and he did so, and the Tartar went and fetched his sword and slew him therewith.

Another man related to me as follows: "I was going," said he, "with seventeen others along a road, and there met us a Tartar horseman, and bade us bind one another's arms. My companions began to do as he bade them, but I said to them, 'He is but one man; wherefore, then, should we not kill him and flee?' They replied, 'We are afraid.' I said, 'This man intends to kill you immediately; let us therefore rather kill him, that perhaps God may deliver us.' But I swear by God that not one of them dared to do this, so I took a knife and slew him, and we fled and escaped." And such occurrences were many.

From: Edward G. Browne, *A Literary History of Persia* (Cambridge: Cambridge University Press, 1902), II, pp. 427–31.

QUESTIONS:

1. What characteristics of the Mongols make them seem so catastrophic and otherworldly to Ibn al-Athir?
2. Does the Mongol catastrophe cause Ibn al-Althir to question his own faith or the guidance of religious authorities? What is the moral of his story, and how does he think good Muslims should react to the catastrophe?

THE PLAGUE

13.2a: *The Muqaddimah* (Ibn Khaldun, before 1406)

Ibn Khaldun (1332–1406) was the son of an Islamic scholar, descendant of a long line of scholar-officials to the dynasties of southern Spain and northwest Africa. These were troubled times for the Iberian Muslim kingdoms, as the Christian Reconquista steadily reduced the extent of Muslim possessions in Spain. Political disunity and instability plagued much of the Muslim world, not to mention the devastation wrought by the Black Death that swept the Muslim world in the 1340s, killing the seventeen-year-old Ibn Khaldun's father. His writing is an influential example of an Islamic scholarly tradition that emphasized the communal development of knowledge and a leading social and pseudogovernmental role for scholars in the wider Muslim world. His writing also reflects the efforts of Muslim scholars to deal with troubled times in terms of their intellectual traditions. In this selection, he offers a theory about how plagues arise.

CAUSES OF PESTILENCES

In the previous (discussion), it has been established that, at the beginning, dynasties are inevitably kind in the exercise of their power and just in their administration. . . . In the later [years] of dynasties, famines and pestilences become numerous. As far as famines are concerned, the reason is that most people at that time refrain from cultivating the soil. For, in the later years of dynasties, there occur attacks on property and tax revenue and, through customs duties, on trading. Or, trouble occurs as the result of the unrest of the subjects and the great number of rebels [who are provoked] by the senility of the dynasty to rebel. Therefore, as a rule, little grain is stored. . . . If for some years nothing is stored, hunger will be general.

The large number of pestilences has its reason in the large number of famines just mentioned. Or, it has its reason in the many disturbances that result from the disintegration of the dynasty. There is much unrest and bloodshed, and plagues occur. The principal reason for the latter is the corruption of the air through [too] large a civilization [population]. It results from the putrefaction and the many evil moistures with which [the air] has contact in a dense civilization. . . . If the corruption is strong, the lung is afflicted with disease. This results in epidemics, which affect the lung in particular. Even if the corruption is not strong or great, putrefaction grows and multiplies under its influence, resulting in many fevers that affect the tempers, and the bodies become sick and perish. The reason for the growth of putrefaction and evil moistures is invariably a dense and abundant civilization such as exists in the later years of a dynasty. Such civilization is the result of the good government, the kindness, the safety, and the light taxation that existed at the beginning of the dynasty. This is obvious. Therefore, it has been clarified by science in the proper place that it is necessary to have empty spaces and waste regions interspersed between civilized areas. This makes circulation of the air possible. It removes the corruption and putrefaction affecting the air after contact with living beings, and brings healthy air. This also is the reason why pestilences occur much more frequently in densely settled cities than elsewhere, as, for instance, in Cairo in the East and Fez in the Maghrib. God determines whatever He wishes.

THE SCIENCE OF MEDICINE

Medicine is a craft that studies the human body in its illness and health. The physician attempts to preserve health and to cure illness with the help of medicines and diets, but first he ascertains the illnesses) peculiar to each limb of the body, and the reasons causing them. He also ascertains the medicines existing for each illness. Physicians deduce the effectiveness of medicines from their composition and powers. They deduce the stage of an illness from signs indicating whether the illness is ripe and will accept the medicine or not. These signs show themselves in the color of the patient, the excretions, and the pulse. The physicians in this imitate the power of nature, which is the controlling element in both health and illness. They imitate nature and help it a little, as the nature of the matter underlying the illness, the season of the year, and the age of the patient may require in each particular case. The science dealing with all these things is called medicine. . . .

Civilized Bedouins have a kind of medicine which is mainly based upon individual experience. They inherit its use from the *shaykhs* and old women of the tribe. Some of it may occasionally be correct. However, that kind of medicine is not based upon any natural norm or upon any conformity of the treatment to the temper of the humors.

The medicine mentioned in religious tradition is of the Bedouin type. It is in no way part of the divine revelation. Such medical matters were merely part of Arab custom and happened to be mentioned in connection with the circumstances of the Prophet [Muhammad], like other things that were customary in his generation. They were not mentioned in order to imply that that particular way of practicing medicine is stipulated by the religious law. Muhammad was sent to teach us the religious law. He was not sent to teach us medicine or any other ordinary matter. In connection with the story of the fecundation of the palms, he said: "You know more about your worldly affairs than I."

None of the statements concerning medicine that occur in sound traditions should be considered to have the force of law. There is nothing to indicate that this is the case. The only thing is that if that type of medicine is used for the sake of a divine blessing and in true faith, it may be very useful. However, that would have nothing to do with humoral medicine but would be the result of true faith. . . .

God guides to that which is correct.

From: Ibn Khaldun, *The Muqaddimah, an Introduction to History*, 3 vols., Franz Rosenthal, transl. (Princeton, NJ: Princeton University Press, 1958), vol. 2, pp. 135–37; vol. 3, pp. 148–51.

QUESTIONS:

1. How is ibn Khaldun's explanation of the plague different from the plague descriptions by Thucydides and Procopius (as well as from al-Maqrizi's description, in source 13.2b below)?
2. What is the moral of the story in this explanation? Does having an explanation with a moral make this a more satisfying account of the plague than simple descriptions?

13.2b: *The Plague in Cairo* (Ahmad al-Maqrizi)

The next selection by Ahmad al-Maqrizi (1364–1442) is one of few accounts of the plague in the Muslim world. Al-Maqrizi lived for most of his life in Egypt and as an Islamic scholar produced considerable work on Egyptian history and biography. His most famous work is his Mawaiz *(Mawaiz wa al-'i'tibar bi dhikr al-khitat wa al-'athar)*, a history of the planning of Cairo and its monuments. In addition to his extensive historical writing, Al-Maqrizi also wrote about coins, weights, and measures in the Muslim world. His account of the plague in Cairo below is from one of his historical works, the Kitab *(kitab al-suluk li-ma 'rifat duwal al-muluk)*.

News reached Cairo from Syria that the plague in Damascus had been less deadly than in Tripoli, Hama, and Aleppo. From [October 1348] death raged with intensity. 1200 people died daily and, as a result, people stopped requesting permits from the administration to bury the dead and many cadavers were abandoned in gardens and on the roads.

In New and Old Cairo, the plague struck women and children at first, then market people, and the numbers of the dead augmented. . . . The [ravages of the] plague intensified in . . . [November] in Cairo and became extremely grave during *Ramadan* [December], which coincided with the arrival of winter. . . . The plague continued to spread so considerably that it became impossible to count how many died. . . .

In [January 1349], new symptoms developed and people began spitting up blood. One sick person came down with internal fever, followed by an unrestrained need to vomit, then spat blood and died. Those around him in his house fell ill, one after the other and in one or two nights they all perished. Everyone lived with the overwhelming preoccupation that death was near. People prepared themselves for death by distributing alms to the poor, reconciled with one another, and multiplied their acts of devotion.

None had time to consult doctors or drink medicinal syrups or take other medications, so rapidly did they die. By [January 7th] bodies had piled up in the streets and markets; [town leaders] appointed burial brigades, and some pious people remained permanently at places of prayer in New and Old Cairo to recite funeral orations over the dead. The situation worsened beyond limits, and no solution appeared possible. Almost the entire royal guard disappeared and the barracks in the sultan's citadel contained no more soldiers. . . .

People began searching [for people to read] the *Qur'an* readers at funerals, and many individuals quit their trades to recite prayers at the head of burial processions. A group of people devoted themselves to applying a coat of clay to the inner sides of the graves. Others volunteered to wash corpses, and still others to carry them. Such volunteers received substantial wages. For example, a *Qur'an* reader earned 10 *dirhams:* the moment he finished with one funeral, he ran off to another. A body carrier demanded six *dirhams* in advance, and still it was hard to find any. A grave-digger wanted 50 *dirhams* per grave. But most of them died before they had a chance to spend their earnings.

Family celebrations and marriages no longer took place. . . . No one had held any festivities during the entire duration of the epidemic, and no voice was heard singing. In an attempt to revive these activities, the *wazir* [prime minister] reduced by a third the taxes paid by the woman responsible for collecting dues on singers. The call to prayer was suspended at many locations, and even at the most important ones, there remained only a single *muezzin* [caller to prayer]. . . .

Most of the mosques and lodges were closed. It was also a known fact that during this epidemic no infant survived more than one or two days after his birth, and his mother usually quickly followed him to the grave.

At [the end of February], all of Upper Egypt was afflicted with the plague. . . . According to information that arrived . . . from . . . other regions, lions, wolves, rabbits, camels, wild asses and boars, and other savage beasts, dropped dead, and were found with scabs on their bodies.

The same thing happened throughout Egypt. When harvest time arrived, many farmers had already perished [and no field hands remained to gather crops]. Soldiers and their young slaves or pages headed for the fields. They tried to recruit workers by promising them half of the proceeds, but they could not find anyone to help them gather the harvest. They threshed the grain with their horses [hoofs], and winnowed the grain themselves, but, unable to carry all the grain back, they had to abandon much of it. Most craft workshops closed, since artisans devoted themselves to disposing of the dead, while others, not less numerous, auctioned off property and textiles [which the dead left behind]. Even though the prices of fabric and other such commodities sold for a fifth of their original value . . . they remained unsold. . . .

From: Ahmad ibn 'Ali al-Makrizi, *kitab al-suluk li-ma 'rifat duwal al-muluk [The Guide to the Knowledge of Dynasties and Kings], 4 vols.*, M. Mustafa Ziada, ed., vol. II, part III (Cairo: Association of Authorship, Translation and Publishing Press, 1958), 779–86, excerpted in Marvin E. Gettleman and Stuart Schaar, eds., *The Middle East and Islamic Reader* (NY: Grove Press, 2003), 52–53.

QUESTIONS:

1. How does al-Maqrizi's account of the plague in Cairo compare to the accounts of plague in Thucydides and Procopius in Chapter 2? What are the similarities and differences?
2. Does the Islamic faith of the population seem to have an effect on social reactions to the plague's devastation?

13.2c: *The Decameron* (Boccacio, 1351)

Giovanni Boccacio (1313–1375) was a Florentine writer and major figure in Renaissance humanist circles. He his best known for *The Decameron,* in which ten young people tell each other stories over ten evenings, making for one hundred stories. But it is the frame that is of interest to us here: the storytellers gather at a country villa outside Florence to escape the outbreak of the Black Death, which Boccacio witnessed. His description of the plague thus opens *The Decameron,* and we excerpt it here.

I say, then, that the sum of thirteen hundred and forty-eight years had elapsed since the fruitful Incarnation of the Son of God, when the noble city of Florence, which for its great beauty excels all others in Italy, was visited by the deadly pestilence. Some say that it descended upon the human race through the influence of the heavenly bodies, others that it was a punishment signifying in God's righteous anger at our iniquitous way of life. But whatever its cause, it had originated some years earlier in the East, where it had claimed countless lives before it unhappily spread westward, growing in strength as it swept relentlessly on from one place to the next.

In the face of its onrush, all the wisdom and ingenuity of man were unavailing. Large quantities of refuse were cleared out of the city by officials specially appointed for the purpose, all sick persons were forbidden entry, and numerous instructions were issued for safeguarding the people's health, but all to no avail. Nor were the countless petitions humbly directed to God by the pious, whether by means of formal processions or in any other guise, any less ineffectual. For in the early spring of the year we have mentioned, the plague began, in a terrifying and extraordinary manner, to make its disastrous effects apparent. It did not take the form it had assumed in the East, where if anyone bled from the nose it was an obvious portent of certain death. On the contrary, its earliest symptom, in men and women alike, was the appearance of certain swellings in the groin or the armpit, some of which were egg-shaped whilst others were roughly the size of the common apple. Sometimes the swellings were large, sometimes not so large, and they were referred to by the populace as *gavòccioli*. From the two areas already mentioned, this deadly *gavòcciolo* would begin to spread, and within a short time it would appear at random all over the body. Later on, the symptoms of the disease changed, and many people began to find dark blotches and bruises on their arms, thighs, and other parts of the body, sometimes large and few in number, at other times tiny and closely spaced. These, to anyone unfortunate enough to contract them, were just as infallible a sign that he would die as the *gavòcciolo* had been earlier, and as indeed it still was.

Against these maladies, it seemed that all the advice of physicians and all the power of medicine were profitless and unavailing. Perhaps the nature of the illness was such that it allowed no remedy; or perhaps those people who were treating the illness (whose numbers had increased enormously because the ranks of the qualified were invaded by people, both men and women, who had never received any training in medicine), being ignorant of its causes, were not prescribing the appropriate cure. At all events, few of those who caught it ever recovered, and in most cases death occurred within three days from the appearance of the symptoms we have described, some people dying more rapidly than others, the majority without any fever or other complications.

But what made this pestilence even more severe was that whenever those suffering from it mixed with people who were still unaffected, it would rush upon these with the speed of a fire racing through dry or oily substances that happened to be placed within its reach. Nor was this the full extent of its evil, for not only did it infect healthy persons who conversed or had any dealings with the sick, making them ill or visiting an equally horrible death upon them, but it also seemed to transfer the sickness to anyone touching the clothes or other objects which had been handled or used by its victims.

These things, and many others of a similar or even worse nature, caused various fears and fantasies to take root in the minds of those who were still alive and well. And almost without exception, they took a single and very inhuman precaution namely to avoid or run away from the sick and their belongings, by which means they all thought that their own health would be preserved.

Some people were of the opinion that a sober and abstemious mode of living considerably reduced the risk of infection. They therefore formed themselves into groups and lived in isolation from everyone else. Having withdrawn to a comfortable abode where there were no sick persons, they locked themselves in and settled down to a peaceable existence, consuming modest quantities of delicate foods and precious wines and avoiding all excesses. They refrained from speaking to outsiders, refused to receive news of the dead or sick, and entertained themselves with music and whatever other amusements they were able to devise.

Others took the opposite view, and maintained that an infallible way of warding off this appalling evil was to drink heavily, enjoy life to the full, go round singing and merrymaking, gratify all of one's cravings whenever the opportunity offered, and shrug the whole thing off as one enormous joke. Moreover, they practiced what they preached to the best of their ability, for they would visit one tavern after another, drinking all day and night to immoderate excess; or alternatively (and this was their more frequent custom), they would do their drinking in various private houses, but only in the ones where the conversation was restricted to subjects that were pleasant or entertaining. Such places were easy to find, for people behaved as though their days were numbered, and treated their belongings and their own persons with equal abandon. Hence most houses had become common property, and any passing stranger could make himself at home as naturally as though he were the rightful owner. But for all their riotous manner of living, these people always took good care to avoid any contact with the sick.

In the face of so much affliction and misery, all respect for the laws of God and man had virtually broken down and been extinguished in our city. For like everybody else, those ministers and executors of the laws who were not either dead or ill were left with so few subordinates that they were unable to discharge any of their duties. Hence everyone was free to behave as he pleased.

There were many other people who steered a middle course between the two already mentioned, neither restricting their diet to the same degree as the first group, nor indulging so freely as the second in drinking and other forms of wantonness, but simply doing no more than satisfy their appetite. Instead of incarcerating themselves, these people moved about freely, holding in their hands a posy of flowers, or fragrant herbs, or one of a wide range of spices, which they applied at frequent intervals to their nostrils, thinking it an excellent idea to fortify the brain with smells of that particular sort; for the stench of dead bodies, sickness, and medicines seemed to fill and pollute the whole of the atmosphere.

Some people, pursuing what was possibly the safer alternative, callously maintained that there was no better or more efficacious remedy against a plague than to run away from it. Swayed by this argument, and sparing no thought for anyone but themselves, large numbers of men and women abandoned their city, their homes, their relatives, their estates and their belongings, and headed for the countryside, either in Florentine territory or, better still, abroad. It was as though they imagined that the wrath of God would not unleash this plague against men for their iniquities irrespective of where they happened to be, but would only be aroused against those who found themselves within the city walls; or possibly they assumed that the whole of the population would be exterminated and that the city's last hour had come.

Hence the countless numbers of people who fell ill, both male and female, were entirely dependent upon either the charity of friends (who were few and far between) or the greed of servants, who remained in short supply despite the attraction of high wages out of all proportion to the services they performed. Furthermore, these latter were men and women of coarse intellect and the majority were unused to such duties, and they did little more than hand things to the invalid when asked to do so and watch over him when he was dying. And in performing this kind of service, they frequently lost their lives as well as their earnings.

As a result of this wholesale desertion of the sick by neighbours, relatives and friends, and in view of the scarcity of servants, there grew up a practice almost never previously heard of, whereby when a woman fell ill, no matter how gracious or beautiful or gently bred she might be, she raised no objection to being attended by a male servant, whether he was young or not. Nor did she have any scruples about showing him every part of her body as freely as she would have displayed it to a woman, provided that the nature of her infirmity required her to do so; and this explains why those women who recovered were possibly less chaste in the period that followed.

Moreover a great many people died who would perhaps have survived had they received some assistance. And hence, what with the lack of appropriate means for tending the sick, and the virulence of the plague, the number of deaths reported in the city whether by day or night was so enormous that it astonished all who heard tell of it, to say nothing of the people who actually witnessed the carnage. And it was perhaps inevitable that among the citizens who survived there arose certain customs that were quite contrary to established tradition.

As for the common people and a large proportion of the bourgeoisie, they presented a much more pathetic spectacle, for the majority of them were constrained, either by their poverty or the hope of survival, to remain in their houses. Being confined to their own parts of the city, they fell ill daily in their thousands, and since they had no one to assist them or attend to their needs, they inevitably perished almost without exception. Many dropped dead in the open streets, both by day and by night, whilst a great many others, though dying in their own houses, drew their neighbours' attention to the fact more by the smell of their rotting corpses than by any other means. And what with these, and the others who were dying all over the city, bodies were here, there and everywhere.

Whenever people died, their neighbours nearly always followed a single, set routine, prompted as much by their fear of being contaminated by the decaying corpse as by any charitable feelings they may have entertained towards the deceased. Either on their own, or with the assistance of bearers whenever these were to be had, they extracted the bodies of the dead from their houses and left then lying outside their front doors, where anybody going about the streets, especially in the early morning, could have observed countless numbers of them. Funeral biers would then be sent for, upon which the dead were taken away, though there were some who, for lack of biers, were carried off on plain boards.

But rather than describe in elaborate detail the calamities we experienced in the city at that time, I must mention that, whilst an ill wind was blowing through Florence itself, the surrounding region was no less badly affected. In the fortified towns, conditions were similar to those in the city itself on a minor scale; but in the scattered hamlets and the countryside proper, the poor unfortunate peasants and their families had no physicians or servants whatever to assist them, and collapsed by the wayside, in their fields, and in their cottages at all hours of the day and night, dying more like animals than human beings. Like the townspeople, they too grew apathetic in their ways, disregarded their affairs, and neglected their possessions. Moreover, they all behaved as though each day was to be their last, and far from making provision for the future by tilling their lands, tending their flocks, and adding to their previous labours, they tried in every way they could think of to squander the assets already in their possession. Thus it came about that oxen, asses, sheep, goats, pigs, chickens, and even dogs (for all their deep fidelity to man) were driven away and allowed to roam freely through the fields, where the crops lay abandoned and had not even been reaped, let alone gathered in. And after a whole day's feasting, many of these animals, as though possessing the power of reason, would return glutted in the evening to their own quarters, without any shepherd to guide them.

But let us leave the countryside and return to the city. What more remains to be said, except that the cruelty of heaven (and possibly, in some measure, also that of man) was so immense and so devastating that between March and July of the year in question, what with the fury of the pestilence and the fact that so many of the sick were inadequately cared for or abandoned in their hour of need because the healthy were too terrified to approach them, it is reliably thought that over a hundred thousand human lives were extinguished within the walls of the city of Florence? Yet before this lethal catastrophe fell upon the city, it is doubtful whether anyone would have guessed it contained so many inhabitants.

From: Horrox, Rosemary, *The Black Death* (Manchester: Manchester University Press, 1994), pp. 26–34.

QUESTIONS:

1. How does Boccacio's account of the plague in Cairo compare to the accounts of plague in Thucydides and Procopius in Chapter 2 (and al-Makrizi's in the previous source)? What are the similarities and differences? Does the Xian faith of the population seem to have an effect on social reactions to the plague's devastation?
2. How are Muslim funerals arranged in Ahmad al-Maqrizi's account of the plague in Cairo? How does his description compare with Boccaccio's of Christian funerals? What cultural values might explain the differences?

13.3: Tradition Reasserted: *Dee Goong An (Celebrated Cases of Judge Dee)*, (Ming, translated in 1949 by Robert van Gulik)

Di Renjie (c. 630–c. 700), or Judge Dee, was a famous magistrate during the Tang Dynasty (618–900). In the fifteenth century, under the Ming Dynasty, Judge Dee became the subject of popular Chinese detective-mystery novels. (So much, by the way, for Edgar Allen Poe or Wilkie Collins as the inventor of the genre.) Nominally, they were set in Tang times, but they reflected much about Ming culture. In 1949, the Dutch diplomat Robert van Gulik (1910–67) discovered an eighteenth century copy of the novel in a Tokyo bookstore and translated it into English. He later wrote an entire series of Judge Dee mysteries based on the character. This excerpt shows us a slice of Chinese culture in the Ming period, after the Mongol Yüan Dynasty had been expelled.

MRS. DJOU REFUSES TO LET HER HUSBAND BE BURIED; JUDGE DEE VISITS THE TEMPLE FOR SPIRITUAL GUIDANCE.

"Since the outside of the corpse shows no traces, its inside must be probed," Judge Dee said firmly. "This is the fixed rule for an autopsy."

He did not allow Mrs. Djou to say another word, and ordered the coroner to proceed.

The coroner poured hot water into the mouth of the corpse, and by exercising pressure with the palms of his hands on its breast and belly, made the water first enter, and then come out again. Then he took a thin lamella of polished silver, of about eight inches long, and slowly pushed it down till it had entered deep down in the throat. He left it there, and turning to the judge, asked him to witness the withdrawal of the lamella.

Judge Dee left his seat and stood next to the corpse while the coroner drew the lamella out again. Its surface did not show the slightest discoloration.

The coroner was perplexed, and said:

"This, Your Honor, is passing strange. I cannot but state that I did not find one single trace of this man having met with a violent death. I beg to advise, however, that an older coroner of established reputation be ordered to perform a second autopsy, to see whether he confirms my findings."

Judge Dee now was in great consternation. He slowly resumed his seat, and said to Mrs. Djou:

"Since no trace of a crime having been committed was revealed by this autopsy, I shall so report to the higher authorities, and take full responsibility for the consequences. In the meantime we cannot leave this corpse lying exposed here. We shall replace it in its coffin, so that it can be interred again."

Before he had quite finished, however, Mrs. Djou had already kicked away one of the trestles from under the empty coffin; it fell down with a crash, and broke to pieces. She cried:

"I maintained that he died of an illness, but you, dog-official, insisted upon an autopsy. And now, having failed to discover any trace of a crime, you want to bury it again as if nothing had happened. What kind of a magistrate are you? Although I am but a poor woman of the common people, you have no right to beat and torture me when am innocent. Yesterday you tried to compel me to make a false confession, to-day you are desecrating a grave. Since you have had the corpse exhumed, it shall not be interred again. Although we are but common people, we need not let ourselves be trod upon in this way. This corpse shall not be interred again until the day this case is solved, and you have lost your black cap!"

She went on reviling Judge Dee, and her mother soon joined in the chorus. Judge Dee could answer nothing in return.

The crowd of onlookers, however, seeing that the judge, whom they knew as an honest official, was thus being insulted in public, were all of the opinion that this was a disgraceful situation. A few elders closed in on Mrs. Djou and her mother, and reprimanded them, saying that since the corpse had already been subjected to the disgrace of the autopsy, it was outrageous to let it lie there exposed in broad daylight. Others added that the judge was an honest official who, although he had erred in this case, had done so in good faith, and after all only for her dead husband's sake. Others again declared that they would not stand for a woman of their village to shout at and curse an official in public. Would not the people from the neighboring hamlets deride us of Huang-hua Village, and say that we did not know the rules of propriety? She had better follow the instructions of the judge, and consent to the corpse being buried again.

Mrs. Djou, seeing that this was the general opinion of the crowd did not think it expedient to insist further. She thought by herself that by her threats and recriminations she had at least achieved that no other coroner would be asked to perform a second autopsy. The main thing was to have the corpse placed again in a coffin, and buried safely underground.

Judge Dee, seeing that the old coffin could not be used anymore, sent a few constables to the village, to buy a temporary coffin. When this had arrived, the corpse was hurriedly dressed, and the coffin closed. For the time being it was to be left there on its bier.

Judge Dee had the necessary documents relating to the exhumation filled out, and then returned to Huang-hua Village, followed by the crowd.

Since it was growing dark already, he decided to stay there for the night in the same hostel. He ordered that Mrs. Bee would be allowed to go home, but that Mrs. Djou be returned to the jail of the tribunal, to be kept there until further notice.

Having issued these orders Judge Dee retired to his room in the hostel, and there sat down, alone with his troubled thoughts.

Then Sergeant Hoong came in, and after having greeted the judge, reported the following:

"Obeying Your Honor's instructions, I have made inquiries with that young man who used to be Bee Hsun's neighbor. I found that he had been quite friendly with Bee Hsun and regrets very much that death separated them. But he could add little to what we know already about the crime itself. He mentioned, though, that when Bee Hsun was still alive, his wife loved to show herself in the streets, joking and laughing in public and altogether did not behave as a self-respecting housewife should. Bee Hsun often scolded her for this, but that always resulted only in some violent quarrels. When, after his death, his wife locked up herself in her house, and refused to see anybody except her mother, it caused no little surprise among the neighbors.

"Now that the autopsy has produced no results", the sergeant added, "how shall we proceed with this case? Although we are firmly convinced that Bee Hsun was murdered, as long as there is no proof, we can hardly again question Mrs. Djou under torture. Moreover, the double murder of Six Mile Village has not been solved either. More than two weeks have elapsed, but still there is no news about Ma Joong and Chiao Tai having traced the murderer. It is true that Your Honor is indifferent with regard to his own reputation, but both cases are heinous crimes which cry for justice. Cannot Your Honor devise some way. . ."

While the sergeant was saying this, he was interrupted by the sounds of loud crying, outside in the courtyard. Fearing that Mrs. Bee had turned up again to annoy Judge Dee, he wanted to go outside to intercept her. But then he heard the constable standing guard outside saying:

"So you are asking for His Excellency the Judge? Well, you may be the wife of that man, but that is no reason to get in such a state. His Excellency is doing what he can. You first rest here a while and explain to me, then I shall report it to the Judge. Now how do you know that that man was your husband?"

Sergeant Hoong went hastily outside and heard that the wife of the unidentified victim of the crime at Six Mile Village had arrived to file her case with the judge. When he had reported this to his master, Judge Dee ordered the woman to be brought in.

She was a woman of about forty, her hair was disheveled, and tears were streaming down her face. Kneeling down in front of the judge, she started wailing loudly, imploring him to avenge her husband's death.

When asked to explain, she told the following:

"My poor husband was called Wang, he was a carter by profession. We live in Liu-shui-kow, about twenty miles from Six Mile Village. On the eve of the murder, the wife of our neighbor became very ill, and begged my husband to go to Six Mile Village at once and fetch her husband, who happened to be staying there for transacting some business. Now my husband was going there anyway with his pushcart to fetch some goods, so he set out that same night expecting to be back early the next morning. But I waited for him the whole next day in vain. First I did not worry, thinking that he might have found some carting to do there. When, however, after three days, our neighbor came back and told me that he had not seen my husband at all, I became very much worried. I waited another few days, and then asked some of our relatives to go out and make inquiries along the road, and in Six Mile Village. They came upon a coffin placed on its bier near the guard house and read the official notice put up by its side. From the description given there, they immediately knew that the unidentified victim was my husband, dastardly done to death by some unknown person. I beg Your Honor to avenge his death!"

Judge Dee was moved by her grief, and said some comforting words, assuring her that everything was being done to apprehend the murderer. He then gave her some silver, and told her to use this sum for having her husband properly buried.

After the widow Wang had left, Judge Dee remained sitting there, sunk in melancholy thoughts. He reflected that since he had sadly failed in his duties as a magistrate, how could he still remain in office, having proved incapable of serving the State and the people?

The waiter brought his dinner in, but Judge Dee felt no appetite and he had to force himself to eat a few morsels. With the dejected sergeant standing by, the meal was finished in dismal silence. Judge Dee went to bed shortly afterwards.

The next morning Judge Dee left the hostel early, and, accompanied by his retinue, went back to the city. He made, however, a detour via Six Mile Village, where he personally ordered the headman to give Mrs. Wang all assistance for having the coffin with her husband's corpse transported to her own village.

As soon as he was seated in his private office, Judge Dee moistened his writing brush, and drew up a report for the higher authorities. He described in full detail how he had committed the crime of desecrating a grave, and recommended himself for appropriate punishment. When he had acquitted himself of this melancholy task, he ordered the servants to prepare a bath, and told them that he would not require any food, as he was going to fast that day.

When he had bathed, and put on clean clothes, he ordered Sergeant Hoong to go to the city temple, and inform the superior that he intended to stay there that night; the main hall of the temple was to be closed to the public after nightfall, and all persons except the priests were to be told to leave.

When night was falling, Judge Dee proceeded to the temple. Arrived before the gate, he sent his escort back, and ascended the main hall alone.

There Sergeant Hoong had already prepared a couch for him in a corner, and a cushion for meditation was placed in front of the altar.

The sergeant added new incense in the burner and then took his leave. He spread his bedding out below on one of the broad steps leading up to the main hall, and there lay down.

Then Judge Dee knelt down on the bare floor in front of the altar, and prayed fervently. He supplicated the Powers on High that they, knowing his earnest desire that justice be done, would deign to show him the right way.

He sat down on the cushion, with crossed legs and his body erect. Closing his eyes, he tried to achieve a tranquil state of mind.

From: Gulik, Robert Hans van, *Celebrated cases of Judge Dee (Dee Goong An): an authentic eighteenth-century Chinese detective novel* (New York: Dover Publications, 1976).

QUESTIONS:

1. Based on this episode, what values, either frame values or those contested on the cultural screen, inform the relationship between the Chinese state and its subjects? That is, what beliefs allow the Ming hierarchy to function?
2. What is the relationship in this episode between what appears to be a fairly sophisticated, evidence based, even scientific approach to evidence and respect for tradition and authority? That is, in what ways are innovation and investigation framed by tradition?

CHAPTER 14

Innovation and Tradition: 1350 to 1550

INTRODUCTION

In this chapter we continue to look at reactions to the fourteenth century crises brought about by the Mongols and the bubonic plague pandemic, examining the crisis in western Europe. Two sources show two of this period of crisis that reveal important developments in European societies. The period of crisis was followed by reconstruction of the Eurasian trade network and its expansion to encompass the Americas. We see these developments through two Chinese accounts and two European accounts of oceanic voyages. Finally, the combination of crisis and expanded network flows produced a culture of innovation in western Europe that is represented in our final source.

14.1: Western Europe in Crisis

14.1a: *Statute of Laborers* (1351)

Parliament, representing the interests of elite landowners, passed the Statute of Laborers in 1351 to reinforce the Ordinance of Laborers of 1349, which had been issued by King Edward III. Both responded to concerns about labor shortages caused by the plague, which hit in late 1348. Commoners (working folk, including peasant serfs) were demanding (and receiving) much higher wages than they had been accustomed to receive before the plague. This law specified acceptable wages. The repetition of the wage restriction in 1349 and 1351 indicates the failure of the measures, ignored by workers and employers alike. Wages, in both real and nominal terms, shot up in the decades after the plague. This result—that labor shortage should lead to higher wages—seems natural to us: supply and demand rule. But it is the exact opposite of the result we should expect from Agrarian hierarchies, in which labor shortages led to lower labor freedom, which is in fact what the Statute aimed to achieve. Its failure is therefore deeply significant.

Whereas lately it was ordained by our lord king and by the assent of the prelates, earls, barons and others of his council, against the malice of servants who were idle and not willing to serve after the pestilence without excessive wages, that such manner of servants, men as well as women, should be bound to serve, receiving the customary salary and wages in the places where they are bound to serve in the twentieth year of the reign of the king that now is [that is, in 1347 before the plague], or five or six years before, and that the same servants refusing to serve in such a manner should be punished by imprisonment of their bodies, as is more plainly contained in the said statute. Whereupon commissions were made to diverse people in every county to enquire and punish all those who offend against the same. And now for as much as it is given to the king to understand in the present parliament by the petition of the commons that the servants having no regard to the ordinance but to their ease and singular covetousness, do withdraw themselves from serving great men and others, unless they have livery and wages double or treble of what they were wont to take in the twentieth year and earlier, to the great damage of the great men and impoverishment of all the commonality; whereof the commonality prays remedy. Wherefore in the parliament by the assent of the prelates, earls, barons, and those of the commonality assembled there, in order to refrain the malice of the servants, there are ordained and established the underwritten articles.

Item that carters, ploughmen drivers of ploughs, shepherds, swineherds, day men, and all other servants shall take the liveries and wages accustomed in the twentieth year or four years before so that in the countryside where the wheat was wont to be given they shall take for the bushel 10 d [enarius, or pence], or wheat at the will of the giver until it be otherwise ordained. And that they be hired to serve by a whole year, or by other usual terms, and not by the day; and that none pay at haymaking time more than a penny a day; and a mower of meadows for the acre 5 d, or 5 d by the day; and reapers of corn in the first week of August 2 d, and the second 3 d and so on until the end of August and less in the country where less was wont to be given, without meat or drink, or other courtesy to be demanded, given, or taken; and that all workmen bring their tools openly in their hands to the merchant towns, and they shall be hired there in a common place and not privately.

Item that none take for the threshing of a quarter of wheat or rye over 2½ d and the quarter of barley, beans, peas and oats 1½ d, if so much were wont to be given. And in the country where it is usual to reap by certain sheaves and to thresh by certain bushels they shall take no more nor in other manner than was wont the said twenty year and before, and that the same servants be sworn two times a year before lords, stewards, bailiffs and constables of every town to observe and perform these ordinances; and that none of them go out of the town where he lives in the winter to serve the summer if he may serve in the same town, taking as before is said. . . . [T]hose who refuse to make such oath, or to not perform as they were sworn to do or have taken upon them shall be put in the stocks by the said lords, stewards, bailiffs and constables of the towns for three days or more or sent to the next gaol, there to remain until they satisfy themselves. And that stocks be made in every town for such occasion, between now and the feast of Pentecost.

Item that carpenters masons and tilers and other workmen of houses shall not take by the day further work except in the manner as they were wont to do. . . . And those who carry by land or by water shall take no more for such carriage to be made than they were wont to do in the said twentieth year and four years before.

Item that cordwainers and shoemakers shall not sell boots or shoes nor any other thing touching their craft, in any other manner than they were wont to do in the said twentieth year.

Item that goldsmiths, saddlers, horsesmiths spurriers, tanners, corriers, tawers of leather, tailors and other workmen, artificers and labourers, and all other servants not here specified, shall be sworn before the justices, and do use their crafts and offices in this manner as they were wont to do the said twentieth year, and in the time before, without refusing the same because of this ordinance, and if any of the said servants, labourers, workmen or artificers, after such oath made, come against this ordinance, he shall be punished by fine and ransom and imprisonment after the discretion of the justices.

Item that the stewards, bailiffs and constables of the said towns be sworn before the same justices to enquire diligently by all the good ways they may, of all them that come against this ordinance and to certify the same justices of their names at all times, when they shall come into the country to make their sessions, so that the same justices upon the certificate of the said stewards, bailiffs, and constables, of the names of the rebels shall cause their bodies to be attached before the justices, to answer of such contempts so that they make fine and ransom to the king in case they be attainted [convicted], and moreover to be commanded to prison there to remain until they have found surety to serve and take and do their work and to sell things vendible in the manner aforesaid. And in case that any of them come against his oath and be thereof attainted, he shall have imprisonment of forty days, and if he is convicted another time, he shall be imprisoned for a quarter of a year so that every time he offends and is convicted he shall have double pain. . . .

Item that the justices make their sessions in all English counties at least four times each year, . . . and also at all times that shall be necessary, according to the discretion of the justices, and those who speak in the presence of the justices or do other things in their absence or presence in encouragement or maintenance of the servants, labourers or craftsmen against this ordinance, shall be grievously punished by the discretion of the justices. And if any of the servants, labourers or artificers flee from one county to another, because of this ordinance, then the sheriffs of the counties where such fugitives shall be found shall cause them to be taken at the commandment of the said justices of the counties from where they flee, and bring them to the chief gaol of the shire there to abide until the next sessions of the justices. And that the sheriffs return the same commandments before the same justices at their next sessions. And that this ordinance be held and kept as well in the city of London as in other cities and boroughs, and other places throughout the land, within franchises as well as without.

From: The National Archives of the UK, "Second Statute of Labourers, 1351," Catalogue reference C 74/1, m. 18, online at http://www.nationalarchives.gov.uk/pathways/citizenship/citizen_subject/transcripts/stat_lab.htm, (transcription and translation of the document), http://www.nationalarchives.gov.uk/pathways/citizenship/citizen_subject/docs/statute_labourers .htm, (image of the original document and archival information).

QUESTIONS:

1. Agrarian hierarchies normally responded to labor shortages by restricting peasant freedom: that is, states and elites would meet potential labor shortages by locking in the available labor. What characteristics of the English peasant economy visible in this source might have made such a response difficult to enforce? (For example, what role do cities play in the distribution of agricultural labor?)
2. What cultural attitudes does the Statute express? How might those attitudes have contributed to the Statute's failure?

14.1b: *The Peasants' Revolt of 1381* (Jean Froissart, 1393)

This account of the great Peasants' Revolt that hit England thirty years after the passage of the Statute of Laborers comes from the *Chronicles* of Jean Froissart (1337–1410). Froissart spoke and wrote in French but had connections with the English royal court. He was not an eyewitness to the revolt, but his narrative gives us a clear picture of the attitudes of the elite towards the commoners. He wrote this section in the early 1390s. Froissart claims that "It was because of the abundance and prosperity in which the common people then lived that this rebellion broke out." Common workers after 1351 did enjoy higher wages and better diets than earlier generations had. The royal government, having failed to regulate wages in 1351, tried to exploit the new wealth of the peasantry in 1381 by instituting a Poll Tax—essentially a head tax, or an amount levied on each person in the kingdom. The tax was new and widely hated, and triggered the revolt (note that Froissart fails to mention it).

While these negotiations and discussions were going on [between John of Gaunt, Duke of Lancaster, and the Scots, with a view to renewing the truce between England and Scotland], there occurred in England great disasters and uprisings of the common people, on account of which the country was almost ruined beyond recovery. Never was any land or realm in such great danger as England at that time. It was because of the abundance and prosperity in which the common people then lived that this rebellion broke out, just as in earlier days the [French peasant revolt], by which the noble land of France suffered grave injury.

These terrible troubles originated in England from a strange circumstance and a trivial cause. That it may serve as a lesson to all good men and true, I will describe that circumstance and its effects as I was informed of them at the time.

It is the custom in England, as in several other countries, for the nobles to have strong powers over their men and to hold them in serfdom: that is, that by right and custom they have to till the lands of the gentry, reap the corn and bring it to the big house, put it in the barn, thresh and winnow it; mow the hay and carry it to the house, cut logs and bring them up, and all such forced tasks; all this the men must do by way of serfage to the masters. In England there is a much greater number than elsewhere of such men who are obliged to serve the prelates and the nobles. And in the counties of Kent, Essex, Sussex and Bedford in particular, there are more than in the whole of the rest of England.

These bad people in the counties just mentioned began to rebel because, they said, they were held too much in subjection, and when the world began there had been no serfs and could not be, unless they had rebelled against their lord, as Lucifer did against God; but they were not of that stature, being neither angels nor spirits, but men formed in the image of their masters, and they were treated as animals. This was a thing they could no longer endure, wishing rather to be all one and the same; and, if they worked for their masters, they wanted to have wages for it. In these machinations they had been greatly encouraged originally by a crack-brained priest of Kent called John Ball, who had been imprisoned several times for his reckless words by the Archbishop of Canterbury. This John Ball had the habit on Sundays after mass, when everyone was coming out of church, of going to the cloisters or the graveyard, assembling the people round him and preaching thus:

'Good people, things cannot go right in England and never will, until goods are held in common and there are no more villeins and gentlefolk, but we are all one and the same. In what way are those whom we call lords greater masters than ourselves? How have they deserved it? Why do they hold us in bondage? If we all spring from a single father and mother, Adam and Eve, how can they claim or prove that they are lords more than us, except by making us produce and grow the wealth which they spend? They are clad in velvet and camlet lined with squirrel and ermine, while we go dressed in coarse cloth. They have the wines, the spices and the good bread: we have the rye, the husks and the straw, and we drink water. They have shelter and ease in their fine manors, and we have hardship and toil, the wind and the rain in the fields. And from us must come, from our labor, the things which keep them in luxury. We are called serfs and beaten if we are slow in our service to them, yet we have no sovereign lord we can complain to, none to hear us and do us justice. Let us go to the King—he is young—and show him how we are oppressed, and tell him that we want things to be changed, or else we will change them ourselves. If we go in good earnest and all together, very many people who are called serfs and are held in subjection will follow us to get their freedom. And when the King sees and hears us, he will remedy the evil, either willingly or otherwise.'

These were the kind of things which John Ball usually preached in the villages on Sundays when the congregations came out from mass, and many of the common people agreed with him. Some, who were up to no good, said: 'He's right!' and out in the fields, or walking together from one village to another, or in their homes, they whispered and repeated among themselves: 'That's what John Ball says, and he's right.'

The Archbishop of Canterbury, being informed of all this, had John Ball arrested and put in prison, where he kept him for two or three months as a punishment. It would have been better if he had condemned him to life imprisonment on the first occasion, or had him put to death, than to do what he did; but he had great scruples about putting him to death and set him free; and when John Ball was out of prison, he went on with his intrigues as before. The things he was doing and saying came to the ears of the common people of London, who were envious of the nobles and the rich. These began saying that the country was badly governed and was being robbed of its wealth by those who called themselves noblemen. So these wicked men in London started to become disaffected and to rebel and they sent word to the people in the counties mentioned to come boldly to London with all their followers, when they would find the city open and the common people on their side. They could then so work on the King that there would be no more serfs in England.

These promises incited the people of Kent, Essex, Sussex, Bedford and the neighboring districts and they set off and went towards London. They were a full sixty thousand and their chief captain was one Wat Tyler. With him as his companions were Jack Straw and John Ball. These three were the leaders and Wat Tyler was the greatest of them. He was a tiler of roofs, and a wicked and nasty fellow he was.

[The crowd marches through Canterbury, sacking the palace of the Archbishop on the way, and makes its way to London, where they have several meetings with King Richard II, at the time only 16 years old, and some of his leading nobles. At one of these, in a field outside of London at Smithfield, the king with perhaps sixty supporters, virtually surrounded by the rebel mob, entered into negotiations with Wat Tyler, who (according to this account) was acting belligerently and seemed to be trying to provoke a fight with the king's supporters.]

Just then the Lord Mayor of London arrived on horseback with a dozen others, all fully armed beneath their robes, and broke through the crowd. He saw how Tyler was behaving and said to him in the sort of language he understood: 'Fellow, how dare you say such things in the King's presence? You're getting above yourself.' The King lost his temper and said to the Mayor: 'Lay hands on him, Mayor.' Meanwhile Tyler was answering: 'I can say and do what I like. What's it to do with you?' 'So, you stinking boor,' said the Mayor, who had once been a King's Advocate, 'you talk like that in the presence of the King, my natural lord? I'll be hanged if you don't pay for it.'

With that he drew a great sword he was wearing and struck. He gave Tyler such a blow on the head that he laid him flat under his horse's feet. No sooner was he down than he was entirely surrounded, so as to hide him from the crowds who were there, who called themselves his men. One of the King's squires called John Standish dismounted and thrust his sword into Tyler's belly so that he died.

Those crowds of evil men soon realized that their leader was dead. They began to mutter: 'They've killed our captain. Come on, we'll slay the lot!' They drew themselves up in the square in a kind of battle-order, each holding before him the bow which he carried. Then the King did an extraordinarily rash thing, but it ended well. As soon as Tyler was dispatched, he left his men, saying: 'Stay here, no one is to follow me,' and went alone towards those half-crazed people, to whom he said: 'Sirs, what more do you want ? You have no other captain but me. I am your king, behave peaceably.' On hearing this, the majority of them were ashamed and began to break up. They were the peace-loving ones. But the bad ones did not disband; instead they formed up for battle and showed that they meant business. The King rode back to his men and asked what should be done next. He was advised to go on towards the country, since it was no use trying to run away. The Mayor said: 'That is the best thing for us to do, for I imagine that we shall soon receive reinforcements from London, from the loyal men on our side who are waiting armed in their houses with their friends.'

While all this was going on, a rumor spread through London that the King was being killed. Because of it, loyal men of all conditions left their houses armed and equipped and made for Smithfield and the fields nearby, where the King now was. Soon they were some seven or eight thousand strong. . . . The leaders conferred together, saying: 'What shall we do? There are our enemies who would gladly have killed us if they thought they had the advantage.' Sir Robert Knollys argued frankly that they should go and fight them and kill them all, but the King refused to agree, saying that he would not have that done. 'But,' said the King, 'I want to have my banners back. We will see how they behave when we ask for them. In any case, by peaceful means or not, I want them back.' 'You're right,' said the Earl of Salisbury. So the three new knights were sent over to get them. They made signs to the villeins [commoners] not to shoot, since they had something to discuss. When they were near enough for their voices to be heard, they said: 'Now listen, the King commands you to give back his banners, and we hope that he will have mercy on you.' The banners were handed over at once and taken back to the King. Any of the villeins who had obtained royal letters [of emancipation from serfdom] were also ordered in the King's name to give them up, on pain of death. Some did so, but not all. The King had them taken and torn up in front of them. It may be said that as soon as the royal banners had been removed, those bad men became just a mob. Most of them threw down their bows and they broke formation and started back for London. Sir Robert Knollys was more than angry that they had not been attacked and all killed. But the King would not hear of it, saying that he would take full vengeance later, as he did.

From: Froissart, Jean, *Chronicles,* Geoffrey Brereton, ed. and transl., pp. 211–213, 226–228, © 1968 Penguin Books.

QUESTIONS:

1. What cultural screen images do the leaders of the peasant uprising project to their followers? What cultural frame values lie behind the actions of most of the rebels in the wake of their leader's death? Are the screen images and frame values in agreement?
2. What attitudes toward the rebels does Froissart himself express? How well do you think he understands the revolt?

CHINA AT SEA

14.2a: *Inscription of World Voyages* (Zheng He, c. 1433)

Between 1405 and 1431, the great Chinese admiral Zheng He led seven expedition of Treasure Fleets from China on behalf of the third Ming Emperor. The Yongle emperor's expeditions combined trade, diplomacy, and military display; and the lands they visited, from southeast Asia to India and beyond to Arabia and east Africa, sent items of trade and tribute back to China. But Ming policy changed after 1431: Yongle's successors sent out no more Treasure Fleets, focusing instead on the Mongol frontier. Officials burnt all of Sheng He's logs. All that remains to us is a long lost stone tablet, erected sometime before Zheng He's death in 1435, on which Zheng He had inscribed the following account of the great Treasure Fleet voyages.

A record of the miraculous answer [to prayers] to the goddess the Celestial Spouse [a Daoist diety revered by maritime travelers].

The Imperial Ming Dynasty unifying seas and continents, surpassing the three dynasties even goes beyond the Han and Tang dynasties. The countries beyond the horizon and from the ends of the earth have all become subjects and to the most western of the western or the most northern of the northern countries, however far they may be, the distance and the routes may be calculated. Thus the barbarians from beyond the seas, though their countries are truly distant . . . have come to audience bearing precious objects and presents.

The Emperor, approving of their loyalty and sincerity, has ordered us, Zheng He and others at the head of several tens of thousands of officers and flag-troops to ascend more than one hundred large ships to go and confer presents on them in order to make manifest the transforming power of the (imperial) virtue and to treat distant people with kindness. From the third year of Yongle [1405] till now we have seven times received the commission of ambassadors to countries of the western ocean. The barbarian countries which we have visited are Zhancheng [Vietnam], Zhaowa [Java, Indonesia], Sanfoqi [Sumatra, Indonesia], and Xianlo [Siam] crossing straight over to Xilanshan [Sri Lanka] in South India, Calicut, [India] and Kezhi [India], we have gone to the western regions of Hulumosi [Ormuz], Aden [Yemen], Mogadishu [Somalia], altogether more than thirty countries large and small. We have traversed more than one hundred thousand *li* [35,000 miles] of immense water spaces and have beheld in the ocean huge waves like mountains rising sky high, and we have set eyes on barbarian regions far away hidden in a blue transparency of light vapors, while our sails loftily unfurled like clouds day and night continued their course rapidly like that of a star, traversing those savage waves as if we were treading a public thoroughfare. Truly this was due to the majesty and the good fortune of the Imperial Court and moreover we owe it to the protecting virtue of the divine Celestial Spouse.

The power of the goddess having indeed been manifested in previous times has been abundantly revealed in the present generation. In the midst of the rushing waters it happened that, when there was a hurricane, suddenly there was a divine lantern shining in the mast, and as soon as this miraculous light appeared the danger was appeased, so that even in the danger of capsizing one felt reassured that there was no cause for fear. When we arrived in the distant countries we captured alive those of the native kings who were not respectful and exterminated those barbarian robbers who were engaged in piracy, so that consequently the sea route was cleansed and pacified and the natives put their trust in it. All this is due to the favors of the goddess.

It is not easy to enumerate completely all the cases where the goddess has answered [my prayers]. Previously in a memorial to the Court we have requested that her virtue be recognized . . . and a temple be built at Nanking on the bank of the river where regular sacrifices should be made forever. We have respectfully received an Imperial commemoration exalting her miraculous favors, which is the highest recompense and praise indeed. However, the miraculous power of the goddess resides wherever one goes. . . .

We have received the high favor of a gracious commission from our sacred Lord [the Yongle Emperor], we carry to the distant barbarians the benefits of respect and good faith [on their part]. Commanding the multitudes on the fleet and being responsible for a quantity of money and valuables in the face of the violence of the winds and the nights, our one fear is not to be able to succeed. How, then, dare we not to serve our dynasty with . . . all our loyalty and the gods with the utmost sincerity? How would it be possible not to realize what is the source of the tranquility of the fleet and the troops and the salvation on the voyage both going and returning? Therefore, we have inscribed the virtue of the [Celestial Spouse] on stone and have also recorded the years and months of the voyages to the barbarian countries . . . in order to leave the memory forever.

I. In the third year of Yongle [1405] commanding the fleet we went to Calicut [India] and other countries. At that time the pirate Chen Zuyi had gathered his followers in the country of Sanfoqi [island of Sumatra], where he plundered the native merchants. When he also advanced to resist our fleet, supernatural soldiers secretly came to the rescue so that after one beating of the drum he was annihilated. In the fifth year [1407] we returned.

II. In the fifth year of Yongle [1407] commanding the fleet we went to Zhaowa [Java], Calicut, Kezhi [India], and Xianle [Siam]. The kings of these countries all sent as tribute precious objects, precious birds and rare animals. In the seventh year [1409] we returned.

III. In the seventh year of Yongle [1409] commanding the fleet we went to the countries (visited) before and took our route by the country of Xilanshan [Sri Lanka]. Its king Alagakkonara was guilty of a gross lack of respect and plotted against the fleet. Owing to the manifest answer to prayer of the goddess, [the plot] was discovered and thereupon that king was captured alive. In the ninth year [1411] on our return the captured king was presented [to the throne as a prisoner]; subsequently he received the Imperial [forgiveness and] favor of returning to his own country.

IV. In the eleventh year of Yongle [1413] commanding the fleet we went to Hulumosi [Ormuz] and other countries. In the country of Samudra [northern tip of Sumatra] there was a false king [named Sekandar] who was marauding and invading his country. The [true] king [Zaynu-'l-Abidin] had sent an envoy to the Palace Gates in order to lodge a complaint. We went there with the official troops under our command and exterminated some and arrested [other rebels], and owing to the silent aid of the goddess, we captured the false king alive. In the thirteenth year [1415] on our return he was presented [to the Emperor as a prisoner]. In that year the king of the country of Manlajia [Malacca, Malaysia] came in person with his wife and son to present tribute.

V. In the fifteenth year of Yongle [1417] commanding the fleet we visited the western regions. The country of Ormuz presented lions, leopards with gold spots and large western horses. The country of Aden [Yemen] presented [giraffes], as well as the long-horned [oryx]. The country of Mogadishu [Somalia] presented [zebras] as well as lions. The country of Brava [Somalia or Kenya] presented camels which run one thousand *li*, as well as camel-birds [ostriches]. The countries of Zhaowa [Java] and Calicut [India] presented animal *miligao* [hides]. They all vied in presenting the marvelous objects preserved in the mountains or hidden in the seas and the beautiful treasures buried in the sand or deposited on the shores. Some sent a maternal uncle of the king, others a paternal uncle or a younger brother of the king in order to present a letter of homage written on gold leaf as well as tribute.

VI. In the nineteenth year of Yongle [1421] commanding the fleet we escorted the ambassadors from Ormuz and the other countries who had been in attendance at the capital for a long time back to their countries. The kings of all these countries prepared even more tribute than previously.

VII. In the sixth year of [Yongle's successor, 1431] once more commanding the fleet we have left for the barbarian countries in order to read to them [an Imperial edict] and to confer presents.

We have anchored in this port awaiting a north wind to take the sea, and recalling how previously we have on several occasions received the benefits of the protection of the divine intelligence we have thus recorded an inscription in stone.

From: Filesi, Teobaldo, *China and Africa in the Middle Ages*, David Morison, transl. (London: Frank Cass, 1972), pp. 61–65.

QUESTIONS:

1. According to the inscription, what were the goals of voyages? Do these goals reflect greater influence of hierarchy values or network values? How?
2. After 1431, the Chinese abruptly stopped their overseas voyages. Based on Zheng He's account and the values that inform it, what might have happened if Chinese Treasure Fleets had continued their voyages for another seventy-five years and had then met Vasco da Gama's Portuguese fleets in the early 1500s?

14.2b: *Ma Huan, Overall Survey of the Ocean Shores* (1451)

Ma Huan (c. 1380–1460) was a Chinese Mulsim voyager and translator who accompanied Zheng He on three of the Treasure Fleet expeditions in 1413, 1421, and 1431. He began his *Overall Survey of the Ocean Shores* after the first voyage and expanded it after each subsequent voyage. He visited many countries, including the three whose descriptions are excerpted here—Calicut, Java, and Mecca—serving as a special envoy to the latter. His descriptions demonstrate his broad interests in foreign lands, as he writes about government, customs, religion, systems of criminal punishment, among other topics, in addition to providing notes about trade goods and the length of the maritime routes connecting the places he visited. His book therefore demonstrates the fact that networks always carried ideas along with material goods. He also represents and contributed to the growth of knowledge generated by network activity.

THE COUNTRY OF KU-LI [CALICUT]

In the fifth year of the Yongle [emperor; 1407] the court ordered the principal envoy the grand eunuch Zheng He and others to deliver an imperial mandate to the king of this country and to bestow on him a patent conferring a title of honour, and the grant of a silver seal, [also] to promote all the chiefs and award them hats and girdles of various grades.

[So Zheng He] went there in command of a large fleet of treasure-ships, and he erected a tablet with a pavilion over it and set up a stone which said 'Though the journey from this country to the Central Country [China] is more than a hundred thousand *li*, yet the people are very similar, happy and prosperous, with identical customs. We have here engraved a stone, a perpetual declaration for ten thousand ages.'

The king of the country is a [warrior caste] man; he is a firm believer in the Buddhist religion [actually, he was Hindu]; [and] he venerates the elephant and the ox.

. . . The king of the country and the people of the country all refrain from eating the flesh of the ox. The great chiefs are Muslim people; [and] they all refrain from eating the flesh of the pig. Formerly there was a king who made a sworn compact with the Muslim people, [saying] 'You do not eat the ox; I do not eat the pig; we will reciprocally respect the taboo'; [and this compact] has been honoured right down to the present day.

. . .

As to the pepper: the inhabitants of the mountainous countryside have established gardens, and it is extensively cultivated. When the period of the tenth moon arrives, the pepper ripens; [and] it is collected, dried in the sun, and sold. Of course, big pepper-collectors come and collect it, and take it up to the official storehouse to be stored; if there is a buyer, an official gives permission for the sale; the duty is calculated according to the amount [of the purchase price] and is paid in to the authorities. Each one ***po-ho*** of pepper is sold for two hundred gold coins.

The Che-ti mostly purchase all kinds of precious stones and pearls, and they manufacture coral beads and other such things.

Foreign ships from every place come there; and the king of the country also sends a chief and a writer and others to watch the sales; thereupon they collect the duty and pay it in to the authorities.

The wealthy people mostly cultivate coconut trees-sometimes a thousand trees, sometimes two thousand or three thousand; this constitutes their property.

THE COUNTRY OF CHAO-WA [JAVA]

As to the place where the king resides: the walls are made of bricks, and are more than three *chang* [about 31 feet] in height; in circumference they are something more than two hundred paces; [and] in the [walls] are set double gates, very well-kept and clean.

The houses are constructed in storeyed form, each being three or four *chang* in height; they lay a plank [flooring, over which] they spread matting [made of] fine rattans, or else patterned grass mats, on which the people sit cross-legged; [and] on the top of the houses they use boards of hard wood as tiles, splitting [the wood into] roofing [material].

The houses in which the people of the country live have thatch for their roofs. Every family has a store-room built of bricks in the ground; . . . [in this] they store the private belongings of the family; [and] upon this they live, sit and sleep.

The people of the country, both men and women, are all particular about their heads; if a man touches their head with his hand, or if there is a misunderstanding about money at a sale, or a battle of words when they are crazy with drunkenness, they at once pull out these knives and stab [each other]. He who is stronger prevails. When [one] man is stabbed to death, if the [other] man runs away and conceals himself for three days before emerging, then he does not forfeit his life; [but] if he is seized at the very moment [of the stabbing], he too is instantly stabbed to death.

The country has no [such] punishment as flogging; no [matter whether] the offence be great or small, they tie both [the offender's] hands behind his back with a fine rattan, and hustle him away for several paces, then they take a *pu-la-t'ou* and stab the offender once or twice in the small of the back or in the floating ribs, causing instant death. According to the local custom of the country no day [passes] without a man being put to death; [it is] very terrible.

Copper coins of the successive dynasties in the Central Country are in current use universally. . . .

The people of the country are very fond of the blue patterned porcelain-ware of the Central Country, also of such things as musk, gold-flecked hemp-silks, and beads. They buy these things in exchange for copper coins.

The king of the country constantly sends chiefs, who load foreign products into a ship, and present them as tribute to the Central Country.

THE COUNTRY OF THE 'HEAVENLY SQUARE' [MECCA]

They profess the Muslim religion. A holy man first expounded and spread the doctrine of . . . this country, and right down to the present day the people of the country all observe the regulations of the doctrine in their actions, not daring to commit the slightest transgression.

The people of this country are stalwart and fine-looking, and their limbs and faces are of a very dark purple colour.

The menfolk bind up their heads; they wear long garments; [and] on their feet they put leather shoes. The women all wear a covering over their heads, and you cannot see their faces.

They speak the A-la-pi [Arabic] language. The law of the country prohibits wine- drinking. The customs of the people are pacific and admirable. There are no poverty-stricken families. They all observe the precepts of their religion, and law-breakers are few. It is in truth a most happy country.

As to the marriage- and funeral-rites: they all conduct themselves in accordance with the regulations of their religion.

If you travel on from here for a journey of more than half a day, you reach the Heavenly Hall mosque, the foreign name for this Hall is K'ai-a-pai [Ka'ba]. . . . The Hall is built with layers of five-coloured stones; in shape it is square and flat-topped. Inside, there are pillars formed of five great beams of sinking incense wood, and a shelf made of yellow gold. Through out the interior of the Hall, the walls are all formed of clay mixed with rose water and ambergris, exhaling a perpetual fragrance. Over [the Hall] is a covering of black hemp-silk. They keep two black lions to guard the door.

Every year on the tenth day of the twelfth moon all the foreign Muslims—in extreme cases making a long journey of one or two years—come to worship inside the Hall.

From: Ma, Huan, Chengjun Feng, and J. V. G. Mills, *Ying-yai sheng-lan. 'The overall survey of the ocean's shores'* [1433], (Cambridge, England: Published for the Hakluyt Society at the University Press, 1970), excerpts from pp. 137–78.

QUESTIONS:

1. What do Ma Huan's observations tell us about the operation of maritime networks in the fifteenth century? What are the similarities and differences from maritime network operations of earlier centuries shown in Chapter 8?
2. Based on what he observes about each country, what is Ma Huan interested in? What does he find agreeable and what does he find peculiar about each place? That is, what do his observations reveal about his frame values and about Chinese frame values more generally?

EUROPE AT SEA

14.3a: *A Journal of the First Voyage* (Vasco da Gama, 1497–98)

Vasco da Gama (1460–1524) made two voyages to India, in 1497–98 and 1502–3. The success of these voyages, despite setbacks including conflicts with locals in both East Africa and Calicut described in this selection, connected western Europe to the lucrative maritime network of the Indian Ocean world. Indeed, da Gama himself launched Portugal on a path not just of participation in this network, but on a mission to establish Portuguese dominance through the exercise of military force at sea. As we noted earlier, the opportunity to pursue this mission arose from Ming China's withdrawal from active participation in the region. Da Gama's official logs of the journeys were lost, so this account is from an anonymous member of the fleet. Its details can be verified through other sources.

In the name of God. Amen. In the year 1497, King Dom Manuel . . . despatched four vessels to make discoveries and go in search of spices. Vasco da Gama was the captain of these vessels. . . .

1497. Mozambique. The people of this country are of ruddy complexion and well made. They are Muhammadans [Muslims], and their language is the same as that of the Moors [Arabic]. Their dresses are of fine linen or cotton stuffs, with variously colored stripes, and of rich and elaborate workmanship. They all wear robes with borders of silk embroidered in gold. They are merchants, and have transactions with white Moors [Arabs], four of whose vessels were at the time in port, laden with gold, silver, cloves, pepper, ginger, and silver rings, as also with quantities of pearls, jewels, and rubies, all of which are used by the people of this country. We understood them to say that all these things, with the exception of the gold, were brought thither by these Moors; and that further on to where we were going, they abounded, and that precious stones, pearls and spices were so plentiful that there was no need to purchase them as they could be collected in baskets. All this we learned through a sailor the Captain [Vasco da Gama] had with him, and who, having formerly been a prisoner among the Moors, understood their language.

In this place and island of Mozambique, there resided a chief who had the title of Sultan. He often came aboard our ships attended by some of his people. The Captain gave him many good things to eat, and made him a present of hats, shirts, corals and many other articles. He was, however, so proud that he treated all we gave him with contempt, and asked for scarlet cloth, of which we had none. . . .

One evening, as we left the ship for the mainland to obtain drinking water, we saw about twenty men on the beach. They were armed with spears, and forbade our landing. After the Captain heard this, he ordered three bombards [small cannon] to be fired upon them, so that we might land. Having effected our landing, these men fled into the bush, and we took as much water as we wanted. [The next day], a Moor rowed out to our ships, and told us that if we wanted more drinking water, that we should go for it, suggesting that we would encounter more trouble and be forced to turn back. The Captain no sooner heard this [threat] than he resolved to go, in order to show that we were able to do them harm if we desired it. We then armed our boats, placing bombards in their poops, and started for the shore. The Moors had constructed [a defensive wall] by lashing planks together . . . [but as we approached] they were at the time walking along the beach, armed with spears, knives, bows, and slingshots, with which they hurled stones at us. But our bombards soon made it so hot for them that they fled behind their walls, but this turned out to their injury rather than their profit. During the three hours that we were occupied in this manner [bombarding the beach] we saw at least two men killed, one on the beach and the other behind the wall. When we were weary of this work we retired to our ships to dine. . . .

[Vasco da Gama sailed from Mozambique to Swahili city-state of Mombasa, a two week voyage]

On Saturday, we cast anchor off Mombasa, but did not enter the port. . . . In front of the city there lay numerous vessels, all dressed in flags. And we, anxious not to be outdone, also dressed our ships, and we actually surpassed their show. . . . We anchored here with much pleasure, for we confidently hoped that on the following day we might go on land and hear [Catholic] mass jointly with the Christians reported to live there in a neighborhood separate from that of the Moors. . . .

But those who had told us [about the Christians] had said it [to trap us], for it was not true. At midnight there approached us a *dhow* with about a hundred men, all armed with cutlasses and shields. When they came to the vessel of the Captain they attempted to board her, armed as they were, but this was not permitted, only four or five of the most distinguished men among them being allowed on board. They remained about a couple of hours, and it seemed to us that they paid us this visit merely to find out whether they might not capture one or the other of our vessels. . . .

These and other wicked tricks were practiced upon us by these dogs, but our Lord did not allow them to succeed, because they were unbelievers.

[The fleet then sailed across the Indian Ocean for 23 days, guided by a Muslim navigator, and came to Calicut, where Ma Huan also visited.].

After we were at anchor, four boats approached us from the land, and they asked of what nation we were. We told them, and they then pointed out Calicut to us. . . . The city of Calicut is inhabited by

Christians [actually Hindus]. They are of tawny complexion. Some of them have big beards and long hair, whilst others clip their hair short or shave the head, merely allowing a tuft to remain on the crown as a sign that they are Christians. They also wear moustaches. They pierce the ears and wear much gold in them. They go naked down to the waist, covering their lower extremities with very fine cotton stuffs. But it is only the most respectable who do this, for the others manage as best they are able. The women of this country, as a rule, are ugly and of small stature. They wear many jewels of gold round the neck, numerous bracelets on their arms, and rings set with precious stones on their toes. All these people are well-disposed and apparently of mild temper. At first sight they seem covetous and ignorant. . . .

When we arrived at Calicut the king was away. The Captain sent two men to him with a message, informing him that an ambassador had arrived from the King of Portugal with letters . . . [The king] sent word to the Captain bidding him welcome [and sent] a pilot . . . with orders to take us to [an anchorage] in front of the city of Calicut. We were told that the anchorage at the place to which we were to go was good . . . and that it was customary for the ships which came to this country to anchor there for the sake of safety. We ourselves did not feel comfortable . . . and we did not anchor as near the shore as the king's pilot desired. . . .

On the following morning . . . the Captain set out to speak to the king, and took with him thirteen men. We put on our best attire, put bombards [small cannon] in our boats, and took with us trumpets and many flags. On landing, the Captain was received by government officials, along with a crowd of many men, armed and unarmed. The reception was friendly, as if the people were pleased to see us, though at first appearances looked threatening, for they carried naked swords in their hands. A palanquin was provided for the captain, such as is used by men of distinction in that country. . . . When we arrived [at the king's palace], men of much distinction and great lords came out to meet the Captain, and joined those who were already in attendance upon him. . . .

The king was in a small court, reclining upon a couch covered with a cloth of green velvet, above which was a good mattress, and upon this again a sheet of cotton stuff, very white and fine, more so than any linen. . . . The Captain, on entering, saluted in the manner of the country: by putting the hands together, then raising them towards Heaven, as is done by Christians when addressing God, and immediately afterwards opening them and shutting fists quickly. . . .

And the Captain told him he was the ambassador of the King of Portugal, who was Lord of many countries and the possessor of great wealth of every description, exceeding that of any king of these parts; that for a period of sixty years his people had annually sent out vessels to make discoveries in the direction of India, as they knew that there were Christian kings there like themselves. This, he said, was the reason which induced them to order this country to be discovered, not because they sought for gold or silver, for of this they had such abundance that they needed not what was to be found in this country. . . . There reigned a king now whose name was Dom Manuel, who had ordered [Da Gama] to build three vessels, of which he had been appointed Captain, and who had ordered him not to return to Portugal until he should have discovered this King of the Christians, on pain of having his head cut off. That two letters had been entrusted to him to be presented in case he succeeded in discovering him . . . and, finally, he had been instructed to say by word of mouth that he [the King of Portugal] desired to be his friend and brother. . . .

[The next morning], the captain got ready the following gifts to be sent to the king: twelve pieces of [cotton cloth], four scarlet hoods, six hats, four strings of coral, a case containing six wash-hand basins, a case of sugar, two casks of oil, and two of honey. And as it is the custom not to send anything to the king without the knowledge of the Moor [his financial advisor], and other officials, the Captain informed them of his intention. They came, and when they saw the present they laughed at it, saying that it was not a thing to offer to a king, that the poorest merchant from Mecca, or any other part of India, gave more, and that if he wanted to make a present it should be in gold, as the king would not accept such things. When the Captain heard this he grew sad, and said that he had brought no gold, that, moreover, he was no merchant, but an ambassador; that he gave of that which he had, which was his own private gift and not the king's; that if the King of Portugal ordered him to return he would entrust him with far richer presents; and that if the king would not accept these things he would send them back to the ships. Upon this they [the government officials] declared that they would not forward his presents, nor consent to his forwarding them himself. When they had gone there came certain Moorish merchants, and they all mocked the presents which the Captain desired to be sent to the king.

From: A Journal of the First Voyage of Vasco da Gama, 1479–1499, E. Ravenstein, transl., Hakluyt Society Series 1, vol. 99 (London: The Hakluyt Society, 1898), pp. 22–68 passim.

QUESTIONS:

1. Characterize the observations and impressions are recorded in the journal. How does the Portuguese attitude towards the people they meet compare with the Chinese attitude found in the two previous sources?
2. Are Portuguese attitudes and observations shaped more by their motives and cultural frame values, or by actual experiences? What frame values do you see here and how do they affect Portuguese interactions? Are they closer to network or hierarchy values?

14.3b: *Letter Describing His First Voyage* (Christopher Columbus, 1493)

Christopher Columbus (1451–1506) was the son of a Genoese woolworker. He became a sailor, visiting locations in the Atlantic world as far flung as Iceland and the west coast of Africa. Determined to find a route across the Atlantic to the fabled riches of the Far East, he sought patronage from the monarchies of Portugal and Spain. After several initial rebuffs, he finally convinced King Ferdinand and Queen Isabella to fund an expedition. Between 1492 and 1504 he made four voyages across the ocean, exploring islands in what we now know is the Caribbean, not the outer regions of East Asia. Between his first and second voyages he wrote a letter to the king and queen describing his discoveries. That letter is excerpted here.

Since I know that you will be pleased at the great victory with which Our Lord has crowned my voyage, I write this to you, from which you will learn how in thirty-three days I passed from the Canary Islands to the Indies, with the fleet which the most illustrious king and queen, our sovereigns, gave to me. There I found very many islands, filled with people innumerable, and of them all I have taken possession for their Highnesses, by proclamation made and with the royal standard unfurled, and no opposition was offered to me.

To the first island which I found I gave the name "San Salvador," in remembrance of the blessed Savior, who had marvelously bestowed all this; the Indians call it "Guanahani." To the second island, I gave the name "Santa Maria de Concepcion" [Rum Cay] to the third, "Fernandina"; to the fourth, "Isabella" . . . and so each island received a new name from me.

When I came to Juana [Cuba], I followed its coast to the westward, and I found it to be so extensive that I thought that it must be the mainland, the province of Cathay [China]. And since there were neither towns nor villages on the seashore, but only small villages whose residents all fled immediately, I continued along the coast, thinking that I could not fail to find great cities and towns. . . .

Hispana [Hispaniola] is a marvel. The sierras and the mountains, the plains, the arable and pasture lands, are so lovely and so rich for planting and sowing, for breeding cattle of every kind, and for building towns and villages. The harbors of the sea here are such as cannot be believed to exist unless they have been seen, and so with the rivers, many and great, and of good water, the majority of which contain gold. In the trees, fruits and plants, there is a great difference from those of Juana [Cuba]. In this island, there are many spices and great mines of gold and of other metals.

The people of this island, and of all the other islands which I have found and of which I have information, all go naked, men and women, as their mothers bore them, although some of the women cover a single place with the leaf of a plant or with a net of cotton which they make for the purpose. They have no iron or steel or weapons, nor are they inclined to use them. This is not because they are not well built and of handsome stature, but because they are very timid. They have no other arms than spears made of reeds, to which they fix a small sharpened stick. They do not dare to make use of these weapons against us, for many times it has happened that I have sent ashore two or three men to some town to have speech with them, and countless people have come out to them, and as soon as they have seen my men approaching, they have fled, a father not even waiting for his son. This is not because we have done them any harm; on the contrary, at every place where I have been and have been able to have speech with them, I have given gifts to them, such as cloth and many other things, receiving nothing in exchange. But they remain by nature incurably timid.

It is true that, once they have been reassured and have lost their fear of us, they are so innocent and so generous with all that they possess, that no one would believe it who has not seen it. They refuse nothing that they possess if it be asked of them. On the contrary, they invite any one to share it and display as much love as if they would give their hearts. They are content with whatever trifle or gift that is given to them, whether it be of value or valueless. . . . I gave them a thousand handsome good things, which I had brought, in order that they might conceive affection for us and, more than that, might become Christians and be inclined to the love and service of your Highnesses and of the whole Spanish nation, and strive to aid us and to give us of the things which they have in abundance and which are necessary to us.

They do not hold any creed nor are they idolaters; they only believe that power and good are in the heavens. . . . This belief is not the result of ignorance, for they are actually of a very acute intelligence, they know how to navigate the seas, and it is amazing how good an account they give of everything. [Instead], this belief is because they have never seen people clothed or ships such as ours.

As soon as I arrived in the Indies, I took by force some natives at the first island that I found in order that they might give me information about these places. And so it was that they soon understood us, and we them, either by speech or signs, and they have been very helpful. I still have them with me, and they are always assured that I come from Heaven, despite all the discussions which they have had with me. They were the first to announce this wherever I went in the islands, and others went running from house to house, and to neighboring towns, crying loudly "Come! Come! See the men from Heaven!" So all, men and women alike, once their fear was set at rest, came out to welcome us, and they all brought something to eat and drink, which they gave with extraordinary affection and generosity.

In all the islands, they have very many canoes, which are like our rowboats, except they are not so broad, because they are made of a single log of wood. But a rowboat would not be able to keep up with them, since their speed is incredible. In these they navigate among all the islands, and carry their goods and conduct trade. In one of these canoes I have seen with seventy and eighty men, each one with his oar.

In all these islands, I saw no great diversity in the appearance of the people or in their manners and language. On the contrary, they all understand one another. . . . and if their Highnesses assent, this will [assist] their conversion to our holy faith of Christ, to which they are very ready and favorably inclined. . . .

In all these islands, it seems to me that each man is content with one wife, except the chiefs or kings who may have as many as twenty wives. It appears to me that the women work more than the men. I have not been able to learn if they hold private property, but it seemed to me that they all shared what they had, especially of eatable things. In these islands I have so far found no human monstrosities, as many expected . . . on the contrary, the whole population is very well formed. They are not black like the people in Guinea [West Africa], but their hair is flowing. . . .

And so I have found no monsters, nor have I heard of any, except on an island called Charis. . . . This island is inhabited by a people who are regarded in all the islands as very fierce, and they are cannibals who eat human flesh. They have many canoes with which they range through all the islands of India and pillage and take whatever they can. They are no more malformed than are the others, except that they have the custom of wearing their hair long like women, and they use bows and arrows. . . . They are ferocious towards these other people who are excessively cowardly, but I regard them as no more fearsome than the others. . . . I have also been told of another island, which they assure me is larger than Hispana, where the people have no hair. In this place there is reportedly incalculable amounts of gold. . . .

To conclude this report . . . their Highnesses can see that I can supply them as much gold as they may need if their Highnesses will continue to assist [my voyages]. Moreover, I will provide them spices and cotton, as much as their Highnesses shall command; and mastic and aloe, as much as they shall order to be shipped; and slaves, as many as they shall order to be shipped and who will be from the idolaters. I believe also that I have found rhubarb and cinnamon, and I shall find a thousand other things of value. . . .

Our thanksgiving must be directed the most to the eternal God, Our Lord, Who gives to all those who walk in His way triumph over things which appear to be impossible, and this was one such glorious example. For although men have talked or have written of these distant lands, all was conjectural and without evidence. . . . It is our Redeemer who has given the victory to our most illustrious king and queen, and to their renowned kingdom . . . and all Christendom ought to feel delight and make great feasts and give solemn thanks to our Lord and Savior Jesus Christ, with many solemn prayers for the great exaltation which they shall have in the turning of so many pagan peoples to our Holy Faith, and afterwards for the temporal benefits, because not only Spain but all Christendom will have hence refreshment and gain.

These deeds that have been accomplished are thus briefly recorded while aboard ship, off the Canary Islands, on the fifteenth of February, in the year one thousand four hundred and ninety-three. I remain, at your orders and your service.

The Admiral

From: Columbus, Christopher, *The Voyages of Christopher Columbus, Being the Journals of his First and Third, and the Letters Concerning his First and Last Voyages*, Cecil Jane, transl. and ed. (London: Argonaut Press, 1930), pp. 259–64.

QUESTIONS:

1. Characterize Columbus' observations. How do they compare to those of da Gama, Ma Huan, and Zheng He? What does he emphasize most? What evidence do you see in the text that Columbus is shaping his account for his audience and his own purposes?
2. Describe the screen image of the peoples of Caribbean that Columbus projects. Describe what you think the Caribbean peoples' screen image of Columbus might look like. What accounts for the differences?

FRAMING INNOVATION

14.4: *Giorgio Vasari: Lives of the Most Eminent Painters, Sculptors, and Architects* (1550)

Leonardo da Vinci (1452-1519): painter and sculptor of florence

Giorgio Vasari (1511–74) was an Italian painter, architect, writer, and historian. He was successful in his own right, more as an architect than a painter. He became best known, however, for his *Lives of the Most Eminent Painters, Sculptors, and Architects*, published in 1550 and dedicated to Grand Duke Cosimo I de' Medici, a major patron of Renaissance artists. The work celebrates the creative genius and competitive nature of great Italian (especially Florentine) artists; his biographies of artists established a lasting genre in art historical writing. He was the first author to use the term "Renaissance" in print, and in general he provides a fine example of the European Renaissance emphasis on innovation and individualism. This selection is his biography of Leonardo da Vinci, painter, inventor, and the quintessential "Renaissance Man."

THE GREATEST GIFTS are often seen, in the course of nature, rained by celestial influences on human creatures; and sometimes, in supernatural fashion, beauty, grace, and talent are united beyond measure in one single person, in a manner that to whatever such an one turns his attention, his every action is so divine, that, surpassing all other men, it makes itself clearly known as a thing bestowed by God (as it is), and not acquired by human art. This was seen by all mankind in Leonardo da Vinci, in whom, besides a beauty of body never sufficiently extolled, there was an infinite grace in all his actions; and so great was his genius, and such its growth, that to whatever difficulties he turned his mind, he solved them with ease. In him was great bodily strength, joined to dexterity, with a spirit and courage ever royal and magnanimous; and the fame of his name so increased, that not only in his lifetime was he held in esteem, but his reputation became even greater among posterity after his death.

Truly marvelous and celestial was Leonardo, the son of Ser Piero da Vinci; and in learning and in the rudiments of letters he would have made great proficience, if he had not been so variable and unstable, for he set himself to learn many things, and then, after having begun them, abandoned them. Thus, in arithmetic, during the few months that he studied it, he made so much progress, that, by continually suggesting doubts and difficulties to the master who was teaching him, he would very often bewilder him. He gave some little attention to music, and quickly resolved to learn to play the lyre, as one who had by nature a spirit most lofty and full of refinement: wherefore he sang divinely to that instrument, improvising upon it. Nevertheless, although he occupied himself with such a variety of things, he never ceased drawing and working in relief, pursuits which suited his fancy more than any other. Ser Piero, having observed this, and having considered the loftiness of his intellect, one day took some of his drawings and carried them to Andrea del Verrocchio, who was much his friend, and besought him straightly to tell him whether Leonardo, by devoting himself to drawing, would make any proficience.

Andrea was astonished to see the extraordinary beginnings of Leonardo, and urged Ser Piero that he should make him study it; wherefore he arranged with Leonardo that he should enter the workshop of Andrea, which Leonardo did with the greatest willingness in the world. And he practiced not one branch of art only, but all those in which drawing played a part; and having an intellect so divine and marvelous that he was also an excellent geometrician, he not only worked in sculpture, making in his youth, in clay, some heads of women that are smiling, of which plaster casts are still taken, and likewise some heads of boys which appeared to have issued from the hand of a master; but in architecture, also, he made many drawings both of groundplans and of other designs of buildings; and he was the first, although but a youth, who suggested the plan of reducing the river Arno to a navigable canal from Pisa to Florence. He made designs of flour mills, fulling mills, and engines, which might be driven by the force of water: and since he wished that his profession should be painting, he studied much in drawing after nature, and sometimes in making models of figures in clay, over which he would lay soft pieces of cloth dipped in clay, and then set himself patiently to draw them on a certain kind of very fine Rheims cloth, or prepared linen: and he executed them in black and white with the point of his brush, so that it was a marvel, as some of them by his hand, which I have in our book of drawings, still bear witness; besides which, he drew on paper with such diligence and so well, that there is no one who has ever equaled him in perfection of finish; and I have one, a head drawn with the style in chiaroscuro, which is divine.

And there was infused in that brain such grace from God, and a power of expression in such sublime accord with the intellect and memory that served it, and he knew so well how to express his conceptions by draughtsmanship, that he vanquished with his discourse, and confuted with his reasoning, every valiant wit. And he was continually making models and designs to show men how to remove mountains with ease, and how to bore them in order to pass from one level to another; and by means of levers, windlasses, and screws, he showed the way to raise and draw great weights, together with methods for emptying harbors, and pumps for removing water from low places, things which his brain never ceased from devising; and of these ideas and labours many drawings may be seen, scattered abroad among our craftsmen; and I myself have seen not a few. He even went so far as to waste his time in drawing knots of cords, made according to an order, that from one end all the rest might follow till the other, so as to fill a round; and one of these is to be seen in stamp, most difficult and beautiful, and in the middle of it are these words, "Leonardus Vinci Accademia." And among these models and designs, there was one by which he often demonstrated to many ingenious citizens, who were then governing Florence, how he proposed to raise the Temple of S. Giovanni in Florence, and place steps under it, without damaging the building; and with such strong reasons did he urge this, that it appeared possible, although each man, after he had departed, would recognize for himself the impossibility of so vast an undertaking.

He was so pleasing in conversation, that he attracted to himself the hearts of men. And although he possessed, one might say, nothing, and worked little, he always kept servants and horses, in which latter he took much delight, and particularly in all other animals, which he managed with the greatest love and patience; and this he showed when often passing by the places where birds were sold, for, taking them with his own hand out of their cages, and having paid to those who sold them the price that was asked, he let them fly away into the air, restoring to them their lost liberty. For which reason nature was pleased so to favor him, that, wherever he turned his thought, brain, and mind, he displayed such divine power in his works, that, in giving them their perfection, no one was ever his peer in readiness, vivacity, excellence, beauty, and grace.

From: "Vasari's Life of Leonardo da Vinci," http://members.efn.org/~acd/vite/VasariLeo.html.

QUESTIONS:

1. What qualities about Leonardo does Vasari emphasize and admire most? That is, what stands out about this screen image of Leonardo? What do these qualities suggest about European (or at least Italian Renaissance) frame values?
2. Reread the source from a traditional Agrarian Era emphasis on tradition. What strikes you as odd here? How would you reemphasize tradition in the life of Leonardo?

Printed in the USA/Agawam, MA
December 14, 2020

765857.009